The Linguistics of Laugh

This book examines what speakers try to achieve by producing 'laughter-talk' (the talk preceding and eliciting an episode of laughter) and, using abundant examples from language corpora, what hearers are signalling when they produce laughter.

In particular, the author focuses on the tactical use of laughter-talk to achieve specific rhetorical and strategic ends: for example, to construct an identity, to make an argumentative point, to threaten someone else's face or save one's own. Although laughter and humour are by no means always related, the book also considers the implications these corpus-based observations may have about humour theory in general.

As one of the first works to have recourse to such a sizeable databank of examples of laughter in spontaneous running talk, this impressive volume will be a point of reference and an inspiration for scholars with an interest in corpus linguistics, discourse, humour, wordplay, irony and laughter-talk as a social phenomenon.

Alan Partington is Associate Professor of Linguistics in the Faculty of Political Science at the University of Bologna, Italy. He is the author of *Patterns and Meanings: Using Corpora for English Language Research and Teaching* and *The Linguistics of Political Argument: The Spin-doctor and the Wolf-pack at the White House* (also published by Routledge).

Routledge Studies in Linguistics

1. **Polari – The Lost Language of Gay Men**
   Paul Baker

2. **The Linguistic Analysis of Jokes**
   Graeme Ritchie

3. **The Irish Language in Ireland**
   From Goídel to globalisation
   Diarmait Mac Giolla Chríost

4. **Conceptualizing Metaphors**
   On Charles Peirce's marginalia
   Ivan Mladenov

5. **The Linguistics of Laughter**
   A corpus-assisted study of laughter-talk
   Alan Partington

The Linguistics of Laughter
A corpus-assisted study of laughter-talk

Alan Partington

LONDON AND NEW YORK

First published 2006
by Routledge
2 Park Square, Milton Park, Abingdon, Oxon, OX14 4RN

Simultaneously published in the USA and Canada
by Routledge
270 Madison Ave, New York NY 10016

*Routledge is an imprint of the Taylor & Francis Group,
an informa business*

Transferred to Digital Printing 2009

© 2006 Alan Partington

Typeset in Times New Roman by
Newgen Imaging Systems (P) Ltd, Chennai, India

All rights reserved. No part of this book may be reprinted or
reproduced or utilised in any form or by any electronic,
mechanical, or other means, now known or hereafter
invented, including photocopying and recording, or in any
information storage or retrieval system, without permission in
writing from the publishers.

British Library Cataloguing in Publication Data
A catalogue record for this book is available from the British Library

Library of Congress Cataloging in Publication Data
A catalog record for this book has been requested

ISBN10: 0–415–38166–5 (hbk)
ISBN10: 0–415–54407–6 (pbk)

ISBN13: 978–0–415–38166–6 (hbk)
ISBN13: 978–0–415–54407–8 (pbk)

Contents

Acknowledgements   vi

Introduction: laughter-talk – research questions and methods   1

1   Joke humour theory and language principles   25

2   Laughter in running discourse: shifts of mode, narrative, role and register   57

3   Face-work and the in-group   82

4   Wordplay, phraseplay and relexicalization   110

5   Teasing and verbal duelling   144

6   Irony and sarcasm   182

7   General conclusions   225

Appendix 1: visual puns and verbal-visual puns   237
Appendix 2: levels of sarcasm   239
Appendix 3: irony and popular historiography   240
Notes   242
Bibliography   248
Name index   256
Subject index   259

Acknowledgements

First of all, I am grateful to the White House Library for making the briefings transcripts publicly available and to C-Span public service television for broadcasting the briefings on their website. I must also thank fellow members of *CorDis*, a computer-assisted research project into modern political English financed by the Italian Ministry for Universities, especially John Morley, Louann Haarman, Alison Duguid and David Brierley, an honorary member, for their invaluable observations on the manuscript. Many thanks too are due to Salvatore Attardo for his comments and encouragement at vital moments. As ever, I am immensely grateful to Peter Levy for the sureness of his linguistic touch, his lateral insights and his cheerful chiding.

Introduction
Laughter-talk – research questions and methods

I.1 Aims

This work investigates the phenomenon of 'laughter-talk', that is, the talk preceding and provoking, intentionally or otherwise, a bout of laughter. More specifically, with the assistance of language corpora, I examine what speakers try to achieve by engaging in laughter-talk and what both speakers and hearers may be signalling when they produce laughter. Of particular interest is the tactical use of laughter-talk to achieve specific rhetorical ends, for example, to construct an identity, to make an argumentative point, to threaten someone else's face or boost one's own.

Although laughter and humour are by no means coterminous, intuition, experience and past literature tell us that they are closely related and so I go on to consider the implications these corpus-based observations may have for humour theory in general.

Past research into the relationship between language and laughter has fallen into two camps. The first type has been, roughly speaking, cognitive-psychological and has concentrated on laughter as a signal of humour. It has tried to answer a question of the type 'what does the human mind, or psyche, find funny, and why?' The data discussed was usually deliberately 'authored' material, either comic literature or what are known in layman's terms as 'canned jokes'. This was the case for both technical and philosophical reasons. Until comparatively recently the means of recording spontaneous episodes of humour were not available, whilst a feeling dominated the field that authored material was a more proper object of study, more interesting and closer to art and literature. Of late, however, some analysts have felt that such entirely decontextualized studies of humour, devoid of due regard to the producer and receiver of the laughter-talk, may leave important questions unexamined.

The second vein of research is socio-anthropological and looks at laughter in its social contexts. Rather than treating laughter as natural, instinctual and beyond our conscious control, in short, as a response to some stimulus entering the mind, attention is paid to issues such as when, where and in what ways people organize, produce, respond to and interpret laughter as part of the ongoing stream of social interaction. Research of this second variety was made possible by the development

2 Laughter-talk

of tape recording. One major criticism that has been levelled at such studies, however, is the high degree to which they are subject to the Observer's Paradox, how both the observer and the process of observation interfere considerably with what is observed. Much of the data is collected relatively informally, by recording friends or colleagues who are often both aware of the presence of the tape recorder and of the object of the research. This inevitably begs questions about the spontaneity and authenticity of such discourse. The amount of data collected in such studies is often relatively small.

In more recent times, the advent of corpus technology, allied to the increasing availability of material in electronic form on the Web, has made it possible to compile large corpora of authentic discourse occurring while subjects are going about their everyday business. This enables the analyst to collect and study considerable numbers of episodes of spontaneous laughter in circumstances where participants interact naturally and are unaware that their linguistic or laughter behaviour is an object of study. The main data for the current work consists of around 180 transcriptions containing circa 1,000,000 words of press conferences (or 'briefings') held at the White House over the past six years. The transcriptions contain indications of where laughter occurs – the word 'laughter' in round or square brackets – and it is possible to recover a degree of audio-visual information regarding the contexts in which it occurred, since the briefings are broadcast over the Web by C-Span television.[1] Thus, one of the innovations of the present work is the use of methodologies and software deriving from Corpus Linguistics (especially concordancing) and the integration of quantitative and qualitative approaches in the study of laughter phenomena.

The main concept driving the current work, then, is the need to compare and contrast current developments in both the cognitive and the discourse/conversational fields of linguistics. Indeed, the contention is that these approaches are compatible and that attention to both is necessary if we wish to build up a picture of why human beings use laughter-talk and how they do so to attain strategic goals in everyday interaction. In brief, in order to understand laughter-talk, we need to develop a model which can encompass and render compatible three elements: a theory of language production and reception, a theory of cognition as it relates to humour and a theory of human social interaction. The availability of large quantities of suitable data along with the technological and methodological capacity to analyse it may shed new light on this most ancient of objects of study, which thinkers from Aristotle, through Hobbes, Freud, Bergson to Woody Allen have found endlessly fascinating and utterly vexing in equal measure.

1.2 Press briefings

The current research into laughter utilizes data from three corpora of White House press briefings. Briefings are press conferences held on a regular basis – in the case of the White House, almost daily. They are a particular type of *institutional talk* (Drew and Heritage eds 1992), which is basically defined as talk between professionals and lay people, but the definition can be stretched, as here, to include talk between two groups of professionals with an audience of lay persons (the TV and Internet audience). In fact, briefings are a particularly fascinating genre of institutional talk in that they combine features of informal talk, given that the participants meet so often and know each other well, and confrontational or 'strategic' talk. The two parties involved – the spokesperson or podium (officially known as the 'White House Press Secretary') and the press – have very different interests and aims in life, which are in conflict on several levels. The podium wishes to project his political ideas and particular view of the world, the press to test that view, often suggesting more critical alternatives. The press hopes to uncover ever more information, including any evidence of weakness, malpractice, internal dissension and so on, the podium ideally wants to give as little away as possible outside the official line. They adopt and exploit different participant roles or *footings* (Goffman 1981; Levinson 1988), command non-symmetrical sets of discursive resources and employ different discourse strategies; they use different metaphors to describe the world and probably even see the whole nature of the business being conducted in different ways (Partington 2003).

What transpires in these briefings can also be extremely important and highly delicate from a political perspective:

> Anything McCurry [press secretary during the Clinton administration] uttered from the podium magically attained the status of official White House policy, and if he deviated later on the administration would be accused of the dreaded sin of flip-flopping.
>
> (Reaves White)[2]

Not only are the podium's words often treated by the press as White House policy, but they risk interpretation by non-American bodies as official US policy. Since they are broadcast both on television and on the Internet, 'any misstep can be beamed instantaneously around the world' (*CNN-allpolitics*). All this exposure, of course, means fame: 'the chief White House spokesman's face is probably as well known as any cabinet member' (*CNN-allpolitics*). In Galtung and Ruge's (1981) terms he is 'newsworthy', has become an 'elite person' in his own right. Many of the journalists, too, are well-known television faces or newspaper by-lines. Clayman and Heritage (2002) suggest that press conferences, including briefings, occupy the same vital space in the US political-media arena as the news interview in the British. An outline of the typical structure of White House press briefings is given in section 2.2.1.

1.3 Corpus-Assisted Discourse Studies

1.3.1 *Quantitative and qualitative approaches combined*

This research into laughter-talk is an instance of a project in the nascent interdisciplinary field of Corpus-Assisted Discourse Studies (CADS). This arose from the realisation that some of the methodology and instruments commonly used in

Corpus Linguistics might be adapted for the study of features of discourse (see especially Louw 1993; Stubbs 1996, 2001; Partington *et al.* 2004). In other words, that it was possible to combine the *quantitative* types of analysis used in Corpus Linguistics, which generally take into consideration large quantities of texts and subject them to statistical analysis, with the *qualitative* methods more typical of discourse studies which examine in detail much smaller amounts of discourse, frequently single texts. In its purest form:

> the quantitative paradigm hinges on a hypothetical-deductive mode of inquiry and a fairly rigid sequence of interventions which foresee the performance of experiments in controlled situations and the statistical measurement of data in order to reach reliable and replicable results which allow for generalisations and the prediction of a cause and effect relationship.
>
> (Haarman *et al.* 2002: 56–57)

whereas:

> qualitative methodology instead proceeds in a non-experimental or exploratory fashion, draws considerably on insight and intuition and derives results from the systematic observation of phenomena in such a way that theories or hypotheses emerge inductively and are said to be 'grounded' in data.
>
> (Haarman *et al.* 2002: 57)

Many experimenters, especially in the social sciences, have questioned this rigid dichotomy, maintaining that elements of both paradigms can usefully be employed in the research process. Just as the experimental researcher subjectively intervenes in the research design when formulating hypotheses and in deciding cut-off points for statistical analysis, so the qualitative researcher cannot be insensitive to quantity in the interpretation of data.[3] In this school of thought, research is 'a dynamic process which links together problems, theories and methods' (Bryman and Burgess 1994: 4) and the researcher is free to shunt back and forth among hypotheses, data-collection, analysis, evaluation and even speculation, as long as these phases are kept separate and the movements among them are closely chartered. Data *creation* (as in, say, arranging circumstances for laughter to occur and then recording it for analysis) is another matter and should only be employed if there is no alternative. In terms of a debate which has recently opened up in the field (Provine 2000; Attardo 2003), a CADS approach to laughter studies is neither entirely *performance* based nor wholly *competence* based, but combines features of both.

What follows, then, is an outline of the CADS methodology employed in the course of the present research. This description is included in the Introduction since the intricacies of the methodology will not always be explained in detail in the following chapters, first, because many readers will be more interested in discourse and humour studies than in Corpus Linguistics and, second, because many of the techniques are fairly repetitive.

1.3.2 Corpus-Assisted Discourse Studies methodology

The initial phases of CADS methodology are as follows:

1   data collection and corpus compilation;
2   data / corpus organization;
3   corpus interrogation.

(1) Data collection and corpus compilation

THE MAIN CORPORA

A number of the corpora used in the current research were compiled for Partington (2003) where briefings were analysed from a number of political and discourse angles including stance and footing, journalistic attribution, politeness phenomena and metaphor.

During this research it became clear that the briefings corpus also constituted an ample database of laughter occurring in semi-spontaneous speech. These bouts of laughter were in transcribed texts but many briefings were also available to audio-visual scrutiny because they are frequently screened as webcasts. This presented the opportunity to examine what makes people laugh in real-life spontaneous speech in a working environment. Moreover it was possible to do so with a degree of 'blindness' missing from some research into authentic discourse, in that the subjects are unaware of the objectives of the research and there is no danger of the subjects being influenced by interaction with the researcher. In the present case the raw data is produced by participants who most probably never in their wildest dreams imagined that their interaction might be studied from the point of view of laughter-talk. Moreover, the data was transcribed by parties (professional transcribers at the White House library) different from the final analyst (myself). The separation of data formulation and data analysis is, of course, fundamental in the elimination of contamination between researcher and subject.

The technology of data collection developed rapidly as this research evolved, that is, from 1998 to the present. The briefings transcripts for the earliest versions of the corpora were collected 'manually' by downloading them one by one from the White House Library website. The very first corpus (*Dems*) was of briefings held during the last years of the Clinton administration, 48 in all, composing a total of 250,000 words of spoken discourse. By watching the webcasts I was able to make notes on interesting features of paralanguage. At this early stage I was not exclusively interested in laughter phenomena but in all aspects of this discourse type.

The second corpus (*Reps*) was compiled in a different fashion. I began to collect a batch of briefings, still downloading one by one, in September–October, 2001, that is, during and immediately after the September 11th attack, in order to study the podium's and the press's reaction to such dramatic events. I subsequently decided to collect batches of briefings at six monthly intervals in order to

6 *Laughter-talk*

construct what is known as a 'monitor' corpus (Sinclair 1982). Since the transcriptions remain on the White House Library website until the end of the administration (they disappear when the administration changes – a 'new broom' policy), I also collected a batch from six months *before* the attack, for purposes of comparison. Each batch contains circa 125,000 words of running discourse. The *Reps* corpus, then, currently consists of a series of subcorpora:

- *Reps0* (Mar/Apr 2001)
- *Reps1* (Sep/Oct 2001)
- *Reps2* (Mar/Apr 2002)
- *Reps3* (Sep/Oct 2002)
- *Reps4* (Mar/Apr 2003)
- *Reps5* (Sep/Apr 2003)

for a total of 750,000 words which, when combined with *Dems*, makes a grand total of 1 million words of briefings. It has subsequently become possible, thanks to expanding software capability and disk storage, to download files from the Web in automatic fashion, using programmes such as *Nettransport* or *Winhttrack*. These programmes are capable of downloading onto a hard-disk or other memory support all the files in a given website. By specifying the briefings section of the White House Library site, *WHBig* was compiled, containing all press secretary briefings held from the beginning of the Republican reign until 17th June 2004 (the last available transcript at the time of compilation), a total of approximately 6 million words.

OTHER CORPORA

One of the axioms of CADS is that discourse study is necessarily comparative in two separate but related ways. First, within an individual discourse type, only by comparing the choices being made by speakers or writers at any point in a discourse with those which are normal, that is, usual within the genre, can we discover how *meaningful* those choices are. Observations from a single source (even an authentic text) are of limited value and are essentially anecdotal: 'by and large, we are not methodologically justified in interpreting the significance of a particular linguistic event unless we can compare it with other similar events' (Partington 1998: 146). Testing observations and findings against corpus data can provide 'background information' against which particular events can be judged.

Second, if we are also interested in the characteristics of the discourse type itself, it is vital to be able to compare its particular features and patterns with those of other discourse types. In this way we discover *how* it is special, and can go on to consider *why*. All genre/register/discourse type analysis is thus properly comparative. In the wider field of discourse studies, this requirement has unfortunately not always been observed in practice.

In sum, CADS analysts hold that, if texts are not compared to other bodies or corpora of texts it is not possible to know or to prove what is normal and only against a known background of what is normal and expected can we detect the unusual and meaningful.

A number of other corpora were utilized in the course of this research as a basis for comparison with briefings discourse. These include several corpora of journalistic texts: a collection of British news interviews (*INTS*) of similar size to the first briefings corpus (250,000 words), a 100-million-word corpus of written British broadsheet newspaper texts (*Papers*) and a circa one-million-word corpus of editorials and reports from British broadsheets and tabloids (*EdsReps*). The *Frown* (one million words of general US English) and its sister *Flob* (one million words of UK English) corpora, the *Colt* corpus of teenager talk and the *Wellington Spoken Corpus* (*WSC*) of general conversation were all used when appropriate. The *British National Corpus* (*BNC*) on the Web was also occasionally consulted (http://www.natcorp.ox.ac.uk/).

(2) Data/corpus organization

EDITING

Corpora can be edited in various ways, a process normally referred to as *mark-up*. Most of the original corpora, *Dems* and *Reps*, have been edited so that, when required, it is possible to treat the journalist's contributions and the podium's contributions as separate subcorpora. Thus, for instance, we can contrast the way journalists typically use a particular expression with the way the podium employs it.

With these corpora subdivisions and this mark-up, it became possible to compare (i) the podium's speech with that of the journalists, (ii) the speech of different podiums and (iii) briefings from different periods (including Democrat and the Republican periods of office).

ISOLATING LAUGHTER EPISODES

This can be carried out in two ways. First, one can go through each file and use the search and cut and paste facilities offered by a Word Processor to extract all episodes where the item *laughter* appears in the transcript. Alternatively, one can run the concordancer (see section I.3.4) to collect all instances of the use of the word *laughter* and then save the resulting concordance list in a separate file. It is possible to ask the program to include considerable co-text around the word or phrase to be sought (the *searchword*), which generally allows the analyst to study the episode in context. The second method clearly saves a great deal of time, but subsequent editing of the file may be needed to put the episodes in the correct chronological order or to remove episodes which appear more than once because one instance of *laughter* has occurred in close proximity to another – a very frequent phenomenon. This second method was the one I used and separate concordances of *laughter* were made for *Dems* and for each of the *Reps* collections. These will be referred to collectively as the 'laughter files'.

8 *Laughter-talk*

Subsequent analysis, classification and evaluation of the laughter bouts is, of course, largely a 'manual', that is, a human task. However, if the concordances of *laughter* are transferred into a word processor file, the analyst can add notes to the raw data. This then allows him or her, at a later date, to concordance the annotated version and call up, for instance, episodes where *wordplay* has occurred, or where *sarcasm* or *facework* are in play (if, of course, these were categories employed). By using the concordancer's *Context* facility, it becomes possible to perform cross-referenced enquiries: for example, to call up all episodes where wordplay *and* facework were deemed to be involved in the laughter-talk.

(3) Corpus interrogation and data analysis

SOFTWARE

A corpus by itself is simply an inert archive. However, it can be 'interrogated' using dedicated software. The packages used to interrogate the various corpora were *MicroConcord* and *WordSmith Tools*, both very widely available.[4] Such software can help supply us with various kinds of information on the frequency of occurrence of lexis, whilst the queen of corpus tools, the *concordancer*, is essentially a collector and collator of examples. Though in themselves quite simple (and easy to use), these tools can provide a great deal of information about the texts contained in a corpus not always easily available to the naked eye.

I.3.3 Some frequency data

Figure I.1 shows the incidence of laughter episodes in the various subcorpora. In *Dems* there are 220 occurrences of [laughter], one every 1,171 words. In *Reps* overall there are 323, an incidence of one laughter episode every 2,340 words. However, in *Reps1*, the briefings which take place during and immediately after 9/11, the incidence drops to one every 3,474 words; understandably it was a

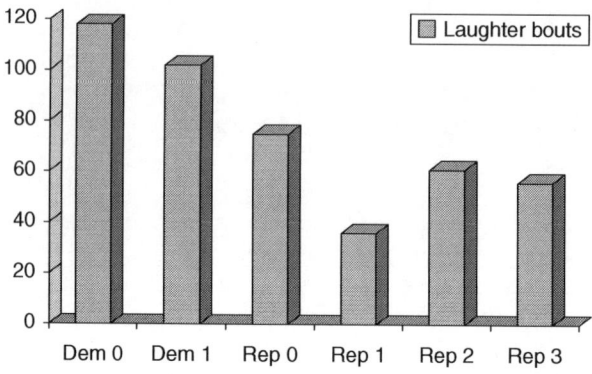

Figure I.1 The relative number of laughter bouts in each of the subcorpora of briefings.

sombre moment. There were other clear indicators too of a particular tension between the press and the podium. There is still more to the question, however. In *Reps0*, the briefings held before the attack, the laughter incidence was analogous to that of *Dems*: one episode every 1,664 words, whilst in *Reps5* the incidence was one every 2,508. The briefings had not recovered their gelastic quality thanks, most probably, to the further serious political and military developments.

WordSmith provides a distribution *Plot* tool which displays in a visual form where any particular word or phrase appears in a file. The distribution of *laughter* in first half of the *Dems* files is shown in Figure I.2.

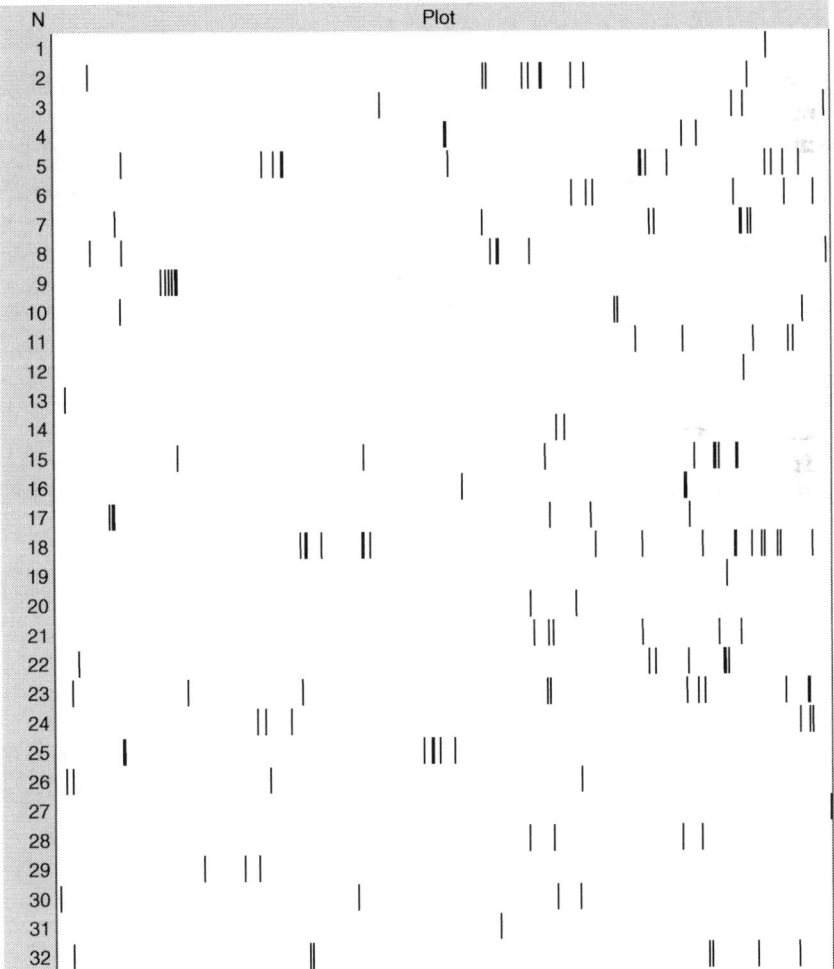

Figure I.2 A plot over time of the incidence of bouts of laughter in 32 briefings in the *Dems* corpus (*Wordsmith Tools*, version 4.0).

10 *Laughter-talk*

This is a graphic demonstration of how bouts of laughter tend to cluster together, in other words, that laughter seems to spawn more laughter. As we shall see in Chapter 2, these constellations occur within phases of *interaction*, whilst the long stretches where laughter is absent tend to indicate phases of *transaction*, when, as it were, the 'real' business of briefings is under way. We can also see that there is also a tendency for laughter – and therefore interaction – to occur towards the end of a briefing.

The *Collocation* facility provided by *WordSmith* gives a list of the most frequent words which appear in the immediate co-text of the searchword. Collocation is one of the most important technical concepts in Corpus Linguistics (Stubbs 2001: 29–30; Hoey 2005: 2–15), but it is defined in slightly different ways (Sinclair 1991: 170; Partington 1998: 15–17) and the terminology can be confusing. Here, it is used to indicate the actual, observed co-occurrence (either noted by a human analyst or picked out of the ocean of a corpus by software) of one lexical item with others within a short span of text. When using the facility, the researcher can decide the span but it is usual to set it at between three to five words to the left and right of the searchword. Those lexical items which are observed to occur within this span are called the *collocates* of the searchword. Thus, if we were to take the word *corpus* in the third sentence in this paragraph as our searchword and set the span at three items either side, the collocates are *ocean, of* (twice), *a, by, software, like*. If, using the *WordSmith Collocation* tool, we ask for all the collocates of the word *corpus* every time it appears in this book and ask for them to be ordered by frequency, we find, not surprisingly, that they include *linguistic* (co-occurring with *corpus* 13 times), *data* (10), *evidence* (7), *discourse* (6) and *briefings* (4). However, and just as predictably, if we spend a moment to reflect, the most common collocates are the grammar words *the* (41) and *in* (14). When issues of frequency are being discussed, the term *collocation(s)* is often employed, but in two ways. In the first, *x* is said to be a frequent or common collocation of *y*, that is, the items *linguistic* and *evidence* are said to be a frequent or common collocations of *corpus*. In the second, on the other hand, it is the *combination* of items *xy*, for example, *linguistic corpus* or *corpus evidence*, which is called a common collocation. By the same token, rare or nonce combinations such as *stone blind* (Edward Thomas) or *a grief ago* (Dylan Thomas) are often referred to as unusual collocations.

WordSmith's so-called *Clusters* facility, meanwhile, gives a list of the most frequent word-strings the searchword appears in. Neither of these tools at first blush furnishes any remarkable information at all on the co-text surrounding *laughter*, which is evidence that there is no such thing as a special vocabulary for conversational laughter. Examples of the use of these two tools are discussed in section I.7.

I.3.4 Concordancing

The concordancer is a collector and collator of examples. It extracts as many instances as the analyst wishes of the searchword or expression under analysis and arranges them in a concordance, that is, a list of unconnected lines of text that have been summoned by the concordance program from a computer corpus, with the searchword located at the centre of each line. The rest of each line contains the immediate co-text to the left and right of the searchword. It is generally possible to specify the number of characters of co-text from around, say, 40 to, realistically, around 500 on each side. Such a list enables the analyst to look for eventual patterns in the surrounding co-text, which proffer clues to the use of the searchword. It allows the observer to discover *patterns* of collocation, that is, how any particular word or expression co-occurs with other words/expressions with particular frequency. These patterns are often not available to unassisted introspection.

These lists can be prepared and edited in several ways. The entries can be *sorted*, that is listed in alphabetical order, according perhaps to the first word to the left (which, if the searchword is a noun, would group together the adjectives preceding it), or to the right (which, if the searchword is an adverb, would group the adjectives that follow it). Lines deemed to be uninteresting or not relevant can be removed by a *Cancel* (or *Zap*) facility. The concordances presented in this work are what I call 'sentence concordances', prepared by allowing a generous amount of co-text which is then pruned to demonstrate the use of the searchword in a – hopefully – comprehensible segment of discourse. The general reader should find these easier to digest than raw concordance lines. The most extensive examples of sentence concordances can be found in sections 1.4.2, 5.1 and 6.2.5.

We have already noted how the concordancer can extract episodes of laughter from the integral briefings texts and arrange them for the analyst's attention. This data extraction use of the concordancer was employed throughout the studies in this work. The clearest cases of its use is in Chapter 5 in trying to arrive at a satisfactory definition of *tease, teasing* and in Chapter 6 where expressions of explicit irony were gathered in various corpora by concordancing *irony/ironic/ironically*, but there were many other instances. For example, having noted from a preliminary perusal of some of the laughter files that certain innocuous-seeming words or phrases seemed to recur more often than expected, for instance, the word *hypothetical* (section 5.3.3), and that any reference to newspapers or the journalist's trade (e.g. Chapter 3, example 29 or Chapter 6, example 32) was frequently associated with laughter, these could be concordanced to see what function they were performing and why they should be associated with laughter. Usually they were indicators of reference to in-group knowledge or activity (Chapter 3). Having noted that certain journalists were indicated by the podium by name, for example, *Helen, Wolf, Kelly*, the names were concordanced and it was possible to study the differences in the way individual journalists interacted with the podium (Chapter 5 on teasing relations).

One of the most useful features of the concordancer is the *Context* tool, which allows the analyst to look for one item occurring in reasonable proximity in the text to another. For instance, a search for *laughter* in the proximity of *Republican** or *Democrat** was conducted to observe whether the other side is ever treated as an object of derision (this happens, but less often than I expected).

12 *Laughter-talk*

The use of the asterisk 'wildcard' (which signifies 'any string of letters, including none'), means that the program looks for the items *Republicans, Democrats* and *Democratic*, as well as simply *Republican* and *Democrat*. The wildcard can save a good deal of time. For example, in Chapter 6 I wanted to know how irony and sarcasm were generally felt by writers to relate to laughter and so I concordanced *ironic** and *sarcas** in the context of *laugh** which provided all instances of permutations of *ironic, ironical, ironically* and *sarcasm, sarcastic* and *sarcastically* with *laugh, laughed, laughing* and *laughter*. Many combinations were fairly predictable: 'an unpleasant mixture of sarcasm and scornful laughter', others a little less so: 'extra laughs attend upon an ironic budgerigar'.

1.3.5 Serendipity

> Serendipity: The faculty of making happy and unexpected discoveries by accident.
> (Oxford English Dictionary)

There is frequently a serendipitous quality to concordance searching, in the sense that one trawl can lead to another which leads to yet another and takes the explorer down new and unexpected avenues. This is both exciting and satisfying in terms of scientific experimental methodology. It provides a further stage of analyst abstraction from the data in that hypotheses can be *suggested by* the data rather than being *imposed on* the data. It thus casts the researcher in a new role, and often the sheer variety of possible avenues which constantly open up means the researcher has to learn the skill of selecting and of predicting which they feel are likely to prove the most rewarding.

One example of how serendipity can come into play is the following. Having read in Seto (1998) how irony is often associated with hyperbolic expressions, including intensifying or emphasizing adverbs such as *truly, certainly* and so on, I concordanced the *Laughter* files for items ending in *-ly* in the context of the item *laughter* in the hope that this would be a reasonably objective way of searching for instances of irony and sarcasm. The search was successful, revealing interesting episodes of joking irony (Chapter 6):

(1)   Q: I'm really hurt that no-one leaked anything to me. (Laughter)

but also of teasing (Chapter 5):

(2)   Q: Like Lester I have a completely unrelated follow-up.

of interpersonal interaction (see section 2.2) with individual members of the audience:

(3)   Q: So you really do like working with the press?
       MR. FLEISCHER: Especially you, April. (Laughter)

and of parody (section 2.5, 2.6):

(4) Q: [...]if those trade-offs are really excellent and the benefits to children and the American people are really terrific [...] (laughter)

in which the journalist rather sarcastically echoes podium-speak. But the *-ly* concordance also contained the item *males-only*, obviously not an intensifier. However, my curiosity aroused, I asked the system for the wider context, which was the following (shortly before the invasion of Iraq):

(5) Q: Ari [...] do you suspect that the New York Times would get behind our war effort if only Iraq were to open a males-only golf club, like Augusta, Georgia? (Laughter)

which seemed to reveal the possibility that journalists could be teasingly sarcastic not just about the podium or the administration but also about other newspapers. I decided to investigate this possibility by concordancing the items *Times* and *Post* (two popular terms in US newspaper titles) in the context of *laughter*. A few more examples of journalist teasing journalist were found but what also caught the eye was that one journalist in particular was nominated very frequently in the co-text, *Les* or *Lester*. The concordance of *Les* and *Lester* revealed his particular tactic of podium 'entrapment'. He produces an apparently innocent quote from a recent newspaper report, often on some fairly obscure topic, in order to entice the podium into a comment that he can subsequently denounce. The reason these citations are often accompanied by audience laughter is that they are, of course, well aware of Lester's technique and anticipate some fun. The particular teasing relation between Lester and the podium is described in section 5.7.

I.4 Definitions and descriptions of laughter types

Defining the object of enquiry in the fields of laughter and humour studies is a notoriously slippery business:

> The study of humor, irony, and other playful forms is plagued by definitional problems [...] Often, authors will expend significant energy explaining and justifying complex terminological distinctions that are bound to crumble at the first close examination. This state of affairs is probably motivated by the fact that terms such as *humor, irony, sarcasm, funny, laughable, ridiculous*, etc., are folk-concepts, with fuzzy boundaries, if any.
>
> (Attardo 2001a)

Perhaps the best way of gaining insights into folk intuitions about word meaning and use is through corpus evidence, which allows us to examine the way people have actually employed these terms. During the course of this work we will interrogate the corpora for this purpose. In the meantime, we can attempt a few informal definitions. There are several ways of describing the *physical* characteristics of laughter: articulatory, acoustic or auditory. For our purposes, we can concentrate on the third and adopt the down-to-earth characterization of *laughter* given by the phoneticians, Bachorowski *et al.*, as 'any perceptibly audible sound that an ordinary person would characterize as a laugh if heard under ordinary everyday circumstances' (2001: 1582). The laughter transcribed in the briefings data has, in fact, been attested by an 'ordinary person' (the transcriber) in reasonably normal circumstances (listening to a recording of the proceedings). Beyond this, in this book we will also be attempting a *functional* definition, less what laughter *is* than what it *does*, or rather, what people do with it.

Laughter-talk was earlier defined informally as the talk preceding and provoking, intentionally or otherwise, a bout of laughter. It thus encompasses both the locutionary moves (what was actually said) and the illocutionary intentions (what we can glean from the context about what the speaker meant to do) inherent in the speakers' move(s) preceding the laughter bout or series of bouts in a cluster of laughter. Laughter itself is part of the perlocutionary effect of the move, but it generally remains necessary to interpret the perlocutionary meaning of the laughter. When the effect is missing, when the illocution has *misfired* and no laughter (or smiling) occurs, we may be in the presence of a failed attempt at laughter-talk.

The question of speaker intentionality or otherwise poses problems for an observer, product-based, approach and any speculation on what speakers were intending to do, based on 'outsider' observation of the data, can never be totally reliable. And yet to exclude observer appraisal altogether would be unproductive. In my hat as a corpus linguist, on the one hand, I look at attested (attested, that is, by someone else) instances of laughter, without taking for granted that any one of them will necessarily be intentionally humorous. On the other hand, in my hat as a discourse analyst, I feel it is important for the observer to go on to evaluate the data and hypothesize on what they might *mean*, and I see no reason to exclude such processes from Corpus-Assisted Discourse Study. I wish to occupy the middle ground between behaviourism and those schools which specialize in speculation largely ungrounded in data or which simply invent examples to support a point.

As regards failed humour, very often, of course, it will leave no direct trace in the linguistic record. I did, however, have access to a certain amount of audio-visual information through the briefings webcasts, which can sometimes provide evidence for speaker intent (smile, smile-voice etc.). Moreover, once a study of the data has begun to reveal speaker acts which typically raise a laugh (e.g. adopting fantasy roles) it might be possible for an analyst to extrapolate and say that when such an act is not greeted with laughter, it might well have been an unsuccessful attempt to elicit laughter. The analyst can then investigate the context, as far as possible, and try to determine why it failed.

It will be noted that the laughter bouts are reported in the original 'raw' form of transcription as found on the Web. I have refrained from re-transcribing them using any of the various systems often found in Conversation Analysis (or CA; especially Jefferson 1985), which attempt to give indications of time, intonation and breathing patterns, and voice quality, for instance:

KRISTIN: u̱hh heh heh
WILSON: ihh he̱h ↑hhe he̱h he̱h he̱h heh heh hah hah.

(Glenn 2003: 11)

There are several reasons for this decision, both technical and methodological. First, for the reader not well-versed in CA, its transcripts can be difficult to interpret. Moreover, some of the decisions about what phonological phenomena to indicate, or mimic, in these systems can appear arbitrary.

In more practical terms, the quality of the audio signal in the briefings broadcasts is often quite poor. It is therefore not always possible to judge the exact duration in time of an individual bout since many bouts fade in and out imperceptibly. On the other hand, it is normally possible to judge whether the laughter is choral or individual. Relative strength or loudness can also generally be appreciated. Indications of the precise nature of the laughter are reported only where it is considered important for the interpretation of the episode, usually as a gloss in the surrounding text. It is hoped that these decisions have led to a readable text for a general audience.

Turning to the visual information, the camera in the briefings broadcasts focuses on the podium with only occasional panning around the room. Visual images of audience laughter are correspondingly rare. In recompense we can study the podium in more detail. Very little work has been done on systematizing proxemics, gesture, facial expressions and so on, for corpus analysis (but see Baldry ed. 2000), and so I use everyday expressions. The first consideration is whether the podium or the audience initiate the laughter. The second is whether there is some form of uptake by the other. In other words, if the audience laughs first does the podium laugh or smile too, or does he adopt some non-laughing (or 'po-faced'; Drew 1987) expression? Or if the podium initiates, does the audience follow suit? Lack of uptake is usually a problem, a hitch in proceedings which will require some kind of remedy. Podium uptake after audience laughter subsequent to his remark usually signals that humour was deliberate and also may well be acknowledging the 'praise' that the audience laughter implies. Podium uptake after a remark from the audience can be more difficult to interpret, especially if the remark was non-affiliative, teasing or sarcastic (Chapter 5 on response to teasing).

As far as the position of the bout is concerned, O'Connell and Kowel list three possibilities, initial ('at the beginning of an articulatory phrase'), medial ('during an articulatory phrase') and terminal or final or 'punctuating' ('at the end of an articulatory phrase', 2004: 472). Initial laughter is practically absent from the transcription. The transcribers make some attempt to distinguish between medial and terminal laughter but the matter is complicated by the delay which is common in laughter onset. Thus what is really a terminal laugh at the end of a speaker's move sometimes gets transcribed in the middle of the next speaker's move. In very general terms, medial laughter can have a quite different significance from terminal.

Whereas the latter usually indicates that a speaker has deliberately indulged in laughter-talk, the former, which can be intrusive and interrupting, often seems to signal that the speaker has unwittingly said something which the audience finds a cause for laughter.

Speech-laughs or '*laughspeak*, a form of blended, laughing speech that communicates emotional tone' (Provine 2000: 37) is not normally transcribed as '(Laughter)' by the White House transcribers.

The default and by far the most common form of laughter in the briefings data, then, is as follows: terminal, choral, audience initiated (following an utterance of the podium or member of the audience) with some degree of podium uptake (smile or laughter), brief to medium in length, soft to medium in intensity. Only deviations from this norm will be given explicit attention in the text.

I.5 Literature on laughter in discourse

In contrast to the vast literature on the phenomenon of laughter, comparatively little has been written on laughter in authentic, running, spontaneous speech. The recent work by Glenn (2003) is one of the very few book-length studies of laughter in interaction. The author includes a survey of the literature on laughter in linguistics and related disciplines.

The review considers the question of how and why laughter developed phylogenetically and ontogenetically. In both the species as a whole and in the individual infant, laughter predates speech. Laughter may be universal and its forms may be extremely similar across diverse cultures and linguistic groups, but the theories explaining its biological origins are most certainly not. Ideas range from laughter being a special form of aggression, derived from the mobbing of an intruder, to its precise opposite, a means of displaying appeasement to potential adversaries. Or it expresses the celebration of 'sudden glory' felt after vanquishing an enemy in combat. Or then again it provides an audible means to signal group safety or good fortune (Glenn 2003: 14). We will return to these ideas in the Conclusion to this work.

In order to correct what he feels is an over-association of the two in the past, Glenn is keen to point out research which emphasizes that 'much human laughter occurs independent of humorous stimuli [...] Descriptors such as "nervous", "insincere", or "wicked" applied to laughter imply something more than simple perception of humor' (2003: 23). He cites Foot (1977) who lists the following 'functions': humorous laughter, social laughter, ignorance laughter, evasion laughter, apologetic laughter, anxiety laughter, derision laughter and joyous laughter. We might bear this list in mind when viewing the examples of laughter in this book. Tickling merits a special mention both as a prompt of non-humorous laughter but also for the role it plays in certain pathologies of the brain (2003: 24). In conclusion to this preliminary overview, Glenn notes how research in the field has tended towards an increasing acknowledgment of the complexities of laughter and 'that many factors, internal and external, affect or stimulate laughter', and that 'treating it solely as a response to a stimulus' is inadequate and misleading (2003: 25). Moreover, much of the methodology which treats laughter as solely instinctual generally describes the phenomenon in isolation from its naturally occurring contexts; descriptions favour loud 'obvious' laughter and the quieter, more subtle conversational laughter is overlooked.

The first systematic studies of laughter in running discourse were developed in the field of Conversation Analysis. However, in much of the early work even here, laughter is still generally seen as an index of humour. Thus Sacks (1978) and Sherzer (1985) both examine puns and jokes, whilst Tannen (1984) records and analyses all the 'humorous occurrences' in the conversations held at a Thanksgiving dinner. Nevertheless, this was ground-breaking work particularly in the way it revealed how humour in conversation functions entirely differently from more authored or 'canned' forms. Tannen's essential and fascinating conclusion is that 'the use of humor played a significant role in the impact that each [member] had on the group' (1984: 143). In other words, the contributions of participants who employed humour extensively were deemed more memorable by other members of the group than those who did not.

The conversation analyst most closely associated with the study of laughter itself is Jefferson. In Jefferson (1979) responses to speaker laughter are analysed and the following three possibilities are envisaged: recipient laughter, recipient silence and recipient non-laughing speech. Recipient laughter (in response to first speaker laughter) constitutes acceptance of a 'laugh invitation'. Recipient silence can indicate a misunderstanding of the utterance and may generate further pursuit of laughter by the first speaker. Recipient non-laughing speech declines the first speaker's laugh invitation, which may have an effect on how the conversation continues as well as on the relationship between the participants.

Jefferson (1984) examines laughter in the non-humorous context of 'troubles talk'. She discovered that, if a speaker laughs when recounting the trouble, listeners generally do *not* see this as an invitation to reply in kind, in stark contrast to normal conversational practice. Jefferson (1985) outlines a system for transcribing instances of laughter in talk.

Jefferson, Sacks and Schegloff (1987) looks at episodes of shared laughter, that is, when participants laugh together and at how they manufacture a sense of group intimacy by, for instance, recounting funny stories, especially about 'improper' topics, such as sex and drunkenness (see section 1.3.6). Running throughout Jefferson's work is an attention to the sequential and cohesive aspects of the phenomenon, how laughter derives from the preceding discourse and influences the nature of subsequent talk.

Modern CA, then, generally seeks to separate laughter from humour in order to treat it as an object of research in itself: 'the recognition that laughter does not provide a direct barometer of perceived humor opens up questions of what other factors might influence its occurrence and what else it might be doing' (Glenn 2003: 26). It treats laughter in two principal ways: as a social (rather than physiological or psychological) phenomenon and as a discursive phenomenon, a means of organizing discourse.

18 *Laughter-talk*

In social terms, as many authors – from Bergson to Provine – have noted, people laugh more, and differently, in company. Considerable attention has been paid to what laughter signals to the other participants. In particular, *speaker* laughter helps frame the discourse as one in which laughter is relevant for some reason (Goffman 1981: 316–319). This could be to communicate play frame (see section 2.3), or embarrassment, or even, as we saw earlier, that troubles are about to be narrated. Thus laughter is an important way of attempting to instruct or persuade interlocutors about how they should receive a speaker's contribution. This can be of considerable interest in the study of 'strategic' talk such as political debates, interviews and briefings.

Recipient laughter is seen as a way of signalling affiliation and alignment. These two terms are frequently confused in the literature. In the present work, affiliation is used to mean the expression of solidarity with another participant on an affective, interpersonal plane, whereas alignment means communicating agreement with what another person has said, that is, approval of the opinions and sentiments he or she has expressed. Recipient laughter then can signal affiliation and/or alignment with first speaker (laughing *with*) or non-affiliation and/or non-alignment (laughing *at*). Or it can signal simply understanding and acknowledgment that the first speaker was attempting laughter-talk.

The power of creating affiliation, and especially the group-bonding effects of shared laughter, means that laughter is an important means of promoting in-group solidarity. In contrast, its potential to express disaffiliation can project an individual or group as external, an out-person/group, and is a significant way of shaming and performing aggressive face attacks. These issues will be taken up in later chapters.

Table I.1 is reported from Stewart (1995) and is an adaptation from Labov and Fanshel (1977), Glenn (1987) and Brown and Levinson (1987) and offers a classification of laughter into several domains and functions:

Table I.1 Conversational uses of laughter

Domain	Supportive functions	Seemingly non-supportive or distancing functions
Metalinguistic	backchannel respond reinforce	interrupt
Evaluative	agree interpret support	disagree challenge reinterpret contradict
Joking	claim common ground tease confim in-group identity	indicate non-acceptance or the inappropriate nature of an utterance

Finally, although not a work in linguistics proper, a special mention is merited by Provine (2000), which reports a wealth of observations and facts about laughter, some highly relevant to the current enterprise, some merely fascinating, other downright bizarre. He conducted a number of social experiments, sending student informants out in the field to collect information on how people laugh and what makes them laugh. His first conclusion is that laughter in everyday interaction is rarely directly related to humour as normally intended (i.e. 'funniness'): 'the next time you are around laughing people', he advises us, 'examine for yourself the general witlessness of pre-laugh comments' (2000: 42; see section 3.1). He found too that females laugh more than males in courtship or semi-courtship encounters but also in same-sex conversations, that laughter can play a key but complicated role in the expression of dominance and subservience and, most fundamentally of all, that 'speakers laugh more than their audience' in normal social intercourse. He then goes on to compare human and chimpanzee laughter, to examine the role of laughter in opera and explore the curious but all-pervasive worlds of 'tickle torture' and 'tickle lust'. He muses on the contagiousness of laughter, how in extreme cases laughter epidemics can occur, including the one which plagued Tanganyika (Tanzania) for over two years in the early 1960s. He tells of various instances of people laughing themselves to death, of how excessive hilarity is one of the early symptoms of spongiform encephalopathy (including *kuru*, a form once endemic in New Guinea contracted by the ritual consumption of ones' relatives), of how victims of strychnine poisoning die with a smile on their face, due to extreme muscular contraction. Provine proves, without a shadow of a doubt, that there is more to laughter than meets the eye or ear.

1.6 Literature on laughter in politics

Little work has so far been conducted on laughter in institutional discourse and very little indeed on laughter in politics, in contrast to the many formal and informal treatments of political *humour*, usually jokes (for example, Yarwood (2004) and Raskin (1985), who dedicates an entire chapter to the topic). Here we report on a couple of significant papers.

Clayman (1992a) studied laughter as one among what he calls 'collective audience responses' during public speeches, which also include applause and booing. As in other public speaking settings, affiliative audience laughter displays audience members' appreciation, or at least acknowledgment, of the speakers' humour, but it does not necessarily represent an unequivocal expression of support for the messages that the speakers attempt to convey. In contrast to applause, which, he claims, usually represents a 'purified' expression of support, shared laughter allows audiences to *affiliate* with speakers without having to unequivocally *align* with the positions they express. This may help to account for the fact that shared laughter occurs in a far greater range of public speaking settings than does applause (see also Greatbatch and Clark 2003).

These conclusions could have important repercussions for the podium in briefings. Perhaps indulging in laughter-talk has less effect on the audience of journalists than he imagines. However, another important consideration is that, since recipient laughter is highly ambiguous and often *does* signal alignment, each individual member of an audience may feel that fellow members concur with the orator's message and his or her own alignment may converge with that the crowd. This at least would be the podium's aspiration.

O'Connell and Kowal, in their study of laughter in TV and radio interviews with Hillary Clinton, in which both political and personal issues are discussed, believe that 'laughter is always perspectival, i.e., it manifests some sort of position taking on the part of the laugher' (2004: 476). The most dramatic example of this in their database, they say, is the following episode, where Hillary Clinton is asked about her possible presidential candidacy:

> INTERVIEWER: you have said Senator Clinton you will not run for president in two thousand four [...] what if your party drafted you
> HILLARY CLINTON: (LAUGHING) that's not gonna happen we have very –
> INTERVIEWER: what if it did what if they came to you and said Senator Hillary Clinton you are the only person in our view who can beat president Bush [...]
> (O'Connell and Kowal 2004: 473 with slight editing)

This, they claim (citing Glenn), is an instance of 'the kind of laughter people produce when faced with a situation demanding politeness yet provoking discomfort' (Glenn 2003: 151), proof, they say, that laughter is by no means always associated with an underlying pleasant emotion or with the communication of the non-serious: 'the topic itself is not at all funny; the laughter was not invited by the interviewer; and Hillary Clinton used her laughter as a ploy to avoid a definitive answer to the question' (O'Connell and Kowal 2004: 476). These claims are perhaps rather strong. As analysts we cannot know for sure whether the signalling inherent in the laughter was voluntary, as the authors imply, or involuntary. Moreover, another gloss would be that her laughter reinterprets the topic as, indeed, a non-serious or 'funny' one in order to avoid having to provide a lengthy response. Nevertheless, it remains the case that laughter communicates stance, the laugher's orientation to the topic and to the interlocutor (affiliation, disaffiliation or neutrality), especially when it is the listener who laughs. Whether on any occasion this signalling is deliberate or not is a question of observer judgement, at times speculation even, and is one of the themes of the current work.

I.7 Laughter: what the corpus says

The corpus is not always the best place to look if one wishes to find the definition of a concept (a dictionary is often better), but it can certainly provide a mine of information on the associations and the social connotations of an item and how people actually use and regard it (Partington 2001: 64–65). So what can we glean from corpora, in particular, the largest corpus we use here, *Papers*, about the lexical items *laugh* and *laughter*?

If we use the *WordSmith* 'Clusters' facility (settings fixed at four-word string and minimum occurrence frequency of five), the most frequent phrases involving the item *laugh** turn out to include the following (in decreasing order):

> *have the last laugh*
> *laughing all the way (to the bank)*
> *a laughing stock*
> *(didn't know whether) to laugh or cry*
> *laughed out of court*
> *a lot / bundle / barrel of laughs*
> *have a good laugh*
> *don't make me laugh*
> *is no laughing matter*
> *(can / to) laugh at themselves*
> *laughed off suggestions that*
> *a hollow laugh from*
> *roared with laughter*
> *would be laughable if*
> *doubled up with laughter*
> *laugh and a joke*
> *the laughter of fools*
> *he who laughs last*
> *to raise a laugh*
> *in fits of laughter*
> *laughed in my / your face*
> *laughed in the face (of adversity* etc.)

There is no doubting the association with energetic fun but it is also noticeable that the word *joke* appears in only one instance. Moreover, just as strong would seem to be the correlation with embarrassment and shame – *a laughing stock, laugh out of court, laughable* – and with aggression, competition or revenge – *have the last laugh* (the table-topper), *laugh in one's face* and *he who laughs last*. That laughter can be entirely dissociated from pleasure is attested by *hollow laugh* and *(I didn't know) whether to laugh or cry*.

In the frequency list of collocates of *laugh**, items such as *comedy, happy* and *funny* certainly appear, but not near the top. What kinds of laugh do people recognize – in other words what adjectives are used before *laugh* in the corpus? Unsurprisingly, they fall into similar semantic groups – 'energetic fun': *hearty, easy, belly*; 'embarrassment': *nervous, embarrassed, uncomfortable*; 'aggression': *baiting, contemptuous*. As well as *hollow*, a laugh can be *bitter* and *wry*. The socially cohesive aspects of laughter are attested by *audience, infectious* and *empathic*.

If we concordance some of the common phrases from the list in the preceding paragraph, we find that laughter can be a fine and noble thing, as witnessed by *laugh in the face of death, adversity, the devil* and *relegation*, though perhaps to *laugh in the face of the law* is somewhat less so. The laudable ability to *laugh at themselves* is a trait shared by as disparate a bunch as the English, the Germans, the Swiss, Jews and Nigerians. The phrase *laugh off suggestions* is one of the most intriguing. The *suggestions* are generally derogatory or demeaning ones for the laugher, for example, *that he would stage a putsch, that he is an empire-builder, that it has lost its way* but the implication is almost always that the reader, however, is to take the *suggestions* seriously. People can either *laugh* or *cry all the way to the bank*. The latter is a subtle accusation of hypocrisy, whereas the first usually means settling a score, getting even, on the part of someone whose decisions have proved justified in the face of earlier criticism or other difficulties. It is generally quite affiliative as, for example, in the headline 'Skoda laughing all the way to the bank' but there are exceptions: 'The Bee-Gees have been laughing all the way to the bank after discovering white suits and how to sing like Pinky and Perky. But this has gone beyond a joke'.

It is interesting to compare *laugh* with *smile*. The latter was found to be almost as frequent, with 6,026 occurrences of *smil** (excluding *Smiley* and *Smilla*) against 6,996 of *laugh**. It appears, however, to take part in far fewer set expressions, the most frequent being *with a smile on his face, have something / plenty / little to smile about, bring a smile to / put a smile on the face of*... and *wipe the smile off his face*. All these are rarely simply descriptions but tend, in newspaper texts at least, to be used metonymically, the *cause* which *brings the smile to* or *wipes the smile off* the face in question being the real emphasis, for example, 'Bossi won his seat, abruptly wiping the smile of the faces of the mainstream politicians' or 'Ford had something to smile about as their Taurus [...] was America's best-selling car'.

The most common adjective before *smile* is *wry* but this is closely followed by *big, broad* and *happy*. When *smiles* are *sweet* or *winning* there is frequently more than a touch of irony: '... a wild, paranoid fantasy in which the Englishman walks hand in hand with the Pope and the IRA, smiling sweetly and plotting murder', 'Ian Katz reports on the painter who has splashed Saddam Hussein's winning smile the length of his beleaguered land'.

I.8 Laughter: humorous and non-humorous

The corpus, then, provides clear evidence of how people feel that laughter and humour, though connected, are not entirely one and the same. As Attardo puts it: 'ample research has demonstrated beyond doubt that humor and laughter, though obviously related, are by no means coextensive' (2003: 1288). He cites research such as Drew's po-faced (serious) responses to humorous teases which 'are precisely non-amused reactions to a humorous turn in conversation' (2003: 1288, and see section 5.4). Conversely, he mentions various non-humorous stimuli (tickling, laughing gas) which are often accompanied by laughter. The frequency of laughter in troubles-telling could also be mentioned. In the previous section, we saw in the corpus how laughter can express aggression, ridicule and embarrassment but also courage and defiance and sense of achievement.

Nevertheless, any attempt to describe how laughter functions in human interaction without reference to humour would be, as Attardo remarks, 'counterintuitive'.

The current author would add 'incomplete' and 'unsatisfying'. If any were needed, the corpus gives ample evidence of the general perception people have of their interrelation. Even authors such as Jefferson, who wished to treat laughter in isolation to study its mechanisms, still eventually have to include talk of humour and '*funny* stories' (Jefferson *et al.* 1987).

I.9   Outline of the work and the research questions we confront

The next chapter, then, Chapter 1, undertakes a critical analysis of the most influential of current cognitive theories regarding verbal joke humour, namely, bisociation. The expression was coined by Koestler (1964) and is defined as the clash of two habitually incompatible frames of reference. We revisit the script-shift theory and propose that a sudden shift of narrative is the mechanism underlying many jokes. No single mechanism, however, can be a sufficient condition for humour and other logical relations, such as evaluation and reversal of evaluation, and real-world, cultural-moral values, especially taboo improprieties, need to be included in any analysis. The last part of the chapter points to analogies which exist between the probable cognitive mechanisms underlying much verbal humour and those found in language production and reception in general, that is, script/schema recall and best-guess inferencing.

In Chapter 2 we begin our analyses of the corpus data. The main research question will be: is there any evidence of mechanisms similar to bisociation and narrative shift at play in conversational laughter-talk? How precisely do they function and how are they realized linguistically? We begin to see how laughter-talk is used strategically by participants and how it contributes to the construction of identity within the group. In Chapter 3 we continue to examine these social aspects using a framework of social relations which draws heavily from Brown and Levinson's Politeness theory. We analyse the different kinds of face on display and at risk in a professional but informal environment. Questions include: how does laughter face-work relate to the notions of in-group and out-group? Just how do participants manoeuvre themselves 'in' and their adversaries 'out'? Is it always best to be in or are there sometimes advantages to being outside? Why do participants sometimes laugh at themselves? How does one recuperate lost face?

In Chapter 4 we turn our attention to wordplay and phraseplay, particularly as instantiated in both the newspaper and briefings corpora. We attempt a description of how puns are structured and consider the question of whether linguistics can help define the *quality* of humour, that is, the difference between a good pun and a bad one, drawing on the concepts of *delexicalization* and *relexicalization* as developed in the field of Corpus Linguistics. Using the newspapers corpora, we then attempt to formulate a taxonomy of the mechanisms used by headline writers to activate wordplay and consider the question: what are the psychological mechanisms readers must use to link the new phraseology they find on the page and the 'original' versions stored in the brain? In examining the puns in briefings we ask: why do participants use wordplay, do they hope to enhance their face or gain strategic advantage? Is punning wordplay always 'disruptive' of discourse, as Norrick recently suggests (1993, 2003), or can it also be used to advance an argument?

In Chapter 5 we return to issues of face, in particular face attacks, especially teasing. Using corpus data as evidence, teasing is defined, in terms of the laughter-talk theories developed here, as a face-threatening act performed (apparently) in non-*bona-fide* mode. We ask: who teases whom, when and for what reason? Is it possible to extrapolate a typology of teasing from the current data? What strategies of response to teasing or ridicule can victims employ and what are their relative merits and demerits in practice? In what circumstances is one strategy preferable to another and why do participants differ in their preferred choices?

Both linguistics and humour studies have recently witnessed a surge of interest in irony and its less attractive sibling, sarcasm. In Chapter 6 we contemplate some of the controversies and disputes concerning irony, waged largely in the absence of authentic data, and consider whether an examination of corpus data can shed new light on them. Is irony bisociative in nature and, if so, how? What does irony convey in written texts (namely, newspapers) and how and why do speakers use it in spoken interaction (briefings)? What is the relationship between irony and sarcasm? In sarcasm, bisociation and aggressive face-work seem to meet. How do they interrelate?

In the Conclusion we endeavour to draw together some of these many threads and consider to what extent we have been able to answer these varied research questions. In particular, how successful in explaining laughter is the three-fold combination of cognitive bisociation theory, the linguistic theories we espoused regarding language production-reception and politeness/face theory? Finally, we speculate briefly on whether what we have uncovered in the course of these authentic data-driven studies can tell us anything about the socio-biological evolution of laughter.

1 Joke humour theory and language principles

> Nature has furnished men with double parts... where that duplicity may be highly useful.
>
> (Boyle)
>
> What subterfuge, what double-dealing, what two-facedness!
>
> (Talmage)

1.1 Bisociation

1.1.1 Koestler and The Act of Creation

The theory of bisociation and how it applies to humour is laid out by Koestler in part one (entitled 'The Jester') of his seminal work *The Act of Creation* first published in 1964. His main endeavour is to draw analogies between the Comic, the Scientific and the Poetic spheres: his 'triptych' or 'three domains of creativity'. 'The logical pattern of the creative process is the same in all three cases', he argues: 'it consists in the discovery of hidden similarities' (1964: 27). The relation of comedy to wisdom, 'that the Jester should be brother to the Sage', is reflected in language, he says, and asks us to consider not only the word *wit(s)*, 'Jester and savant must both "live on their wits"' (1964: 28), which stems from *witan*, 'understanding', and eventually goes back to the Sanskrit *veda*, 'knowledge', but also *spirituel* (Fr) which may mean either witty or spiritually profound and *amuse* from *à-muser* (Fr) 'to muse' or 'ponder'.[1]

In all three domains, an act of creation results when our more or less automatized routines of thinking and behaving are somehow superseded by the unexpected juxtaposition or connection of 'previously unconnected matrices of experience'. This is the bisociative act. These matrices of experience are variously referred to by Koestler as 'frames of reference', 'associative contexts', 'types of logic', 'codes of behaviour', 'universes of discourse' and 'schemata'. If the process of their connection is a *collision* then humour will ensue, if a *fusion*, intellectual understanding, if a *confrontation*, an aesthetic experience. Pinker, in a critique of Koestler's ideas, outlines how bisociation works in the particular domain of humour which:

> begins with a train of thought in one frame of reference that bumps up against an anomaly: an event or statement that makes no sense in the context of what has come before. The anomaly can be resolved by shifting to a different frame of reference, one in which the event does make sense.
>
> (Pinker 1997: 549)

Koestler discusses almost exclusively canned jokes, probably because, firstly, of the relative difficulty at the time he writes of collecting conversational data, then, the fact that the latter tends not to appear particularly comic out of context and, finally, because pre-formulated jokes, being a literary genre and in a sense 'authored', must have struck him as being a more appropriate analogy with works in his other creative domains, especially the Poetic. One of the main topics of discussion in the current work will be the relevance or otherwise of bisociation theory to laughter-talk beyond canned jokes but, before we extrapolate, in this chapter we will concentrate on jokes in order to explicate and examine the theory itself. Pinker claims that Koestler's joke examples have dated and so he offers the following in illustration:

(1)   A mountain climber slips over a precipice and clings to a rope over a thousand-foot drop. In fear and despair, he looks to the heavens and cries, 'Is there anyone up there who can help me?' A voice from above booms, 'You will be saved if you show your faith by letting go of the rope.' The man looks down, then up, and shouts, 'Is there anyone else up there who can help me?'

(Pinker 1997: 550)

The joke begins by – very rapidly and efficiently – evoking the frame of reference of a religious miracle story in which God saves people because of their unbounded faith. There is then a hiatus or transition in which the hearer is skilfully encouraged to adopt the mountaineer's viewpoint 'looks down, then up' and the frame of reference is now his, his physical and mental predicament expressed in an everyday logic 'in which people have a healthy respect for the laws of gravity and are sceptical of anyone who claims to defy them' (Pinker 1997: 550). The result is the unexpected (in terms of the original religious script) refusal of divine advice.

Koestler warns us though that 'unexpectedness alone is not enough to produce a comic effect' (1964: 33). The second matrix (here the mountaineer's scepticism) must also be 'perfectly logical' in itself, and it is the clash of logics that begets laughter. The relationship between the two parts of a joke is obviously of vital importance and will be the object of our attention throughout this study. The concept of what constitutes a 'clash' (rather than 'confrontation' or 'fusion') is not fully explored by Koestler. There is, for instance, a relation of *bathos* in joke (1) above: the first frame of reference, the religious story, is in high style whereas the second is in low, everyday mode (a discussion of bathos for humorous effects can be found in section 2.6). Pinker claims that in all humour 'someone's dignity has been downgraded' in the second frame. It remains to be seen whether this is necessarily or typically the case.

Finally, it must be remembered that there is an overarching 'frame of reference' in the above – that of the canned joke genre. In this frame, paradoxically, it is to be expected that something unexpected will occur. This is not necessarily the case when the frame of reference is conversation, and it will be interesting to examine the role of the unexpected in conversational laughter-talk.

Koestler's only mention of humour beyond jokes and anecdotes is a brief comment on what he calls 'the higher forms of sustained humour, such as the satire or comic poem' (1964: 37). Whereas in jokes there exists 'a single point of culmination', these latter, he claims, 'do not rely on a single effect but on a series of minor explosions' since the humorous narrative 'oscillates between two frames of reference – say the romantic fantasy world of Don Quixote, and Sancho's cunning horse-sense' (1964: 37) – which, we might note, is an archetypal bathetic relationship.

1.1.2 *The Semantic Script Theory of jokes*

Although he realizes how important it is to define precisely what the first half and second half of a joke encapsulate and spends considerable time examining what precisely a matrix or a frame of reference might be, Koestler was writing too early to take advantage of the research conducted in the fields of Artificial Intelligence into the mental and behavioural phenomenon of *scripts*. He was nevertheless aware of Bartlett's work on *schemata*, the historical precursor to scripts, and recognizes their importance to his theory:

> We learn by assimilating experiences and grouping them into ordered schemata, into stable patterns of unity in variety. They enable us to cope with events and situations by applying the rules of the game appropriate to them.
> (Koestler 1964: 44)

Our memory is structured into schemata, which are then used as the basis on which we organize our normal day-to-day behaviour. They are 'condensations of learning into habit' and without them we would have to analyse afresh every situation we met, no matter how often we had been in it before. But Koestler's interest lies in moments where man ceases to be a creature of habit. The bisociative act, by connecting previously unconnected matrices of experience, provides a flash of new insight by showing a familiar situation in a new way and 'makes us "understand what it is to be awake, to be living on several planes at once" (to quote T.S. Eliot)' (1964: 45). Humour is one of the ways the schemata of habit are broken or superseded.

Raskin (1985) develops a theory of joke humour which is also dualistic in nature. Rather than matrix or frame he adopts the term *script* and formulates the

Semantic Script Theory of Humor (SSTH), which constitutes a considerable advance on previous formulations of joke theory. He outlines it as follows:

> A text can be characterized as a single-joke-carrying text if both of the [following] conditions are satisfied:
>
> (i) the text is compatible, fully or in part, with two different scripts;
> (ii) the two scripts with which the text is compatible are opposite.
>
> (Raskin 1985: 99)

The theory is illustrated by the following joke (slight editing):

(2) A man wrapped in hat and scarf makes his way to the local doctor's house. 'Is the doctor at home?' he asks in a hoarse voice. 'No,' replies the doctor's pretty young wife. 'Come right in.'

This text is said to contain two scripts, one of VISITING THE DOCTOR and the other of ADULTERY. As for the all-important question of the relationship between the two parts, Raskin tells us that they are *overlapping* and *opposite* 'and it is this oppositeness which creates the joke' (Raskin 1985: 100).

The term 'overlapping' is glossed by Attardo as follows: 'during the process of combining scripts [we will encounter] stretches of text that are compatible with more than one "reading" i.e. would fit more than one script'. In the Doctor's Wife joke, all but the final part, the punch-line consisting of the wife's invitation to 'Come right in', is compatible with both scripts (though, clearly, we are meant to adopt the more obvious one of VISITING THE DOCTOR). The overlap between two scripts may be partial or total. 'If the overlap is total, the text in its entirety is compatible with both scripts; if the overlap is partial, some parts of the text [...] will not be compatible with one or the other script' (Attardo 1994: 203). In other words, the second script either does away with the first, replacing it (as in the Doctor's Wife joke, in which the punchline renders the 'visiting the doctor' reading most unlikely), or joins it, cohabiting with it and creating an ambiguous text ('double-' or dual-meaning). Raskin's example of the latter is the Village Vicar joke (slight editing):

(3) An English bishop gets a note from the vicar of a village in his diocese: 'Milord, I regret to inform you of my wife's death. Can you possibly send me a substitute for the weekend?'

where both meanings (substitute for his wife and substitute for him) are both technically compatible with the text.

The segment of the text which introduces the second script – in the Doctor's Wife text, the final part, the wife's invitation – is called by Raskin the *scriptswitch trigger* (in other theories it is known as the *disjunctor*). It works by forcing the hearer/reader to perform a procedure which Attardo calls *backtracking*

(1994: 140), that is, going back over the text to reassess it in the light of the new information:

> When the hearer reaches the disjunctor, he/she realises that the interpretation of the text up to that point is either untenable or another previously unnoticed interpretation is also possible, and that the two are not compatible (i.e. they are incongruous). The hearer is forced to return to the beginning of the text (i.e. to backtrack) and parse it again in the light of the new contextual information.
> (Attardo 1994: 140)

Since the term script-shift might imply that the second script necessarily replaces the first and since the term disjunctor is not self-explanatory, we will adopt the expression *backtrack trigger* in this study.

Nevertheless, 'the overlapping of two scripts is not necessarily a cause of humor *per se*' (Attardo 1994: 203), they must also, the theory claims, be opposite. Raskin spends some time defining the oppositeness of scripts, arguments which we will discuss in section 1.3.4.

In the meantime, however, in order, first, to evaluate and perhaps extend the script theory of jokes and, second, to examine the relationship that may exist between scripts as envisaged in cognitive theory and scripts or schemata as concepts in linguistic theory, we need to consider in some detail the concept of script itself and its precise relevance to jokes.

1.2 Script theory

1.2.1 Learning and memory

The closely related schema (Bartlett 1932), frame (Minsky 1975) and script theories (Schank and Abelson 1977; Schank 1986, 1991) are theories first and foremost of learning and memory. Bartlett's seminal work is entitled *Remembering* whilst Schank and Abelson state plainly that their book is, 'in a sense, entirely about memory [...] human memory organization' (Schank and Abelson 1977: 17). These theories are obviously mentalist in character, in that they take for granted the existence of mind:

> American social psychology had its roots in Gestalt psychology and therefore did not succumb to the excesses of behaviorism the way human experimental psychology did. The phenomenology of mental life maintained a central role.
> (Schank and Abelson 1977: 10)

The core of all three theories is the argument that the mind plays an *active* role in the organization of memory.

The Schank and Abelson theory argues that many of the experiences, or 'sequences of events' that humans encounter are similar to or reminiscent of others, in other words, much of life consists of meeting with roughly similar experiences. It is reasonable to assume, they continue, that human memory must include the capability of recognizing repeated or similar sequences of events. When sufficient experiences of a certain type have been met, the memory 'as an economy measure' stores the sequences of events as a 'standardized generalized episode which we will call a script' (1977: 19). The script contains an outline description of the typical events in their proper sequence. Thus, after having eaten in restaurants (Schank and Abelson's recurrent example) a number of times, an individual's memory will have constructed a *restaurant script* ($RESTAURANT in their notation) of how the events contingent upon a visit to a restaurant normally unfold (arrive, enter, allow the waiter/waitress to show you to a table, etc.) and for each subsequent visit to a restaurant 'rather than list the details of what happened [...] memory simply stores the items in this particular episode that were significantly different from the standard script as the only items specifically in the description of that episode' (1977: 19). A script then 'is a structure that describes appropriate sequences of events in a particular context' and consists of 'slots and requirements about what can fill those slots'. 'Slot-fillers' can be particular events or sequences of events, that is (sub)scripts (e.g. choosing what to eat and drink).

A script differs from a *concept* in that it must unfold ('be written' 1977: 42) from one particular role's point of view – the *restaurant script* for the customer is different from that of the waiter. The concept of eating in a restaurant, then, can be said to be a conglomeration of scripts. In this personalization, scripts resemble templates for narratives, templates which have certain fixed elements (it is difficult to imagine a restaurant with no serving staff), and variable features which can alter on occasion but about which actors will have differing strengths of expectation (we strongly expect a written menu, but some restaurants do without; the quality of food is entirely variable and to be discovered on each visit).

So far we have tried to define scripts in terms of their contribution to memory, but script theory has aroused the greatest interest in those fields which attempt to explain human *understanding* (including, indeed especially, that of discourse).[2] Script theory was elaborated in the domain of Artificial Intelligence as an attempt to solve some of the problems researchers encountered in trying to teach machines to understand human communication, in particular the problem of how 'the appropriate ingredients for extracting the meaning of a sentence [...] are often nowhere to be found within the sentence' (Schank and Abelson 1977: 9). The researchers recognized that acquired background knowledge of both situation and texts/discourses was of overwhelming importance in interpreting the simplest utterances, for instance:

(4) I went to three drugstores this morning.

implies that the speaker did not find what they were looking for in the first two. The problem is the same as that which interests Grice, who asserts that with the utterance:

(5) [Mr] X is meeting a woman this evening.

the speaker is normally implying (or 'implicating') that 'the person to be met was someone other than Mr X's wife, mother, sister or perhaps even close Platonic friend' (Grice 1975: 50).

Scripts, it is claimed, are used to '*interpret* and *participate in* (my emphasis) events we have been through many times' (Schank and Abelson 1977: 37). Although the interpretation of a situation is of course frequently the prelude to participation in it, most of Schank and Abelson's discussion concentrates on the first of these and examines the ways subjects understand stories, sequential narratives and so on.

Other researchers, too, have been attracted to script/frame/schema theory as accounting for discourse understanding. Rumelhart (1976), for instance, asserts that 'the process of understanding a passage consists in finding a schema which will account for it' (although this, as we shall see, is a considerable over-simplification). Charniak writes that frames explain at least in part the 'process of fitting what one is told into the framework of what one already knows' (Charniak 1979, in Brown and Yule 1983: 239). This is, of course, what makes their ideas so valuable to the study of joke-comprehension.

For Schank and Abelson, proof that humans use scripts comes in the form of what they call *causal chains*. 'People, in speaking and writing,' they note, 'consistently leave out information that they feel can easily be inferred by the listener or reader' (1977: 22). In particular in a context where A causes B and B causes C, when the path is 'obvious', humans communicate 'A, then C'. For example, compare the utterances:

(6) John burned his hand because he touched the stove.
John burned his hand because he forgot the stove was on.

The first means what it says causally, but in the second, 'forgetting' does not cause 'burning' except by a missing process – that of absent-mindedly touching the stove. The following:

(7) John cried because Mary said she loved Bill.

'is a meaningful, well-constructed sentence [...] Yet, it is literally quite silly'. And though such sentences do not generally cause problems in human communication, 'in designing a theory of understanding, there is a great deal to worry about' (Schank and Abelson 1977: 23). The only explanation of how humans cope so effortlessly with this kind of utterance is that they have the necessary interpretative information, especially the missing links, already stored away, largely in the form of scripts. Scripts, say Schank and Abelson (1977: 45), are in effect maxi-causal chains and when two people share a script, a vast amount of information can remain implicit, unsaid. To quote their example, all a speaker has to recount is:

(8)   John went to a restaurant;
      He ordered chicken;
      He left a large tip.

And, having called up (or *activated*) the $RESTAURANT, all the procedures between entering and ordering and between ordering and tipping are assumed by the hearer:

> we fill in, as if we had actually heard them, the events on the default path of the applied script, as long as we are simply filling in the steps between explicitly stated points.
>
> (Schank and Abelson 1977: 45)

In fact speakers will tend to mention the bare minimum and leave the hearer to assume as much as possible in order to concentrate on what cannot be assumed, the deviations from the default script, which will, of course, generally be the *point* of the narration. Hearers will expect the same, will expect not to be burdened with information they can safely assume and indeed, if assumable procedures are explicitly mentioned ('John ate the chicken'), they are liable to cast around for the special significance of its inclusion. All this is of course in accord with Sperber and Wilson's (1995) general communicative principle of *relevance* which states that, in normal circumstances, speakers attempt to achieve *optimal relevance*, that is, they try to communicate meaning at the lowest possible processing cost to the hearer. This implies that, from the hearer's point of view, they will presume that any apparent extra demands on them are being made because extra information is being conveyed.

It is important in the analysis of humour to stress that script theory implies that understanding is an active process. Scripts enable the hearer to both fill in the missing information and also, crucially to jokes, *predict* what will occur in a given situation: 'we are claiming that understanding is predictive in its nature' (Schank and Abelson 1977: 76).

There is, of course, a (rather exasperating) type of joke-riddle which exploits the use of scripts and the tendency to take the assumable for granted: witness the following:

(9)   'Do you stir your coffee with you right hand or your left?'
      'Neither – I use a spoon.'

(Raskin 1985: 26, from Mindess 1971)

Similarly, the old music hall chestnut:

(10) 'Who was that woman I saw you with last night?'
'That was no woman, that was my wife.'

exploits the very assumption noted by Grice and mentioned above that 'Mr X is meeting a woman' is conventionally taken to imply that the rendezvous is not with a woman that X already knows well.

1.2.2 Script interaction

We have already mentioned that both Koestler and Raskin argue that more than one script is involved in jokes and so we need to examine how scripts interrelate.

Schank and Abelson outline several ways in which two scripts can interact. First, a main script can be interrupted by another so-called *distracting script* occurring within its boundaries. The main script in such cases is said to be *in abeyance*. An example might be the meeting and greeting of a friend who unexpectedly enters the restaurant. Sometimes, however, the distracting script can be a problem or *obstacle* to the script's completion. To use Schank and Abelson's example, if the waitress brings a hot dog instead of the hamburger that was ordered, *corrective action* needs to be undertaken, which normally takes the form of a *loop*, that is, a repetition of the part of the script (ordering) in which the obstacle occurred. In other words, the actors go back over the course of the script to the part where the problem occurred and replay that part. As Schank and Abelson also point out, there may be an emotional accompaniment such as anger, regret, sadness and so on.

In the second form of script interaction, a new script may put an end to a previous one, preventing its natural completion. Discovering the restaurant was closed, or that one had forgotten one's wallet/purse, or being offended by the service and leaving would all be script terminators.

Finally two or more scripts can simply be active at the same time. Schank and Abelson cite the example of 'John was wooing his girlfriend in the restaurant', where $RESTAURANT and $ROMANCER are both alive. In such cases, of course, 'when two scripts are active at once they compete for incoming items of information. Sometimes the events that fit one affect the events of the other... any new item is potentially in either one' (1977: 58). If we were to meet in the course of this narrative a sentence like 'John asked her for some money' we might infer either that he needed it to pay the bill, that he was wooing this particular girl because she had money or, of course, both. Schank and Abelson call such a state of affairs *scriptural ambiguity*. Like all forms of ambiguity,[3] in cases of normal communication, scriptural ambiguity is normally either suppressed (i.e. disambiguated) by the context or resolved later in proceedings. Many creative discourses, however, including jokes, of course, thrive on it.

1.2.3 Types of script

So far this discussion has been concerned with the kind of script in which to a large extent:

1) the situation is specified;
2) the several players have interlocking roles to follow;
3) the players share an understanding of what is supposed to happen.

(Schank and Abelson 1977: 61)

In other words, the customer and waitress typically both do what the other expects. This is normally the prevailing case in real life, otherwise interaction would be extremely difficult and prolonged. In terms of the subject matter of this study, political language and, in particular, briefings, 'it is characteristic of institutionalized public situations with defined goals [...] that the social interactions be stylized' (1977: 61) so that everyone involved stands the best possible chance of following the interaction. There is a very real sense, then, in which we can talk of the waitress and customer in a restaurant or the podium and journalist in briefings as *playing the roles* of waitress, customer, podium and questioner since they are following a number of scripts pre-ordained for their social or institutional role in order to facilitate the business in hand.

However, Schank and Abelson also postulate the existence of *personal scripts* which actors may be following alongside and over and above the standardized social ones. 'Suppose that one of the parties wants to direct the interaction into channels other than those defined by the situational script' (1977: 61–62). The customer may wish to make a date with the waitress, in which case he will both follow the $RESTAURANT and instantiate a flirting script. Sometimes participants will be aware of their participation in other actors' personal scripts, sometimes not (as in a successful confidence trick), sometimes they will cooperate, sometimes not. In any case, importantly, they are almost always goal-oriented.[4]

Personal scripts may be relevant to the present study in two ways. First of all, the participants in political interviews or briefings may well – probably it is typically the case – have personal scripts they are following either openly or covertly, alongside their institutional roles. Second, much humour seems to work by the sudden and unexpected revelation of a personal narrative being followed by one of the characters in the text (as the doctor's wife with her amorous intentions, or the mountaineer who prefers to save his skin rather than his soul).

1.2.4 Problems with script theory

Although a great deal of experimental evidence has been accumulated to support at least the part of script theory which describes their use in understanding discourse (e.g. Tannen and Wallatt 1999), a number of questions were also raised from the start.

One frequent objection to script theory is that, as Brown and Yule point out, by itself, it predicts that 'a lot less human discourse should occur than actually occurs' (1983: 240), although the illustrations of this argument they produce are rather unfair. They ask the question: why, for instance, have a newspaper report of a car crash if people already have all the relevant stereotypical information? The answer is of course that organs of mass media cannot rely on everyone in their audience having a full and appropriate script of all recurrent phenomena. Moreover, in any case, such news report do in fact take vast amounts of detail as given: that there was a driver or that the car had wheels will hardly be mentioned unless relevant and, if they are, they will be accompanied by the definite article, a sign they are considered as given information.[5]

Nevertheless the objection is fundamentally legitimate; humans do spend time going over old ground, telling others what they can be reasonably expected to already know. Script theory describes the exchange of what we might call strictly cognitive information, whereas humans are interested in much more than this when they converse. Script theory has to be accompanied by approaches which take account of social and psychological phenomena such as, for example, identity display and bonding. Canned joke-telling itself, of course, has its socio-psychological functions, although much of the ludic quality of jokes lies in their presentation *as if they were vital information*, delivered with urgent voice and frequently introduced as 'news' – 'have you heard about' etc. Humour which makes a point, of course, is by definition cognitively informative as well as ludic.

Yet another criticism of script theory is that it is too powerful. Any text can call up very large numbers of scripts. Brown and Yule ask us to consider the following article from the *Sunday Times*:

> The Cathedral congregation had watched on television monitors as Pope and Archbishop met, in front of a British Caledonian helicopter, on the dewy grass of a Canterbury recreation ground.
>
> (1983: 240)

Which scripts are selected by readers? Perhaps $CATHEDRAL, $TELEVISION WATCHING and $MEETING. But what of $RIDING IN a HELICOPTER or $WHAT TO DO IN a RECREATION GROUND? 'The outstanding problem for Schank's theory' they argue, 'is to find a principled means of limiting the number of conceptualizations required for the understanding of a sentence' (1983: 244). 'These questions are not trivial' they add. Maybe not, but they do appear to be envisaged and dealt with in Schank and Abelson's treatise, which stresses the difference between *strong* and *weak* activation. In the above newspaper text, given its extreme brevity, all the scripts suggested by Brown and Yule will be weakly activated in the mind of a competent reader, who will, however, wait until more text and more information is given before deciding which of the scripts is to be strongly activated or *instantiated*. The principle of relevance as outlined earlier will militate against unnecessary early strong activations. The other scripts will not be discarded but will remain in the background; they can be referred to anew (and their components will then take *the*, for example, *the helicopter*) and can even take over as instantiated script should the text so develop.

36 Joke humour theory and language principles

There are, however, a number of even more fundamental questions to be answered. For example, how many times does one have to have experience of a situation to internalize its features into a script? Or consider the following set of related issues. How can anyone do anything for the first time (say, buy a car)?[6] Can people have a hearsay script, that is, one you have not experienced yourself but have been told about or even explicitly taught? If so, how do these differ from the standard experiential scripts? Similarly, what is the status of scripts in fiction, that is, event sequences that never actually happened, and, more outlandishly still, do we have 'unreal scripts', that is, stereotypical information about events that could never happen?

More detailed answers to these questions will be attempted in the following sections. Suffice it to say here that a script theory that did not envisage hearsay and second-hand learning would be a poor thing indeed. The construction of such scripts would seem to be the point of both (theoretical) education and (practical) training. A very large number of scripts would seem to be constructed by the assimilation of a mixture of both first- and second-hand experience. One might hazard a hypothetical psychological mechanism. The first scripts we learn in childhood we learn from our own perspective. As we mature we become aware of the scripts being followed by the people we interact with and we slowly learn to imaginatively empathize, to put ourselves in their place. Finally, in a third stage, abstract imagination can construct even fictional scripts by a combination of analogy with scripts we are already familiar with and a general knowledge of human requirements, goals and plan-making abilities. How we acquire this form of knowledge is the topic of the following section.

1.2.5 Needs, goals and plans

There is one important part of Schank and Abelson's theory which is frequently overlooked, namely their description of how understanding occurs when an actor has no script for a particular situation. It will have been noted how, in the explanation in section 1.2.1 of how humans process utterances such as:

(6) John burned his hand because he forgot the stove was on.

or

(7) John cried because Mary said she loved Bill.

It was asserted that they do so with ease because they have the necessary interpretative information, especially the missing links, already stored away, largely in the form of scripts. But note the hedge 'largely', because they also, according to Schank and Abelson, make use of another type of preconstituted knowledge. The kind of information contained in scripts is described as *specific* knowledge, but we also have access to what they call *general* knowledge which:

> enables a person to understand and interpret another person's actions simply because the other person is a human being with certain standard needs who lives in a world which has certain standard methods of getting those needs fulfilled.
>
> (Schank and Abelson 1977: 37)

Because we inhabit the same sort of bodies in the same sort of world, we share many similar needs with our fellow human animals, thus 'if someone asks you for a glass of water, you need not ask why he wants it' (Schank and Abelson 1977: 37). Moreover, we readily assume (sometimes erroneously) that our fellows will have much the same goals as we do or at least that we can envisage having. Thus we are able to interpret 'John cried because Mary said she loved Bill' partly because we know human males often desire the exclusive affection of a particular female and, on discovering that they do not possess it, are liable to feel pain. Furthermore, we also assume (sometimes just as erroneously) that our fellows are rational beings who will follow some kind of reasonable plan to achieve those goals. We use this knowledge of plan-making, say Schank and Abelson, to interpret even the most seemingly disconnected sentences:

(11)   John knew that his wife's operation would be very expensive.
       There was always Uncle Harry...
       He reached for the suburban phone book.

If, as hearers/readers, we can discern a plan being followed by a character in the narrative we will happily use it to interpret the text. 'By finding a plan, an understander can make guesses about the intentions of an action (*sic*, read *actor*) in an unfolding story and use these guesses to make sense of the story' (Schank and Abelson 1977: 70). Compare the straightforward:

(12)   Willa was hungry.
       She went to look in the fridge.

Such a plan is so common we would call it part of a script. But Schank and Abelson ask us to compare:

(13)   Willa was hungry.
       She took out the Michelin Guide.

and

(14)   Willa was hungry.
       She took out 'Concepts in Artificial Intelligence'.

Only (13) is readily interpretable as a pre-plan or the first step in a plan to obtain (good) food.

Note that, although the guessing of goals and plans are 'the mechanisms that underlie scripts', that is, it constitutes the main means by which we construct our scripts, understanding via scripts tends to have priority. If we can interpret an event by finding a script, then we will do so, since it saves much processing time and effort. Only if we fail to interpret it do we fall back on general knowledge inferencing. The first is 'quick and dirty' whilst the second requires the on-line or nonce construction of a *mental model* that will fit the data.

1.2.6 Mental models

A mental model is 'a representation in the form of an internal model of the state of affairs characterized by the sentence' (Brown and Yule 1983: 251) (we might prefer the term *utterance*). A form of mental model theory, proposed by Johnson-Laird (1981a, 1981b, 1983), differs somewhat from that proposed here. It relies not on inference from the first basics of human goals, but entails a heuristic approach, affirming that people construct a sort of 'best model' on the available evidence, inferencing, that is, from features of the context of situation. The two versions are not necessarily incompatible and the Johnson-Laird approach may well be useful for discourses where human purpose and planning are not relevant. In any case, various evidence is cited for the existence of mental models. For instance, subjects in recall experiments tend to provide a model of information they have been asked to remember, rather than the information in its original form (Anderson *et al.* 1976). What we might call 'jumping-to-a-conclusion' reading is further evidence: a sentence such as 'This book fills a much-needed gap' is readily interpreted, according to Johnson-Laird (1981a), as praise for the book. It is also evidence, surely, of an overpowering innate human *desire* to comprehend.

We are now in a position to confront some of the questions raised at the end of the previous section, namely, how we do anything for the first time, how we cope with fictional events and, especially, how we assimilate third-hand experiences. Taking this latter first, since:

> a major function of language is to enable one person to have another's experience of the world by proxy;
>
> (Johnson-Laird 1981b: 139)

whenever we hear, read about or are taught a certain event sequence we have never experienced personally, we set about first of all, building a mental model to accommodate it:

> instead of a direct apprehension of a state of affairs, the listener constructs a model of them based on a speaker's remarks.
>
> (Johnson-Laird 1981b: 139)

If this model is productive, in other words, if it helps to produce satisfactory future behaviour in real life (for example, after being told by others how they bought a car we manage to buy one ourselves) we are liable to begin to solidify the model into a script.

The situation regarding fictional, even impossible or 'unreal', discourse scripts is entirely analogous. If a model enables the reader to successfully predict later developments in a discourse it is likely to congeal into a script. If I read 'the alien battle-fleet set out for Earth' – presuming alien nature to be similar to human – I will predict their goal is conquest, the battle-fleet part of the plan, and that aliens are an aggressive lot to boot. If the expected invasion occurs, my mental model will be reinforced. If instead the battle-fleet is actually coming to rescue our troubled planet, then I will revise my model. In this way are formed fictional genre expectations, which are nothing more than the set of scripts we have acquired for the particular genre or discourse type. Canned jokes, of course, are an assortment of fictional discourse types, each of which comes laden with its expectations or scripts (including, as we have said, the expectation of the unexpected). But all sophisticated literature, including jokes, operates by the exploitation, the reworking and reanimating of expectations; none but the most hackneyed or ritualistic of fiction works only by recalling scripts. There is almost always an interplay of the two methods of discourse construction – script recall and inference-driven model building.

1.3 A script-and-inference theory of jokes

1.3.1 *From script to narrative*

We are now able to return to the main theme of this work and consider the relevance of these considerations to laughter-talk. We can conclude that the Semantic Script Theory of joke Humor (SSTH, see section 1.1.2), as formulated by Raskin, although constituting perhaps the most complete systematic statement of joke humour of recent times, does not fully explain how all jokes work. Some jokes will indeed involve the 'overlapping' of two scripts. But it is contended here that many jokes depend instead on the movement from the script to the mental model, and perhaps back again, from the quick and straightforward process of recall to the hard work of best-guess inferencing, from the stereotypical to the relatively novel. This sudden shift helps account for the role of the unexpected in humour. It is a surprise for the instantiated script to be so brusquely interrupted and for us to be asked to switch not only scripts but sometimes entire procedures.

We can see how the process works with the two jokes we recounted earlier in the chapter. First, the Doctor's Wife:

(2) A man wrapped in hat and scarf makes his way to the local doctor's house. 'Is the doctor at home?' he asks in a hoarse voice. 'No' replies the doctor's pretty young wife. 'Come right in.'

If we recall, Raskin describes this as containing the two overlapping scripts of $VISITING THE DOCTOR and $ADULTERY. The text certainly begins by inviting the reader/hearer to call up a script involving a man going to the doctor. On meeting the wife's words 'No, come on in' we are forced to perform, as Schank and Abelson would have it, a loop, to replay the joke with remedial action, since the $VISITING THE DOCTOR (for treatment) no longer allows us an adequate interpretation of the sequence of events. The remedial action is the inferencing process which now kicks in and we 'make guesses about the intentions of an [actor] in an unfolding story and use these guesses to make sense of the story' (Schank and Abelson 1977: 70). We begin to conjecture about the motives of the doctor's wife in particular, being the one who utters the backtrack trigger. We know that a highly popular – to say the least – *goal* of human behaviour is sex, and since we know enough about the joke discourse conventions to know that characters in them are very frequently involved in the search for sex, this is one of our first conjectures – or mental models – and it explains the turn of events admirably. However, the joke remains ambiguous, in that two readings are still possible. Either the wife is attempting to seduce the patient, or he is no patient at all but her lover arriving on an assignation. In other words we cannot choose between seduction and adultery, and this too is an argument against a simple script-to-script interpretation of this text.

Returning to Pinker's Mountaineer joke:

(1) A mountain climber slips over a precipice and clings to a rope over a thousand-foot drop. In fear and despair, he looks to the heaven and cries: 'Is there anyone up there who can help me?' A voice from above booms: 'You will be saved if you show your faith by letting go of the rope.' The man looks down, then up, and shouts, 'Is there anyone *else* up there who can help me?'

This joke is explicitly about *plans*. The first script we are meant to instantiate here – a 'climber suspended over a terrible drop' – is, thankfully, for most of us at least, a hearsay one we have met mostly through fiction (including other jokes). This then develops into a 'praying to God for a miracle' script. In contrast to the Doctor's Wife, here, a new script – that of 'asking for a second opinion' – is unambiguously instantiated by the end, but this does not in itself explain why the text is funny. The humour lies in the pay-off from the inferential work we have to do in the transition between the $MIRACLE and $SECOND OPINION. The man's goal throughout is, of course, self-preservation – another motivation needing little explanation. The joke turns upon him rejecting God's plan and upsetting the normal development of the script. We have constructed a mental model of a terrified but impertinent individual whose suspicious and unheroic reactions are all too much like ours.

It needs to be stressed that the script-inference theory is still bisociative. In fact it helps to revive one of Koestler's most important arguments, that the new part of a joke has to have its own logic and, since the vast majority of jokes involve human characters, the new 'logic' is often that of human desire and planning – frequently a personal, individual and context-dependent one as opposed to the generality expressed in the original script, as in the Mountaineer joke. Although Pinker failed to find it funny, it is profitable to look at one of Koestler's illustrations of bisociation in jokes (taken from Freud: slight editing):

(15) A Marquis at the court of Louis XIV enters his wife's boudoir and finds her in the arms of a Bishop. He walks calmly to the window and starts blessing the people on the street below.

'What are you doing?' asks the wife in astonishment.
'Monseigneur is performing my functions,' replied the Marquis, 'so I am performing his!'

Our dramatic expectations, argues Koestler, are raised most economically by the activation of an adultery script ('what happens when the husband finds his wife in bed with another man') and are debunked by the Marquis's unexpected reaction. But the script-to-script theory fails to elucidate such a joke, partly because it is impossible to construe a second script. Is it *impersonating someone*? – far too vague to be a script, or is it *impersonating a Monseigneur*? – not a script too many of us will have acquired, one suspects. There is only a limited amount of inferencing work to be carried out in this particular joke. Given the obscurity of the Marquis's actions, his explanation carries out most of the inferencing for us (and this is probably why Pinker finds it disappointing). However, the explanation allows the inclusion of a joke within a joke (the real point of the text) which is the euphemistic phraseplay on the expression 'performing my functions'.

Given the frequent difficulty of interpreting the second part of jokes in terms of simple scripts, where necessary, we will adopt the superordinate expression *narrative* to include both scripts and non-script sequences of events: the bisociative theory adopted here, then, proposes that a large number of jokes consist of two separate narratives.

A narrative can be defined as an event or sequence of events which unfold from a particular perspective. To follow a narrative, as in all story-telling (fictional or factual), the listener is required to perform an act of imagination, of fantasy, and adopt a non-self perspective. If the narrative is a script, he or she will also be asked to draw upon their memory. But they may well also be required to infer what is happening using their knowledge of how the world (sometimes a fantasy world) and its inhabitants normally function. The joke-teller also *a fortiori* achieves an act of fantasy but disrupts the listener's original reading in one or both of the following ways: either by revealing that the script s/he has chosen is the wrong one or/and by upsetting their expectations of how the world should operate.

1.3.2 Script and non-script narratives in jokes

Some jokes, then, involve simply the substitution of one script narrative for another, as in the following children's joke (from Wells 1982):

(16) A feller went into the park and he went up to the park-keeper and he says:
 'Have you got any manure I can put on my rhubarb?'
 And the park-keeper goes:
 'No, come on in here. We put custard on ours.'

where the gardening script is abruptly reinterpreted as a culinary one with a – for the average child – delightfully revolting effect.

Other children's jokes seem to go to the opposite extreme (from Attardo et al. 2002):

(17) Why did the elephant sit on the marshmallow?
      Because he did not want to fall in the hot chocolate.

It is hard to divine any script instantiation in such jokes of the absurd.

Many jokes however play with a mixture of script and non-script narratives. One type, the tricolon or three-part joke, illustrates this interplay well:

(18) An Englishman, an Irishman and a Scotsman were in a pub, talking about their sons. 'My son was born on St George's Day,' commented the Englishman. 'So we obviously decided to call him George'. 'That's a real coincidence,' remarked the Scot. 'My son was born on St Andrew's Day, so obviously we decided to call him Andrew.'
      'That's incredible, what a coincidence,' said the Irishman. 'Exactly the same thing happened with my son Pancake.'

Shrove Tuesday is 'Pancake Day' in Britain. Whether naming sons after patron saints is a script in the sense intended by Schank and Abelson is a moot question.[7] The main point is that, in the tricolon joke, the narrative is repeated so that it *becomes* a script or 'acquired information', and this repetition sets up expectations about the series, the model being followed. The third part of the tricolon is then employed to upset these expectations in some way. Here is another tricolon joke:

(19) There are three Irishmen stranded on an island. Suddenly a fairy appears and offers to grant each one of them one wish. The first one asks to be intelligent. Instantly, he is turned into a Scotsman and he swims off the island. The next one asks to be even more intelligent than the previous one. So, instantly he is turned into a Welshman. He builds a boat and sails off the island. The third Irishman asks to become even more intelligent than the previous two. The fairy turns him into a woman, and she walks across the bridge.

The joke begins with a mix of three joke-scripts, the $DESERT ISLAND, the $GODMOTHER-THREE WISHES and the $ENGLISHMAN, IRISHMAN AND SCOTSMAN. The novel, non-script information is the nature of the wish – to be made intelligent – and the transformation into a Scotsman and Welshman. A script is built up within the world of the joke of $HOW TO GET OFF THE ISLAND. The script expectations are doubly defeated in the third section of the tricolon. Not only is no intelligence required to leave the island, the intelligent third member of the trio, instead of being the expected 'Englishman' (in the English version of the joke of course), is a woman, and the joke is partly on the listener, especially if male and English.

Tricolon jokes, then, employ a sort of 'garden path' mechanism. However, in (18) one of the characters in the joke misapplies the son-naming narrative, whereas in (19) it is the joke-teller who redirects the narrative. In cases similar to the latter, the joke contains a 'superior logic' hyper-script. In cases similar to the former, however, where a joke character upsets the script, we can have either a superiority or inferiority (stupidity) logic hyper-script (section 1.3.8, and on superiority theory see section 7.3).

1.3.3 What kind of incongruity is funny?

'If there is one generalization that can be extracted from the literature about humour, it is that humour involves *incongruity*' (Ritchie 2004: 46). Both Koestler and Raskin's ideas clearly depend heavily on the notion that the two narratives in a joke are somehow incongruous. Koestler, as we have said, talks of a clash, whereas Raskin talks of his two scripts being 'opposite'. But the question which, as Ritchie notes, often goes unaddressed in much theorizing about humour is 'what kind of incongruity is funny?' (2004: 63).

1.3.4 Oppositeness

Raskin lists five of what for him are the most common oppositions: good/bad, life/death, obscene/non-obscene, money/no-money and high/low stature, which he claims are 'essential to human life' (Raskin 1985: 113). He also goes on, however, to list a good number of paired items which are very difficult to see as 'opposite', for example, disease/money, writer/postman, Jaguar/calendar, stalemate/wife. He explains that these are 'examples of local antonyms, i.e. two linguistic entities whose meanings are opposite only within a particular discourse and solely for the purposes of this discourse (cf. Lyons 1977, 271–279)' (Raskin 1985: 108). In (2), as we have seen, doctor and lover are said to be opposed.

Ritchie (2004: 69–80) offers a none-too-friendly critique of the SSTH. His main reproach is the underdefinition of terms and the lack of clarity of concepts employed, including, and most crucially, that of script opposition. Many of the illustrations of oppositeness in Raskin, he argues, are obscure or far-fetched and so it is not possible to divine the precise nature of 'oppositeness'. In logical terms, if *any* two scripts when juxtaposed in a text can be described as 'opposite', then opposite means nothing more than 'different'. In any two-term universe of discourse the two terms are in some sense opposed, but unless this opposition has some value, some meaning in the world outside, in the world of the joke-teller and receiver, then we are no nearer to a definition of what humans find comic. As for the 'five most common oppositions' listed in the previous paragraph, whilst it has long been recognized that many jokes evoke (preoccupations about) death, sex, bodily functions, penury and social status, it is doubtful whether jokes which deal with these matters necessarily also explicitly contain a script outlining their 'opposites'. The Mountaineer joke, for example, only makes sense in the context of human fear of dying but it would be a vast oversimplification to analyse it as consisting of one script representing life and the second death (for one thing, the mountaineer does not die).

Ritchie also criticizes Attardo's development of the SSTH into what he calls the General Theory of Verbal Humor (GTVH). At times Attardo also talks of local antonymy as the difference between the relevant elements of two scripts (Attardo 2001) but elsewhere (Attardo *et al.* 2002) he seems to feel that simple non-identity is the measure of the difference, though non-identity would seem to be merely another term for 'different'. The question remains of why two narratives placed in conjunction should sometimes be funny, sometimes not, as well as the question of the quality of humour – why some jokes containing two narratives are funnier than others. The answer must lie, to a large extent at least, in the way they interrelate.

1.3.5 Logical mechanisms

In order to confront the crucial question of the way the two scripts or narratives interact in the joke to create humour, Attardo and Raskin (1991) propose the idea of *logical mechanisms*, which account for 'the way in which the two [scripts] in the joke are brought together' (Ruch *et al.* 1993: 125). Attardo *et al.* (2002) list no less than twenty-seven mechanisms, including role-reversal, garden-path, exaggeration, figure-ground reversal, ignoring the obvious and false analogy. A joke may rely on more than one logical mechanism. They go on to admit, however, that 'it seems likely that at a fairly abstract level there exists only a handful of [logical mechanisms]; perhaps further research will be able to reduce them to a single very abstract mechanism' (2002: 29). In the following section I would like to discuss three proposals of my own which seem to be at work in a very large number of jokes. The first two are logical mechanisms, namely, the proper-to-improper shift and the reversal of evaluation. The third, quirky logic, is less a mechanism for relating narratives, more a play on the listener's real-world expectations. All three are closely interrelated.

1.3.6 The proper- improper narrative shift

When a joke turns on the proper-improper narrative shift, the second narrative introduces behaviour that is somehow improper in two ways. It is, first of all, anomalous in terms of the original script, but it is also 'objectively' improper in terms of 'real-world' behaviour. This is a major departure from Raskin's definition of oppositeness, which remains a logical concept and takes little account of socio-pragmatics.

The opposition proper-improper is one of the most fundamental of all in the construction of jokes, and reveals a great deal of what we find comic and why we indulge in laughter. Probably the most common sort of impropriety in joke texts is the sexual sort. In the Doctor's Wife we are presented with the contrast between visiting the doctor to be treated (normal and proper) and visiting doctor's wife for a tryst (unexpected and improper by the socio-sexual mores of society). In the Village Vicar, one reading is a perfectly proper request by the vicar to be substituted, the second depends upon the impropriety of asking for a substitute wife (and therefore sexual partner).

There are of course numerous other variations on the proper-to-improper shift. One is blasphemy as illustrated in the Mountaineer joke, which comprises a right and proper request for divine help substituted by a most improper rejection of the same, along with the suspicion of God that this implies. Scatological jokes need little explanation, such themes and the accompanying language being in themselves taboo. Their straightforwardness means they usually hold little appeal for adults but the following:

(20) Why do farts smell?
For the deaf.

manages to combine a scatological theme with a special unexpected shift, given that a different *type* of epistemological explanation is produced. Instead of something about internal bodily plumbing we get a teleological account (with more than a touch of the absurd). It is a kind of pun on the word *why*.

Many more jokes play with other kinds of social conventions, expectations and, of course, pretensions. Raskin's duchess and driver joke is a good example:

(21) Duchess to driver: 'What's your name?'
'Thomas, maam'
'Your second name – I never call chauffeur's by their first name'
'Darling, maam'
'Drive on Thomas.'

The snobbish duchess is forced to choose between two social improprieties, and chooses the solution with no sexual overtones.

Sometimes the impropriety lies in behaviour which is improper in a particular type of individual. See, for example, (25) below, in which the marriage broker joke ends up denigrating the bride, and the following:

(22) Vice president Dick Cheney gets a call from his 'boss', George W. Bush.
'I've got a problem,' says W.
'What's the matter?' asks Cheney.
'Well, you told me to keep busy in the Oval Office, so, I got a jigsaw puzzle, but it's too hard. None of the pieces fit together and I can't find any edges.'
'What's it a picture of?' asks Cheney.
'A big rooster,' replies W.
'All right,' sighs Cheney, 'I'll come over and have a look.'
So he leaves his office and heads over to the Oval Office. W points at the jigsaw on his desk.
Cheney looks at the desk and then turns to W and says, 'For crying out loud, George – put the cornflakes back in the box.'

Stupidity is of course another kind of inappropriate behaviour and is very common in jokes (see section 1.3.8). It is particularly inappropriate in the President. Note too that the humour also largely depends on the reputation of the participants – the same joke featuring Mr Clinton, whose reputation was rather different in his later years in office, would be less effective.

In sum then, it has, of course, long been noted that a great many jokes are plays on taboo subjects – bodily functions, sex, social gaffes. Another great canon comprises those jokes based around some unusual, often stupid behaviour. They can all, however, be recognized as subtypes of the proper-to-improper narrative shift model.

1.3.7 *Reversal of evaluation*

The following joke contains an example of the reversal of evaluation mechanism (evaluation is being used in the sense defined by Hunston: 'the indication that something is good or bad', 2004: 157):

(23) A group of students from East Germany are all killed in a car crash. They discover that hell, too, is divided into an eastern and western sector. Given the choice, those who see themselves as ideologically sound opt for the eastern hell. A fact-finding delegation arrives from the western hell; they complain 'Conditions on our western side are terrible; we've been boiled in oil three times already and roasted half a dozen times. How are things with you, in the eastern hell?' 'Fine,' is the answer. 'They've run out of fuel.'

(adapted from Larsen 1980, 94–95)

Under this mechanism, what is normally evaluated as good, appropriate, fitting, useful, beautiful and so on, finds itself evaluated, in the second narrative, as the opposite – bad, inappropriate, ugly and so on – or, of course, vice versa. In this instance, the waste and inefficiency normally associated with Soviet bloc regimes and normally viewed as a defect is reinterpreted in the new context as a benefit. By the same token, the relative efficiency of the West German state suddenly becomes very bad for one's health.

There is clearly a strong association between the proper-to-improper and evaluation reversal mechanisms; whenever what is normally seen in the real world as proper is suddenly re-evaluated as improper as we have both mechanisms in play. The Mountaineer joke is a good example. The impropriety of rejecting God's advice is suddenly reassessed as rather sensible in the second narrative.

It should be noted in particular that the reversal of normal evaluation effected in and by the second narrative in such jokes presents situations which by their very nature are novel and unpredictable. This is the strongest evidence that these second narratives cannot be treated simply as a script taking the place of another. 'Inefficiency is a good thing' (Eastern Hell joke) would be an odd script in anyone's psychology.

Not all reversal of evaluation jokes are political, of course. Here is a more racy example (adapted from Attardo et al. 2002: 10):

(24)   Mr Smith got himself a new secretary. She was young, sweet, and very polite. One day while taking dictation, she noticed his fly was open. When leaving the room, she said, 'Mr Smith, your barracks door is open.' He did not understand her remark. But, later on, he happened to look down and saw his zipper was open.
He decided to have some fun with his secretary. Calling her in, he asked, 'By the way, Miss Jones, when you saw my barracks door open this morning, did you also notice a soldier standing to attention?' The secretary, replied, 'Why, no sir. All I saw was a wrinkled little veteran sitting on two duffel bags.'

which combines reversal with a satisfying moral come-uppance (which plays a part, as we shall see, in both teasing and irony).

Related to this type of joke is perhaps the reversal-of-role joke, of which one of Freud's Jewish marriage broker tales (*Schadchen* stories) is a classic example:

(25)   The bridegroom was most disagreeably surprised when the bride was introduced to him, and drew the broker on one side and whispered: 'Why have you brought me here? She's ugly and old, she squints and has bad teeth and bleary eyes...' – 'You needn't lower your voice' interrupted the broker 'she's deaf as well'.

As well as reversal of evaluation here we have reversal of evaluator; the broker should be the last person to point out defects in the bride.

The previous two examples again underline how closely related are the proper-to-improper shift and evaluation reversal. Whenever there is a moral element involved in the evaluation, the two mechanisms are conflated. In fact, we can conclude that the former is, in fact, a subcategory of the latter. In (26), from Raskin, the conventional positive moral suppositions that nuns are chaste and in (27) that wives are devoted are turned on their heads:

(26)   A nun is attacked and raped by twelve bandits in the desert. When they are done with her and flee the nun stands up and says, 'That was nice. Just enough and quite sinless.'

(27)   A woman accompanied her husband to the doctor's office.
After his check-up, the doctor called the wife into his office alone.
He said, 'Your husband is suffering from a very severe stress disorder. If you don't follow my instructions carefully, your husband will surely die.
'Each morning, fix him a healthy breakfast. Be pleasant at all times. For lunch make him a nutritious meal. For dinner prepare an especially nice meal for him.

'Don't burden him with chores. Don't discuss your problems with him; it will only make his stress worse.
Do not nag him. Most importantly, make love to him regularly.
'If you can do this for the next 10 months to a year, I think your husband will regain his health completely.'
On the way home, the husband asked his wife, 'What did the doctor say?'
'Oh, he said you're going to die,' she replied.

1.3.8 The absurd, the abnormal and quirky logic in jokes

If we stretch the notion of impropriety a little, we may begin to attempt a treatment of jokes of the absurd. These are very common and Ritchie includes a couple of examples:

(28) O'Riley was on trial for armed robbery. The jury came out and announced, 'Not guilty.'
'Wonderful,' said O'Riley, 'does that mean I can keep the money?'
(29) Fat Ethel sat down at the lunch counter and ordered a whole fruit cake. 'Shall I cut it into four or eight pieces?' asked the waitress. 'Four,' said Ethel, 'I'm on a diet'.

Whilst Koestler (1964: 36), reports what he calls 'this venerable chestnut' (first recorded in Schopenhauer):

(30) A convict was playing cards with his gaolers. On discovering that he cheated they kicked him out of gaol.

There is no real ambiguity in the lead up to the punchline, and the punchline itself therefore is not a backtrack trigger, no backtracking is necessary. Nevertheless, Koestler still argues that such constructions are clearly bisociative: 'two conventional rules ("offenders are punished by being locked up" and "cheats are punished by being kicked out"), each of them self-consistent, collide in a given situation' (1964: 36). But clashes of logic are not necessarily humorous and the reason why these jokes are funny also needs to be explained by reference to everyday real-world evaluations. Ritchie includes the 'absurd' under an umbrella category of inappropriateness but the question remains of why some absurd acts should be presented as laughable and others not.

We have already stressed (in section 1.3.6) how the improper behaviour of the joke characters has to be seen to be 'objectively' improper in terms of 'real-world' behaviour. There is no doubt that O'Riley's outburst would be just about the most inappropriate possible in the circumstances, whilst Ethel is, to say the least, working to a different logic from the rest of us. Part of the humour, of course, is that O'Riley and Ethel are the butts of comic stupidity humour. The gaolers' idiotic punishment of the convict in (30), moreover, is just what he wants.

Joke humour theory and language principles 49

However, there is also a class of absurd jokes in which the quirky logic of one of the participants is actually not stupidity but superior logic. Several of Freud's jokes are of this nature, and the logician, the character who turns everyday reason on its head, is the comic hero of the tale (slight editing):

(31) A gentleman enters a pastry cook's shop and orders a cake. He leaves, then takes it back and exchanges it for a glass of liqueur. He drinks it and is about to leave without paying. The shopkeeper stops him. 'What do you want?' asks the customer – 'You haven't paid for the liqueur' – 'But I gave you the cake in exchange for it' – 'You didn't pay for that either' – 'But I hadn't eaten it!'

(1960: 69)

Freud seems to think that it is 'faulty logic' which causes these stories to be comic, but faulty logic in itself is not humorous. And surely we are laughing *with* rather than *at* the gentleman, with his superior intellectual skills and one-upmanship. The audience empathizes with what, in real life, would be clever victory in a conflict of *face*. The relationship of face and laughter is one of the main topics of this work.

But what, if anything, is improper about the behaviour of the comic hero? Apart from leaving without paying, the answer is that it offends the mild social taboo against cunning, distortion and spin. It is bare-faced cheek and, were we to be on the losing end of such behaviour in the real world, we would accuse the perpetrator of fraudulence. Thus there is a degree of tension for the hearer of this class of jokes; as we said, we feel some admiration for the jester, relief that we do not have to counter his logic ourselves and a small delight in the breaching of a taboo.

But if jokes like these do not involve an explicit second narrative, can their humorous effect be seen as bisociative in any way? To a large degree it can, since another narrative, consisting of normal logic and everyday behaviour, is always 'in the air' in such jokes. We compare the odd or quirky logic with our own background knowledge of what would be customary, default, 'right and proper' reasoning in the situation. The joke narrative evokes a comparative one in the mind of the hearer – what O'Riley should have done (kept quiet), what Ethel should have said ('just give me a small piece'), how the gentleman should have behaved (paid for his drink) – without which comparison the actual joke text would have no humorous force. The normal, precisely because it *is* normal, does not need to be stated explicitly.

We shall meet the same kind of evocation of an unmentioned, inexplicit 'other version' in the study of wordplay (Chapter 4) and irony (Chapter 6). Laughter engendered by the unusual and the abnormal (in the sense of out of the ordinary or which infringes the rules) in conversational discourse will be discussed in detail in Chapter 3. How individuals can be teased on account of their supposedly illogical behaviour will be examined in Chapter 5.

1.4 Scripts and logical analysis/inferencing in language processing: lexicogrammar

Human understanding, not only of jokes but of all discourse, perhaps even of all behaviour, is an active process which utilizes two basic procedures. Sometimes we can confidently pull out large blocks from memory but sometimes we need to work things out from basic principles.

The equivalents, or the expression, of these two mechanisms, script-recall and inferencing, have recently begun to be studied in the field of grammar as relevant not only to the reception but also to the construction of utterances. Sinclair (1987), in his theory of lexicogrammar, talks of, on the one hand, the *idiom* or *collocational* principle, which sees a text as largely composed of preconstituted blocks of language and, on the other, the *open-choice* principle of language, which sees a text as 'the result of a very large number of complex choices', largely word by word (1987: 319). In Sinclair (2004) these two principles are also referred to as the *phraseological tendency* (equivalent to the *idiom*), 'the tendency of a speaker/writer to choose several words at a time' and the *terminological tendency* (equivalent to the *open-choice*), 'the tendency of language users to protect the meaning of a word or phrase so that every time it is used it guarantees delivery of a known meaning' (2004: 170). We need to look in some detail at these two language principles, since their interaction will be vital in understanding how wordplay and phraseplay function (Chapter 4).

1.4.1 Open choice and inferencing

The second of these principles, the open-choice, has been the traditional way of describing language, just as, before research into scripts and schemata began, cognitive studies privileged the view of mental reasoning in terms of inferential processing. Open choice sees language production as a continuous series of open-ended choices, 'a series of slots which have to be filled from a lexicon' (Sinclair 1987: 320), the only restraints being grammatical, that is, that only items from certain word classes may appear in a given slot. Thus an utterance such as *the cat sat on the mat* is first prepared mentally as:

Noun Phrase *followed by* Verb Phrase *followed by* Prepositional Phrase.

The production process of this sequence is further broken down as follows. The noun phrase opens with a determiner *the*; one of the classes of items that can 'legally' follow a determiner is a noun, so we can insert *cat*. A noun phrase Subject must (sooner or later) be followed by a verb phrase and we choose SIT + *past tense*, that is *sat*. Our knowledge of English grammar tells us that *sat* (belonging to the class of so-called intransitive verbs) can be followed either by nothing (thus ending the phrase: *the cat sat*), or by an adverbial, for example, *the cat sat down*, or by a preposition as, here, *on*, in which case a noun phrase must follow. Whether or not this is the actual procedure followed by the human mind in utterance construction or whether it is simply a convenient Popperian model was one of the burning questions of traditional grammarians' debate.

The analogy between the open choice/terminological principle and inferencing from first basics is thus very close. As we have seen, knowledge inferencing enables a hearer to build up a model of what is happening at any particular juncture by applying a set of rules derived from what the individual knows of the normal behaviour of people and objects. Similarly, in linguistic terms, when interpreting utterances, hearers check whether the input they are receiving is decipherable by applying a set of rules derived from what that individual knows of the normal behaviour and interaction of lexical items and syntactic classes, that is, their internalized grammar of the language.

The analogy between cognitive and grammatical inferencing is supported by the observations from many parts that a great deal of real-life language, especially spoken language, is not entirely grammatically well-formed but nevertheless is interpretable. Lapses, false starts, interruptions, failure to finish phrases are all commonplace. Here is a selection from the briefings:

(32) You talked yesterday about Senator Byrd had a valid point when he talked about [...]

(33) No, but neither is he someone that's easy to control or to tell him what to say.

whilst the following, if not quite ungrammatical, contains enough replanning to lose its way:

(34) I think I answered that by saying I don't think I can answer that now, based on what we don't know.

And yet, except in extreme cases, discourse interaction is not impeded, participants carry on regardless. The simplest explanation is surely that we make a 'best guess' about what the 'imperfect' utterance must have been, in other words we make an inference, build a mental model of what the other person meant to say, based on both our knowledge of the language and our experience of human interaction, including which mistakes or inadequacies are most likely to occur.

1.4.2 The idiom principle and script-recall

The *idiom* principle, on the other hand, states that the openness of choice is not available to the same extent at every point along the syntagmatic progression of an utterance, but that 'the language user has available to him a large number of preconstructed or semi-preconstructed phrases that constitute single choices, even though they appear to be analysable into segments' (Sinclair 1987: 320).

52 Joke humour theory and language principles

Bolinger (1976) calls these chunks of language 'prefabrications' or 'prefabs'. Others have talked of multi-word units (Zgusta 1987; Baker and McCarthy 1990).

Sinclair illustrates the principle by means of the common phrase *out of the corner of my eye*, as found in *but I'm watching out of the corner of my eye*. 'There are seven words in the phrase,' he says, 'and they all simultaneously choose one unit of meaning, to do with peripheral vision' (2004: 171). There is some room for internal variation: *my* can be a different possessive depending on the owner of the eye, and *out of* can occasionally cede its place to *from*. 'So here we have a seven-word phrase which realizes one overall choice and at most two subsidiary choices' (2004: 171). The picture is confirmed and expanded by the following selection of sentence concordance lines from the *Papers* corpus:

1   Seeing the movement out of the corner of his eye, Faldo was distracted.
2   [...] tricks of the trade that can win or lose a show,' he says, observing the judges out of the corner of his eye.
3   He could appear to be dozing but was always peeping out of the corner of his eye.
4   Out of the corner of his eye the scrum-half sees a black shirt and instinctively goes the other way.
5   Out of the corner of my eye I could see the sales assistant spraying and polishing.
6   A widowed father, who lives happily with his daughter, watches out of the corner of his eye as she seems to be pushing past the best age for marriage.

There were twenty-seven occurrences in all, of which only two were not accompanied by a verb of seeing (one, from a boxing report referred to a cut, in another, someone wipes away a tear). When the verb preceded the expression there was a wide variety, for example, SEE, WATCH, OBSERVE, NOTICE. But when it comes after, in all cases but one it was a form of SEE. Non-concrete uses were predictably rare, but the last example in the above list shows that they are possible.

We can now represent the expression notationally as: {SEE} + [*out of*/*from*] *the corner of* [possessive] *eye*, where the curly brackets indicate a semantic set, whilst the parts outside brackets are stable and the parts inside are variable. Nor can such a phrase be dismissed as 'idiom' and therefore 'anomalous', not subject to the normal working of language and so dismissible. If it is argued that *corner* in *corner of the eye* is figurative, then there is little of language which is not figurative. This is, of course, precisely the case. Consider ordinary expressions such as *the rib cage, the seat of his trousers, the roof of her mouth, the bridge of his nose* – the list is endless. Barthes asserts that all language consists of dead metaphor. In systemic terms we might say language is *analogous*, that is, all complex concepts are described (almost by definition) by analogy to fewer basic, simpler ones.

Bolinger's solution is to admit that such expressions are idiomatic but 'idiomaticity is a vastly more pervasive phenomenon than we ever imagined' and needs accounting for. Sinclair's point is similar: it *represents* one of the ways language works and cannot, as it has been for centuries, be left to lie forgotten in a linguistic attic.

Authors in the area of lexical grammar have provided many similar illustrations of the idiom/ phraseological principle. Pawley and Syder (1983) talk of *lexicalized sentence stems*, whilst most revealingly for our purposes Barlow and Kemmer (1994; Barlow 1996) employ the similar notion of the linguistic *schema*. These are all analogous to the (semi) preconstructed phrase consisting of a combination of fixed parts and variable parts. Pawley and Syder illustrate the notion with the example of the conventional expressions of apology:

> I'm sorry to keep you waiting.
> I'm so sorry to have kept you waiting.
> Mr X is sorry to keep you waiting all this time.
>
> (1983: 210)

These are variations on the grammatical frame:

[NP] BE *sorry to* KEEP *you waiting*.

which allows for certain fairly conventional insertions ('pragmatic padding') such as *so, terribly, all this time*, which in this case are all intensifiers with the function of assuaging the hearer's face. Barlow (1996: 15) cites *to let oneself go* (i.e LET [possessive]+ *self go*) and *to lose one's way* (LOSE [possessive] *way*) as examples of his expression frames or schemata. He also suggests reasons why their study had for so long been neglected. The standard generative schools have failed to cope with them since they 'do not fit in particularly well in the lexicon (because the units are too large and contain too much that is regular)' whilst they also 'do not fit in the syntax (because they are in some sense a unit)' (Barlow 1996: 15).

The most exciting current work in the field is Hoey's notion of lexical priming, which has close parallels with script theory, translating many of the latter's insights about how we learn to behave into how we learn a language. Lexical priming is a self-reproducing phenomenon whereby the normal language user learns by repeated acquaintance with a lexical item along with processes of analogy with other similar items, the typical behaviour of that item in interaction. In particular, we learn which other lexical items it co-occurs with regularly (*collocation*), which semantic sets it occurs with (*semantic association*; other authors would favour the term *semantic preference*; see Sinclair 2004: 33–34; Partington 2004), which grammatical categories it co-occurs with or avoids and which grammatical positions it favours or disfavours (*colligation*), which positions in an utterance or sentence or paragraph or entire text it tends to prefer or avoid occurring in (*textual collocation*) and whether it tends to participate in cohesion or not. The user then, of course, reproduces this behaviour in his/her own linguistic performance. The lexical item itself is said to be primed to behave in these particular ways. Thus, for example, the item *winter* is primed to collocate

54 Joke humour theory and language principles

with *in, that, during the*, etc. As regards colligational behaviour, the expression *in winter* is primed to occur with the present tense in clauses expressing relational processes. It displays a semantic preference to occur with expressions of 'timeless truths', for example: 'In winter, Hammerfest is a thirty-hour ride by bus from Oslo [...]'. In terms of textual collocation, in some kinds of discourse (e.g. travel writing) *in winter* is probably weakly primed to appear at the beginning of a sentence, as in the previous sentence. It is only weakly primed to occur in cohesive chains. In Hoey's terms, the fact that *winter* is normally classified as a nominal, a noun, is entirely a result of its set of combinational primings, otherwise called its *priming prosody* (2005: 165–168). Nevertheless, Hoey is at great pains to stress that normal priming prosodies can always be overridden by users, as in the example he provides: 'The expedition returns to England, having rescued the men left to *winter* on Elephant Island' (2005: 155). Creativity with language is largely a process of overriding or exploiting normal primings. In section 2.5 (on register play) and Chapter 4 (on wordplay) we will observe a number of instances of how this is performed for humorous effect.

Hoey reinterprets the kind of linguistic schemata we have discussed earlier in terms of semantic preference, that is, as we said, the tendency of a lexical item to co-occur with other items from a particular semantic field, and underlines how creative the process can be. He shows, for instance, how by steady acquaintance with phrases associating a number, an hour and journey with a vehicle, for example:

a three-hour *car* ride
a five-hour *coach* ride
a half-hour *train* ride
a two-hour ride by *four wheel drive vehicle*

speakers are primed to recognize both similar phrases they have heard before but can also interpret novel, fresh ones like, say, 'a 27-hour meander by sledge' (2005: 17). We saw that script use is an *active* mental process which helps us make sense of the new by reference to the old. Hoey's theory of lexical priming, including semantic preference, explains how the same is true in language reception.

The analogy of linguistic schemata with knowledge schemata or scripts, then, seems clear. Of scripts we have already said that they too are templates consisting of some fixed routines and some variable ones, and that they too can often accommodate insertions. Just as scripts are typically made up of other scripts and go on themselves to compose larger ones, lexical-semantic templates too tend to *nest*, to use Hoey's term. For instance, the template we discussed in the preceding lines, *a* + [number-time] + [vehicle] *ride* is primed to nest within another template [Locality A] is *a* + [number-time] + [vehicle] *ride from* [Locality B], as in the example already cited: 'In winter, Hammerfest is a thirty-hour ride by bus from Oslo [...]'.

Not least of the analogy is that they serve similar purposes, to save mental processing time and effort. There is, however, a trade-off involved. If it is the case that the language user needs to store in his memory *both* the single vocabulary items *and* a lexicon of (semi-) preconstructed phrases, the number of which is probably in excess of the number of vocabulary items used productively by the individual, then it would seem counterproductive to store linguistic information in this way. The reason why this happens must be that the effort saved by making far fewer slot-filling choices in *real-time* – that is in the process of communication – easily outweighs the disadvantages of unwieldy storage. As Ladefoged has said:

> The indications from neurophysiology and psychology are that, instead of storing a small number of primitives and organizing them in terms of a (relatively) large number of rules, we store a large number of complex items which we manipulate with comparatively simple operations. The central nervous system is like a special kind of computer which has rapid access to items in a very large memory, but comparatively little ability to process these items when they have been taken out of memory.
> (Ladefoged 1972: 282)

More recently, Nattinger and DeCarrico too have noted that:

> In formulating performance models of language processing, researchers endeavour to offer direct descriptions of psychological categories and processes, attempting to describe languages in terms of how they are perceived, stored, remembered and produced. These researchers feel that the storage capacity of memory is vast, but that the speed for processing those memories is not (Crick 1979: 219), so that we must learn short cuts for making efficient use of this processing time.
> (Nattinger and DeCarrico 1992: 31)

Principal among these short cuts is the use of multi-word units.

A still more powerful reason for the employment of semi-preconstructed phrases probably lies in the way it facilitates communication processing on the part of the hearer. Language consisting of a relatively high number of fixed phrases is generally more predictable than that which is not (Oller and Streiff 1975). In real-time language decoding, hearers need all the help they can get. Redundancy in communication is often explained in this way and the idiom principle probably has the same functional origins.

To complete the analogies between the script recall-inferencing duality in cognition and idiom-open choice in language, just as Schank and Abelson claim that script-based understanding is the hearer's default approach, that, in simple terms, script recall is more frequently employed than inferencing, both Barlow and Sinclair argue that production and interpretation at utterance level is also dominated by schemata. Barlow tells us that '*most* of language consists of semi-regular, semi-fixed phrases or units', whilst Sinclair even suggests a figure: 'early estimates were that up to 80 per cent of the occurrence of words could be through co-selections, which would leave, of course, only 20 per cent for the sort of independent paradigmatic choices of the grammar' (2004: 171).

56 *Joke humour theory and language principles*

On the basis of these similarities the following hypothesis will be investigated in Chapter 4. Just as joke humour functions through the interplay of the script and inference work, through the defeating of script-based expectations deliberately set up by the joke-maker, the fundamental mechanism underlying most forms of phraseplay is the interchange between the idiom and the open-choice principles, between linguistic schemata and analytic interpretation, in a process we will call *relexicalization*.

2 Laughter in running discourse
Shifts of mode, narrative, role and register

> just when you least expect it
> just what you least expect
> (Pet Shop Boys)

In the previous chapter we discussed the theory of bisociation particularly as relevant to joke humour. We also carried out a critical appraisal of the bisociative Semantic Shift Theory of joke Humour, which necessitated an examination of script theory itself. We proposed that human cognition relies on two general principles, script recall and inferencing, and that human interactive communication relies on two analogous principles of language, the phraseological and the open-choice. We proposed the superordinate term *narrative* to include both script-based and inference-based narrated sequences of events. We then hazarded the hypothesis that much laughter-talk involves the sudden shift from one narrative to another or from one language principal to another (with the caveat, of course, that this alone is not a sufficient condition for humour).

In this chapter we will examine the relevance of bisociation, not to canned jokes, but to episodes of laughter in authentic running spoken discourse, or rather in one type of discourse, namely, press briefings, as represented in the *Dems* and *Reps* corpora.

2.1 Briefings as institutional talk

Press briefings are one particular form of *institutional talk*. This is generally defined as talk between professionals and lay people or between, as here, two groups of professionals (watched by an audience of both lay people and professionals on TV and the Internet).

Institutional talk is largely instrumental, is both talk *at* work and talk *for* work, in the sense that it aims to accomplish the work of the relevant institution, whilst, in contrast, one of the defining characteristics of normal conversation is that it is not principally necessitated by a practical task (Cook 1989: 51). A word of caution, however. This is not to say that conversation is not goal-oriented, that participants do not have aims and strategies to achieve those aims. As Harris remarks, 'most linguistic contexts contain elements of the "strategic", even those which might be considered the prototype of discourse oriented to reaching an understanding' (1995: 122). The difference is that in institutional talk the *overall aims* are principally defined by the nature of the work being done and the institutions being served. Conversational participants may well not have any overall aims in this sense at all. Institutional interaction:

> involves an orientation by at least one of the participants to some core goal, task or identity (or set of them) conventionally associated with the institution in question. In short, institutional talk is normally informed by *goal orientations* of a relatively restricted conventional form.
>
> (Drew and Heritage 1992: 22)

Drew and Heritage are here talking about relatively long-term goals and not the kind of goals which exist at the micro, speech act level, although the latter are to an extent determined by the former.

Institutional settings also, predictably, impose particular limitations on the kind of language behaviour which can be produced. The interaction:

> may often involve *special and particular constraints* on what one or both of the participants will treat as allowable contributions to the business in hand.
>
> (Drew and Heritage 1992: 22)

In other words, each kind of institutional setting tends to have a set of conventions associated with it regulating how participants speak, behave and interact.

However, it is necessary to make a distinction between highly formal institutional settings and more informal ones. The behaviour expected of a professional in the first kind (e.g. a barrister/attorney in court) is highly constrained and any deviations will either be very minor or heavily censured. In less formal environments, on the other hand, there may well be more room for manoeuvre, the conventions may be fewer or more relaxable. For example, interpersonal communication between participants on more than one social level, a 'business' level but also more unofficial planes, may sometimes be possible. In these briefings, the participants generally know each other very well, and the way the talk moves from one speech-style or register (for a definition see section 2.5.1) to another, often for laughter purposes, will be one of the topics of this chapter.

Of utmost importance is the fact that the informality of this discourse type makes phases of *play* possible, involving the invention of situations, roles (or *personae*) and language associated with these roles. It is during these play phases that the majority of the laughter occurs. Play is a concept as complex as humour and much has been written on it. A brief discussion for the purposes of the current study will be undertaken in section 2.3.

2.2 Transaction and interaction in institutional talk

A number of authors (Brown and Yule 1983; R. Lakoff 1989; Kasper 1990) have proposed the existence of two general categories of language use: the *transactional* and the *interactional*. Broadly and informally speaking, transactional language is used to convey content; interactional language is used to express and maintain social relationships. One of the most important sites of transactional language is in institutional talk. The distinction is very similar to that of Habermas (1984) between *communicative* discourse, essentially forms of conversation, which 'is oriented to reaching an understanding' (Harris 1995: 121) and *strategic* discourse which 'is oriented to success' and 'is basically instrumental in mode, power-laden and often located in institutional sites' (Harris 1995: 121).

As Brown and Yule point out, the division of transactional and interactional language is 'an analytic convenience,' and few natural language interchanges 'would be used to fulfil only one function, to the total exclusion of the other' (1983:1). For example, asking for a third party's telephone number could be an example of transaction in a conversation. Nevertheless, we will find it useful here to distinguish between transactional and interactional discourse *modes*. When speakers are in the first of these modes, their attention is concentrated 'on the optimally efficient transmission of information'. They are 'task-focused' and the 'need for truthfulness, clarity and brevity' are the overriding concerns (Kasper 1990: 205). When speakers are operating in interactional mode, by contrast, their 'primary goal [is] the establishment and maintenance of social relationships' (Kasper 1990: 205): more particularly, they aim to use language 'to negotiate role-relationships, peer-solidarity, the exchange of turns in a conversation, the saving of face of both speaker and hearer' (Brown and Yule 1983: 3).

By talking of the transactional and interactional as modes of discourse (rather than as functions), we are able to maintain a useful distinction between these and what Halliday (1994) calls the ideational or experiential and interpersonal functions of language. As regards the first of these, we use language to talk about ideas, to describe events and states and entities in our experience of the world, including the worlds in our own minds. As for the second, we use language to interact with others, establish relations and attempt to influence their behaviour (Thompson 1996: 28). There is an overall correspondence between the modes and the functions inasmuch as transactional discourse will be dominated by ideational use and interactional discourse by interpersonal use. But we may well find aspects of interpersonal function at play during transactional sessions and some ideational information transfer can occur within interactional exchanges. Transaction and interaction are thus also psychological notions, especially with regard to institutional settings: speakers are in transactional mode when they *feel* they are doing institutional business, otherwise they are in interactional mode. And whenever they feel that special attention is being paid to interpersonal matters (face attack for example), they may well feel themselves to no longer be in transactional mode and to be free of the accompanying responsibilities.

60 Laughter in running discourse

Another consequence of this distinction is that it allows for simulation and even duplicity, the possibility of conducting interpersonal work under the guise of transaction, and vice versa.

2.2.1 Transaction in the briefings

When the participants are in what we have called transactional mode they are doing the business of briefings, in other words, they are involved in the exchange of political information. In very general terms, most tokens of institutional talk consist of an opening sequence, consisting of greetings, followed by an explanation by the so-called gatekeeping participant of what the event will consist of, followed in turn by a series of question and response exchanges (Q-R) and concluded by closing and leave-taking sequences. The distinction we made earlier between the transactional/ interactional and the ideational/interpersonal polarities can help us describe the opening and closing phases. In much of discourse analysis, salutations are regarded as interpersonal activity. And yet they are an integral part of an entire transactional event in institutional settings. In such environments, they are best considered as interpersonal events occurring in a transactional mode. They are also frequently formalized and stereotypical, emphasizing how participants *feel* they are part of the transactional mode. In these briefings, the greetings and leave-taking sessions are extremely brief, peremptory even (presumably because, first, the participants meet so frequently and, second, they feel duty-bound to get down to business). The podium will usually give a short prepared introduction outlining what the administration has done or is thinking of doing that day and then will 'take questions' for the rest of the event.

There are, however, different hues to transactional briefings business, some of which we need to recognize. Many of the exchanges are very formal, polite and unrevealing:

(1) Q: Sorry, can you comment on some breaking news? The Palestinian cabinet was approved. Can you just give us the White House position on that and what it means for the road map going forward now?

MR. FLEISCHER: The President looks forward to working with the Palestinian Authority and the Palestinian people, as well as the Israeli government and the Israeli people, to advance the cause of peace in the Middle East. The United States will shortly release the road map formally to the various parties. Our hope is that they will work diligently and hard to advance the cause of peace. Thank you.

We should note how standard politeness signals, usually treated in discourse literature as interpersonal events, are used to carry out transactional work. *Sorry* is used as a brief introduction, whilst *Thank you* serves to communicate 'I have dealt with you and this question and am now moving on to someone else'.

Laughter in running discourse 61

In other exchanges, the podium gives some information he is asked for and tries to correct any misapprehensions he feels the questioner might have:

(2) Q: Ari, on the AIDS initiative, have you seen any sign from the other African countries, with the exception of Uganda and the Caribbean countries, that they are making changes to alleviate the AIDS crisis? And has there been any cooperation from Tahabo and Mbeki in South Africa?
   MR. FLEISCHER: Well, keep in mind, this initiative is specific to the countries that were named as part of the initiative. It's not every country in Africa. It is the countries with whom we have a working relationship [...]

But this is only part of the podium's move. He goes on:

(3) [...] There's an absolute moral calling, in the President's judgment, to the people of the United States to help those in need in Africa and the Caribbean that have been ravaged by this. And of course, we will work through these systems in place to make certain that the money and the aid go to the people who need it, not to the governments who might siphon it off. Those countries – and there are countries that have troublesome records – are not part of this.

He adds on his own messages about his President's moral integrity but also that American tax-dollars will not be squandered, perhaps to forestall what he feels is the questioner's hidden agenda.

However the exchanges are frequently much more animated than this:

(4) Q: On the energy bill, even if it were passed, it's not going to reap any benefits for years. So what can the President do immediately on the price of gas?
   MR. MCCLELLAN: John, first of all, you hit on a very good point. We continue – we continue to go from crisis to crisis when it comes to – whether it's electricity, or whether it's gas prices. We need comprehensive solutions, not patchwork crisis management. We wouldn't be in this situation today if Senate Democrats were not holding up the national energy plan that the President proposed back in May of 2001. In terms of the current gas price situation, the President, like most Americans, is concerned about rising gas prices. And we will continue to act to make sure that there is no price gouging going on [...more of the same...]
   Q: When he was running for President, the President said that President Clinton should get on the phone with the OPEC cartel and say, we expect you to open up your spigots. But it doesn't appear that he's doing that –
   MR. MCCLELLAN: Well, I think that's wrong. No, this – go ahead.
   Q: Well, excuse me, I was just going to ask, could you tell us what calls the President has made?

MR. MCCLELLAN: This administration remains actively engaged with our friends in OPEC, as well as non-OPEC producers from around the world. Secretary Abraham, Secretary Powell, the White House, we are in constant discussions with producers from around the world. Condi Rice has certainly been in touch with individuals in OPEC, and we will continue working for America's consumers to make our views known to our friends in OPEC, as well as other producers around the world.

The journalists are not satisfied with the podium's responses and press him for more details of the President's behaviour:

(5) Q: But he's not making calls, himself?
MR. MCCLELLAN: I'm sorry?
Q: He's not making calls, himself?
MR. MCCLELLAN: The President makes his views known on a regular basis to leaders, and this administration remains actively engaged in discussions – over the last few days, today, we remain actively engaged in discussions with our friends in OPEC, as well as others.
Q: Scott, our friends in OPEC don't seem to be paying any attention. It seems as if the President has been unpersuasive with our friends in OPEC. Is it fair to conclude that –
MR. MCCLELLAN: Well, I disagree with your characterization.
Q: Well, they're jacking the price on us. Is it fair to conclude that he's not – what he's doing isn't working?
MR. MCCLELLAN: Well, that's why I emphasized that we stay in close discussion with our friends in OPEC [...]

Episodes such as this show how the transactional business can be peppered by interpersonal acts. Note the use of first names, the way the podium (rather patronizingly) praises the questioner ('you hit on a good question'), how five moves are introduced by *well*, which each time expresses curt disagreement with the other speaker's formulation, how the questioner repeats somewhat sarcastically the podium's expression 'our friends in OPEC' and backs this up with some colourful, colloquial language 'they're jacking the price on us'. Although the podium's facial expression throughout is of polite attention, the underlying feeling is of tension such that the episode is on the verge of being perceived as a face attack, of the psychological discourse scales being tipped into interactional mode. We will see, especially in Chapter 5, a number of episodes where the scales are well and truly tipped. Merrison (2002) investigates the role of face in task-oriented dialogue and discusses the interplay of face wants with transactional wants. Analogous to Brown and Levinson's (1987) notion of *face-threatening act* (FTA), he proposes the existence of the *transaction-threatening act* (TTA). Some of the questioners' moves in the passage above would seem to fall into this category.

2.2.2 Interaction in the briefings

We can now contrast the transactional episodes with a couple of more interactional ones. The vast majority of these are very brief. Here, however, is a rare lengthy one which took place at the end of Mr McCurry's very last briefing:

(6) Q: What are you going to miss the most about being the spokesperson?
MR. MCCURRY: I'll miss the give-and-take here in the briefing room. I enjoy this – it's kind of fun.
[...]
Q: Which is exactly why I want to ask you this question. Who does a press secretary work for? Does he work for the press? Does he work for the President?
MR. MCCURRY: [...] you work for both sides of this equation. I like to tell people, my office is perfectly situated as a geographic metaphor here in the White House – 50 feet in one direction is the Oval Office, and 50 feet away is here where we are dealing with you. And that's the role of the Press Secretary, to be equidistant between two combatants in this adversarial relationship.
Q: Well, you've done a good job, Mike.
MR. MCCURRY: Thanks, sweets. (Laughter)
Q: Under the circumstances.
MR. MCCURRY: Helen and I always had a thing for each other. (Laughter)
This is the 539th time that I've stood here and briefed, and then probably another 250 times beyond that in places far-flung, around and about. And it has been fun. The other thing I said when I started was I wanted to have some fun doing it, and some days have been less fun than other days, but on balance it's always been an honor to work here [...]
Q: You leave with your honor intact.
MR. MCCURRY: Thank you. It's a good way to end.
Q: And what are your plans, Mike?
Q: What's next?
MR. MCCURRY: Play a little golf, make a little money, do a lot of Little League coaching and volunteering in my schools.
Q: Mike, are you going to write a book?
MR. MCCURRY: No. Well, not immediately. I might – (Laughter)
My agent advised me never to say 'no'. (Laughter)
[...]
Q: What would you write about?
MR. MCCURRY: About the changes we're going through as a culture, as we try to communicate about public policy and the Information Age.
Q: Sounds boring.
MR. MCCURRY: Sounds dull. (Laughter) No, it sounds like a text book that might get ordered over and over on –
Q: Can you share what your best moment and your worst moment was in your position? Does today fit into any of these categories?
MR. MCCURRY: Best moments –
Q: Today. (Laughter)

64   *Laughter in running discourse*

>   MR. MCCURRY: Packing up and leaving. (Laughter) No. Actually – the worst moments and the ones that I've struggled with, ironically, we touched on today, and that's the tragedy in the Balkans [...]

Notice that the predominant format, preserving a vestige of transaction, is still the Q-R and the Q-R-E ('Sounds boring' being a clear example of evaluation [E]). The moves, however, are very short and there is a rapid shift of topic, both of which are symptomatic of interaction.

Other typical features of interaction are the interruptions and 'chipping in' (when one journalist repeats or reinforces another journalist's contribution, for example, 'What are your plans, Mike?' echoed by 'What's next?'). The episode includes a number of very clear attempts to produce humour, the adoption of comic roles (see section 2.4) and colloquial language. In short, it is suffused by play.

This second episode plays with the briefings format itself:

(7)   MR. FLEISCHER: John, I don't think it's any secret, going back any number of administrations and including this administration, that Israel is an ally, Israel is a democracy. The United States and Israel do share much, have much in common, and that's a well-known position.
Q: First of all, congratulations. When the bells are ringing? (Laughter)
MR. FLEISCHER: Oh, that was a question? (Laughter)
Q: No, I was just commenting on it.
MR. FLEISCHER: What's the question?
Q: When is the wedding date?
Q: Monsoon wedding?
MR. FLEISCHER: I can fall back into presidential spokesman speak and say we're working on modalities, working on the timing.
Q: When we have something to announce –
MR. FLEISCHER: When we have something to announce, we'll announce it. (Laughter) All I say is it will be – I'll let you know when it will be. I think it will be –
Q: Will we be invited?
MR. FLEISCHER: Les? Do you really want that answer? (Laughter)
Q: Congratulations, Ari.
MR. FLEISCHER: Thank you.
Q: My question is, two weeks ago – section of India Globe ran the same story today Washington Times is running [...]

This is, in effect, a kind of parody in interactional mode of briefings transaction. In the extract I have included the move before the interactional session begins to show how the switch into interactional mode is typically very sudden and is usually performed by a newly elected speaker. Occasionally, on the other hand, it is introduced in a speaker's second move following a sort of comic 'set-up' routine, as in example (8) (at the time, the American and French governments were at loggerheads over military intervention in Iraq):

(8) Q: Ari, I have two questions. What's happening to those millions of U.S. dollars in hundred dollar bills found at presidential palaces and residences in Baghdad? And has the Secret Service determined the money is real?
MR. FLEISCHER: The last update I had was that it did appear that the money is real. It will be saved and used for the people of Iraq.
Q: I have another question. Is it true that when the President goes to the G8 meeting in France next month, he is going to sleep across the border in Switzerland?
MR. FLEISCHER: It is not. (Laughter) It is not true.

As in both these episodes, the mode transition is typically highly unexpected. From these examples we begin to discern what we might call the first level of bisociation in authentic running discourse: the sudden shift of language *mode*, the unexpected switch from transaction to interaction which prepares fertile ground for laughter-talk.

We might say that there are generally two stages in the preparation for laughter-talk. The first is the transition to interactional mode. The second stage is entering into play frame.

2.3 Play

There are two principal reasons why participants in briefings break into interactional mode: either because of aggression, because a transaction-threatening act is felt to have occurred, or because someone wants to play. There may be a mixture of these two motivations when teasing or banter sessions are entered into.

But what precisely is *play* and how does it relate to verbal humour? The term is widely adopted in discourse analysis and elsewhere, and since it is used in the field as a semi-technical term, it merits some descriptive attention.

Dictionaries and concordances are of little initial use in defining it for our purposes. The first are inevitably too wide-ranging, and not a little circular. *Webster's Encyclopedic Unabridged Dictionary of English* (henceforth *Webster's*), for example, defines *play* as 'exercise or action by way of amusement or recreation' or 'fun, jest, or trifling as opposed to earnest', leaving us with the need to define a host of fresh terms. As regards concordancing, the item *play* (as the noun) in general (or *heterogeneric*) corpora tends to collocate with a wide number of lexical items, but is rarely used in the sense usually intended in discourse analysis. It also collocates in widely differing ways in different domains. In business journalism we find expressions such as *in play* (meaning the object of some sort of bid), *high venture capital play* and *power play*, all of which seem very much in earnest as opposed to 'fun, jest or trifling'. In news sections it usually refers to a theatre play or sport (especially chess) but we also find the occasional set expression such as *child's play, foul play, to make great play of*, and as a verb: *play hardball* and *the games statesmen play*.

Outside linguistics, there is a vast literature on the topic, much of which insists that play is a natural and vitally important form of behaviour (Huizinga 1949;

Bateson 1955; Fry 1963). Many authors have felt intuitively that a relationship exists between humour and play. Freud talks of jokes or wit arising out of the pleasure of play. Berger broaches the important notion of the 'play frame':

> It seems evident that humor invokes setting up a frame of some sort that tells people that whatever is in the frame is 'humorous'. The complexities of establishing this frame and communicating to others that 'play' is going on are central concerns for the cognitive theorists
>
> (1987: 10)

That is, in order that others should understand that a particular act or utterance is intended as humorous, it is necessary to somehow signal that the activity one is engaged in is playful, that one is acting within a play frame. It should be noted that this use of the term *frame* is different from that intended by Minsky (1975). Boxer and Cortés-Conde (1997) insist that the concept of play frame is as necessary in conversational joking as in joke-telling. But within linguistics itself very few authors tell us what play or the play frame is. In his otherwise excellent wide-ranging analysis of linguistic theories of humour, Attardo (1994) devotes one short paragraph to the topic. Norrick (1993) feels it safest to give a list of play activities, which includes anecdotes, joint narratives, wordplay, mocking, sarcasm and teasing. But the question of what to include is not unproblematic. Grainger (2002) notes how Ragan (1990) lists things differently from Norrick and sees as play only those activities which are affectively bonding, excluding joking and teasing, which are seen as potentially interpersonally threatening. Nor is the question of how (and when) the play frame is signalled always addressed. Tannen and Wallatt (1999) are an exception. They recount an anecdote of a friend's dog who would understand that its master wished to play when he slipped into a southern states accent: 'people (and dogs)', they conclude, 'identify frames in interaction by association with linguistic and paralinguistic cues – the way the words are uttered – in addition to what they say' (1999: 350). Norrick notes that in conversational contexts, once the play frame has been introduced, it tends to get prolonged (2003: 1346–1347). As regards breifings, this was demonstrated easily and clearly using the Dispersion Plot facility from the *WordSmith* suite of programmes. This tool plots and displays in linear fashion where in a text the current search word appears. The 'hits' for the transcription item [Laughter] are very typically found clustered closely together (see Table I.2 in Chapter I.3.3).

Play, then, is a folk concept of complex and probably indeterminate boundaries. However, if it is a term to be used in scientific research – as it so often is in the literature – a degree of rigour and a working definition or at least a description need to be attempted. Two authors who, together, may help are Raskin (1985) and Cook (2000). Raskin (1985), following upon work by Searle and Grice, proposes an interesting distinction between *bona fide* and non-*bona fide* modes of communication. *Bona fide* is 'the "ordinary" information-conveying mode (no lying, acting, joking, etc.)', whilst in non-*bona fide* mode 'speakers are not committed to the truth of what they say' or rather, they signal somehow that what they say is not necessarily meant to be taken wholly literally or truthfully. In his discussion of joke humour, Raskin supplies a technical description of non-*bona fide* behaviour which draws on all four of Grice's cooperative maxims but the most relevant point is that the maxim of quality – 'tell only what you know to be true' – is clearly relaxed in non-*bona fide* communication. From the hearer's point of view, if s/he can't process an utterance by either fitting it into a known script or by squaring it with the contextual facts of which s/he is aware, s/he has the option of either rejecting it or switching from the default assumption of the speaker's being in *bona fide* mode to being in non-*bona fide* mode.

One important motivation for laughter in 'spontaneous' spoken discourse is to signal that non-*bona fide* communication has been intended on the part of the speaker, or recognized on the part of the hearer, even if they do not necessarily find the utterance particularly humorous.

Raskin goes on to use his theory to explain the four different occasions on which joking may occur (S = speaker, H = hearer):

A (i)   S makes the joke unintentionally;
A(ii)   S makes the joke intentionally;

B (i)   H does not expect a joke;
B(ii)   H expects a joke.

In A(i), the speaker is engaged in *bona fide* communication. The hearer may laugh either as a signal that they have detected something amiss or to inform the speaker that what s/he has said has misfired.

In A(ii), the speaker is in non-*bona-fide* mode and aware of the overlap of meaning.

In B(i), the hearer will at first try to interpret the utterance as if the speaker were in *bona fide* mode, but eventually cotton on that the speaker is joking, 'because, in our culture, joke telling is a much more socially acceptable form of behaviour than, for instance, lying'.

In B(ii) the hearer is 'attuned' and does not attempt to apply *bona fide* interpretation rules.

Raskin's work deals with jokes, but these are not the only form of non-*bona fide* behaviour; there is also, as the discussion above implies, lying. The difference is that joke-telling is cooperative behaviour, lying is not. In other words, there is fiction and deception involved in both, but only in one is the deception meant to be discovered – either by issuing some signal of non-*bona fide* mode or by making one's utterance obviously at odds with contextual facts and so forcing the hearer to assume non-*bona fide* mode. In any case, 'humor seems to be the next most socially acceptable form of communication in our society after *bona-fide* communcation'. Moreover, 'the easy shift from *bona-fide* communication to joke telling as the most accessible and acceptable form of non-*bona-fide* communication may be underlaid by the basic concept of play, which is readily assumed by people as a natural form of behaviour'.

For Raskin, it would seem, humour is an amalgamation of non-*bona-fide* communication with 'play', but he still shies away from telling us quite what the latter consists of.

Cook (2000) attacks the problem on two fronts; he asks both what the nature of play in general and language play in particular might be and also what functions it serves. The latter might be the more fruitful starting point. Play often combines elements of competition and collaboration. In terms of the latter it both strengthens social bonds, signalling and enhancing an individual's membership of an in-group, and it also proves that the individual *can* collaborate and is reliable:

> [...] humans play fair by each other (both in the literal and metaphorical senses) not necessarily for reasons of altruism, but because if they do not their fellows may be unwilling to collaborate with them again and in addition may spread news of their unreliability.
>
> (Cook 2000: 104)

In terms of the former, very many activities defined as 'play' contain some form of competition, sometimes for a prize but often simply for self display (or dis-play). For this reason participants often vie to display superior skill, mental, physical or verbal. The association of play with skill explains why the term is often transferred metaphorically to other – 'serious' – activities which require skill (such as *power-play* or, as Cook observes *swordplay*, 2000:111).[1] Play, then, probably channels aggression into socially acceptable forms of expression. Whether they are harmless or not is another matter.

As for defining the nature of play, Cook draws on Fry:

> Play ... is behaviour which depends on the mutual recognition (through meta-communcation, internal or external) that that behaviour does not mean the same thing as does that behaviour (fighting, etc.) which play represents.
>
> (1963: 123)

Bateson, too, argues that in order for both animals and humans to engage in play activities, they must first of all be capable of distinguishing between play and non-play and also be able to transmit and receive the metacommunicative message 'this is play' [1955 (1972): 177–193]. Laughter is obviously one of the most important markers of this message. Play, then, is defined as metabehaviour. This definition has the merit of allowing us to include word- and phraseplay in the phenomenon, where language is employed metalinguistically and reflexively, language drawing attention to language. From another perspective, it can be described as language as *mention* rather than as *use* (section 6.2.1).

We need to bear in mind, however, another general aspect of play which is its immense creativity and its close association with the imagination. In a chapter entitled 'The meanings of language play: imaginary worlds', Cook lists some of the play activities (language and non) which involve creative imagining, including fiction, mime-mimicry, acting, disguise, make-belief and fantasizing. He notes how little attention fiction and story-telling has received in both psychology and linguistics and also how narration helps construct and reinforce group solidarity, a point which will be important to the present study. He even speculates that play gives rise to language itself and that, working together, they make complex thought and social organization possible:

> It might be that both ontogenetically and phylogenetically, the first function of language is the creation of imaginative worlds: whether lies, games, fictions or fantasies. From this use could have emerged the capacity for intricate social organization and complex knowledge.
> (Cook 2000: 47)

Be that as it may, play and the imagination certainly have the socio-biological function of training the mind to be flexible and adaptable to unforeseen circumstances and keeping these skills alive, even in times of relative social stability.

It might be thought that another important part of the description of play would be its pleasurability, at least for some of its participants. However, Cook liquidates pleasure in a single paragraph. 'The enjoyment of play' he affirms 'is an epiphenomenon rather than a cause'. In other words, feelings of pleasure are associated with play in order to ensure its survival as an activity, as with sex, parenting, friendship and even eating and sleeping. In evolutionary terms, we play not because it gives us pleasure but because we have needed it to survive. This may well be the case, but it is also true that, from a personal psychological rather than evolutionary perspective, we play because we enjoy it.

Finally, play is also ultimately to be defined in terms of opposition. It is the one term in a duality, the other term variously being notions such as 'work', 'serious activity' and 'real-life', depending on the context. This explains too, as mentioned earlier, the general sense that humans have of play providing relief from these other activities.

2.4 Narratives and role play

2.4.1 *Repeated narratives*

Play, then, is characterized by dissimulation, invention, fantasy. When participants in the briefings come out to play, what precisely do they invent? The following examples provide a few clues:

(9) Q: Ari, there's a tape running now – it may want to – it may affect what you just said.
MR. FLEISCHER: Now, as we speak?
Q: As we speak, yes.
MR. FLEISCHER: How do you know? You're sitting here. (Laughter) You don't have one of those little –
Q: Because I've got the same communication devices you do.

Q: He's emplanted. (Laughter)
Q: It's in his teeth. (Laughter)
Q: — that shows Saddam actually touring bombed-out parts of Baghdad.
(10) MR. WILSON: I didn't realize we were going to be on camera. Let me just sort of get my hair squared away here. (Laughter)

One or other of the participants frequently invents a fantasy narrative, involving perhaps relevant fictional roles (or personae) along with appropriate language. In example (9) we have an espionage and then in (10) a 'man surprised to be on television' fantasy narrative.

A number of narratives are evoked repeatedly and have become humorous in-scripts for the group, whilst the particular roles associated with them have become in-group personae. One of the simplest and most common is the 'briefings as a game show' narrative, in which the podium becomes the contestant, usually facing difficult or trick questions:

(11) Q: Joe, on China —
MR. LOCKHART: Sure. An easy one, China. (Laughter)
(12) Q: I've got a question about the President's choice to head the St. Lawrence Seaway. There appears to be a gentleman from California with no —
MR. MCCURRY: This is stump Mike time. (Laughter)

Closely linked is the podium in a 'tough job' narrative:

(13) MR. LOCKHART: I thought this was my honeymoon week? No?
Q: It was. (Laughter)
MR. LOCKHART: This was my honeymoon?
Q: You're having it. (Laughter)
(14) [...] what is the estimated cost of this latest trip and how precisely is this cost-effective? And is the President still receiving the pastoral counseling that was announced last fall?
MR. LOCKHART: Whew, connect those two in an answer. (Laughter)

also recalled in an example we have already seen:

(15) MR. MCCURRY: Best moments —
Q: Today. (Laughter)
MR. MCCURRY: Packing up and leaving. (Laughter)

which is associated with 'ordinary guy caught up in tough job' podium persona (a question has been put about who pays for Mrs Clinton's foreign trips and the podium has indicated the State Department):

(16) Q: Joe, is there a difference between the State Department and the taxpayers?
MR. LOCKHART: No. (Laughter) It just sounded a lot better if I said State Department. (Laughter)

The 'regular guy' persona can even slip into the self-deprecating 'rather dumber-than-average' guy:

(17) Q: Joe, is The New York Times one of the papers that you read carefully?
MR. LOCKHART: Some days, but they use a lot of big words, so it's sometimes hard to understand. (Laughter)

On other occasions, though, we come across the 'podium as tough guy' role/narrative:

(18) MR. FLEISCHER: I treat you like I treat everybody else.
[...]
Q: That's not saying much. (Laughter)

and see Chapter 3, examples (23), (28) and (49). From which it is a small step to the narrative of 'podium and press as adversaries':

(19) MR. FLEISCHER: [...] You know, there is an enemy who wants to know, so I'm not going to give any indications about –
Q: That's not us, right? (Laughter)

Here we find a reinterpretation of the expression *an enemy who wants to know*. It is apparently self-deprecatory but in reality the press also love casting themselves or being cast by the podium in a role of rigorous task-masters.

Different podiums display a distinct preference for different play roles. Of the Democrats, Mr McCurry enjoyed being the 'tough-but-regular guy', whilst Mr Lockhart was far more likely to slip into a self-deprecatory persona. The Republican, Mr Fleischer, in contrast, preferred 'figure of authority' roles, variations on parent, judge, master of ceremonies and schoolmaster:

(20) Q: That was my question, but I have another.
MR. FLEISCHER: The three of you must have passed notes. (Laughter)
(21) MR. FLEISCHER: Les, that's three questions, not two. You need to pick one.
Q: Well – let's see –
MR. FLEISCHER: You're taking too long [...] (Laughter)
(22) MR. FLEISCHER: By the way, whose seat do you – who is not showing up for their briefings anymore? (Laughter)
Q: The Washington Post.
MR. FLEISCHER: Oh. Well, I can't call on them now. Maybe they're mysteriously in another seat.

which tends to cast the press audience in the role/persona of recalcitrant children:

(23) MR. FLEISCHER: Kelly, didn't you have yours already? (Laughter)
Q: I did. Other people get more than one. (Laughter)
MR. FLEISCHER: You did. Remember, this is our orderly system. And then we come back to the front, and you ask something, and we go to – Connie. (Laughter)

He upbraids Kelly for trying to obtain an extra turn when she has just asked a question. Turns are expressed as some kind of treat and Kelly has finished hers already. Note how Kelly falls into the role assigned her.

Yet another recurrent in-script is that of 'money-making'. This particular narrative is interesting for its ethical undertones. Both sides in these briefings tend to claim the moral high ground, the podium on behalf of his well-intentioned President, the press as upstanding representatives of the American public. But occasionally there is sneaking recognition that both sides are rather well paid for their ethical concerns. Mr McCurry again on his retirement:

(24) Q: Have you learned anything in five and a half years from this press and from this White House?
MR. MCCURRY: Yes, quite a bit about it. But I'm going to go out and make people pay to hear it from now on. (Laughter)

But the other podiums also sometimes embrace this narrative, which always seems to raise a laugh with the press (see Chapter 3, example 36). The shift of emphasis from 'memoires' to money is clearly a bathetic one. Bathos will be discussed in more detail in the following pages.

2.4.2 Occasional narratives

A good number of fantasy narratives occur only once in the corpus. One of these is 'briefings as theatre':

(25) MR. FLEISCHER: Bob. We're going to keep moving. We're losing our audience. People are walking out. (Laughter)

another is 'negotiation', 'bargaining':

(26) Q: Wait, wait, wait. You said 30 days was a non-starter. Now you're saying that 24 –
MR. FLEISCHER: Four weeks, obviously, is 28 days. Four days ago I was asked about 30 days. That makes it 26. No, that's a non-starter.
Q: How about three weeks? (Laughter)
MR. FLEISCHER: Are you negotiating for someone? (Laughter)

Some narratives seem to depend on the adoption rather of a mood or a character-type than a specific role, for example, comic resignation:

(27) MR. FLEISCHER: I was, as you know, not in Washington on Sunday, I was traveling with the President. So forgive me if I missed an editorial.
Q: You'll take it. All right. (Laughter)

Taking the question is briefings-speak meaning passing it on to someone else and not answering it now, hence the journalist's mock disappointment and scepticism.

Generosity too can compose a comic 'mood-narrative'. One journalist here cedes the floor with exaggerated good grace:

(28) Q: Please, proceed.
Q: – sorry – the Russians aren't part of that. Sorry, Sam.
Q: No, whatever time you require. (Laughter)

as, predictably perhaps, can cynicism:

(29)   [...] So the President is very pleased to be able to make the announcement today about giving Governor's Island to the people of New York.
   Q: Did you choose a Monday because Congress wasn't around? (Laughter)

and see example (48). In section 5.3.4 we will examine the face-threatening potential of the cynicism tease.

2.4.3   Evaluation reversal

One interesting and effective type of narrative shift is evaluation reversal, whereby something which is normally expected to be appraised as good or bad is suddenly re-presented as the opposite. We saw in the previous chapter (section 1.3.7) how evaluation reversal was the basis of a large class of canned jokes. The best example from the corpus is the following:

(30)   Q: The Associated Press reports that on Sunday in Middlebury, Vermont, where you gave a speech and were given an alumni achievement award, there were more than 500 protestors.
   MR. FLEISCHER: Oh, it was more than that. (Laughter)

The questioner intends to imply that *more than 500 protesters* is in some way a stigmatization of the podium and/or his Republican masters. In his response the podium very skilfully reverses the evaluation, transforming it into a compliment. He manages to imply that the more protesters one has the better, the more prestige you enjoy.

Very closely related is the ploy of turning the other speaker's narrative against them. The exchange continues:

(31)   Q: WVMT in Burlington reports that you thoughtfully pointed out that their protest banner was posted backwards and you also told them, 'the hardest part of my job is knowing what not to say'. And my question: How could you tell them this when you so often do not say with such evident skill?
   MR. FLEISCHER: (Laughter) Well, in keeping with the spirit of not saying anything, Les, let's go to Dave. (Laughter)

The questioner's move is in effect a good-natured jibe. The podium cleverly reinterprets quite literally 'not saying anything'. A couple of moves later he follows up with a further quip:

(32)   MR. FLEISCHER: And on the poster, I was just trying to be helpful

In the following episode the roles are exchanged:

(33)   MR. FLEISCHER: [...] the best way for our nation to win this war is through the forthright sharing of information. And that's important.

74 *Laughter in running discourse*

> Q: Well, in that spirit, can you share the evidence against bin Laden? (Laughter)

This time the journalist reinterprets bathetically the podium's high-minded 'sharing of information' to mean 'why not let us in on a few details?'

2.5 Register play

2.5.1 *Definitions*

Most work in linguistics into the study of register has taken its cue from Halliday (1978) and Hasan and Halliday (1989), who define a register as 'a cluster of associated features having a greater than random [...] tendency to co-occur' in a given situation. This formal definition has been the basis for the highly productive work carried out by Biber and colleagues on variation in texts (for instance, Biber 1988, 1995; Biber, Conrad and Reppen 1998; Biber *et al.* 1999).

For our purposes here, we can define a register as a way of speaking or writing regularly associated by a set of participants with a certain set of contextual circumstances. Thus register is recognized as a linguistic but also as a social and a psychological entity. It is linguistic in being characterized by a particular vocabulary and phraseology, a particular syntax, a particular discourse organization and, if spoken, very possibly by special intonation patterns and voice quality. It is social in that there is a consensus in a given discourse community about which features normally belong to or are appropriate in a given context, that is, whether the register matches the situation. And it is psychological in that any individual member of the community can recognize whether a piece of discourse which has been produced is appropriate in the current situation.

'Register humour' is defined by Attardo as 'humor caused by an incongruity originating in the clash between two registers' (1994: 230). What precisely we might mean by 'incongruity' and 'clash' and how such concepts relate to laughter-talk has been discussed in the previous chapter. In the terms being adopted here, register humour involves a conflict of priming prosodies and can occur when a mismatch is perceived between speech events which have actually been produced and those that might be expected in the current situation. In practice, as Attardo implies, the speech events produced are normally felt to belong rightfully to, to be characteristic of, a different situation from the one actually pertaining, in other words, that a speaker/writer has fallen into a *different* register and is conjuring up a fantasy situation. In this sudden switching between language forms, register humour is clearly bisociative. Presumably, as with other forms of humour, register mismatch will be appreciated differently depending on whether the audience feels the speaker/writer is acting deliberately or has simply made a mistake. When register play is intentional, it is usually possible to point to particular features of vocabulary, syntax, voice quality and so on, which are being used as deliberate signals that a different register is being evoked. Even when unintentional, it is often not difficult to divine which particular features of an utterance an audience is reacting to when it laughs. What is also interesting for the analyst is the question why a speaker departs from a given register, either deliberately or otherwise. Here are some simple examples of both kinds from the briefings, the unintentional departure first:

(34) Q: Does the President regard Paul Sarbanes of Maryland as a Senator of many good accomplishments, or not?

The register of the first part of the question is somewhat formal, including as it does the expression *regard as* and *many good accomplishments*, but the utterance concludes with the highly colloquial question tag *or not?* The podium is alerted that something is amiss:

(35) MR. LOCKHART: What's the trick here? (Laughter) What did he say? That would be a total, unqualified yes. Now, your follow-up?

The speaker (Mr Lester Kinsolving, see section 5.7) is in a hurry to get his pre-question out of the way in order then to pull some negative 'fact' about the Senator out of his hat and put the podium on the spot.

Here, by contrast, is an instance of intentional register play:

(36) MR. MCCURRY: No, the President said – I asked him earlier, I said, do you feel you pay a fair amount in taxes. And he said, it sure looks like it. (Laughter)

The podium's anecdote also begins in a manner conventionally appropriate to briefings narratives, employing the 'briefings word' *earlier*, the mid-formal *do you feel* (more formal, say, than *do you think* but less than *in your opinion*). The syntactic formulation of the reported question to the President is thus in briefings-speak, as the audience will have recognized. The President's reported reply is, on the other hand, highly colloquial, *it sure looks like it* being an emphatic vernacular way of saying 'yes'. The speaker deliberately falls into a friendly, familiar register both to make his audience laugh but also, of course, to portray the President as a 'regular guy'. This is a fairly common way of depicting the President and would fall into the class of recurrent play-roles listed earlier in this chapter.

In this third example it is hard to tell whether the register shift is deliberate or not:

(37) Q: [...] he said 'I'll have more to say about Joe and about Mike this fall when we actually make the change.' My question is, could we expect a visitation here from the President and an opportunity to ask him some other questions? (Laughter)

The item *visitation* (rather than *visit*) is redolent of religion – in the *Papers* corpus it co-occurs with *angels*, the *Virgin Mary* and *aliens* – and in the present context causes some hilarity. But was the speaker being deliberately sarcastic in casting the President in such company?

2.5.2 Transaction to interaction and back again

In the first two examples – (34) and (36) – the movement is from a 'higher' to a 'lower' register, traditional bathos, whilst the third, example (37), introduces an item from a higher register, an effect we shall call *upgrading*. By 'lower', we intend the register(s) appropriate to normal, everyday conversation, by 'higher' we are referring to registers appropriate to more restricted circumstances. The 'high-low' metaphor is widely used in linguistics in discussions of language variety. Scannell (1991:12) talks of conversation as the 'bed-rock' form of talk, which implies that all other spoken discourse type are derivative and are presumably 'rock strata' lying *above* it. Other ways of talking about this or similar phenomena use terms such as *formal* and *informal*, whilst in socio-phonetics it is common to talk about more and less *careful* forms of utterance production.

Given the existence of the two modes at work in these briefings, the transactional and the interactional, is it the case that the first is characterized by the use of higher registers and the second lower? In reality, matters turn out to be a little more complicated. Participants seem to feel that normal transactional business mode is a kind of default, the way, as it were, we should be speaking, and it is felt to be neither high nor low. It is often, in fact, jokingly contrasted with high register:

(38) Q: [...] Ari, after having passed two tax cut packages, Congress is coming back to start to digest the concomitant spending –
MR. FLEISCHER: Concomitant.
Q: Yes. I can't say that in my TV work, but – (Laughter) –

Concomitant is a high-falutin' word and the podium adopts the 'regular guy' persona by commenting on its use. Much register play consists in the use by one side or the other of a higher than expected register and this high register tends to be in imitation of what the participants feel is the language of politics, administration or diplomacy, but not necessarily of their own business:

(39) Q: Has the President gotten any response from the Senate on the proposal he made yesterday on means testing Medicare?
MR. MCCURRY: A number of senators have responded publicly and we're encouraged by those who are supportive and not discouraged by those who are not. (Laughter)

There is more than an element of self-parody here of course, but such high registers are considered by the participants to be an exception rather than the norm for briefings transaction.

On the other hand, the interactional phases of the discourse generally take place in a more conversational register than the transactional and there is the awareness that lower, more colloquial registers than the one they normally use are available, especially for comic effect:

(40) Q: [...] unless Mrs. Clinton makes up her mind whether she wants to run. Will the President try to nudge a decision out of her in the interest of the party?
MR. LOCKHART: You've got to be kidding me. (Laughter)

and see 'it sure looks like it' in example (36). There is no doubt that the sudden transition from transactional to interactional is usually accompanied by a fall in register. This may well be one of the reasons it holds such comic possibilities:

(41) MR. FLEISCHER: Lester, the President's position on all these matters is that people should be hired on the basis of merit, and hired in accordance with the laws of our land.
Q: Great. I really appreciate these answers today, Ari. I'm very touched. (Laughter)

Something which regularly elicits repeated bouts laughter is the use of features of transaction, largely vocabulary and syntax, within interactional sessions to express interpersonal meanings. In other words, what the press and podium particularly enjoy is playing around with the modes. We have already come across an example in (7) where both sides playfully discuss Mr Fleischer's upcoming marriage, pretending it is a political event and using, as Ari himself proclaims: 'presidential spokesman speak' – with a question and answer format. Other occurrences of the same also raise a laugh:

(42) MR. FLEISCHER: Jim, in a different seat?
Q: Yes. I was trying to shake you from this geographical hang-up that you have. (Laughter)
MR. FLEISCHER: But you haven't changed rows; you've just changed sides in the same row.
Q: I wanted to ease it in on you. I didn't want to shock you too much –
MR. FLEISCHER: Horizontal move, not a vertical move (Laughter)
Q: Left to right.
(43) Q: What kind of coverage are the reporters going to have? I mean, how much access are they going to be able to see?
MR. MCCURRY: Traditional and customary. (Laughter)
Q: Will there be a pool at the Rockefeller house every day?
MR. MCCURRY: The coverage opportunities will be designed to afford those who are there to cover the President plenty of time for their own relaxation and vacation. (Laughter)

In the second of these, the podium uses high language to convey to the journalists that they will not be allowed to see much of the President during his vacation.
Thus the podium can parody his own style, and so can the press:

(44) Q: Mike, in perhaps your last Japan question-answer – (Laughter)

This was also delivered in an especially sententious manner, in what we might term 'role-play voice' (see Tannen 1984: 130–143 on mock speech patterns for role-playing). Predictably, and as already noted in the introductory Chapter, the journalists parody the podium's language in jest: 'but if those trade-offs are really excellent and the benefits to children and the American people are really terrific, better than you can imagine...' (laughter) and see section 5.3.3. This kind of parody, of course, can also be interpreted as an in-joke.

2.6 Bathos and upgrading

Bathos, the movement from high to low, is widely recognized as a traditional comic technique. It is, of course, not always principally a fall in register which is involved: sometimes ideas are involved, sometimes it is simply, as Bergson reminds us, 'a great cause which resolves itself in a small effect', the juxtaposition of the two being unexpected. Others talk of comic deflation. Here is an example:

(45) Q: The Vice President will be here?
MR. LOCKHART: He is very knowledgeable on the environment. He could speak to you in a way that you could use tomorrow instead of today, but he won't be here. (Laughter)

We even find an example of its use combined with reverse irony, bathetic praise on the occasion of a political nomination, where being in possession of an excellent degree from Harvard is depicted as something to be ashamed of:

(46) Q: How does he expect to get it through?
MR. MCCURRY: By hard work. By the persuasive arguments [...] on behalf of Governor Weld; and by the overall superior record and qualifications of the nominee – save his summa cum laude degree from Harvard. (Laughter)

The speaker thus manages to praise his client without hubris.

In the episodes we examined here – (45) and (46) – the bathetic shift is found in a single speaker's move, but it is also frequently used to great effect by a second speaker to shift the emphasis of a previous speaker's move. We have already witnessed a case in example (33) and here are two more:

(47) Q: [...] Does the President think that his hands-off policy has contributed in any way to the hopelessness and the rising violence in the Middle East? And, anticipating your answer, I have a follow-on. (Laughter)
MR. FLEISCHER: Why don't you just get it all out of the way, Helen? (Laughter)

The first speaker (Helen) rather sarcastically implies that the podium's response will be somehow unsatisfactory, presumably either evasive or anodyne, but manages to remain, technically at least, in transactional mode. The podium attempts to reinterpret her narrative in a way more favourable to himself, implying that she is unreasonable or has personal issues, whereas he is patient and long-suffering. However, to do so he has to slip into a more interactional mode, addressing her with more interpersonal emphasis than transactional mode will generally support. In the next example:

(48) MR. BERGER: [...] You know deadlines are a double-edged sword. On the one hand, deadlines provide a –
Q: Selling point. (Laughter)

Laughter in running discourse 79

by interrupting the other speaker and finishing his utterance for him – a phenomenon known as *other's turn completion* – the second speaker (Helen once more) deflates the podium's high blown rhetoric and at the same time rejects his serious frame and his narrative of administration openness and fairness, replacing it with one of sham and deviousness. The second speaker thus manages to overturn the previous speaker's frame, narrative and register.

On a lighter note, the podium occasionally uses a kind of bathetic response to praise, a self-deprecation along with regular guy role-play that goes down well with his audience:

(49)   Q: Some of your fellow White House officials have remarked in recent weeks that your status has increased to a kind of superstar level –
       MR. MCCURRY: Those are just the envious ones.

and see Chapter 3, example (40). The converse technique, upgrading from low to high, is much less recognized in the literature on humour, probably because it is generally subsumed into the general category of parody. There are a number of examples in this corpus, however. See example (43) and the following:

(50)   And do you really think many people believe he is really happy about this, Joe?
       MR. LOCKHART: I have no reason to dispute the joy he expressed so openly in front of you. (Laughter) Next.

The middle register of the question is met with a much higher register in the response, all of which is a comic way of saying simply 'yes'.

In general terms in these briefings, upgrading is probably the most common type of deliberate register mismatch:

(51)   And I will certainly enjoy whatever notoriety I have, and I will certainly use it to the good fortune of my family in the future. (Laughter)

The speaker – Mr McCurry again on his retirement – matches a 'low' narrative – the money-making in-script, with high language, as well as adopting a high, noble, modest fantasy persona. The parody this time is not only of a language style but also of those politicians who, in true Pecksniff-like fashion, talk of their family while feathering their nest.

In this final example we find bathos and upgrading in quick succession (on the Clinton-Lewinsky case):

(52)   [...] isn't the sole alternative what *Reuters News Agency* quoted Angie Dickinson saying in Hollywood: Clinton has a very horny appetite, and I find that quite reasonable.
       MR. MCCURRY: Is that a medical diagnosis, or was that a – (Laughter).

The questioner, Mr Kinsolving again, pursues his original line in middle register, employing typical briefings question syntax and vocabulary, until reaching the expression *horny appetite*, which is decidedly colloquial. The podium responds to this fall in register as well as the sexual slant of the discourse by moving into interpersonal mode in asking his question on the *medical diagnosis*.

80 *Laughter in running discourse*

The questioner himself, however, moves back into typical transactional middle-to-high register:

(53) Q: I wonder, would you agree, disagree, or give that an icy 'no comment'?

while the podium winds up the exchange with a piece of rather suggestive upgrading of his own, using podium-speak to refer obliquely to sex:

(54) MR. MCCURRY: I'm not familiar enough with Angie Dickinson to know whether she's been in a position to render such an astute and explicit diagnosis, but I doubt that she has any informed ability to make that decision.

2.7 Colourful language

In his analysis of audience laughter during the 1988 US presidential debates, Clayman (1992a) notes that in one of the sites of what he calls 'affiliative laughter' one of the speakers has indulged in some sort of far-fetched, metaphorical description. In the briefings too, what we might term 'colourful language' often seems to be enough to occasion laughter:

(55) MR. FLEISCHER: No. With all due respect, I think you're fishing off a dock that doesn't exist. (Laughter)

There is considerable evidence that participants find colourful language striking and memorable. In one of his early briefings, Mr Fleischer asserts that, thanks to his President's ability to work with the Democrats, 'you can hear the sound of *gridlock breaking*' (my emphasis), a metaphor meaning 'to get things moving again'. Several moves go by until someone decides to ask: 'Ari, what is the sound of gridlock breaking?', which affords general mirth and prolonged laughter. At first, understandably, the laughter is slightly delayed (one person in fact laughs much later than the others) but the audience eventually recall the expression, which was used only once and a good two minutes earlier.

On several other occasions a striking metaphor is picked out and re-employed by another speaker:

(56) Q: You said the NSC meeting today was to discuss a variety of military matters that are pending, a phrase that would seem to be eight months pregnant with meaning. (Laughter) [...]
MR. FLEISCHER: I'm trying to do the math. When does eight months go back to? (Laughter) And are you suggesting there will be a baby born in one month? (Laughter)

(57) MR. FLEISCHER: [...] let me put it to you this way; the President is going the last mile for diplomacy. We shall see if the other nations on the Security Council are willing to entertain that last mile. We shall see.
Q: Is the last mile 10 days long?
MR. FLEISCHER: Not going – (Laughter)

As the second example shows, colourful language can be dangerous: it can be picked up and used against the other speaker sarcastically, often through a *reductio ad absurdum*.

The significance of the audience laughter in simple cases such as (55) and the first bout in (56) would seem to be simple recognition of out-of-the-ordinary language and that non-serious, non-*bona fide* mode has been employed. In the second bout of (56) and in (57), however, we find this recognition value accompanied by teasing. In Clayman's terms we would have to talk of a combination of or rapid interchange between affiliative (recognition) and non-affiliative (teasing) laughter in such episodes.

2.8 Conclusion

We set out at the beginning of this chapter to discover the relevance of the bisociative theory of humour to authentic speech in a particular discourse type. Our main observation is that the bisociative shift was very frequently involved in the laughter-talk in the material examined. We have found it in considerable variety. We have found shifts of mode, from the transitional to the interactional, shifts of frame, from the serious to the play, shifts of narrative of endless diversity (potentially as many kinds as there are contexts), shifts of role (from a professional into a play or fantasy persona) and finally, shifts of register, from high to low, from business to personal, and back again.

However, and most intriguingly, we have also discovered that bisociation in authentic discourse is no idle phenomenon, no end in itself as it sometimes appears to be in joke research. On the contrary, these sudden transitions of narrative, with their accompanying switches of role and language are very frequently performed with a rhetorical purpose (where, by *rhetoric*, we intend 'the art of persuasion', Cockcroft and Cockcroft 1992). Participants adopt fantasy narratives and roles which favour their side of an argument, which help to project their professed view of the world and which reflect well on themselves and their clients. Different participants adopt different strategies. Of the podiums, one will project himself as a schoolmaster and his audience as a class of unruly schoolchildren, another will portray himself as a tough trouble-shooter and yet another as living in the doghouse (Chapter 4, example 55). All will choose narratives which project their President as a long-suffering fellow citizen and, of course, as that most valued of figures in US society, a regular guy. Of the journalists, some will tend to humour the podium's narratives, others will contest them, some to the point of arrogating to themselves the role of professional cynic.

Bisociation, then, particularly narrative shift, in the adversarial but often good-humoured environment of this discourse type is not neutral, not disinterested or inert, but a useful tactical ploy to disarm the opposition and drive home a point. Laughter-talk is often as good a way as any of gaining the upper hand in an argument.

3 Face-work and the in-group

> People sometimes divide others into those you laugh at and those you laugh with. The young Auden was someone you could laugh-at-with.
>
> (Stephen Spender)

3.1 Introduction

Perhaps the most striking of findings in Provine's study of what he calls 'convivial humour' in authentic social situations was how 'only about ten to twenty percent of pre-laugh comments were estimated by [...] assistants to be even remotely humorous' (2000: 40). The funniest pre-laugh comments include such gems as 'He tried to blow his nose but he missed' and 'Do you date within your species?' but these are rarities. Most seem entirely innocuous: 'See you guys later', 'I hope we all do well', 'Are you sure?' and suchlike. This is, of course, entirely consonant with folk experience of spontaneous laughter-talk – 'you had to be there'.

The discovery that most conversational laughter '*is not a response to jokes or other formal attempts at humor* forces a reevaluation of what laughter signals' (Provine 2000: 42, his italics). Studies of laughter which are preoccupied with humour 'are of limited relevance in understanding most laughter'. He goes on to compare the complexity of conversational laughter with that of stand-up comedy, which, he claims, has unfortunately served as the 'prototype of much laugh research and philosophical inquiry' (2000: 43). The former is mundane, the latter based on jokes. The first requires intimate contact, in the second the comic is physically and socially distant. The comic typically refrains from laughter, whilst Provine studies show how, in conversational laughter, speakers actually laugh *more* than audiences (2000: 27).

The briefings constitute a sort of half-way house between Provine's entirely casual exchanges and comedy performance. The podium, it is true, can have a touch of the stand-up comic about him in his distance and delivery of quips, but this is balanced by the social intimacy between the two sides and many of the episodes of laughter-talk in the briefings are not immediately humorous to an outside observer and need a considerable effort of empathy on the part of an outsider to be appreciated. So why do people laugh in such circumstance? Can we shed light on the conditions in which such laughter occurs?

First of all, a large proportion of such episodes fall into two types: laughter at some kind of 'hitch or glitch' in the smooth running of the briefings and laughter occasioned by some direct reference to the fact of, as it were, 'doing the business of briefings'. There is clearly some overlap between the two on many occasions, especially when some break-down of normal proceedings excites comment on what went wrong.

A couple of examples will suffice here whilst a more detailed examination will follow the theoretical discussion. Perhaps the simplest kind of hitch is when some kind of purely physical impediment to the smooth running of proceedings arises:

(1) Mr Hunt is correct that that occurred in April, but –
     Q: Would that be the Surgeon General?
     MR. MCCURRY: Say what?
     Q: The Surgeon General?
     MR. MCCURRY: I can't hear you. What? (Laughter)

The podium presumably simply can't hear the question. This is a marked event, it should not normally happen, which is enough for it to occasion laughter.

Someone not knowing what they might be expected to know is a common cause of laughter:

(2) Q: Abacha's death?
     MR. MCCURRY: Have we put out any formal statement? I'm asking you. (Laughter)
(3) Q: Two-part, Joe. Does the President believe that Kazan should be receiving a special Oscar or not? (Laughter) It's been in the news Joe.
     MR. LOCKHART: I know. What's the controversy?
     Q: He turned them all in –
     MR. LOCKHART: I saw a headline. I don't know what it is.
     Q: He turned them all in
     MR. LOCKHART: Oh, he turned them all in. (Laughter)
     Q: He turned in people that he believed were sympathetic to the communists.

and see example (13), where it is the journalist who does not know his business too well.

Part of the laughter here may, of course, be due to the unexpected reversal of roles, the podium normally being the one to reply to, not ask, the questions. Surprise reversal, as we see throughout this work, is often implicated in laughter-talk. The podium, however, is not the only one to be so caught out:

(4) Q: Joe, do you wish to amend or revise the 'gloat-free zone' comment you made yesterday?
     MR. LOCKHART: Why?
     Q: I don't know. (Laughter)

In general any action, any deed, any piece of behaviour, deliberate or otherwise, which could be construed as someone not doing their job properly seems to be a potential cause for laughter: for instance, should the podium jump the gun (Mr Joe Lockhart has begun to speculate on which parts of Texas the President will visit, Mr Toiv is a member of the President's staff):

(5) MR. TOIV: Joe, we're not ready to announce Texas.
    MR. LOCKHART: OK (Laughter) [...]
    MR. TOIV: We don't have any specifics.

or even simply be unsure:

(6) Q: Not Texas?
    MR. LOCKHART: No, it could be Texas. That's what I'm trying to indicate here. But we're not sure yet. (Laughter)

or need to find the right piece of paper for a read-out:

(7) Q: What's the White House view of Fidel Castro's announcement making Christmas a permanent holiday in Cuba?
    MR. LOCKHART: I'll tell you in a second. (Laughter) We welcome any move [...]

then laughter is likely to ensue. Making a factual error is also deemed, not surprisingly, a good reason to laugh:

(8) Q: Why have there been no consequences for Secretary Rubin for publicly criticizing the steel –
    Q: O'Neill.
    Q: O'Neill.
    Q: Oh, Secretary O'Neill, thank you. (Laughter)

The laughter which accompanies hitches or *faux pas* would normally be put down to the audience's reaction to a participant's (potential) embarrassment. But this begs the question of why another's embarrassment should be deemed a cause for laughter, a question we will address later.

Turning briefly to the second kind of laughter-talk, namely, direct comments on the business of briefings themselves, we find a large number of metadiscursive 'asides':

(9) Q: Was that yet another indicator, as far as the White House is concerned, about the partisan environment surrounding the proceeding?
    Q: Say yes. (Laughter)
(10) Q: I've got a question about the President's choice to head the St. Lawrence Seaway. There appears to be a gentleman from California with no –
    MR. MCCURRY: This is stump Mike time. (Laughter)

and in the following the aside is, as it were, waiting to happen:

(11) Q: What was for lunch today?

MR. FLEISCHER: It was a buffet, there was rice, there was fillet, there was salad, bread.
Q: Was there chicken too?
MR. FLEISCHER: If there was chicken there, I didn't see it.
Q: What was dessert?
MR. FLEISCHER: Dessert was something chocolate with something ice cream inside it. (Laughter)
Q: What wines?
MR. FLEISCHER: This must be the classic definition of a slow news day. (Laughter) I'm new here, but –

What seems to happen in such cases is that the business of briefings itself is suspended for a time in order for metadiscursive remarks to be made. The movement is certainly from transactional to interactional mode, but this is a particular form of interaction in which the topic of conversational mode is the business of briefings itself.

We might note in passing that many of the asides appear to involve a good dose of aggression:

(12) Q: [...] Is it safe to assume now that the objectives have changed to be what you've just read – I remember what you read, so you don't need to read it again – (Laughter) –

The laughter in such cases may well be a result of a mixture of causes – comment on business along with display of aggression – and will be considered in more detail in our discussion of the effects of hostile speech moves.

As mentioned earlier, one of the most frequent stimuli for comments on business are, predictably, the kind of hitches we have listed, so the laughter results from a combination of blunder or lapses and the metadiscursive comment it provokes:

(13) MR. MCCURRY: This is the Florida provision? I'm not familiar enough –
Q: I knew you would ask me that. They only sent me – [inaudible] – back of this story. (Laughter)

The podium admits to not knowing much about the topic but the journalist too, embarrassingly, is unable to supply more details.

Why should committing some minor transgression or displaying some shortcoming constitute an occasion for laughter? And why should explicit comment on the business in hand be greeted by laughter? The first question will be considered by reference to the concepts of *politeness* and *face* and the degree to which a speaker's face is 'on the line', particularly in situations involving an audience. The answer to the second question lies in the immense importance generally accorded by participants to being part of the in-group in a given social setting. As will be seen, these two sources of laughter are very closely connected since there is a natural association between face-work and in- and out-group posturing and manoeuvring.

3.2 Politeness theory and *face*

3.2.1 The model

The theory we shall employ to explain why hitches and glitches occasion laughter in the current data is the *Politeness* theory developed by Brown and Levinson (1987). This theory grew out of the authors' initial perception that politeness has 'a sociological significance altogether beyond the level of table manners and etiquette books'. Instead, they argue: 'from a grossly ethological perspective [...] the problem for any social group is to control its internal aggression while retaining the potential for aggression both in internal social control and [...] in external competitive relations with other groups.' At the same time as exerting this control, the possibility of 'communication between potentially aggressive parties' must be created and maintained (1987: 1).

To explain how these conflicting impulses – aggression and cooperation – are managed, Brown and Levinson propose a kind of 'economic' model of social relationships (Cherry 1988), in which politeness helps an individual to maximize in cost/benefit terms (i.e. to achieve the greatest benefit at the lowest cost, Brown and Levinson 1987: 17) their acquisition of 'goods and services'. These include all social wants, from tangible possessions through love and attention to privacy. Their theory evolves from the dual axioms that model human beings are first of all rational entities and at the same time driven by needs and desires. These axioms are interdependent: humans are rational precisely inasmuch as they are capable of developing strategies to achieve their goals (their needs and desires). Moreover, all normal adult members of society have, and recognize that other members have, what is known as *face* (a term borrowed from Goffman (1967) and from the English folk usage). Face is defined as 'the public self-image that every member wants to claim for himself' and consists of two related types:

> *negative face*: the basic claim to territories, personal preserves, rights to non-distraction – i.e. to freedom of action and freedom from imposition;
> *positive face*: the positive consistent self-image or 'personality' (crucially including the desire that this self-image be appreciated and approved of) claimed by interactants.
>
> (Brown and Levinson 1987: 61)

Negative face, the desire for freedom from imposition and freedom of action, is recognizable as more or less the kind of phenomenon we mean when we normally refer to politeness – we pay attention to another's negative face every time we knock on their door to request their permission to enter. Positive face is less straightforward, but it comprises 'the desire to be ratified, understood, approved of, liked or admired' by at least some others, presumably those we in turn approve of and admire. One important further step in the theory is that this positive face includes the desire to have one's *goals* thought of as desirable. Although the precise characteristics and delimitations of both types of face will differ from culture to culture (including of course the exact nature of goals generally thought worthy of approbation – the suggestion has been made that some societies give more weight to one type of face, negative or positive, than the other), there is an assumption that face itself is a universal phenomenon. It is the consequence of the need for the human animal – possibly the most aggressive animal on the planet – to cohabit with other similar animals in society and to cooperate with them in order to protect and pursue its interests.

3.2.2 Threatening face

The theory also asserts that face is extremely sensitive, volatile and vulnerable. It claims we pay vast amounts of attention to protecting and enhancing our own face and in ensuring that we do not threaten or even seem to threaten that of others, and we expect others to do the same for us. It maintains that even much of normal social interaction is potentially threatening to either or both the speaker's or hearer's face. Any action which puts pressure on the hearer to do something – an order, request, suggestion, reminder and so on – potentially threatens their negative face, as would any act (giving a gift, paying a compliment) which entails the hearer incurring a debt. Any action which could be construed as demonstrating a lack of care for the hearer's desires and goals is a potential threat to the latter's positive face, for example, criticism and disapproval but also contradiction, challenge, even interruption or simply the failure to show alignment and agreement with their views (in section 5.1 we will also mention how interlocutors in conversation generally behave under a 'with me or against me' assumption). Actions which threaten face are conventionally denominated *face-threatening acts* or FTAs.

Speakers put their *own* negative face at risk in a number of ways, such as by expressing thanks or accepting an offer (thereby recognizing a debt). They risk their own positive face when, for example, they apologize or confess guilt or responsibility (thereby acknowledging some previous shortcoming). Most importantly for the present study, in the presence of an audience, any recognizable mistake, misdemeanour or *faux pas* committed by a speaker constitutes a threat for that speaker's face, as we saw in the earlier examples – a situation which usually requires some sort of attention and redress.

We do not, however, treat all our interlocutors in the same way at all times. We adopt different politeness strategies according to context, and it is part of adult communicative competence (Hymes 1971) to judge which is the correct strategy for a particular situation. For example, greater indirectness in requesting is usually perceived as directly proportional to politeness. But speakers cannot always choose to err on the side of caution, to be hyper-indirect. If the circumstances are not right, they will be seen as joking, facetious or making a more serious request than they actually are, thereby arousing unnecessary suspicion or anxiety. Speaker 'strategies' are by and large unconscious, though they can in some circumstances open up to introspection. For example, they may come to the surface when communication breaks down and participants need to reassess them.

Brown and Levinson list three 'sociological variables' that speakers employ in choosing the degree of politeness to use and in calculating the amount of threat to their own face:

(i) the 'social distance' of the speaker and the hearer (D);
(ii) the relative 'power' of the speaker over the hearer (P);
(iii) the absolute ranking of impositions in the particular culture (R).

The greater the social distance between the interlocutors (e. g., if they know each other very little), the more politeness is generally expected. The greater the (perceived) relative power of hearer over speaker, the more politeness is recommended. The heavier the imposition made on the hearer (the more of their time required, or the greater the favour requested), the more politeness will generally have to be used.

In the years following Brown and Levinson's original outline in 1978, plenty of objections, major and minor, have been proffered. Several authors have questioned the universality of their theory especially in regard to non-European societies, and a number of refinements have been suggested – that the effect of power and distance on politeness is not deterministic, that the importance of *affect* (e.g. whether or not the interlocutors like each other) be reappraised, that *rudeness* receive more attention (R. Lakoff 1989, 2003). Of particular relevance to the present study, Brown and Levinson themselves admit that in their original work the effects of the presence or otherwise of an audience were underanalysed. An audience will exert an influence on 'definitions of situational "formality"' and so will influence 'P, D, R assessments' and thus also 'assessments of FTA danger' (1987: 16). In other words, we can predict that participants are still more sensitive about face when the interaction is witnessed by others. As we have already underlined, the context of the briefings includes several audiences, both present and distant.

On the whole, however, the edifice of their ideas of politeness as *strategic conflict management* has weathered the scrutiny of time and criticism very well. The ramifications of politeness theory have been explored in many and varied discourse types from, for instance, the clinical interview (Rowland 1999a), to patient–nurse interaction (Grainger 2002) to teacher–student dialogue in the teaching of mathematics (Rowland 1999b, Bills 2000). As Holtgraves points out, however, a great deal of the research into politeness 'has examined hypothetical politeness or the perception of theoretically generated politeness strategies' (1997: 235) without availing itself of naturally occurring language data. The present study is, of course, entirely based on authentic examples. Moreover Harris notes that 'politeness has also been much less examined in relationship to institutional contexts and/or discourse types other than ordinary conversation' (2001: 452). Briefings, as we have witnessed, represent a mixture of types combining transactional institutional talk with discourse of a more spontaneous and conversational nature. For a fuller treatment of politeness interplay in the briefings see Partington (2003: 124–155).

3.2.3 Face *in lexicography and corpora*

Dictionaries, if they touch upon it all, do not cover this sense of the word *face* at all well. The *WUEB* includes it briefly under *lose face*, defined as 'to suffer a fall in the prestige in which one is held'. Chamber's 20th Century has both *lose face*, 'lose prestige' and *save one's face* 'to avoid humiliation or appearance by climbing down', which seems to raise as many questions as it resolves (how do we now define 'appearance' and 'climbing down'?).

The word *face* in the context of *los** and *sav** was concordanced in *WHBig*, the *5Mil* newspaper corpus and the *Flob* and *Frown* general corpora. Although the two items *saving face* and *losing face* were generally not very common, the results were most intriguing. The owners of the face being lost or to be saved were, most frequently of all, the Chinese government:

1 There is plenty of common ground for resolving the dispute quietly, without China losing **face**.
2 Patten went public with the plan apparently without much consultation with the Chinese. This mortified Beijing, which felt it had lost **face**.
3 Deng Xiaoping could not tolerate the loss of **face** of postponement.

then politicians of both Eastern and United Germany:

4 Only the canny Mr Genscher, who knew the East Germans' minds, could have thought of letting the regime save **face** by 'expelling' their own people across their own territory.
5 [...] if Britain shows signs that it cannot ratify Maastricht, then Germany will lead the core to the promised land. Members of Mr Kohl's Christian Democrat party want a Europe that embraces more than five, if only to save **face**.

or the Soviet regime:

6 If the 1957 explanation was false, the theory runs, then the subsequent loss of **face** would have been too great for a correction to be issued in Gromyko's lifetime.

or North Korea:

7 On North Korea, what would be so terrible about meeting North Korea unilaterally, **face**-to-**face**, if that would help them save their **face**?

or the United Nations:

8 Why won't you say whether we're willing to give up some power to the UN, some control over the multination force? As least they will be able to save **face**.

or the European Central Bank:

9 Instead, the central bank yesterday sought to pull off the seemingly impossible: to satisfy international pressure; to minimize its loss of **face**; to convince the world that it remained as tough as ever; and to send an encouraging domestic signal [...].

The only non-official, non-political entities to have face were sports teams, one cricket and one football. The only individuals mentioned by name were Deng Xiaoping, Lord Carrington (at the time, British Foreign Secretary and the only non-foreign political entity deemed to have face) and Aristide, the Haitian dictator. No private, person-in-the-street in any of these corpora is ever discussed in terms of having face to lose or save. The only group which is said to itself claim or admit to having face is the IRA:

10 The Unionists are saying that the IRA will never completely give up their arms, and the IRA has been saying that they would lose **face** if they accept this decommissioning.

Those seen as having face, then, tend to be authoritarian regimes, alien power bodies generally regarded by the cultures the speakers/writers belong to as – in another sense of the word – 'faceless' regimes. In modern lexicogrammatical terms, *face* has an unfavourable *prosody*, that is, it co-occurs with items of a bad evaluative sense or connotation. In fact, if any entity is said to have face to save or lose, the hearer can fairly safely assume that the speaker views this entity unfavourably, even if this evaluation is not made explicit. Possible examples of this kind of hidden prosody are line 9, from the *Independent* newspaper – the European Central Bank is, in fact, not generally viewed with particular affection in the British press – and line 8, from *WHBig* – the United Nations was definitely out of favour in United States political circles in the period leading up to the conflict in Iraq. Equally, one strongly suspects that, as regards line 10, no actual member of the IRA itself will have stated explicitly 'we will lose face if we decommission some of our weapons'. *Lose face* and *save face* are 'over-the-fence' items (Partington 1998: 74–76), words or phrases used of others, not of oneself.

All this is a far cry from the ways Goffman and Brown and Levinson see the phenomenon. For politeness theory, face is a universal human attribute, although, most interestingly, the latter do underline the parallel between personal and international face: 'politeness', they say, is 'like formal diplomatic protocol (for which it must surely be the model)' (1987: 1). Just for once, we might be justified in treating this lack of overt mention of personal everyday face in the corpora as a paradoxical kind of confirmation of its existence in that, as Brown and Levinson constantly imply, people are so acutely sensitive, so anxious about face they cannot even bring themselves to admit having it.

3.2.4 Positive face and the in-group

We have defined positive face as 'the desire to be ratified, understood, approved of, liked or admired' by some set of others. The degree to which this kind of face can exist independently of other people, especially of the social group to which an individual belongs or aspires to belong is a moot question. We might surmise that Robinson Crusoe's face needs (before meeting Friday) were highly particular and probably less impelling than those of us in normal society. In any case, it is clear that it is of paramount importance for most individuals to protect and enhance their face in the face, as it were, of others.

Brown and Levinson's descriptions often seem to be biased in favour of dyadic one-to-one conversation and, of their own admission, group dynamics are somewhat underexamined. We might redefine 'the desire to be ratified, understood, approved of, liked or admired' by others as 'the need to feel part of a group', the desire to be an 'insider' of the 'in-group'. Brown and Levinson's main focus is on analysing how speakers 'pay attention to' (both assuaging and menacing) the hearer's face. However, we can predict that participants in discourse, especially when there is an audience and still more so when that audience, as in the briefings, constitutes an in-group, will spend a great deal of time, effort and attention in managing their position in relation to that group. Brown and Levinson list the following as the three main 'strategies' (or hyper-strategies) of redressing the hearer's positive face (S = speaker, H = hearer):

- claim common ground;
- convey that S and H are cooperators;
- fulfil H's wants.

(Brown and Levinson 1987: 102)

They are obviously also very useful ploys for a speaker who wishes to infiltrate, to gain inclusion in the in-group.

The precise definition of 'in-group' need not concern us here, but regularity of contact among members as well as a degree of shared interests are important components. We can safely assume that the audience of journalists constitutes such a group: they know each other well, they congregate at the White House and presumably elsewhere almost daily and despite a high degree of professional competitiveness, they all share the same task of news gathering (or news devising).

The position of the podium as regards the in-group is on the other hand quite delicate. One of the principal topics of the present work is how the various podiums orient to the group via laughter-talk. One strategy could be to stress common interests with his audience, but this may not always be possible for a number of reasons. The audience may reject his overtures, at considerable cost to his face. Or it may be of strategic advantage to claim higher ground in relation to the group, for instance, when he adopts a role of authority or expert. In any case, his professional role as spokesperson for the administration disallows complete membership, at least during phases of transaction – it is his job to be outside the group. Conversely how does the in-group behave in response? When do they accept his advances and when do they treat them with hostility and suspicion?

In the following sections we will examine in-group dynamics via the use of laughter-talk. We will analyse how laughter-talk is used by the group to express its solidarity, and how it can help define and signal reactions to a potential outsider as well as how participants use it in the attempt to gain and affirm group-inclusion.

3.3 Politeness and laughter

In the light of this discussion, we can attempt to answer the two questions which arose in section 3.1: why hitches and glitches are often greeted with laughter and why metadiscursive asides on briefings business can also induce laughter.

3.3.1 Incidents and accidents

As regards the first of these, in the context of briefings, then, any accident, misre-membering, oversight, miscalculation or downright clanger perpetrated by a speaker, either the podium or a journalist, implicates a potential loss of professional prestige. An ideal podium or journalist would be free from such shortcomings; when they occur in practice they are a fall from grace, a temporary one at least. Sometimes, the audio-visual evidence shows that the podium smiles or even occasionally initiates the laughter, which lends weight to Goffman's observations (1981) on how laughter signals a speaker's awareness of his or her own gaffe and acts as a prelude to some excuse or account paving the way for a return to normality. In other words, laughter helps the perpetrator negotiate repair. On other occasions, for example (7) or (10), the podium's smile seems to indicate that he is committing a 'mock gaffe' and is playing to the gallery. In either case, the smile or laughter of the perpetrator indicates their awareness of the abnormality and therefore their intention to return to the straight and narrow. Gavioli (1995), in a comparative study of service encounters in British and Italian bookshops,[1] also observes how assistants often laugh when for some reason they cannot satisfy a customer's requirements – a requested book is not available or he or she cannot answer a customer's question, and so on. Here too the laughter is a signal of a problem, perhaps even an admission of fallibility, and acts as a prologue to repair, which can involve apologies, accounts of why the book is not there, information on where to find it and promises to take further action.

Returning to the briefings, the hearer or audience laughter which follows a podium hitch, first and foremost, also expresses and signals the recognition that a problem has occurred. What however is the value of such laughter or rather, how does the author of the incident/accident evaluate it? Laughter is notoriously ambiguous in value, it can be either affiliative or disaffiliative. As Glenn (2003) points out, laughter is affiliative when it is used to remedy breakdowns and thus is typically apparent in situations of possible embarrassment and anxiety, as in the briefings, but also, for example, in hospital talk (Regan 1990, Grainger 2002). Audience affiliation expresses some kind of temporary inclusion of the perpetrator in the in-group. However, laughter can obviously also indicate derision and hostility. Disaffiliative laughter most definitely positions the victim outside the in-group.

We might surmise, however, that a third possibility exists. Laughter may signal simple recognition that a breakdown has occurred and been noticed but does not necessarily entail anything more. Glenn notes how 'in response to teases and improprieties, laughter shows willingness to go along but (by itself) stops short of outright affiliation with what is going on' and also that 'recipient laughter can show appreciation only [...] rather than affiliation with what the laughable is doing' (2003: 122, a *laughable* is anything that occasions laughter). The same is true of error-produced laughter. The problem for whoever is facing the laughter is to interpret quite which of the possibilities is being signalled.

Brown and Levinson, of course, define affiliation as redressing the other's positive face. They list 'joke' among their standard positive politeness strategies useful for emphasizing common ground: 'since jokes are based on mutual shared background knowledge and values, jokes may be used to stress that shared background or those shared values' and 'for putting H at ease'. Of particular relevance here, the very first positive politeness strategy they list is 'notice, or attend to H (his interests, wants, needs, goods)' (1987: 103). One important aspect of 'notice', they say, is that 'when H makes an FTA against himself (a breakdown of body control, or any *faux pas*), S should "notice" it and indicate that he's not embarrassed by it [...] He can do this by a joke, or teasing H about his penchant for *faux pas*, for example: "God you're farty tonight"' (Brown and Levinson 1987: 104).

There are examples of a similar kind of notice in the briefings, especially when the hitch is substantial and could hardly be glossed over. This first occasion is a podium lapse, Dublin, of course, being in the *Republic* of Ireland:

(14) Q: Where in Northern Ireland will the two leaders meet?
 MR. FLEISCHER: Dublin.
 Q: No, no.
 [...]
 Q: A historic development, Ari. (Laughter)

while in the following a journalist is at fault:

(15) Q: Why have there been no consequences for Secretary Rubin for publicly criticizing the steel –
 Q: O'Neill.
 Q: O'Neill.
 Q: Oh, Secretary O'Neill, thank you. (Laughter)
 MR. FLEISCHER: Did you have to correct him? I was going to work with him. (Laughter)

This kind of notice is probably the normal, default operation in informal face-to-face conversation. In the briefings context, though, there are often constraints on time and on availability of turn and so detailed notice like the examples given earlier is not always apparent. We might, however, treat the laughter which often greets such breakdowns as the minimal form of mention. It signals simple recognition that some marked activity has occurred but at the same time is ambiguous in terms of affiliation, or otherwise, with the perpetrator. It might be an offer to repair the breakdown, ease the speaker's loss of face and get on with things, but any kind of notice also brings the *faux pas* to the surface of discourse and reifies it. Or it might simply be non-committal and the laughers may have decided to wait upon further turns of events, in particular, to see what the rest of the group feels about things.

The next question then is: how can a perpetrator react in these circumstances? Is there any way he or she can redeem themselves, to recover at least some of the lost professional face or to somehow make up for the loss? We can examine one or two of the 'extrication' strategies adopted in the briefings. One might expect simple apology to be one such strategy but no instances were found of apologies in a laughter episode, although there were several not accompanied by laughter.[2] We do however find apology followed by further play as in examples (14) and (15). In the second example, the perpetrator resorts to a hyperbolic self-deprecating sarcasm: 'And I was thinking I was doing so well this time. Sorry. It's President Bush, right?' He adopts a rather indeterminate play-fantasy persona of 'beginner' or 'game contestant' which, incidentally, involves oblique metadiscursive comment on briefings.

Note how the perpetrator's move follows upon the podium's tease: 'Did you have to correct him? I was going to work with him.' As Glenn remarks, errors 'provide a potential basis for subsequent teasing' (2003: 131). But since teasing can also help form the basis of intimacy ('bonding' as well as 'biting', Boxer and Cortés-Conde 1997), the journalist plays along with the tease, indeed builds on it, in the attempt to secure group affiliation. Very frequently 'one error having served as a laughable, speakers produce another, similar error, to provide for more shared laughs' (Glenn 2003: 131), in other words, in order to transform laughing *at* into laughing *with*.

3.3.2 Self-deprecation as 'exit strategy'

Self-deprecation, then, is probably the most common ingredient in perpetrator response strategies, as we first saw in examples (6) and (7) earlier, where the speaker adopts a 'bumbling' persona which both appeals for audience sympathy but also, paradoxically, by being a play role, implies that this is not the speaker's true, normal behaviour. A still clearer example is the following:

(16)   MR. LOCKHART: Okay, well, I'm choosing not to answer that hypothetical. (Laughter)
   Q: As long as it's not a general principle, that's –
   MR. LOCKHART: It should be. (Laughter) I'm just not smart enough to remember it. (Laughter)

As Zajdman remarks, self-denigration is, at first blush, very strange behaviour:

> The phenomenon of humor directed against one's self has been especially interesting to psychologists. The fact that someone may choose to humiliate him/herself in the presence of others seemed very peculiar to them.
>
> (1995: 337)

The solution offered is that the hearer assumes that:

> nobody in his/her right mind is hostile to him/herself. Therefore when a self-denigrating FTA is performed, this is interpreted as humorous, and cognitive consistence remains preserved.
>
> (1995: 337)

Boxer and Cortés-Conde add that 'Joking and self-denigrating humor are safer forms of humor than teasing' (1997: 282) but also that self-denigration 'unlike joking or teasing, will always involve identity display' (1997: 284).

Grainger, in her study of nurse-patient relationships, notes how self-denigration marks or projects a relationship as intimate:

> the nurse's comment ('your mother must have had hell with you') is preceded by the patient's self-denigrating comment 'cheeky isn't I?' which not only is face-threatening to herself, but also invites the nurse to threaten her positive face wants. Any possibility of 'bite' to this teasing is therefore reduced as the relationship is 'set up' as intimate, and the patient positions herself as the less powerful (child-like) participant with a reference to 'cheeky' behaviour.
>
> (Grainger 2002)

Different participants seem to employ the technique in different ways. The journalists tend to confine self-deprecatory humour to situations of face repair, usually to extricate themselves after some blunder, in accord with the observations of the *Language in the Worksite* project:

> Workers sometimes use humour as a self-depreciation device, to defuse the pressure when they know they haven't acted as they should have, or have done something stupid. Co-workers tend to be more sympathetic when this approach is taken.
>
> (from website: http://www.vuw.ac.nz/lals/research/lwp/research/humour.aspx)

In the terms adopted in this work, we will interpret such use of self-deprecatory humour as a kind of compensatory face-shift: when competence face has been irremediably compromised by some kind of blunder, a victim will often seize the option of boosting his or her affective face in recompense (see section 3.3.4).

However, one of the podiums, Mr Lockhart, seems to use it as a general strategy. He employs it in various ways; first, for the sort of self-display mentioned by Grainger, second, to avoid the question, as in (16), or perhaps to soften the face-threat involved in a non-answer and, third, often along with the 'tough-job' narrative, to endear himself to the audience. In an interview with the commentator Terry Gross (16 Jan. 2002) he confesses to using this form of humour tactically:

Terry Gross: Did any of your jokes get you into trouble?
Joe Lockhart: Occasionally [...] Humor is probably the, if not the best, one of the best weapons you can use in disarming an aggressive press corps. It's particularly useful if you can do it at your own expense rather than someone else's expense. But there are times when in trying to loosen things up you go over the line and you generally pay for those.

Brown and Levinson talk of self-denigration and 'dishonorifics' (e.g. 'welcome to my *hovel*') (1987: 182) as part of a general system of inference whereby to raise the other is to imply a lowering of the self and a lowering of the self implies a raising of the other (1987: 39).

3.3.3 *More reactive strategies*

However, self-deprecation is not the only strategy at participants' disposal. On occasion they employ more reactive policies:

(17) MR. MCCURRY: [...] the Internal Revenue Service will open local offices on Saturdays –
Q: That's been announced.
MR. MCCURRY: – for the next six weeks. I know. I'm just taking advantage.
(Laughter)

The podium does not excuse himself but provides a joking account for his giving old news, hinting at a 'briefings-as-role-play' in-script (see section 3.3.5). An *account* is meant here in the semi-technical sense of providing an explanation or justification for one's previous behaviour (Tholander and Aronsson 2002: 566–567). In the next example, the topic is which states of the Union the President might include in a forthcoming visit:

(18) MR. FLEISCHER: Incidentally, I said all 50 states are options. I should back up, it may not be fully the whole gamut of all 50 being options, but many are.
Q: Hawaii. (Laughter)
MR. FLEISCHER: Hawaii? Do I hear Hawaii, John Roberts?
Q: And Alaska.
MR. FLEISCHER: And Alaska.
Q: Just on that very point, I just want to ask, could you explain [...]

This episode is open to several interpretations. Is the first journalist jokingly implying that the President is very unlikely to venture as far afield as Hawaii or that he may choose it as a good place to have a holiday. Mr Fleischer rather cleverly turns the remark to his advantage by transforming it into a kind of quiz or rather an auction wherein the nominated members of the audience have to supply unusual or far-away states.

It is also quite common to find participants taking action *before* they have performed any self-inflicted face damage out of fear of not coming up to scratch:

(19) Q: Joe, on China –
    MR. LOCKHART: Sure. An easy one, China. (Laughter)

There are, then, various extrication strategies a perpetrator can perform in front of an audience. The possibilities seem to include:

- apologize, generally with some sort of play;
- deflect the criticism;
- involve others in the error;
- perform pre-emptive remedial action.

Finally, we saw in Chapter 1 how one of the most important logical mechanisms in jokes was the proper-to-improper narrative shift. The mechanism we have studied in this section, laughter provoked by hitches and glitches, is its real-life analogy. Both depend on the expectations of normal behaviour being upset. The hitch or glitch is clearly – in different ways and to different degrees – 'improper' behaviour which occurs suddenly and unexpectedly to interrupt the proper course of affairs.

3.3.4 Competence face and affective face

Almost all of these strategies appear to involve the speaker attempting not to recuperate their lost professional positive face, which is irredeemably if temporarily diminished by the error or shortcoming, but by bolstering another kind of face altogether, one which is bound up with affect. In fact, these observations seem to require us to reconsider the nature of face in interaction. It would appear that people have two principal sorts of positive face: a *competence* and an *affective* face. We bolster our competence face by convincing others that we are capable, authoritative and in control. This, as we have said, is the kind of face which is compromised by error, oversight or any kind of perceived inefficiency. Competence face is not always compatible with the expression of in-group solidarity, in fact, speakers who choose to adopt the role of authority or expert may well in consequence have to forfeit common ground with their audience. In practice, a skilful speaker will limit the damage by persuading the group that he or she is adopting an authority/expert role in order to serve its ultimate interest.

We reinforce our affective face, instead, by persuading our peers that we are, first of all, non-threatening, but also congenial and good to be around. The desire to appear non-threatening is, anthropologically, directly related to the aspiration to belong to the in-group and is thus normally expressed by trying to appear as similar in as many ways as possible to the other members. We attempt to stress this belonging in manifold fashion, one of which is through the employment of humour itself (if a sense of humour is valued by the group), another is by attacking or teasing others, temporarily casting them in the role of outsider to accentuate the sense of solidarity and affiliation of the remaining members (see Chapter 5).

There are other related aspects to consider. The importance of one kind of face over the other will depend on situation and on personality. Competence face is loosely associated with formality, affective face with informality. Institutional settings are an area where much work directed at competence face can be expected. As regards briefings discourse in particular, we have seen in Chapter 2 how the participants interrelate in two modes, the transactional and the interactional. For the former, professional competence face is vital, in the latter, the ability to appear congenial is highly prized. Participants have to strike a balance between the two. The problem for any individual is that the two types of face-work are frequently incompatible. As we said, attempts to build up competence face, to appear authoritative, bear a high risk of appearing non-affiliative, of claiming superiority to the group and supremacy over it. Conversely, too much indulgence in humour is liable to undermine competence face, as the following illustrates (the context is the joking suggestion of changing the epithet 'French' to 'freedom' following the reluctance of the French government to support military action in Iraq; my italics):

(20) Q: Ari, the House has changed the menus to freedom fries on Air Force One as freedom toast. There are now some Republicans on Capitol Hill, about 60, who want to step that up a level and cancel a Marine contract worth almost $1 billion dollars with the Marines. [...]
MR. FLEISCHER: I have heard people, particularly some of those who wear these type of shirts wonder whether you call it a freedom cuff shirt or not [...](Laughter)
Q: But what about stepping it up – *I understand you like to make jokes*, but what about people stepping it up to [...]

Accusations of 'making jokes' inappropriately can be considerably threatening to competence face.

We have seen evidence that the various podiums strike the balance in different ways and we shall see that different journalists do as well.

We have also observed that, through the use of self-deprecatory humour and of the other remedial strategies listed here, when competence face has been irremediably compromised by some kind of blunder, the perpetrator will often seize the option of boosting his or her affective face in recompense.

3.3.5 *Comment on the business in hand*

We have already come across a good number of occasions on which participants make some kind of metadiscursive comment, a sort of aside, on the business in hand and even quite banal ones seem regularly to raise a laugh:

(21) MR. MCCURRY: [...] these stops would occur after the APEC meeting, which is November 17th to 18th. We'll have more to say on this – actually, Mr. Lockhart will have more to say on it – (Laughter)

the reference here being simply to the fact that Mr McCurry is about to retire. One of the leitmotifs, or recurrent joking in-references, of another of the podiums, Mr Fleischer, is his constant allusion to the turn-taking mechanism of briefings, that each journalist will get their turn, must wait their turn, must not hog the floor ('only two' means only two turns: Les is notoriously verbose and so this is an in-joke, see section 5.7):

(22) MR. FLEISCHER: [...] Only two today, Les. (laughter)
(23) Q: Ari, I have a follow-up. My other one, my second one, Ari –
      MR. FLEISCHER: How can you follow up when I didn't answer your first question? (Laughter)
(24) MR. FLEISCHER: This is four follow-ups.
      Q: Who's counting? (Laughter)

Explicit reference to in-group activity is noted by Brown and Levinson as one of the strategies of positive politeness; it functions of course by implying the affiliation of the speaker to the group in question. Partington (2003) notes how, in the briefings, a variety of informalisms – informality being a striking feature of this discourse type – have this function of referring to a stock of common knowledge and common language. These include the use of first names, frequently abbreviated (Helen, Sam, Mike), suggesting how well we know each other, the use of slang (*a ballpark (figure), my dime*) and in-group technical jargon (*soft money*) as well as a myriad of colloquialisms:[3]

(25) MR. MCCURRY: We'll have David – David and Mary Ellen will be in a position to *run through* the schedule and brief on it later. Maybe you guys can just *jump up* and do that at the end.
(26) MR. MCCURRY: [...] The President *dropped by* for about 15 minutes.
(27) MR. MCCURRY: [...] So they are going to *get together* and *chat*. (The President with Senator Dolez).

Along with *you guys, cronies, off-message* and many more. Such language has a number of overlapping effects. Official business is thus familiarized, de-bureaucratized. It calls up the 'we-are-all-regular-guys' in-script. It projects a sense of common ground.

The laughter that greets in-group reference, in all probability, simply signals recognition of the allusion, a sort of back-channel gesture. Politeness theory predicts that individuals often go to great lengths to mark their belonging to the in-group. Failure to signal recognition of an in-group reference could be taken as failure of understanding, implying that one is not really an in-group member. It is thus a very astute ploy by, especially, the podium to play on the insecurity of the individuals in the group to assert his own membership thereof.

Nevertheless, the laughter often results not from simple in-group reference alone, but its combination with other mechanisms of laughter-talk. Mr Fleischer's incessant mentions of turn-taking, for example, usually also have a teasing or sarcastic value: someone is generally the butt of the comment (see Chapter 2, example 23, where he appears to treat Kelly as an unruly child). One of the most common and effective ways of bonding with the in-group and projecting one's own belonging is to cast someone else as an outsider, as representing something other than the 'us'. Teasing, as we shall see in Chapter 5, is ambiguous in this sense, it plays with the possibility of outcasting some individual; it both assigns them the role of outsider but in a non-*bona fide* fashion, thus implying that, in reality, they *are* part of the in-group. The audience laughter (abundant in this case) signals both recognition of the allusion and relief of tension at not being the butt oneself.

In-group allusion generally involves the sudden intrusion of the interactional mode into the transactional, the usual prerequisite of laughter events in this type of discourse, as we remarked in Chapter 2. We have also seen the bathetic mechanism in play, including episodes where a speaker comments on his or her own move:

(28) MR. MCCURRY: [A lengthy homily on the virtues of his party...] an economic program that is working exceedingly well for this country is perfectly within fair game as the President articulates his case.
Q: The Treasury says that –
MR. MCCURRY: Want a little bit more of that? (Laughter)
Q: No, that's enough. (Laughter)
Q: Maybe later.
MR. MCCURRY: I don't think they're going to ask that question again.

In this case, the speaker admits to having been tedious or bombastic, that is, to making heavy demands on the audience's negative face (if we recall, the desire to be left in peace to pursue one's own interests) but jokingly reverses the evaluation of the move, turning it into a boast and a threat. The essence of such allusions is that the speaker steps outside his normal institutional role of podium or press representative and comments on affairs as if he was simply a private individual, a regular guy. In this way, the business of briefings itself is revealed as a playing of roles. The laughter results from the switch of mode and the sudden relaxation of professional restraints (see Chapter 2, example 16). But even such a switch to 'average guy' can itself be a playing with roles or personae. In fact, this is probably the normal state of affairs: an individual is rarely simply him/herself (whatever that may mean) in a context such as briefings. Even intimacy-display is used functionally, often in quite intricate ways. We have already observed a couple of episodes where the podium comments on briefings as if they were a kind of competition or game show, with himself as contestant: 'This is stump Mike time' and 'Sure, an easy one, China'. This persona has the added value of portraying the podium in a tough job and complimenting the press as uncompromising task-masters. This compliment is most effective when it is paid obliquely:

(29) Did the newspapers get this story wrong [...]?
MR. FLEISCHER: Never say a newspaper got something wrong, at least publicly. (Laughter)

Face-work and the in-group 101

(30) MR. FLEISCHER: Les, I get blamed every day for things I did or did not do or say.
Q: But you weren't blamed for this.
MR. FLEISCHER: Not in this building, I wasn't. (Laughter) At least not by people on the federal payroll with whom I work. (Laughter)

In other words, in the second of these, I was not blamed by my working colleagues, but I would never exclude being inculpated by you people. This is apparently a subtle indirect face attack on his audience, but since – as we saw in Chapter 2 – his audience adores being assigned the role of uncompromising persecutors of the administration, he is even more subtlely massaging their egos.

Predictably, the press too like to evoke the play in-script of the adversarial relationship just for fun:

(31) Q: Can I follow up?
MR. FLEISCHER: Please. Could I stop you if I tried? (Laughter)
Q: It would be an interesting contest to see – (Laughter)

and see Chapter 2, example (19) [Mr Fleischer: You know, there is an enemy who wants to know – Q: That's not us, right? (Laughter)].

Other in-jokes revolve around shared knowledge and as such are frequently rather obscure to the outside observer. They often depend upon the reputation of some member and are mildly sarcastic:

(32) Sam, if you're late, we're not going to wait for you. (Laughter)

is relatively easy to interpret; presumably Sam has a reputation for tardiness. Similarly:

(33) MR. FLEISCHER: [...] OK James has patiently waited.
Q: And Les Kinsolving is patiently waiting.
MR. FLEISCHER: I understand. Well, let's not use the word patiently, but – James. (Laughter)

is a joke because the journalist in question has earned a reputation as being hyperactive. Finally, we have already observed in the previous chapter how *playing with the typical register* of briefings can constitute an in-joke:

(34) Q: Has the President gotten any response from the Senate on the proposal he made yesterday on means testing Medicare?
MR. MCCURRY: A number of senators have responded publicly and we're encouraged by those who are supportive and not discouraged by those who are not. (Laughter)

In conclusion, we might surmise that one other principal reason why comments on business so frequently raise a laugh is that they have much in common with *play* as defined/described in section 2.3. Comments on business, or metadiscursive asides, is one form of the metabehaviour which Fry proposed as the common denominator of play activities. Goffman, in his discussion of radio announcer talk, makes mention of the 'bracket laugh' which announcers use 'to show that what they have been saying is not part of the text proper but a comment on it' and to 'frame' it as play (1981: 317). In briefings, in contrast, it is rarely the speaker who initiates the laughter – this would be considered unsophisticated and would defeat the object, which is to let the audience revel in their recognition of signals of what is going on.

3.4 Threatening the other's face

3.4.1 *Differing politeness norms according to discourse type and context*

Up to this point we have concentrated on how speakers and the audience react to hitches and glitches, on how speakers attempt to remedy self-inflicted face-loss, and also on how a sense of in-group belonging is constructed and projected. But not all face-loss is self-inflicted and an in-group generally presupposes the existence of an out-group. Speakers will often chose less generous and more antagonistic strategies to get what they want and much face-work in the briefings is not supportive of others but rather hostile and belligerent. We have already recorded a couple of instances in (12) and (20).

However, by no means all face threats are carried out deliberately or as the result of aggressive intent. Particularly in work settings such as the briefings, paying attention to another's face is often a secondary consideration to that of pursuing the business in hand. In fact, in different discourse situations, politeness norms and expectations of how one's face is to be treated can alter radically and, as we noted earlier, it is an important part of a participant's communicative competence to know what comprises normal face activity in a particular context; it is, indeed, part of background in-group knowledge. As regards negative face, in normal circumstances:

> Questions of any kind are an attack on the interviewee's negative face, in that they infringe upon the questionee's right to be unimpeded.
>
> (Best 1996: 4.31)

But when the respondent is *paid* to reply to questions, or has otherwise volunteered to fill the interviewee role, according to Jucker they relinquish normal rights to negative face:

> The interviewee has undertaken to be publicly questioned on a certain topic and therefore his/her negative face is for the time being to some extent put out of force.
>
> (Jucker 1986: 73)

This corresponds to the practice of interview neutralism, widely commented on in recent literature (Heritage and Greatbatch 1991, Clayman 1992b, Partington 2003: 90–93, 106–108).[4]

As regards positive face, 'the podium's positive face and that of his clients is routinely under threat from questioners' (Partington 2003: 154). Examining, testing and asking questions of – all of which in politeness terms are subsumed into 'threatening' – the prestige, the reputation for good and efficient practice, in other words, the *competence face* of the podium's clients, and indeed, the podium himself, is in fact the whole point of the exercise of the press interrogation.

However, the briefings situation, as we have found, is complex, given the ease with which transactional mode, with its particular face norms and expectations, can convert to interaction, where the expectations are very different. A number of interesting questions arise. The podium for instance, might expect his face – because it is his personal face – to be respected during the more conversational moments than during the business sessions. But how distinct are the two kinds of faces in practice? In addition, granted the close association of the podium with his superiors, at least during phases of transaction, how sensitive is the podium to face attacks on the President or other chief figures in the administration, does their face ever get mixed up or conflated? And how do the various podiums treat the journalists' face(s) both as a group and individuals? In general, then, we need to ascertain what is considered normal unmarked face behaviour during the business of briefings and what is considered marked and over-aggressive face-work. Given the association of laughter with aggression, laughter episodes can throw a deal of light on this topic.

The following sections will contain a brief overview of some of the face friction and conflict which is apparent in the corpus. A fuller treatment of the topic will be undertaken in Chapter 5.

3.4.2 *Negative face threats: threatening and complimenting*

We mentioned earlier how norms change in different discourse contexts and a number of the threats to a hearer's negative face listed by Brown and Levinson become normal expected working practice in interviews or briefings, for instance, requests (including requests for information), extracting promises ('when will you tell us'), reminders ('the other day, when you were asked...'), expressions of strong emotions towards the hearer (or someone associated with them). But there are ways and means of expressing requests, some of which border on ordering, on *telling* someone what to do, generally considered highly face-threatening, as in example (12).

Threats too are on the Brown and Levinson list. Such threats as there are, whether from journalist to podium or vice versa, are always taken by the audience as non-serious in accordance with the 'great face-threat paradox', that is, the heavier the FTA, the less likely it is to be taken seriously – at 'face' value – and threats are very grave indeed. We have already come across the threat to leave Sam behind if he is late (example 32) and we also find:

(35)   Q: I have a follow up to David, because he didn't follow up enough.
             (Laughter)

that is, I'm going to give you a harder time than he did.

On Brown and Levinson's list of threats to negative face we also find 'compliments' which, along with expressions of admiration or envy, 'predicate some desire of S towards H or H's goods'. The problem for the addressee of the compliment is how to react. Brown and Levinson (following Pomerantz 1978) cite response to compliments as a central instance of 'conflicting requirements' of face. Does one accept the compliment, the preferred response and therefore infringe the constraint against a speaker indulging in self-praise, or does one turn it down and therefore disagree with the compliment payer?

> To preserve something of the preference for agreement and the constraint, various intermediate turn-types are often used: agreements with praise-downgrade; agreements about praiseworthiness but with praise shifted to a third party; return compliments.
>
> (Brown and Levinson 1987: 39)

Direct compliments from the podium to the press tend to take the form of 'good question' but the transcripts rarely indicate any reply. However, we have already come across various hidden, indirect compliments paid by the podium (the podium has just denied any connection between the administration and three ex-consultants to the Democratic party who are advising one of the sides in the Israeli election campaign):

(36) MR. LOCKHART: Well, I mean – pursuing your craft, and being compensated fairly for it is something that everyone in this room understands – (laughter).

He might be seen as implying that his audience is somewhat mercenary. At first sight, this seems a risky move but he knows his audience well enough to indulge them with the 'we are all men and women of the world' in-narrative. It combines two narratives, one face-threatening the other complimentary. One journalist chooses to react playfully to the first of these:

(37) Q: I have a retort, but I'm not going to state it. (Laughter)

The retort presumably being along the lines of 'just look who's talking'. The podium therefore, just as playfully, assuages him with a real compliment:

(38) MR. LOCKHART: I think you deserve a raise, though, so let's listen. (Laughter)

Compliments from the press to the podium are rare but interesting; being very marked, they require a response. The simplest is the following (on Mr McCurry's final session before retiring):

(39) Q: First of all, I wish you all the best, you have done a great job as Press Secretary here.
MR. MCCURRY: Thank you. You want to know, though, if we're going to India and Pakistan. (Laughter)

The praise is, in Brown and Levinson's terms, *downgraded* by the podium's minimal attention or notice to it and his moving swiftly on. But what has not been noted in the literature on complimenting and responses to compliments is how very generally they are accompanied by laughter. Compliments create politeness tension in both the giver and the receiver, especially in male-dominated circles like these briefings where giving and accepting direct compliments is taboo. Which also means they are occasions for play:

(40) Q: You've had one of the most civil staffs we've ever dealt with.
MR. MCCURRY: That's good. They're ordered to be that way. (Laughter)

The podium's response here is of a type not catalogued by Brown and Levinson. There is an initial 'agreement about praiseworthiness' but with a joking denigratory *account* hard on its heels. This constitutes yet another instance of comic bathos but at least some of its effect lies in its being pretty close to the bone; unusual podium frankness about the workings of the administration is equivalent to a shift into the interactional mode and is always greeted with laughter:

(41) MR. FLEISCHER: I think the President – whenever Presidents say they read it, you can read that to be he was briefed. (Laughter)
Q: Frankness. (Laughter)
Q: Refreshing. (Laughter)
MR. FLEISCHER: I've enjoyed working here, thank you. (Laughter)

In sum, self-deprecation by the receiver of a compliment is both beneficial for his/her own face and also removes potential for embarrassment on the part of the giver, and laughter so very frequently follows hard upon any form of tension relief.

3.4.3 *Positive face threats*

In briefings, deliberate and aggressive positive face threats can be directed either from journalist to podium or from podium to journalist.

- *From journalist to podium*

We have already observed that attacking the interviewee's face is to a large degree the purpose of the modern political interview/briefing. A good number of the positive face threats listed by Brown and Levinson (1987: 66–67) are, therefore, normal unmarked behaviour in briefings. These include criticism, complaints, accusations, contradictions, disagreements, challenges and also, of course, 'raising of dangerously [...] divisive topics, e.g. politics' (1987: 67). There is then an 'allowable' level of face-threat which varies among discourse types. One suspects, however, that the way in which these speech acts are delivered will, in practice, have considerable effect on how face-threatening they are considered by addressee and audience.

Moreover, the podium, like other institutional respondents has two faces to defend, his own personal face and the professional one of his clients in the administration. With this in mind, Partington (2003) proposes the following as a classification of threats to the podium's face in White House briefings, in order of increasing severity. A questioner may ask for, encourage or force one or more of the following acts, in order of seriousness:

1   state or justify your own opinion;
2   admit you personally were wrong;
3   state or justify your client's opinion or action;
4   state or confirm your client's course of future action;
5   admit disagreement among different clients;
6   admit something your client *said* was wrong;
7   admit something your client *did* was wrong.

The gravest face threats, then, are those aimed at the President, and the balder and more explicit they are the more audience laughter they provoke. Consider:

(42) MR. BERGER: First of all, if I answer any more questions I'll be accused of going on too long.
      Q: You're going on half as long as the President did. (Laughter)

and the following (on the White House not intervening to regulate tobacco companies):

(43) Q: [1] If it was important enough for the President to step into the baseball strike, why not important enough to step in and resolve this –
      Q: [2] Because that was a big mistake. (Laughter)

which comprises another form of threat to positive face from Brown and Levinson's list, namely 'disruptively interrupting H's talk' (1987: 67).

Accusations aimed at the administration, of course, come in a variety of types. There are, however, some more personal imputations and one of the most frequent, often delivered indirectly as a mention rather than censure, is of evasiveness and related sorts of cunning:

(44) Q: [...] The President does not agree with Sharpton, does he, Ari? And I know you won't evade, because that would suggest that he does. (Laughter)
(45) Q: Come on Ari, that is a monstrous evasion. (Laughter)
(46) Q: [...] or will your charming and courteous evasion indicate, Ari, that not a dam' thing has been done [...]

But the press are generally fairly tolerant of podium evasiveness and general sophistry; indeed it becomes an in-joke which the podium can exploit to general hilarity:

(47) Q: I do not have two questions, only a two-part question, if I may. (Laughter)

MR. FLEISCHER: You can stand at this podium if you keep up language like that. (Laughter)
Q: I could never fill those shoes, Ari. (Laughter)

(48) MR. FLEISCHER: Do you have a question I can evade? (Laughter)

- *From podium to journalist*

Under normal conversational circumstances, failure to answer a question 'properly' would usually be taken as a snub, a face attack. Here, given the appreciation that some information will necessarily be sensitive and need to be 'classified' (though perceptions differ, of course, as to how much, and this was especially apparent in the briefings immediately after the September 11th attacks), the press are used to less-than-complete answers.[5] However, the way in which a question is turned down is important:

(49) Q: [...] Can you tell us if that military strike or retaliation, or whatever, is coming within hours, days, weeks or months? Can you give us some kind of time frame?
MR. FLEISCHER: Of course not. (Laughter)

Such abruptness is marked behaviour and becomes an occasion for laughter. Similarly, any whiff of sarcasm is face-threatening, especially before an audience (section 6.3):

(50) Q: [...] It would also be understandable if you were reluctant to tell us military operations, the duration of such.
MR. FLEISCHER: So you're asking me to tell you the duration of the military operation? (Laughter)
Q: No, I'm not asking you the duration of any military operations. I'm asking you to tell us, is Musharraf speaking to his people?

The journalist's nose is clearly out of joint. Mr Fleischer, as these episodes show, is the most aggressive of the podiums represented in the corpus, in fact, this aggression becomes part of his in-group reputation and he is able to exploit it to humorous effect:

(51) Q: Will we be invited?
MR. FLEISCHER: Les? Do you really want that answer? (Laughter)

Finally, just as the journalists, with varying degrees of severity and seriousness, sometimes accuse the podium of not doing his job to satisfaction, the podium can object to questioner's prejudice, miscalculation or, in this case, loose thinking:

(52) MR. FLEISCHER: And what's the name of that official?
Q: The official is unnamed. But it is –
MR. FLEISCHER: Then how do you know he's 'top'? (Laughter)
Q: It says, according to the New York Times. So is this official mistaken?
MR. FLEISCHER: You don't know the person's name.

3.5 Conclusions

Analysing laughter-talk in authentic discourse can tell us something about face relations, whilst at the same time the study of face in group-work also tells us a great deal about why we laugh in company. As regards the latter, we have seen a variety of face moves which tend to provoke laughter. First of these is in-group reference, which reinforces a sense of belonging, and all the podiums use it strategically, though in different ways. These references range from Mr Fleischer's constant comments on turn-taking procedure to 'in-jokes', which generally consist of sarcasm at the expense of some out-group set or individual such as the opposition party or some member of the audience who is picked on and depicted as an outsider for the occasion (John Kasich is a Republican Senator, the *DNC* is the *Democratic National Committee*; Wolf Blitzer is the grey-bearded *CNN* correspondent):

(53) MR. MCCURRY: John Kasich went so far to say if it worked he'd turn himself into a Democrat. And we've got the DNC sending him a membership application now. (Laughter)
(54) MR. BERGER: If you're too young, ask Wolf. (Laughter)

Other laughter-provoking moves include, first, the set of oversights, *faux pas* and so on, that we have classified as hitches and glitches, second, aggressive FTAs and, finally, self-denigratory moves. These have in common the potential to threaten face, for the perpetrator, the victim and the speaker respectively, but what role does laughter play in them? It seems to be used primarily as a way of construing the potentially embarrassing act as non-*bona fide*, as not to be taken seriously, as not *being* taken seriously, in fact. The alternative, taking it seriously, would be highly disruptive. The author of the hitch would have to be condemned as incompetent. A genuine act of aggression would have to be addressed and either ratified (justified) or censured. Authentic self-denigration is both extremely embarrassing for an audience (Brown and Levinson classify it as 'emotional leakage') and normally requires considerable repair work. Laughter instead transports these moves from the realm of the real into play frame. Given it depends on this sudden change of frame (Chapter 2), even this kind of conversational laughter-talk – not normally seen as such – can be interpreted as bisociative.

Turning to the related question of what laughter-talk might imply for Politeness theory, first of all, the observations here, both from the briefings and from the other corpora, seem to offer confirmation of Brown and Levinson's intuitions about our extreme sensitivity to face. However, and true to its multifunctional, multifaceted nature, laughter-talk also allows face tensions to be referred to explicitly and defused, as when the two sides in briefings make joking reference to the antagonistic relationship existing between them.

We have also observed how the face of absent parties – the President, other politicians, a political party – can be mocked and defended by proxy, as it were. We have also seen how different protagonists adopt different strategies to protect and recuperate their own face and to deal with that of others, even in highly analogous circumstances. Moreover, we have perhaps been able to gather some clues as to the effect of the presence of an audience on 'face battles'. There is considerable audio-visual evidence provided by the RealPlayer Webcasts, which focus predominantly on the podium, of his playing to the gallery: Mr Fleischer's ironic-sarcastic tone and facial expressions, Mr Lockhart's exaggerated wide-eyed patience with a troublesome questioner, Mr McCurry's flat intonational, 'exaggerated deadpan' delivery of his quips.

However, the main conclusion in this regard is as follows. The principal function of laughter-talk in this particular discourse situation is to situate oneself in relation to a group in three possible ways. First, as an insider when using aggressive humour against another out-party. Second, when one wishes to adopt an expert persona, as an outsider, superior to the group. And finally, when one indulges in self-denigratory humour, as an outsider but one 'inferior' to the group, non-threatening and pleading for clemency and sympathy. It can be seen from this just how central laughter-talk is to face-play. We are reminded of Brown and Levinson's original vision of politeness as the management of two conflicting impulses: first, socialization, the desire to belong to the in-group (in briefings, belonging is often projected as part of a strategy, particularly by the podium) and, second, the control of aggression and especially the channelling of aggression for strategic purposes, for individual advantage. A considerable amount of tension can arise from this conflict of impulses. Laughter has often been associated in the literature with the expression of aggression but it might be more precise, at least here, to think that laughter is associated with the *management* of aggression and the tension aggression arouses.

Finally, we have investigated briefly how speakers, at least in the type of setting under consideration here (but it seems highly unlikely it should be confined to such contexts), have not one type of face but two distinct ones: competence face and affective face. We speculated how the needs of the two kinds of face often come into conflict and that different protagonists place differing value on each and choose their strategies accordingly. There is considerable future research to be done on these topics. Here, we have considered how strategies differ according to personality, but how, for instance, do they differ in terms of changing situations, the sex and age of speakers or how well interactants know each other? Moreover, do different cultures handle these matters in different ways?

In Chapter 4, we shift emphasis and look at how bisociation is relevant to wordplay, a rather more traditional object of the linguistic study of humour.

4 Wordplay, phraseplay and relexicalization

A pun is its own reword.
    (Redfern)

4.1 Linguistic research into wordplay

In past linguistic studies of humour (as opposed to psychological, medical, literary or aesthetic studies), the lion's share of attention has been paid to plays on words and puns. Of all the forms of humour they are the most obviously based on the creative use of language, the most clearly dependent on a form of wording, and therefore many authors have felt them to be the only kind of humour to constitute a proper object of linguistic study. In terms of Cicero's celebrated distinction between jokes 'about the thing' (*re*) and 'about what is said' (*dicto*),[1] in other words between playing with an idea or a situation and playing on words, puns are felt to fall squarely into the second category. Even the slightest change in the wording of a pun, of course, renders it meaningless or at least humourless. It will be seen in this chapter, however, that many puns play with ideas as well as words. We will see too how puns in natural discourse make conceptual points: 'there is a continuous stretch from the pun through the play on words (*jeu de mots*) to the play of ideas (*jeu d'esprit*)' (Koestler 1964: 66).[2] In particular, we will see how, in spontaneous running discourse like briefings, they also make argumentative points.

Attardo, however, is more than a little critical of the results of past linguistic research in this area. 'Large parts of the territory of punning phenomena still remain uncharted' he notes. He tries to remain polite: 'this is not to say that the efforts of linguists have been wasted' but their 'prevalently taxonomic approach' has dictated ' "low intensity" explanatory patterns' (1994: 108). In other words, linguistics has given us lists of different kinds of puns but has done precious little to explain how they work as a category. This is because 'taxonomies lack explanatory power. Classification is no substitute for analysis and theory building' (Attardo 1994: 112). 'Naming the parts does not show us what makes the gun go off' (Mahood 1979: 19). Nevertheless, taxonomy imposes some order on the world under study, which can be a necessary precondition to explanation.

Wordplay, phraseplay and relexicalization 111

Ritchie is equally critical of past research in this area and suggests practical or circumstantial problems in the study of naturally occurring wordplay:

> Puns which occur spontaneously in everyday life are not often very funny and are rarely recorded for later use; hence there is no obvious source of collected spontaneous puns.
>
> (Ritchie 2004: 114)

The advent of corpora containing considerable quantities of spontaneous discourse may well help to remedy problems of data availability.

Another main problem has simply been definitional. The expression *play on words* denotes an enormously wide variety of phenomena and some order needs to be set. The category includes, among many others, the following:[3]

- blendings (or *porte-manteau* words) for example; *anecdotage* (*anecdote* + *dotage*, that is, how the aged ramble on); *humpage* (*the hump* + *umbrage*, that is, to take offence and keep it);
- reversals, such as metathesis, for example, *dog collar* (for a clergyman's *God collar*) including spoonerism, for example, *a half-warmed fish* (i.e. half-formed wish), or word inversion, for example, '*What's the definition of a hangover?*' '*The wrath of grapes*' or palindromes, for example, *dogma, I am God*;
- chiasmus, for example, *I say what I mean, at least I mean what I say*;
- zeugma (or 'yokewit': Redfern 1984: 95), for example, *They roused him with jam and judicious advice; And even the Baker, though stupid and stout*...(Carroll: *The Hunting of the Snark*);
- anagrams, for example, *Mother-in-law – Woman Hitler; Election results – Lies, let's recount*;
- Malapropisms, for example, *the very pineapple of politeness, If Gower had stopped that (cricket ball) he would have decapitated his hand*;
- Tom Swifties (or Wellerisms): '*The doctor had to remove my left ventricle*', said Tom, half-heartedly; '*I have a split personality*', said Tom, being Frank; '*This must be an aerobics class*', Tom worked out; '*Who discovered radium?*' asked Marie curiously;
- resegmentation or metanalysis, for example, *four candles – fork handles, 'Culture: Who Needs It?' by Phyllis Stein* (philistine);
- reverse coinages, for example, *speakable* (from *unspeakable*), *underwhelmed* (from *overwhelmed*), *underawed* (from *overawed*), *if not actually disgruntled, he was far from being gruntled*.
- 'not-as-they-seems', for example, *a Family Butcher* ('how much to do mine?'),[4] *a cat burglar* (stole our best mouser), *shepherd's pie* (take two plump shepherds...).

One very notable exception to the blandness of past research in this field is Redfern's most witty, learned and elegant study of puns (and French *calembours*) from a stylistic perspective. He too is critical of some linguistic approaches,

112   Wordplay, phraseplay and relexicalization

rightfully sarcastic even: 'Let the linguistic scientist speak: "Unless one is a poet or regards language as a plaything, one tends to regard ambiguity as an undesirable, if not pathological state in language." Presumably because it upsets the computers' (1984: 9–10). A passionate paladin of the art of wordplay, Redfern reminds us that by no means all instances are meant to be comic: 'St Bernard was presumably not seeking a laugh when he said: "Non doctores sed seductores, non pastores sed impostores"' (1984: 7). Shakespeare's inveterate punning is sometimes comic but just as often grim: 'I see it feelingly' says the freshly blinded Gloucester; 'ask for me tomorrow and you will find me a grave man' says the dying Mercutio. Cook (2000), too, remembers that wordplay has a most noble and serious history and in days gone by was held in far higher esteem than now. The Delphic oracle pronounced itself in riddles (causing no end of mayhem). Odysseus, mythology's great wordsmith, uses a double-meaning to get himself out of a spot ('My name is Nobody'). Even Jesus cannot resist the pun: 'Thou art Peter, and upon this rock I shall build my church' (Matthew 16: 18, in Cook 2000: 81), πέτρος being of course both 'Peter' and 'rock' in Greek. Puns executed by the metaphysical poets are ennobled by the title of conceits (or 'big-headed ideas', Redfern 1984: 98).

However, puns have had their enemies too down the years (Redfern calls them these 'misologists', these 'sniffers at words'), but never as much as today. 'In the contemporary science-dominated world, punning is kept at arm's length; people frequently apologize for punning (by saying, for example, "no pun intended")' (Cook 2000: 81). 'Europeans [...] are trained to admire irony but to disapprove of puns' (Ahl 1988: 21). But the *coup-de-grace* for the prestige of puns was delivered by modern linguistic theory of language development and change. In ancient times words were invested with a magic which resided in the sense that the word somehow captured, contained and controlled the essence of its referent. It was, of course, natural that, in Latin, *cave* should be a akin to *canem* because dogs can be dangerous, and that the *Dominicani* (Dominicans) should be *Domini canes* (the hounds of the Lord), especially when they implemented the Inquisition.[5] This presupposed of course that there could be only one True language. In ancient times, the True language was whatever the mother tongue happened to be, of course, but in the Middle Ages the sceptre was held by Latin and in early modern times by Hebrew. In the more prosaic nowadays, word resemblance is held to be an accident of phonological development and any appeal that wordplay holds is entirely melodic and no longer metaphysic.

The reasons why, despite their low esteem, puns continue to be used so frequently – even in serious institutional discourse – is that, first of all, they are often not recognized or classified as puns and, second, they can be used to dramatic strategic effect. They can be a highly effective rhetorical weapon. Among the opponents of puns was Aristotle, who saw them as a danger to philosophy (Ulmer 1988). He finds support in Duisit: 'Tout intellectuel est désarçonné par le spectacle du calembour' ('All intellectuals are thrown at the sight of a pun', quoted in Redfern 1984: 4). They are, of course, quite right. They harness two meanings in a non-logical way, they can thrust together quite disparate entities, causing an analogy to be drawn between them which in cold logic would be untenable. But rhetoric is not logic and, in verbal duelling, arguments which are striking, memorable and beautiful may prevail over those which are merely consistent:

> that which brings together in the human mind the things or the ideas designated by the same sound or by closely related sounds which call out naturally to each other [...] is the very essence of the pun; it has been one of the most powerful factors of the human mind.
> (Paulhan 1897, translated by Redfern 1984: 12)

4.2 Defining the pun

4.2.1 Identity and resemblance

Those interested in the variety of wordplay are referred to Attardo's 'taxonomy of taxonomies' (1994: 112) and Redfern (1984). Here we must attempt a definition of the kind of puns of interest to the current work. Punning is probably the most obviously bisociative of all forms of humour. As Koestler explains:

> The pun is the bisociation of a single phonetic form with two meanings – two strings of thought tied together by an acoustic knot.
> (1964: 65)

Attardo also notes that 'though couched in different theoretical frameworks, all linguistic (and non-linguistic) analyses agree on the fact that puns involve two senses' (1964: 128). But all verbal puns are based upon the same fundamental mechanism: they are plays on *sounds*, or rather, on the resemblance between two sets of sequences of sounds (Koestler's 'acoustic knot'). (It must be stressed that puns generally do not play with single words but entire phrases; they are a form of *amphibology*).[6]

There is a certain tradition that distinguishes between homonymic puns and homophonic puns (see, for example, Reah 1998: 17–18). Examples of these two different kinds can be found in section 4.2.3. However, it will be argued here that a more fundamental distinction is between 'exact' puns and 'near' puns. In an exact pun, two sound sequences which are *identical* are called into play, whereas in the near pun, two sequences are involved which *resemble* each other either phonologically or, in texts primarily meant to be read, visually. Since speech precedes writing both ontogenetically and phylogenetically, we will concentrate on sound. Each of the sound sequences is designed to be associated (in the context of the particular joke text) with a distinct meaning. We might represent this notationally as $SS_1(M_1)$ and $SS_2(M_2)$, where $SS_1 = SS_2$ (exact pun) or $SS_1 \approx SS_2$ (near pun) (SS = sound sequence and M = meaning). It is of course the relationship between M_1 and M_2 which is the *point* of the pun and which will partly determine its quality, whether or not and to what degree it is judged effective or humorous (see section 4.2.4).

Both Attardo and Ritchie (2004: 112–116) point out, however, that ambiguity in itself is not a sufficient condition for punning, that is, the potential existence of two meanings of a single sound sequence does not automatically make it a pun. Indeed, as Attardo reminds us, 'all words are ambiguous, vague, or unspecified if they are not taken in context' (1994: 133). 'Mere ambiguity is not enough to create a pun', he adds, 'otherwise how could one differentiate between a pun and an ambiguous utterance such as "Flying planes can be dangerous"' (1994: 133). In similar vein, Ritchie argues that the ambiguity of *shell* ('discarded marine carapace'/'artillery round') does not make a pun out of 'John found a shell on the beach'.

What else is needed then to transform ambiguity into a pun? Attardo suggests two elements. First, that the meanings be 'opposed'. This, however, is reminiscent of Raskin's theory of opposition in jokes in general and can be discounted for the reasons of over-generality we recounted in Chapter 1. The second is that puns are, as Attardo puts it, 'concocted', though I would prefer 'authored'. In other words, someone has to deliberately manufacture, or at least point out, the ambiguity. It is not hard to conceive of both Attardo and Ritchie's examples of non-punning ambiguity being transformed into puns by, as it were, 'wilful intervention':

(1) A: John found a shell on the beach. (Where *shell* means 'discarded marine carapace')
    B: That's a coincidence. Yesterday, I found a hand grenade. (Forcing *shell* to mean 'artillery round')

The punster has to somehow alter features of the context of an utterance to force a second reading – in the previous example by introducing vocabulary pertaining to explosive devices and thus overriding *beach*'s normal priming to co-occur with *sea-shell*. In fact most punning jokes can be understood in terms of lexical priming (see section 1.4.2). The punster relies on the hearers' being primed to perceive $SS_1(M_1)$, before springing an unexpected $SS_2(M_2)$ on them (see section 4.3).

All puns are deliberate, then, in the sense of knowingly constructed, but some puns are pre-pondered – here we shall adopt the term *scripted* – and generally have a single author, whilst others are unscripted and arise spontaneously in the flow of discourse. The latter are born when one of the interactants perceives the possibility of a second interpretation, that is $SS_2(M_2)$, of some part of some previous utterance and produces the pun by bringing it to the attention of the other participant(s), as in example (1). On occasion, the hearer can create or 'author' even, the pun by producing some kind of back channel behaviour (laughing, groaning, 'That's a good one', and so on) which draws attention to another possible meaning of the first speaker's utterance. The newspaper puns examined in section 4.5 are, of course, of the scripted sort, but we shall see examples of both kinds from the briefings, including puns which are constructed collaboratively.

4.2.2 Near puns

The way puns work is probably best illustrated by considering near puns first. In one type, the so-called syntagmatic pun, both SS_1 and SS_2 are physically present.

The celebrated:

(2) 'non Angli sed angeli'

(attributed Pope Gregory I or 'the Great')

(not Angles but angels), where SS_1 is 'Angli' and SS_2 is 'angeli', is an example.[7]

However, in the majority of jokes based on near puns the hearer is presented with just one of the sound strings (from Redfern 1984: 18–19):

(3) A man forgets to buy his wife her favourite anemones for her birthday. The shop has only some greenery left, which he purchases. But the forgiving wife exclaims on his return: 'With fronds like these, who needs anemones?'

and is required to recover (from the mental lexicon) the other ('with friends like these, who needs enemies?'). Why is this funny (for those who find it so)?[8] There is an intellectual delight in the sheer unexpectedness of the juxtaposition and the ingenuity in the reworking of the story. In terms of the relationship between M_1 and M_2 there is also a sort of evaluation reversal: 'a formula normally used in a hostile context is here twisted for reuse in a conciliatory one' (Redfern 1984: 19).

4.2.3 Exact puns

Turning to exact puns, the simplest of these may exploit either homonymy (words alike in sound and spelling) or homophony (words alike in sound only): in either case the working and effect is identical and in both homonym and homophone puns only one sound sequence is present. An oft-quoted example of a homonym joke is the following:

(4) 'Do you believe in clubs for young people?'
    'Only when kindness fails.'

The sound sequence *club* can express at least two homonyms (or M_1 and M_2 in the notation adopted above), which are 'association of people' and 'heavy weapon'. The initially favoured narrative reading, elicited by M_1, then, is: 'do you think young people should be encouraged to join associations?', whilst the second narrative reading, exploiting M_2, reinterprets the question as 'do you think it may sometimes be necessary to discipline young people with heavy weapons?' (clearly a highly improper proposition, and therein lies much of the humour – see 1.3.6 on impropriety in jokes).

The following, instead is a homophone joke:

(5) 'Why is a defective condom called a Welsh letter?'
    'Because it has a leak in it.'

A *French letter* is a colloquial term for a condom, whilst the *leek* (homophone of *leak*) is a national symbol of Wales.

4.2.4 Good puns and bad? Motivation

One of the burning questions of linguistic research into humour is whether linguistic tools can help us define the *quality* of humour, in particular, whether it can enable us to distinguish a good pun from a bad one.

The optimists appeal to the traditional distinction between the justified or motivated and the non-motivated or hollow pun (other terminological variations exist). Taking the latter first, both Freud and Norrick recount episodes where they encountered hollow puns personally. Freud (1960: 112) recounts how:

(6) at the end of a meal to which I had been invited as a guest, a pudding of the kind known as a '*Roulade*' was served. It requires some skill on the part of the cook to make it; so one of the guests asked. 'Made in the house?' To which the host replied: 'Yes, indeed. A home *roulade*.'

The effect relies on the hearer knowing that an important political issue of the time was Irish *home rule*. Freud uses the episode as an occasion to 'throw light on the condition which seems to determine whether a joke is to be called a "good" or "bad" one' (it will be noted that he is actually talking throughout about puns rather than jokes in general). We derive enjoyment, according to Freudian joke theory, from 'being transported by the use of the same or a similar word from one circle of ideas to another, remote one'. But 'if there is not at the same time a link between those circles of ideas which has a significant sense, then I shall have made a "bad" joke'. There is little connection of sense between Irish independence and a home-baked dessert and so, in the terms adopted here, the home *roulade* pun would be classified as non-motivated. To call it an example of 'bad' humour, however, may be going too far. Freud himself admits that 'when those of us present heard this improvised joke it gave us pleasure [...] and made us laugh' (1960: 12) (his way of saying 'you had to be there'). It had the advantage of topicality and bathos – a juxtaposition of the momentous and the trivial. Humour reception and evaluation are notoriously hugely dependent on context and whether or not the audience is primed for laughter.

A 'good' pun, on the other hand, Freud continues, is occasioned when 'the similarity between the words' – we might prefer 'sound sequences' – 'is shown to be really accompanied by another, important similarity in their sense' (1960: 147). He provides an example from Italian 'the well known cry *Traduttore – Traditore!*' (1960: 36) (*translator – traitor*, which almost works in English, but not quite). To summarize and recapitulate, then, in the terms adopted here, a motivated pun occurs when in conditions of $SS_1(M_1)$, $SS_2(M_2)$ there is some natural or contextual connection between M_1 and M_2.

Norrick (2003: 1335–1336) also provides an interesting example (two friends are discussing dolphin behaviour):

(7) And it seems to be a completely egalitarian bond.
There isn't a leader in a dolphin – do they have pods?

Wordplay, phraseplay and relexicalization 117

> I don't know what they're called.
> Whales are pods. I don't know what dolphins are.
> I guess they're *pods* too. *Pod*dies. Anyway (laughing). Yeah but I mean –
> They're poddy animals.
> (laughs)
> (laughs)
> Oooh. That's – that's like a blow to the midriff, y'know. (laughing)

The pun, of course, depends upon the phonemic similarity (in a North American pronunciation) between *poddy* and *party*, which in turn depends upon an acquaintance with the collocational expression *party animal*. Note how the pun is constructed collaboratively and also how both parties laugh, whilst the recipient of the punch line also feigns physical pain – which reminds us of the modern ambivalence towards punning discussed earlier. The question, however, remains: is this an instance of motivated or non-motivated wordplay? At first sight there would seem to be little connection between dolphins and human party-goers. However, on closer inspection, since it is the group behaviour of the animals which is being discussed, a certain link between dolphin gregariousness and partying becomes apparent. We can conclude that motivation and non-motivation in wordplay is not a polar matter but there exists a cline of motivation along which we can place any individual pun.

A final word on the topic of quality. In general, as we have said, motivated puns will be judged superior to unmotivated ones. And when the motivation is also sustained by a certain sophistication of reference, the results can be most agreeable. I cannot resist including the following as my finale to this section (from Attardo, originally from *Asterix*):

(8) Numérobis: [an architect from Alexandria] 'Je suis mon cher ami, très heureux de te voir.'
    Panoramix: [to the others] 'C'est un alexandrin'.

The play is on an *Alexandrian* and an *alexandrine*, a 12-syllable classical French meter of which Numérobis's greeting is an example.

4.2.5 Derivation and disruption

Two final considerations remain. First, it should be noted how one of the meanings of the sound sequence involved in a pun can be considered as primary and the other derivative. In Freud's joke, *home rule* is the primary SS(M) and *home roulade*, a nonce creation, is derived from it for the purpose of joking. Similarly, in Norrick's example *party animal* is a pre-existing sound sequence from which *poddy animal*, another nonce, is derived. We will see how, in very many cases, the 'original' SS(M) will be more abstract or figurative than the derived version, which will often involve a concrete, tangible entity (as, for instance, *home rule* is a concept whilst *home roulade* is a physical object).[9] This is yet another example of the bathos which is so often a component of humour.

The second consideration arises from a very different definition of 'motivated', a discourse definition. Norrick argues more than once (1993; 2003) that punning, in contrast to other forms of humour such as jokes and especially anecdotes, is always, as he puts it, *disruptive* of conversation, it has, in this sense, no conversational motivation. It brings conversation to an abrupt halt by, he claims, introducing extraneous subject matter. In episode (7), *poddy animals* 'introduces information unrelated to the topic of dolphins or intelligence', thus violating the requirement that participants make their contributions relevant (Sperber and Wilson 1995). My own view is that the disruptive nature of wordplay is explained by its abruptly switching attention away from the subject matter in hand (*re*) to language (*dicto*), from what is being said to the words used to say it. Be this as it may, later in this section we will see episodes where wordplay is only apparently disruptive of discourse argumentation but, in reality, is used strategically to advance it.

4.3 A linguistic account of wordplay

We saw in section 4.1 how Attardo and others felt that linguistics had until now largely failed to offer a satisfactory explanation of wordplay. However, theoretical developments in the field of lexicology over the past fifteen or so years, largely fuelled by corpus research, may be providing us with new insights. In this section and the one following I will offer an account of at least some forms of wordplay making reference in particular to the concepts of lexical priming (see section 1.4.2), collocation (see section I.3.3), semantic preference (section 1.4.2), relexicalization and delexicalization.

4.3.1 Collocation and semantic preference

Towards the end of Chapter 1 we introduced the notion of lexical priming and mentioned how speakers could consciously override the normal combinatorial primings or priming prosody of a phrase for special effect, to create what elsewhere I have termed 'unusuality' (Partington 1998: 121–143). As Hoey points out 'when a choice of one priming is overwhelmed by another, more dominant priming [the result] is either ambiguity or humour' (2005: 170). He discusses an example of unscripted wordplay, namely the occurrence in an advertisement for an evening's entertainment of the phrase *a night to be missed*, which he interprets as a *confusion of primings*. The writer somehow mixed up the phrases *a chance/opportunity not to be missed* and *a night to remember*.

In this chapter, we shall be more concerned with scripted wordplay, where primings are deliberately 'confused' by the punster. One common mechanism is to upset normal collocational combination, as in (7), where the collocation *party animal* is transformed into *poddy animal*. In (4) and (5), on the other hand, we find plays on priming prosody at the level of semantic preference. As regards the first, we noted how the initial favoured reading of 'Do you believe in clubs for young people?' was likely to be 'do you think young people should be encouraged

Wordplay, phraseplay and relexicalization 119

to join clubs? But how can the joke teller be sure this will be the hearer's favoured first reading? The answer, of course, is that *clubs for* has a semantic preference for the semantic set of expressions indicating particular groups of human beings. In *Papers*, *clubs for* is followed by, among others, *businesswomen, children, collectors, pupils* and *young people*.

In (5) the collocational expression *French letter* becomes *Welsh letter; letter* now being made to combine with a different item from the semantic set of {national adjectives}. There is also, of course, reference to the collocational combination *Welsh leek* (four occurrences in *Papers*).

4.3.2 Relexicalization of preconstructed phrases

At the end of Chapter 1 we examined the linguistic argument that the idiom or phraseological principle of language was the dominant, default mode of interpreting discourse but, should this fail (in the sense of failing to explain the text), hearers retain the option of applying the open-choice principle. It is always possible to treat even tightly idiomatic phrases as if they were capable of analysis into smaller units. Here it will be further contended that it is the interplay, the enforced switching from one mode of interpretation to another which is at the heart of a great part of wordplay. A few simple illustrations:

(9) Is the tomb of Karl Marx just another communist plot?
(10) A: What happens if the parachute doesn't open?
B: That's known as 'jumping to a conclusion'.

These work by forcing the hearer to reinterpret the normally preconstructed phrases *communist plot* and *jumping to a conclusion* as *communist + plot* ('grave space') and *jumping + to + a conclusion* ('leaping to one's death'), which are not recognizable preconstructed phrases and whose meaning must be grasped by using the open choice analytical mechanism. We will call this process *relexicalization*, that is, the 'freeing up' of the parts of a normally frozen, preconstructed lexical unit. In the terms adopted in (9) and (10), some contextual aspect of the text forces a sound sequence to be reinterpreted grammatically (syntactically or morphologically), revealing an M_2 very different from the more salient or more expected M_1. In terms of lexical priming theory, the normal priming prosody that the sound sequences be interpreted as a unit is overridden. The effect achieved is a general revitalization of the language at that point of the text. Novelty breathes life into the discourse. Relexicalization is one of the fundamental linguistic process underlying many forms of 'phraseplay'. The kinds of (semi) preconstructed phrases which appear in such plays are of practically any sort, from proverbs and sayings to quotations, idioms, even simple common collocations (as *communist plot*). A rich source, as we shall see, are film, book, TV programme titles and the like.

M_2 is, of course, unearthed through a process of enforced backtracking similar to that outlined in terms of joke humour in Chapter 1. Hoey (2005: 82) discusses

120 *Wordplay, phraseplay and relexicalization*

a verbal-visual pun, from film, where the backtrack trigger is visual:

> In the film *Airplane*, we are told of a pilot who is no longer permitted to fly because he has a 'drinking problem'. The next shot shows him spilling a non-alcoholic drink all over himself; his problem is in fact that he misses his mouth when he tries to drink.

In Hoey's terms, in the absence of context, a US audience is primed to associate the common collocation *drinking problem* with an M_1 of alcoholism. The follow-up shot of the drink being spilled relexicalizes *drinking problem* into the less salient *problem (with) drinking*. This process of relexicalizing a common collocation is particularly frequent in newspaper headlines, as we shall see in section 4.5, and example (49) is an instance from the briefings.

The following – the first a Jewish joke from Redfern, the second a shaggy-dog pun – reveal another aspect to the interpretative mechanism (the *mokel* is the man who performs circumcision):

(11) After the [ceremony], the rabbi collects the fees, but it's the mokel who collects all the tips.

(12) RACING NEWS: Riding the favourite at Cheltenham, a jockey was well ahead of the field. Suddenly he was hit on the head by a turkey and a string of sausages.

He managed to keep control of his mount and pulled back into the lead, only to be struck by a box of Christmas crackers and a dozen mince pies as he went over the last fence.

With great skill he managed to steer the horse to the front of the field once more when, on the run in, he was struck on the head by a bottle of sherry and a Christmas pudding.

Thus distracted, he succeeded in coming only second. He immediately went to the stewards to complain that he had been seriously hampered.

The first, of course, relexicalizes the set phrase *collect* [a/the] *tip* and the second the colligational template BE [intensifier] *hampered*. The evidence of the *Papers* corpus suggests that the priming for this colligation is very strong: *seriously* co-occurs with *hampered* ten times, *severely hampered* is slightly more common (12) with *badly hampered* coming in third (6). The joke's effect depends partly on knowing that *hampered* is a semi-technical term in horse-racing referring to any occasion when a rider's progress is impeded. It is also necessary to be in possession of the cultural knowledge that a Christmas *hamper* is a basket containing the foodstuffs incorporated in the joke – the essential ingredients of a traditional British Christmas. Hoey stresses that different people will have different lexical primings due to different real world experiences which explains in part how jokes and wordplay can have varying effects on individuals. The punning above will fail for people with no experience of horse-racing or the British Christmas.

I wrote in the definition of relexicalization that the hearer resorts to the open choice mode to reinterpret the (semi) preconstructed phrase when their first, or 'salient', reading fails to interpret the text satisfactorily. But in these two cases, the primary collocational readings make perfect sense – the *mokel* could well receive tips from grateful relatives and the rider was, in anyone's book, well and truly impeded. However, of course, neither of the 'straight' primings, the default collocational readings is funny. The hearer knows these texts are meant as jokes and so begins a backtrack to find a humorous reading. We need therefore to refine our definition of what it means to interpret a joke text satisfactorily – it must not only make sense but also 'make humour'.

4.3.3 Delexicalization

There is a type of relexicalization pun which is of special interest both to lexical grammarians and to logicians of language. Freud cites a couple of puns exploiting zeugma based on the verb *take* (the effect depending on the different status of the verb complement):

(13) 1ST MAN: 'Have you taken a bath?'
      2ND MAN: 'Why, is there one missing?'
(14) Two men going past a café.
      1ST MAN: 'Let's go inside and take something'
      2ND MAN: 'But the place is full of people!'

Freud explains that the effect of these texts depends on the reinterpretation of the verb *take*; in his terms, both jokes at first imply the 'empty' use and then enforce a rereading with the 'full' use. In modern lexicogrammar terminology, the verb in phrases such as *take a bath, take a sandwich, have a meal, do a read-through* is said to be *delexicalized*, that is, it adds no separate meaning but is a kind of syntactic support for the phrase which functions as a single preconstructed unit. In other words, a speaker who uses the phrase *take a bath* to mean 'bathe' is making a single lexical choice, a single 'dip' into their mental lexicon. The delexicalized use of these phrases, at least in normal conversation, is far more frequent than any 'full' use, and normal language users are therefore primed to adopt a first reading of, respectively, *did you bathe?* and *let's eat something*.

Sinclair defines the process of the delexicalization of an item as the 'reduction of the distinctive contribution' it makes to the meaning of the piece of utterance in which it occurs. 'There is' he claims, 'a broad tendency for frequent words, or frequent senses of words, to have less of a clear and independent meaning' (1991: 113) and he cites as examples *take* in *take a look at this, make* in *make up your mind* and *of* in *of course*. With very frequent words we should talk about their general *uses* rather than their specific *meanings*. He emphasizes just how common the phenomenon is. Since most 'normal text' consists of the frequent senses of frequent words, most of discourse is to some degree delexicalized. Thus in Freud's two jokes, (13) and (14), the second character's reply in each case reinstates the 'distinctive contribution' that *take* makes to the phrase, treating *take a bath* and *take something* as two combined units (or two choices from the mental lexicon) that is 'remove' + 'a bath' and 'remove' + 'unspecified object'.

122 *Wordplay, phraseplay and relexicalization*

In passing, we might note that Freud seems to take a special interest and enjoyment in jokes which depend upon this reinterpretation of 'empty' conventional phrases with fuller meanings, and discusses other examples including:

(15) 'How are you getting along?' the blind man asks the lame man.
      'As you can see', the lame man replies to the blind man.

(1960: 37)

The following children's joke, recorded by Wells (1982: audiotape), is also based around *take* but is an elegant variation on the mechanism:

(16) There's this man. He come off his holidays from India. He brought this crocodile with him, you see. And he's going round the corner, taking it for walks and this policeman bumps into him. He says:
      'Eh, what are you doing with that crocodile? You should take it to the zoo.'
      'All right, I'll take it.'
      Next day he sees him walking round the corner with the crocodile again. So the policeman says:
      'I thought I told you to take that crocodile to the zoo.'
      'I did. Now I'm taking it to the pictures.'

The context forces a first or salient reading of the phrase template *take* [someone] *to* {a place of public amusement} which is along the lines of 'take the crocodile to the zoo for public safety'. The crocodile owner's interpretation and our backtrack reading is based on the more common – but in this context more unexpected – narrative whereby someone is *accompanied* to the zoo for their entertainment or education. On this occasion, it is the first reading which is *more* fully lexicalized and *less* frequent than the second; a marked occurrence.

We have already noted the association between logic and delexicalization. Much of the wordplay in the *Alice* books by Lewis Carroll (by profession, of course, a mathematician) examines the concept:

(17) '[...] and even Stigand, the patriotic archbishop of Canterbury, found it advisable –'
      'Found what?' said the Duck.
      'Found it,' the Mouse replied rather crossly: 'of course you know what "it" means.'
      'I know what "it" means well enough, when *I* find a thing,' said the Duck: 'it's generally a frog or a worm. The question is, what did the archbishop find?'

It, of course, is frequently used in this totally delexicalized fashion. Phrases like *find it advisable, find it inconceivable, find it convenient* are perfect examples of indivisible preconstructed phrases whose meaning is spread throughout the unit. The Duck attempts to discover a real-world exophoric referent for the term and isolate some meaning for it; the humour actually lies in his perverse refusal to delexicalize.

Wordplay, phraseplay and relexicalization 123

Another example of delexicalization for comic effect comes when Alice meets the Cheshire Cat:

(18)   ALICE: '[...] and I wish you wouldn't keep appearing and vanishing so suddenly: you make me quite giddy!'
'All right', said the Cat; and this time it vanished quite slowly, beginning with the end of the tail, and ending with the grin, which remained some time after the rest of it had gone.

The Cat responds to Alice's objection to his vanishing 'so suddenly' by disappearing slowly, because he treats the individual items as being fully lexicalized, the item *suddenly*, in particular, being treated as an adverb of manner. Alice, however, uttered the phrase 'so suddenly' as a unitary intensifier. The problem for Alice is that, given the – it must be admitted – rather unusual scenario of a disappearing cat, there is no suitable preconstructed intensifier she can use in the context. It is well known that a great number of verbs collocate with particular intensifiers, for example, *work... hard, hurt... bad(ly), insist... doggedly, guard... jealously, endure... patiently* (Bolinger 1972: 246–250). *Vanish* is primed to collocate with *completely, entirely* and *altogether* (in *Papers* at least) but this is not what Alice wishes to say in this context. As Bolinger points out, the intensifier is often, in his terms, 'semantically redundant' in the sense that the semantic content of the intensifier is already more or less present in the verb, for example, *Why does he strut so vainly*? or *Don't stare at me so intently* (examples from Bolinger, 1972). Such utterances might have been simply *Why does he strut so/in such a way*? or *Don't stare at me so/in that way* but speakers will often prefer to add an intensifier for hyperbolic effect, especially when asking the hearer to *stop* doing something. This is the position Alice finds herself in, but the best intensifier she can find is *suddenly*. The Cat treats the intensifier as not at all redundant, relexicalizes the phrase and obeys to the letter.

4.3.4   Reconstruction of an original version

This is not the only way in which relexicalization functions, however. There is another kind which occurs in those puns we have so far classified as 'near' puns, those in which a (semi) preconstructed phrase is presented in some modified form. The altered phrase is the one which appears in the text. The hearer has to use the actually occurring form to realize the preconstructed phrase from which it derives. A couple of simple examples:

(19)   It would appear that I am dying beyond my means.
                                                                (attributed to Oscar Wilde)
(20)   Once the parents were out of the way
         It was every child for itself.
                                                                (Roger McGough: *Hearts and Flowers*)

Here, of course, there is no particular intellectual challenge in reconstructing the original; the normal primings involved in *living beyond one's means* and *every man for himself* have been reversed. It is simply the effect of novelty which is being sought. Occasionally, however, especially in the shaggy dog pun, the humorous effect lies in the ingenuous reworking of a phrase. Consider the following political example:

(21) CNN/REUTERS: News reports have filtered out early this morning that US forces have swooped on an Iraqi Primary School and detained 6th Grade teacher Mohammed Al-Hazar. Sources indicate that, when arrested, Al-Hazar was in possession of a ruler, a protractor, a set square and a calculator. US President George W Bush immediately stated that this was clear and overwhelming evidence that Iraq did indeed possess weapons of maths instruction.

which exploits of course the expression *weapons of mass destruction* (Ritchie discusses these *story puns* at some length, 2004: 120–122). Spoonerism jokes, among many others, work in a similar reconstructive way (example from Redfern):

(22) What's the difference between a conjuror and a psychologist?
A conjuror gets rabbits out of hats.

and therefore, of course, a psychologist *gets habits out of rats*.

We will examine these kinds of puns in more detail in section 4.5. Note however that the kind of wordplay examined here is by no means exclusive to humour, as shown by the following examples, one from a novel, the other from poetry (my italics):

(23) That night in Southern Australia brought its first snuffle of *tidings of great horror*.
(A. Burgess: *The End of the World News*)

(24) And God still sits aloft in the array
That we have wrought him, stone deaf and *stone blind*.
(E. Thomas: *February Afternoon*)

The first exploits the preconstructed *tidings of great joy*, the new version being its opposite. The second contains both the original collocation *stone deaf* and the new one *stone blind*. The effect here is more complex. By applying *stone* in an unusual collocational context, the poet not only extracts a particularly strong intensification of *blind* (the novelty of an intensifier-adjective collocation makes the intensification particularly forceful), but also of *deaf*, in effect, relexicalizing the preceding set expression. God becomes both deaf as stone and blind as stone.

To summarize here. This examination of the manner in which plays on words function lends strong evidence not only for the psychological reality of linguistic schemata but also for the argument that the default principle in interpreting normal communication is the idiomatic or phraseological mode. Many authors have remarked on the deliberately deceptive aspects of both jokes and puns, how they play with primings, raising expectations to upset them and how, siren-like, they entice their hearers onto the rocks. However, as Attardo points out, there has never been a satisfactory account of the linguistic mechanisms wordplay depends upon. Relexicalization as outlined here seems to offer the basis of a powerful and elegant explanatory hypothesis. It describes how puns depend on the interplay of the phraseological (set-piece) and the open-choice (analytical) language principles, the sudden shift from the first to the second. It thus parallels exactly the cognitive theory of joke humour we described in Chapter 1, which relates how jokes exploit the interaction of the script/schema (set-piece) recall and inferencing (analytical) cognitive procedures. This would also help explain why wordplay is generally considered a humorous phenomenon.

4.4 Metanalysis

A brief mention was made in section 4.1 of the phenomenon known as punning *metanalysis*, that is, the reinterpretation or rereading of the way a word or phrase is divided syntactically: '*Metanalysis*: Reinterpretation of the division between words or syntactic units' (*Shorter Oxford English Dictionary*). Examples of word metanalysis from Attardo (1994) include:

(25) If it's feasible, let's fease it.
(26) He may not have been actually disgruntled, but he was certainly far from gruntled.[10]

From newspapers:

(27) THIS IS THE BUGGER
    Ex-cop John Pole, the man who bugged our phones (accompanied by photograph)

where *feasible* is treated as an adjective deriving from a non-existent verb (i.e. *fease* + *ible*), *disgruntled* as the negation of the non-existent *gruntled* (i.e. *dis* + *gruntled*) and *bugger* as 'one who bugs' (i.e. *bug(g)* + *er*).

One particular form of metanalysis is illustrated in the following extract from the *Papers* corpus (my emphasis):

> When upset by such thoughts, I take comfort from harmless pursuits. As a head, I wished my staff to be *couth* and my pupils *hevelled*, with their work at all times *descript*. I now reveal the key for uncertain parents searching for their good school. The qualities are '*effable*' – which I define as clearly *utterable* and easily discernible, and capable of expression by the young.

The removal of a negative prefix from, respectively *uncouth, dishevelled, nondescript, ineffable* and *unutterable* gives the nonce items listed. The writer could have added *speakable* and *flappable*. This is the type of humour headteachers generally find amusing. Of these, only *couth* appears again in *Papers* (actually, three times, it is in danger of becoming hackneyed). Somewhat similar are reverse coinages such as *underwhelmed* or *underawed*.

126   *Wordplay, phraseplay and relexicalization*

The joke potential of metanalysis puns depends largely on the distance between the meanings of the two sound sequences involved (from Attardo *et al.*, 2002):

(28)   TEACHER: 'Use the word "fascinate" in a sentence.'
CHILD: 'There are ten buttons on my coat, but I can only fasten eight.'

The humour depends partly on the child's ingenuousness (or ingenuity) and partly on the bathetic fall in register. Further joke potential of metanalysis puns resides in their ability to lead the hearer astray for subsequent enlightenment:

(29)   A pregnant woman from West Virginia was involved in a car accident and fell into a coma. When she awoke in hospital days later, the woman noticed that she was no longer carrying a child, and asked, 'Doc, what happened to my baby?'
The doctor replied, 'Ma'am, you've had twins! You're the proud mother of a handsome baby boy and a beautiful baby girl. Also, you should know that while you were in a coma, your brother named the children for you.'
'Oh, no!' shrieked the woman. 'Not my brother! He's the family idiot!'
The doctor replied, 'Well, ma'am, your brother named your daughter Denise.'
'That's no so bad,' smiled the woman. Then, hesitantly, she asked, 'What's the boy's name?'
'Denephew.'

It should be clear that the phenomenon is entirely analogous to that described in the preceding section. Metanalysis is another form of relexicalization of either a single lexical item or a short phrase. It frees up the segments of a string or sound sequence (SS) to be rearranged – morphologically and/or phonologically – to provide a second meaning (M_2). On occasion, it allows one to coin, by the normal processes of inference we have already described, lexical items which do not technically exist in the mental lexicon.

A good number of canned jokes function via the metanalysis not of single words but of a phrase. A couple of examples from Ritchie illustrate the mechanism well:

(30)   A lady went into a clothing store and asked: 'may I try on that dress in the window?'
'Well, replied the sales clerk doubtfully, 'don't you think it would be better to use the dressing room?'

(31)   POSTMASTER: here's your five-cent stamp.
SHOPPER (with arms full of bundles): Do I have to stick it on myself?
POSTMASTER: Nope. On the envelope.

These rather trying texts combine the forced narrative reinterpretation typical of jokes with syntactic metanalysis. The punchline forces the hearer to reinterpret the syntax of the penultimate move of the other character in the text. In (30) the priming [may I try on] + [that dress in the window] is forcibly overridden by a new reading [may I try on that dress] + [in the window]. Similarly, in (31), [do I have to stick it on] + [myself] becomes [do I have to] + [stick it on myself], the adverb *on* being reclassified as a preposition. Whether metanalysis in itself is humorous or not is debatable. The examples here become jokes because the second implied narratives are both slightly improper and contain an element of teasing. A series of children's jokes based on the theme of 'the World's Greatest Books' work by metanalysing a seemingly innocuous 'author's name'; the humour is in the relation between the new M_2 and the book topic which often contains an element of taboo: *The Haunted House* by Hugo First ('you go first'), *Cliff Tragedy* by Eileen Dover ('I leaned over'), *What Boys Love* by E. Norma Stitts ('enormous tits').

The following exchange (from Brandreth 1982: 224; the author claims it really happened) takes place between an army medical officer and rating and combines several of the techniques we have discussed:

(32) M.O.: How are your bowels working?
       R.: Haven't been issued with any, sir.
       M.O.: I mean, are you constipated?
       R.: No, sir, I volunteered.
       M.O.: Heavens, man, don't you know the King's English?
       R.: No, sir, is he?

The second exchange contains a weak near pun (constipated – conscripted) and the third is the metanalysis of the expression *the King's English* (into 'don't you know (that) the King is English?'). It is a useful illustration of how subversive wordplay can be, both of linguistic and in this case wordly authority.

4.5 Corpus data 1: puns in newspaper headlines

After this lengthy theoretical discussion the next two sections are devoted to analysis of authentic wordplay in two corpora, one consisting of newspapers, the second, the briefings, that is, *Dems* and *Reps* combined.

As regards the first, Redfern spends a chapter on punning in various 'sub-literary' genres such as advertising and newspaper headlines. In these areas, economy is paramount, and so puns – 'two meanings for the price of one' (Redfern 1984: 130) – are very popular.

4.5.1 Exact puns in headlines

In Partington (1998) I reported the results of an investigation into wordplay in a corpus of approximately 2500 headlines collected from the *Independent*, a UK broadsheet. It was found to be most frequent in the arts section, followed by sports, then business, whereas the news sections were the poorest, presumably owing to the stricter time constraints which apply to them. It often takes time to play with language.

The following list contains a selection of (more or less) exact puns. The original expression on which the wordplay depends is given below each headline:

(33) BUNHILL: Russian sailors left *all at sea* for America's Cup
       BE all at sea = To be in a state of confusion.

128 *Wordplay, phraseplay and relexicalization*

(34) GOLF: *Faldo makes many a slip 'twixt cup and lip*
 There's many a slip twixt cup and lip.
(35) Hoping to enter a Euro lottery? *Don't bet on it*: Maria Scott describes how German lotteries are being promoted here in defiance of the law
 Don't bet on it = don't be too sure about something.
(36) DESIGN/Some day you might be *sitting on a small fortune*: Fashionable young furniture makers of recent years have proved to be worth investing in
 sitting on a fortune = to be in possession (especially unawares) of a source of wealth.
(37) CITY: Closing a deal is *not his Forte*
 not [someone's] *forte* = not their strong point.

Finally, an example from the *Daily Mail* (in Morley 1998):

(38) CAUGHT FLAT FOOTED!
 1,000 policemen
 500 squad cars
 But kidnapper gets away with it
 Flat-foot = policeman.

In every case, the authors of these headlines have relexicalized a set phrase – SS(M_1), the expression reported under each headline – and have implied a second meaning to the phrase – SS(M_2), the headline itself – which is dependent on the subject matter of the article in question. In all of these the wordplay is motivated, both meanings coexisting. This is the most common variety of exact puns found in the material.[11]

Sometimes, if the rereading is felt to be a little obscure we are given a gloss, as in (35), (36) and (38). Otherwise we must read on to discover the new sense, that is, to understand why a trite phrase has been employed to introduce this particular story.

The simplest of these is (33). The expression *BE all at sea* has a metaphorical sense of 'to be thoroughly confused', which the Russian sailors no doubt are. But they are also quite literally *at sea*. We have already noted how second readings are very often concrete readings of more figurative originals. The proverb in (34): *There's many a slip 'twixt cup and lip*, expresses the popular wisdom that making a plan and carrying it out successfully are not always the same thing. And so, one of the meanings is that Faldo may not find winning the tournament as easy as expected. But the items *cup* and *lip* have literal meanings too – the *cup* is the tournament trophy, and the *lip* is the edge of the golf hole which the player was having difficulty in getting beyond. *Don't bet on* in (36) has the double sense of 'don't rely on' and 'don't wager your money on', whilst the *sitting* in (37) may be done (figuratively) on a source of wealth or (literally) on a piece of furniture. In (38) both meanings are figurative, the *flat-foots* ('policemen' by supposed synecdoche) are *caught flat-footed* ('unprepared'). Deciphering the second sense of (37) depends on knowing that *Forte* is also the name of a businessman

Wordplay, phraseplay and relexicalization 129

(Sir Charles Forte), who, evidently, is having difficulty *closing a deal*. Plays on proper names (both empty and motivated) are fairly common in headlines.

4.5.2 Non-exact puns in headlines

Non-exact puns were found to be considerably more frequent than exact ones in this particular discourse type.

Newspaper texts are, of course, meant principally to be read rather than spoken. This gives rise to the possibility of playing with the visual shape of words, for example (my glosses):

(39) Beaten by the belle
 (The boxer, Mike Tyson, is sent to prison on the testimony of a young woman.)
(40) First class male
 (Review of 'Rogue Male': the protagonist-narrator is both upper class and a tough guy.)

which, of course are reworkings, of *beaten by the bell* and *first class mail*. These are sometimes classified as *homophone* puns since *belle* and *bell, male* and *mail* are different words pronounced the same way. More importantly, however, they are *heterographs*. They present a word string which is different in some way from the (semi-)preconstructed item they are recalling (in the letters on the page rather than in the sound waves in the air) and they function in exactly the same way as the near puns we have discussed in the previous sections.

In Partington (1998) it was argued that the preconstructed phrase underlying written near puns can undergo one of four different sorts of changes in their surface realization:

a) *substitution*;
b) *abbreviation*: as in 'Once a Catholic' (where...*always a Catholic* does not appear in the text);
c) *insertion*: as in 'Iain Gale gives three artists the chance to put the palette knife in', which inserts *palette* in the idiom *put the knife in* ('criticize');
d) *rephrasing* i.e. *reordering of parts*: as in 'Another catch for the early birds', which rephrases the proverb *it's the early bird that catches the worm*.

These are, in effect, the four basic classes of change permissible on any kind of information string.

Taking the first of these mechanisms, the substitution can be minimal, even a single letter or phoneme, as in 'A fridge too far' (original: *A Bridge Too Far*), or 'Bonfire of the Sanities' (for *Vanities*), or a single grammatical item, as in 'Murder of the Cathedral' (*of* for *in*) or a single lexical word, as in 'The naked and the well-read' (*well-read* for *dead*). On occasion, however, the substitution process can be drastic, as in 'Elway does it his way', an extreme case of grammatical and lexical substitution. Of the five lexical items which make up the original quotation (the Sinatra song – *I did it my way*), as many as three have been replaced, the only ones which remain unaltered are *it* and *way*. This begs the question of how the text receiver is expected to recognize the original. We might hazard the following explanation. Each of the words in the new version is related to the one in the corresponding position in the original – thus *I* and *Elway* are both personal phrase subjects, *does* and *did* are parts of the same verb and *his* stands in the same relation to *Elway* as *my* to *I*. Clearly what is being recognized is the phrase pattern, the lexical schema of the form [Personal subject (i.e. proper name/pronoun)] DO *it* [possessive] *way*. Thus punning provides, once again, very strong psychological evidence for the existence of priming prosody and that the brain stores not just single lexical items but patterns of collocation, colligation and semantic preferences.

In, for example, the 'Murder of the Cathedral' headline, the story being about the neglect of historical monuments, the pun is highly motivated. But what do we make of headlines such as 'Beaten by the belle'? The literal, relexicalized sense, that the boxer Mike Tyson has been jailed on the evidence of a young woman who claimed she was sexually assaulted by him, fits the text. But the original idiomatic expression *beaten by the bell*, meaning 'to run out of time', is sometimes conventionally applied to a situation where a boxer is cheated of imminent victory by his opponent's surviving the count because the bell ends the round.[12] This has no possible application to the context of the story, it is simply used because it is reminiscent of the world of boxing to give a certain flavour to the story, and possibly remind a distracted reader who Mr Tyson is. We might include this among semi-motivated forms of wordplay, and call it 'reminiscent flavour' punning. Its use is extremely common in English tabloid newspapers.

The following is an example of the second mechanism of change, abbreviation:

(41)   ACCOUNTANCY & MANAGEMENT: *For what we are about to receive*. Simon Pincombe finds that company administrators and receivers are among those destined to do well this year
For what we are about to receive, may the Lord make us truly thankful.

Here, the gloss tells us that *receivers* are *about to receive* some financial reward (i.e. *do well*). What is interesting is that only half the original preconstructed phrase is given and the vital information – that receivers should give thanks to the Lord – is contained in the missing part, the one that the hearer must supply from their mental lexicon. This is a fairly typical procedure, especially if the preconstructed phrase is long.

In the following:

(42)   DANCE/*FROM LITTLE ACORNS*: Judith Mackrell reviews Mikhail Baryshnikov and the White Oak Dance Project at Sadler's Wells
From little acorns, great oak trees grow.

we again have only half the proverb. We can infer that the author expects great things from the modest beginnings of the ballet. This is, of course, the traditional reading of this proverb, and this example is barely a pun at all; the wordplay lies in the echo, the evocation of the missing part of the proverb through the item *oak* in the project's title. Often, in practice, the only basis for the evocation of a particular phrase is some word connected to the story.

The third mechanism of phrase change is insertion or expansion, where items are added to the original preconstructed expression. The simplest example is 'Play up and play the word game' where *word* is inserted into the famous line from Henry Newbolt's poem. Of course, *word game* is itself a recognizable collocation. In 'Iain Gale gave three artists the chance to put the palette knife in', the popular metaphor *put the knife in*, meaning 'criticize viciously' is expanded by the insertion of *palette* knife, that is, an artist's knife. It is a particularly effective comic introduction to a light-hearted article in which painters get the opportunity to criticize the work of art critics who see themselves as budding artists. They were not kind.

The fourth and final mechanism of headline alteration is rephrasing or reformulation, which, along with substitution, is the most common. When discussing 'Elway does it his way', it was argued that the phraseology was what the text receiver recognized, but when the rephrasing of a quotation or saying is particularly drastic, this can no longer be the case. What is it in 'Are the first cuts the deepest?' which enables the reader to recognize the song title *The first cut is the deepest*, or in 'to conquer at the Stoop' which recalls the Goldsmith play *She stoops to conquer*? The answer must be that the reader simply recognizes the co-occurrence of two or three items in the new version – *first, cut(s)* and *deepest* in the first and *stoop(s)* and *conquer* in the second. In the *Elway* example, we hypothesized that the mental recognition works at the level of the lemma, since the reader was expected to pick up the relationship between *does* and *did*. However, here, the new *Stoop* has not changed morphologically but has undergone a drastic grammatical and semantic transformation. It is no longer of the same word class; from being a verb ('to lower/debase oneself') it has become a noun (the name of *Harlequins Rugby Club*'s stadium). The clue to recognizing the original verb form would seem to be entirely graphic or phonological. In fact, readers get no semantic clues to help them recognize the original since items in the new version tend to be used in entirely novel senses, as was mentioned earlier. These instances constitute further evidence that the brain's ability to store and recall lexical items which have been primed to co-occur is extremely powerful. There seem, then, to be two distinct cognitive mechanisms of which hearers avail themselves to link the new version to the original: the *identification of a phrase structure* and *co-occurring-item recognition*.

4.5.3 Verbal cascading

To finish this examination, we will look at a couple of headline building techniques which use wordplay but which are not puns or which are on the outer reaches of the phenomenon.

Many headlines depend for their effect, not on the exploitation of any specific expression, but on the combining of words and phrases which belong to some particular lexico-semantic class.

132 *Wordplay, phraseplay and relexicalization*

The *Independent* sporting headlines are particularly rich in the use of this technique:

(43) Midfield *engine fuels* Anfield *drive*;
(44) Guscott's *magic* ruins Gloucester's *fairy-tale*;
(45) Quins *maul* sleeping *Tigers*.

And the tabloids use the mechanism incessantly:

(46) FISHY!
      Cops *swallowed* kidnapper's red *herring...hook, line* and *sinker*.

We might call this technique of wordplay *verbal cascading*. When there is no real semantic link between the word set employed and the content of the story this can appear a very poor contrivance indeed.

4.6 Corpus data 2: wordplay in interactive discourse

In the previous sections of this chapter we made a number of observations on the structure of punning wordplay and how language users employ it. These included how puns are self-evidently bisociative in nature, two meanings being conjoined in Koestler's 'acoustic knot'. The differentiation between motivated and non-motivated wordplays was considered, as well as how this was related to their 'quality', their 'goodness' or 'badness'. We saw too how exact and non-exact puns are often used by speakers and writers in different ways. Exact puns tend to function (like other bisociative jokes) by forcing the hearer to reinterpret a particular sound sequence in a new way by placing it in a novel context ('May I try on that dress in the window?' – 'Why not use the changing room?'; Hoping to enter a Euro lottery? *Don't bet on it*). Non-exact puns (of which we determined the existence of four types) often also challenge the hearer/reader to reconstruct an 'original' sound sequence of which the one actually uttered is a derivative (as *home rule* must be recovered mentally by the receiver from the uttered sequence *home roulade*). We noted too that the derived sound sequence is very frequently a literal relexicalization of a more figurative original. The challenge is usually fairly mild but on occasion can be more arduous. An oft-quoted example is *Punch* magazine's cartoon of General Napier's forced annexation of the Indian province of Sind, captioned *Peccavi!* ('I have *sinned*'). The aggressive nature of joking in general and wordplay in particular, the way it can constitute a challenge to the hearer, has been noted (Sherzer 1985). Norrick argues convincingly, however, that it tends to be at worst a pseudo-challenge, and that when the hearer passes the test by 'getting' the joke, solidarity or rapport is reinforced (2003: 1342, 1348). This is one of the reasons it is so frequent in newspapers, which are keen to construct a rapport with their readership to encourage their loyalty. Finally, we also commented in passing on the antipathy with which punning is frequently treated in many circles despite, or maybe because of, its pervasiveness.

4.6.1 The importance of wording: playing with definitions

We can now look at how relevant these considerations might be to the study of wordplay in authentic interactional discourse, in the working environment of the briefings. Before looking at the data we need to remember that the participants involved in these interactions are very particular. Both the journalists and their foil, the podium, are wordsmiths by trade. The press pays the utmost attention to the use of language as object, especially the precise form of words used in administration communiqués and responses of government officials to their questions. Political journalists do not report fires or road accidents and very frequently the object of their questions is the use of language itself. As Fairclough reminds us, politics is not just conducted *through* language, but much of politics *is* language: 'politics partly consists in the disputes which occur in language and over language' (1989: 23). The nature of the language used shapes the nature of the news reported, and different formulations of the news can offer competing accounts of reality. The briefings are also broadcast around the world and the transcripts are available to perusal by friends and foes, ranging from other journalists to foreign governments.

It is no surprise then to find on occasion a very scrupulous, even pernickety, attitude to word usage. An (occasionally) self-reflective press even joke about the closeness of their attention to words:

(47) MR. FLEISCHER: John, as the President said, Israel needs to continue its withdrawal, and that's what the President believes [...]
Q: He said, now. And now it's seems he's saying, now doesn't necessarily mean now.
[Several other questions]
Q: I hesitate to return to this question of pullout in Ramallah, but since we spent so much time in past years arguing over the definition of 'is' around here, we can now do the definition of 'now'. (Laughter)
Q: Or 'pullout'.

The terms *define* and *definition* are extremely frequent in the briefings. There are 114 occurrences in the two corpora, roughly one every 6,500 words. This compares to one in every 47,000 words in another spoken corpus, the *Wellington*. There is plenty of evidence that close attention to language and playing around with the definition of terms has the status of an in-script, an in-group joke:

(48) MR. FLEISCHER: I'll try to let you know. I think it's going to be midday, midday-ish.
Q: Do you mean noon, or 2:00 p.m. or –
MR. FLEISCHER: Noon is a good description of midday. (Laughter) That's why I said it as artfully and as accordion-like as I could: midday-ish, i-s-h.
Q: What's your broad definition of midday, Ari?
MR. FLEISCHER: Generally, it begins sometime in the mid- to late morning, and travels through to the early to mid-afternoon, with the forefront being clearly in the center. (Laughter)

Notice the parody of briefings talk in the question 'what's *your broad definition* of midday...?' (see section 2.6).

4.6.2 Scripted puns

Although it is not always possible to tell, some puns which occur in the corpus have all the hallmarks of being scripted, that is, prepared in advance of the moment of utterance (section 4.2.1). Not surprisingly, given what we have said about the lowly status of punning among sophisticates such as an audience of journalists, they are rare. On the other hand and perhaps surprisingly, they seem in practice to be reasonably well-received. Maybe their very occasionalness can relieve the monotony of a question-answer session. In the scripted material, the most patently premanufactured pun in a question is the following:

(49) Q: I have an arms control question. What's the condition in the President's arm? Is his control any better than it was a year ago at this time? (Laughter) And can we expect to see him at some opening day or some early season game throwing out the first pitch?

This is, of course, a syntagmatic pun, usually defined as one in which both sound sequences are present in the text (Ritchie 2004: 127), namely, 'arms control' and 'control...in his arm'. To describe wordplay in interactive discourse, however, we will need to refine this definition a little. The true syntagmatic pun in conversation occurs when both sound sequences are in the same speaker's move. This will permit us to distinguish between these and reformulation puns discussed later, in which the second sequence occurs in another speaker's move. Pure syntagmatic puns – Ritchie cites Mae West's famous 'It is better to be looked over than to be overlooked' (2004: 127) – need a certain degree of careful formulation, and generally have a certain contrived quality about them when they appear in conversation, as here. They are also correspondingly rare.

This pun is clearly bathetic, there is a shift from the high, formal, political narrative to a lower, familiar, sporting one. However, it is rather unusual in form since there is no apparent corresponding shift from transactional to interactional mode; in other words, the speaker carries on from start to finish as if his move was a serious political question.

There are a few instances in the corpus where the podium seems to produce a prescripted pun. The first is a kind of story pun about the attachment of Texans to their homeland:

(50) MR. FLEISCHER: [...] And I've seen this before in a lot of people, interestingly, from Texas; they love Texas in a special way. Returning home means a lot to them. And raising children in Texas means a lot to them.
I have one family friend from Beaumont, Texas, and they had a daughter who was born in Washington, D.C., and the grandmother brought up soil from Beaumont and put it underneath the hospital

Wordplay, phraseplay and relexicalization 135

mattress, April, so that way she could say that her granddaughter was born on Texas soil. (Laughter) So I think it's something special about that. April, you might want to try that, as well.
We'll get you some Baltimore soil. (Laughter)

My suspicions that the story is not entirely spontaneous is based on the fact that it is occasioned by a question about the retirement and return to Texas of a senior White House official – a topic the podium may well have anticipated.

The wordplay, of course, lies in the relexicalization of the semi-preconstructed phrase *born on* [placename] *soil*. Soil is reinterpreted as 'territory' rather than 'earth' (although of course the latter is the usually salient meaning of soil when used outside this set expression). We might note in passing the bathetic insinuation in his teasing of April: one might reasonably act in such a manner if one hails from a big, important state such as Texas, but not if one is from humble Baltimore.

A third likely candidate as a piece of pre-prepared wordplay is the following. The talk has revolved around Mr and Mrs Clinton's plans for a second honeymoon. Mr Lockhart has just taken on the mantle of press secretary. The concomitance of the two events may well have encouraged the press secretary's staff to prepare a suitable quip:

(51)   Q: Joe, this is the honeymoon weekend for the Clintons. When was Mrs. Clinton's trip –
MR. LOCKHART: I thought this was my honeymoon week? No?
Q: It was. (Laughter)
MR. LOCKHART: This was my honeymoon?
Q: You're having it. (Laughter)
MR. LOCKHART: Bye. (Laughter) I told someone – someone asked me last week how long I thought the honeymoon would last, and I said it would end the first day somewhere between good and afternoon. (Laughter)

This episode involves, first of all, a relexicalization of *honeymoon* in its core sense to *honeymoon week*, the first week in a new job. The last part of the repartee, however, is the most interesting. The division of the generally indivisible set phrase 'good afternoon' is another instance of wordplay *insertion* and with it Mr Lockhart evokes the 'tough job' narrative, casting the press in its favourite role of rigorous task masters with all the ego-massaging this involves. We begin to glimpse how wordplay in interaction can be used with specific strategic purpose.

4.6.3 *Unscripted or spontaneous wordplay*

Turning to the spontaneous episodes of wordplay, our first example is as unscripted as possible:

(52)   Q: Who's going out?
MR. MCCURRY: Ms. Terzano, our very capable Deputy Press Secretary, will be there to handle your questions during the period the President is vacating. (Laughter)

136 *Wordplay, phraseplay and relexicalization*

The press seize upon the podium's slip of the tongue, his malapropism of *vacating* for *vacationing* with its scatological undertones. There are other fairly uncomplicated puns:

(53) Q: What about the Ebola outbreak?
      MR. MCCURRY: The President got an update on the two monkeys that are in quarantine in Texas from Leon Panetta, who spoke to Dr. Shalala. Do you want me to monkey around with this further? (Laughter)

(54) Q: Mike, I know you don't want to talk about the train wreck coming, but just one last thing. (Laughter) Could you tell –
      MR. MCCURRY: There's a train wreck – (laughter) –
      Q: I know and it's something to look forward to. (Laughter)

(55) Q: Is the General in the doghouse here?
      MR. LOCKHART: Here? There is no doghouse here; if there was, I'd live there. (Laughter)

The first is a rather silly syntagmatic joke, which receives a patter of polite laughter, partly because humans find the topic of monkeys somehow funny and partly because 'monkey around' probably falls into the category of colourful language (section 2.7). The other two are instances of a more common type of wordplay in these briefings, in which the second speaker picks out a part of the preceding speaker's move to create a pun, what earlier we decided to call reformulation puns. In the first the metaphorical *train wreck* (a disaster, more precisely here, the potential collision of the government and Congress) is playfully reinterpreted by the podium as a real one, whilst in the second Mr Lockhart relexicalizes and de-metaphorizes the set expression *BE in the doghouse* conjuring up a comic fantasy narrative of his own putative life in a kennel. The function of the pun in these three episodes appears to be the same; simply to amuse, create rapport and reinforce the podium's *persona* as congenial regular guy.

But puns can be less innocent. We might consider the following (the topic of talk has been how Mr Clinton's personality might be overshadowing that of Mr Gore in the run-up to the Presidential election):

(56) Q: Joe, you're saying that he doesn't have to do anything, that naturally attention shifts to the presidential election. And certainly that's true in some respects, but the President is a larger-than-life figure and he's somebody who gets attention every time he opens his mouth.
      MR. LOCKHART: Well, we're going to put him on a diet.(Laughter) He's going to be smaller, thinner, less noticeable.

We might recall Norrick's argument about the conversational disruptiveness of punning, how it interrupts the flow. One might even surmise that punning would be doubly distracting in a discourse type such as briefings, where the main aim of the exercise is transactional. Punning, first of all, wrenches the talk from transactional mode and positions it squarely in the interactional. In second place, it effectively also brings the interaction to a shuddering halt. The above episode constitutes a good example of this. The podium is using the reformulation pun, taking *larger than life* and relexicalizing it in a literal fashion in order to distract the audience's attention and in effect to evade the question, to which he has no real answer. However, given the experience and tenacity of the wise heads in the audience, it is a tactic that rarely works. Questioners return to the topic, as the next move in this exchange demonstrates:

(57) Q: Whenever he opens his mouth he gets a lot of attention. He doesn't have to do much.

The podium again tries using humour to avoid answering:

(58) MR. LOCKHART: You need to stop me before I hurt again. (Laughter)

But he is tracked down relentlessly and eventually has to give a serious though somewhat blustering response:

(59) Q: If there's no – if you don't plan to make some kind of effort to put him off the stage, whatever he does he's going to potentially overshadow the Vice President.
MR. LOCKHART: I don't think so. I think that the President fighting for a patients' bill of rights, minimum wage, prescription drugs through Medicare, gun safety legislation and a lot of other legislative priorities, where the Republicans and the special interests are standing in the way, and where the Governor of Texas is standing in the way or doing nothing to promote this – I don't see how that can negatively impact any Democrat in this country.

However, although rarely entirely successful for purposes of evasion, the disruptive nature of punning may well serve a useful purpose in giving the podium a certain breathing space to work out a suitable response (the *NSC* is the *National Security Council*):

(60) Q: You said the NSC meeting today was to discuss a variety of military matters that are pending, a phrase that would seem to be eight months pregnant with meaning. (Laughter) Was the same thing discussed with the congressional leaders?
MR. FLEISCHER: I'm trying to do the math. When does eight months go back to? (Laughter) And are you suggesting there will be a baby born in one month? (Laughter)
Q: Perhaps less than a month. Was the same general set of issues discussed with congressional leaders?

Once again the podium's reinterpretation is from a figurative to a literal sense of the expression in question.

The following episode involves the kind of relexicalization we have come across earlier:

(61) Q: You spoke of the hope that there would be continued free press, that there could be a free press. Are you happy that we have a free press in the United States?
MR. LOCKHART: Very happy. Don't I look happy? (Laughter)

138 Wordplay, phraseplay and relexicalization

The podium relexicalizes the conventional phrase BE happy that/about where happy has become delexicalized to mean something like simply 'satisfied' and reloads it with its original fully lexicalized meaning of 'content'. The process is analogous with what occurs in examples (13) and (14) discussed earlier, where Freud talks of reinvesting 'empty' phrases with their 'full' senses. In any case, any disruption is minimal in that the podium also deals with the question, even if it is a rather elegant dismissal, saying 'of course I am satisfied that the US has a free press'.

The following exchange is particularly illuminating:

(62)   Q: One of those critics is Gary Bauer, who – it seems that you can't pick up a newspaper without him criticizing the President for something. What does the President think of Gary Bauer?
       MR. FLEISCHER: He thinks it's a democracy, and Mr. Bauer is entitled to his opinion. It makes for good cable, I guess.
       Q: But they don't talk? Do they ever communicate?
       MR. FLEISCHER: Mr. Bauer communicates through cable. (Laughter)

Here we observe how the very disruptiveness of punning can be put to strategic argumentative effect. To the question 'But they don't talk? Do they ever communicate?' the podium does not produce a direct unequivocal answer 'no' but one which is apparently a non-sequitur, a statement of a fact that everyone in the room already knows – Mr Bauer conducts a TV show. He has playfully relexicalized the item *communicate* meaning 'talk to each other' to signify 'broadcast', 'communicate to the masses'. The disruptiveness of punning can be used as a kind of evident conversational non-cooperativeness, in the Gricean sense. The hearer is then obliged to cast around for a reason why the speaker is being uncooperative, in this case, concluding that the podium is performing a sarcastic attack on Mr Bauer's kind of cheap TV shots at the President.

Earlier we interpreted Norrick's argument about the disruptive or interruptive effect of punning as arising from its suddenly switching attention from the conversational matter in hand to some aspect of the language being used. But when the topic of discourse is language itself, this disruptive effect may well be attenuated, complex and subtle, indeed, as we have begun to see, it may often be an argumentatively exploitable resource. The superficial disruption can be used to make a deeper level point.

4.6.4 Recovery work

Nevertheless, punning is generally disruptive of the surface of discourse, and normal service usually needs somehow to be resumed, that is, participants need to pick up the threads of transactional briefings business. One option is that illustrated in the episode (56)–(59) in which the questioner simply ignores the podium's attempts at evasion. However, if the rest of the audience is responding to the laughter-work of one's interlocutor, this can be a difficult road to take and some kind of temporary 'playing along' strategy may be advisable. As was pointed out earlier, wordplay can be doubly distracting in a discourse such as briefings since not only does it interrupt the interaction, it has already *a priori* forced the discourse out of transactional and into interactional mode. A speaker whose transaction – their question – has been interrupted by a pun may decide to spend some time in interactional mode before resuming the transaction, to both humour the interlocutor and signal to the rest of the audience that they can take a joke:

(63) Q: Since your revelation about this –
MR. LOCKHART: What's a revelation?
Q: It's in the Bible. (Laughter)
Q: What you did on the platform there. There have been two columns written [...]

(64) Q: Joe, does the Archer – Joe?
MR. LOCKHART: Yes.
Q: Does the Archer Social Security –
MR. LOCKHART: I just can't get the word "bouquet" out of my mouth. (Laughter) Sorry.
Q: Does the bouquet of proposals from Congressman Archer – (Laughter) –
MR. LOCKHART: Well done. (Laughter)

In the first episode, the pun is constructed collaboratively by the podium and a second journalist. This makes it difficult to ignore and so the original questioner plays along, although very briefly.

In the second, the podium's attention has been distracted by an earlier use of the colourful item *bouquet*. His apparent apology for his lack of attention is actually a pun. The questioner then not only plays along but even tops Mr Lockhart's pun with one of his own and yet still manages to stay in transactional mode, but the hope that transaction could continue is rather forlorn and in fact the pun is commented on. We might note in passing how the podium excuses his own punning ('Sorry') but praises that of his interlocutor ('Well done'), reminding us both of the ambivalence felt towards wordplay and also how the podium desires to gratify his audience's positive face.

In this final example here (my emphasis, Karen Hughes was a member of the White House staff):

(65) Q: [...] And yesterday President Bush *embraced* your upcoming nuptials by *kissing* you. And he – (laughter) –
MR. FLEISCHER: Let's keep that off the record. (Laughter)
Q: And he's *embracing* this decision by Karen Hughes to go back to Texas, primarily for her son and the fact that she's homesick [...]

the second journalist actually uses a pun – moving for once from the physical to the metaphorical – to actually get the briefing *back* on tracks and into transactional mode.

4.6.5 Wordplay as weapon

The set of examples considered in this section all contain examples of wordplay reformulation of part of another's move to gain some kind of argumentative advantage (Partington 2003: 177–190). In the following we find in the first case a mild and in the second a rather aggressive threat or warning:

(66) Q: I have a follow up to David, because he didn't follow up enough. (Laughter)

(67) [...] what sort of advice they're giving? Can you perhaps take that?
MR. TOIV: Can I take that question? Sure, I can take that question.
Q: What are you going to do with it? (Laughter)

The examples are similar in that speakers are relexicalizing fossilized, technical briefings vocabulary, in the first case *follow up* and in the second *take the question*. *Follow up* can be used as a noun, as in the first part of the questioner's move, or as a verb, for example, *if I can just follow up on that*. However, this is the only occasion in the briefings where it is relexicalized to become a gradable verb – 'he didn't follow up enough'. What of course is being implied is that the podium was let off some hook and the current questioner is going to hang him back on it.

To *take the question* generally means that the podium will find out more information on a topic and will report back to the troupe at a later date. The questioner relexicalizes *take* to mean 'be in possession of' (we have already seen in section 4.3.3 how the verb *take* is a frequent candidate for relexicalization). The podium is being warned to make sure he comes back with an answer.

The following couple of instances occur in the same section of talk when the subject is whether or not the US administration spies upon its allies as well as its potential enemies. Various questioners are in effect trying to trick, bully or cajole the podium into saying more than he ought, to admit to something by implication. It is a fencing match with the podium very much on the back foot:

(68) MR. FLEISCHER: The policy is the same about any country; we do not talk about intelligence.
Q: I'm trying to square that with earlier in a briefing when you reminded us that Colin Powell spoke about wiretaps of Iraqi officials.
MR. FLEISCHER: Sure, and as you know, that was after a very lengthy declassification process involving the situation uniquely in Iraq.
Q: Well, all we're asking you here to do is if you can, in effect, declassify – (Laughter) What is the difference? You declassify stuff that helps make your case on Iraq. We're asking you if you're bugging our allies. It seems to be –
MR. FLEISCHER: Well, first of all, I'm not making any presumption that it is classified. I'm not saying whether there is or is not anything of the kind that you are asking.

Q: Well, if there's not of a kind, that's why I don't understand why you can't say it's not of the kind.

MR. FLEISCHER: Because then you're playing a process of elimination around the world, which is a process we do not –

Q: Well, we've already eliminated one, Iraq. (Laughter) How about a couple more, the two that are mentioned in this memo, that very clearly –

The first reformulation is of the podium's words 'lengthy declassification process'. The journalist immediately relexicalizes *declassify* to mean 'tell us what we want to know', making fun of administration rhetoric into the bargain. The second reformulation of 'process of elimination' to 'we've already eliminated one, Iraq', that is, you've admitted we spy on Iraq, has an almost prophetic double meaning.

In these final episodes the roles are reversed:

(69) Q: Is he equally committed to the contingency fund?

MR. FLEISCHER: The President's contingency fund? Yes. And the reason the President has proposed a contingency fund is to deal with contingencies. (Laughter)

The apparent tautology involving *contingency* seems to imply that even the questioner ought to be able to work this one out. Podiums of both political colours frequently find it convenient to insist that their words 'speak for themselves', mean what they say, nothing more, nothing less. Journalists, equally, find it convenient to imply that further interpretation or greater detail is necessary, or even that political/diplomatic language needs 'relexicalizing' into everyday meaning (Partington 2003: 173–177).

The following episode contrasts these different philosophies with comic exasperation:

(70) MR. FLEISCHER: The President welcomed this development. The President thinks what's important now is for all parties to focus on their responsibilities, and those responsibilities include efforts to promote peace, security and reform in Palestinian institutions.

Q: Should they pull back further?

MR. FLEISCHER: The President welcomed the development.

Q: So are you satisfied with it?

MR. FLEISCHER: The President welcomed it.

Q: So you're saying he welcomed it? (Laughter)

MR. FLEISCHER: Let me rephrase it. The President welcomed it. (Laughter)

Q: Need to have a little ticker that gives translations. You know, this is what "welcomed" really means. (Laughter)

On the evidence here, then, we need to revise the account of punning as disruptive behaviour. In argumentative discourse such as this the disruption is often only

142 *Wordplay, phraseplay and relexicalization*

apparent and the wordplay is in fact entirely motivated and integrated into the give-and-take of battle, helping score points, forcing the opponent into a difficult situation, making them do what you want them to, whether that be disclose more information, admit they are behaving inappropriately or withdraw a certain line of questioning.

4.6.6 *Conclusions on wordplay in interaction*

To conclude, wordplay in authentic discourse turns out to be complex and multifaceted both structurally and functionally.

In terms of structure, we have found occasional syntagmatic puns where both sound sequences are in a single move of the same speaker. More common are relexicalizations where a second speaker repeats part of the previous turn to different effect:

(71) Q: Can you assure us – just to wind this up, can you assure us that –
 MR. LOCKHART: You are winding me up.

We have also come across creative tautology, examples of metanalysis and seen how both the punning and the recovery work can be carried out collaboratively over a series of different speaker moves.

The simplest function of wordplay in this discourse type is to assuage the interlocutor's face, to amuse, to build rapport and to flatter one's audience, particularly on the part of the podium, several of whose puns are self-effacing or complimentary of his audience. On other occasions it can be an attempt at evasion or winning time. Perhaps most often, though, speakers pick out part of another speaker's move to use it against them: to score a point, to issue a pre-emptive warning or simply to tease or mock them.

The most successful puns in interactive discourse are those which perform more than one function at a time. The topic of the following question is government policy on the environment (my emphasis):

(72) Q: Ari, with respect, there are some people who don't quite see it that way, and they were out there this morning, talking about some of the rollbacks in arsenic, his reversal on carbon dioxide [...] *they said that the President came to town saying that he would change the climate in Washington; we didn't know that it was the actual climate that he was talking about.* (Laughter) And I'm wondering if the White House is concerned that they're giving the Democrats a very big stick with which to whack the President between now and a year November.

The phrase *change the climate*, originally intended metaphorically as the political climate, is reinterpreted to refer to the physical climate, the air we breathe (we noted earlier how often puns convert the metaphorical into the concrete). The speaker here manages to, first of all, amuse his audience and perhaps win their alignment, second to make a sarcastic joke at the President's expense, and finally to make a serious political point. The fact that the pun is so well-integrated into the discourse, so minimally disruptive, means that the speaker does not have to carry out any real recovery work. This is a good example of wordplay which is motivated – and therefore effective – in every sense.

5 Teasing and verbal duelling

> The one thing the Devil cannot stand is laughter.
> (Martin Luther)
>
> I have never made but one prayer to God, a very short one:
> 'O Lord, make my enemies ridiculous.'
> (Voltaire)

5.1 Introduction: definitions of *teasing*

The phenomenon known as teasing is easier to recognize than to define. Attardo maintains that it is generally associated with humour but is also seen as a distinct form: 'teasing differs from other types of humorous interaction because of the presence of an element of "criticism"' (1994: 321), although it would seem to share this function with satire and, often, comic parody. Others note its use for social control: 'according to Drew, teasing is a way of correcting the behaviour of the interlocutor, and so fits in the Bergsonian perspective of humour as a social corrective' (Attardo 1994: 321). Others again stress its connection with shaming, that is, teasing is the deliberate attempt to provoke embarrassment by accusing the target of having failed to be, act or think in accordance with the standards which the community accepts as proper (both the standards and the community are, of course, construed by the teaser). A number of the episodes that will be examined in this chapter have already been discussed earlier as evidence of other forms of laughter-talk. This is evidence that laughter is so often the result of a combination of different causes and forces.

Brown and Levinson take a somewhat different approach and mention teasing briefly as 'a good example of socially acceptable rudeness' (1987: 97). They include it as one of the 'set of cases where non-redress occurs' (1987: 97). They have little else to add except a brief discussion of ritual insults, where they point out that the use of 'conventionalized (ritualized) insults as a mechanism for stressing solidarity' is explained by the fact that 'in intimate relations there may be presumed to be minimal danger of face threats. This gives rise to the use of bald on-record insults or jokes as a way of asserting such intimacy' (1987: 221).

Like all politeness presumptions, however, this can be exploited by speakers to assert not intimacy but aggression/agonism. We will examine this strategic use during the course of this chapter.

Tholander and Aronsson (2002), in reviewing past studies, list three main functions of teasing from the point of view of the teaser:

1   social control (especially of adults over children);
2   affiliation: demonstrating alliance with and against other participants;[1]
3   performance: attracting attention, outperforming other participants in verbal competition.

and one function from the point of view of the target, that of peer socialization, whereby being teased is part of learning the rules of belonging. There are often other more local subfunctions at particular moments in the interaction and these can be of considerable interest in political discourse. Boxer and Cortés-Conde (1997) concentrate on the affiliation function and distinguish between teasing which 'bonds' and that which 'bites'. It bonds by 'displaying a past history' (1997: 285), reassuring the teased that the teaser knows them well and is interested in their interests. Koestler briefly mentions 'friendly teasing' (1964: 53–54), defined as a combination of aggression and affection. He considers it a sophisticated form of humour and speculates (as does Pinker 1997) that this amicable form of teasing might be of late ontogenetic and phylogenetic development, absent both in children and from earlier cultures. Boxer and Cortés-Conde (1997) also stress the role of teasing in both simple identity display and also *relational* identity building, 'the negotiation of a relational identity with others and through others' (1997: 282), which enables participants to construct 'a sense of membership in a group' (1997: 276). In their data, teasing is most common among intimates and least seen among strangers, largely because, in the latter case, there is no 'past history' to exploit and it is often not known whether relational identity building will be worthwhile or possible. We might add that its potential for and association with agonism make it a high risk strategy, to be avoided in relations with non-intimates where misunderstandings are likely to occur.

Grainger (2002), however, discusses an interesting exception to this rule. She notes how teasing can be a frequent and valuable resource in hospital discourse in order to, as Brown and Levinson (1987) term it, *re-rank* (to reduce in this case) the social distance between staff and patients who are very recent acquaintances. Her data consists of recordings and transcriptions of nurses bathing elderly patients, situations where – as is common in the medical sphere – the personal hygiene tasks are 'both medically necessary and personally face-threatening' (2002). It might be predicted, she points out, that negative politeness techniques would abound (*please, sorry, excuse me* etc.), but instead her data is full of positive politeness joke-play and especially teasing:

NURSE: Fill this bath up now
PATIENT: Drown me is it?

146 *Teasing and verbal duelling*

NURSE: Yeh drown you [...] I'm gonna pour so much water over your head with the jug
PATIENT: I'm not coming to this place no more
NURSE: (laughs) Don't ruin our fun Mary [...]

(Grainger 2002; with light editing)

Such direct threats and affronts so obviously flout politeness norms that they can build rapport by signalling a relationship that eschews such superficial conventions (Norrick 1993: 73); as Grainger says 'by casually mentioning them, the effect is to counteract them' (2002). Since there has been no time for the participants to construct an intimate relationship, they simply assume one, invent one. In order to do so, participants exploit contextual, especially psychological factors such as what they know or can safely assume about their interlocutors' intentions, as well as general, shared knowledge and experience of teasing, a common and socially recognized type of interaction. They put to good use, in other words, the peer socialization function of teasing mentioned earlier.

Grainger does not, however, neglect the ominous side of teasing, that is, its function as social control of patients and the risks it can carry of alienating the patient if unwelcome or exaggerated. Of especial interest here (because we will also come across it in briefings) are her observations on the potential aggressive and controlling function of tease *questions*, which either force the target to answer (undermining their negative face) or leave them feeling uneasy or ridiculous (undermining their positive face):

NURSE: You look so handsome we'll have to get you a date won't we? Have you got any money? To take out? And get them a meal?
PATIENT: No
NURSE: Oh they're all fussy in here see they want to be treated like ladies
PATIENT: (3 syllables)
[...]
NURSE: What do you like blondes or brunettes? Eh?
PATIENT: Blondes [...]

(Grainger 2002)

The nurse may well have simply been attempting to include the patient in her banter but, as we have noted, the inherent risk of teasing is its ambiguity, its potential for perlocutionary mismatch between intention and effect. The problem is inescapable. Teasing builds solidarity precisely because the potential of an utterance to threaten or wound is deactivated by context but, especially among non-intimates who can make misguided assumptions about context and fellow participants, non-intentional reactivation is a constant danger. To summarize, Grainger argues that joke-play is invaluable in medical situations where drastic re-ranking is required but adds the salutary reminder that 'it is not enough [...] for the nursing literature to advocate the use of humour as a therapeutic tool, without understanding the relational dynamics in a particular situation' (2002). The effect of particular relational dynamics on teasing and joking in the briefings will be the object of study in this chapter.

What is needed at this point, however, is a working definition of teasing. Dictionary entries, such as:

> to irritate or provoke with persistent petty distractions, trifling raillery, or other annoyance, often in sport;
>
> (*Webster's*)

> To worry or irritate by persistent action which vexes or annoys; now esp. in lighter sense, to disturb by persistent petty annoyance, out of mere mischief or sport; to bother or plague in a petty way;
>
> (*O.E.D*)

> If you tease someone, you make fun of them, for example by embarrassing them or by making them believe something that is not true;
>
> (*Collins-Cobuild*)

seem to fail to capture the spirit of the phenomena described by Boxer and Cortés-Conde or by Grainger, while one dictionary's definition – 'to laugh at, joke about or *intentionally* annoy' – actually seems to be contradicted by one of its example: 'I was only teasing (= joking) I *didn't mean to* upset you' (*Cambridge International Dictionary*: my emphasis).

The corpus evidence, on the other hand, paints a very complex picture of the word. I prepared concordances of *tease(s)* and *teasing* from newspaper corpora, *Frown, Flob, Colt* and the other spoken sections of the *BNC* which demonstrated how its meaning is highly context sensitive and depends upon who the participants are and the situation they are in. When one adult teases another, the associations are often sexual: present satisfaction is being denied but the promise of possible future fulfilment is hinted at. This is occasionally explicit:

(1) Earlier this evening, seduction had been verbal – words **teased**, provoked. Now, immersed in the familiar world of his scent, talk was no longer an issue. He draped an arm over her shoulder as they walked toward his house [...]

(*Frown*)

but more often implicit, a matter of hints and allusions:

(2) [...] asks him to call her Lula Lula and offers him an apple. Clay responds with nervous politeness to her overtures, with bewildered politeness to the way she abruptly turns her back at the height of a **tease**.

(*Newspapers*)

(3) and because he would **tease** me now and then, I thought he liked me enough so that I could ask him to go out to dinner with me.

(*Frown*)

This sexual sense is, of course, the one inherent in *strip-tease* and other such uses of the word. This present-denial-for-future-promise marks the use of the word in other situations, frequently in games:

(4) Without it the masquerade loses some of its charm and fascination, as a **teasing** game, a quiz on identity, a test of reality;

(*Newspapers*)

in sports, where we find many *teasing kicks, crosses, balls* etc. which promise a score:

(5) For once, the **teasing** kicking of Davies, who produced a superbly weighted ball for Wyler to score, was not sufficient;

(*Newspapers*)

and in public performance where hopes are raised in audiences of future entertainment:

(6) Can handsome engaging Paul be a murderer? The solution doesn't quite come up to the **teasing** opening [...]

(*Newspapers*)

(7) It **teases** and intrigues from the start – a decoy solo planted in the orchestra to be picked off by the real one.

(*Newspapers*)

Note that the reception of such teasing by the teased is also varied. It can excite but also irritate, given its strong element of manipulation. And very frequently, of course, it can frustrate when the future promise fails to materialize.

In contrast, when participants are children, schoolchildren especially, the word takes on a much darker sense, much closer to mockery, taunting or any verbal abuse which stops short of physical violence:

(8) In Table 3 we list the most common responses given as to why children think they themselves are **teased**. These are that the teaser is being provocative, wanting a confrontation or even a fight;

(*Flob*)

(9) If you are not going to punish bullies then they have no incentive to stop **teasing** and victimising children more vulnerable that them.

(*Newspapers*)

(10) Research shows that these children are **teased** and ostracised by their schoolmates so that they grow up isolated and withdrawn.

(*Newspapers*)

(11) He had always skipped swimming because he got **teased** about his bones sticking out. Ribs like a xylophone, they said. Play us a tune, Hoomey. Is there a woodpecker in the changing room? No, it's Hoomey shivering.

(*Newspapers*)

It frequently co-occurs with modifiers and other terms which underline its aggressive or sadistic nature, such as *mercilessly, ruthlessly, detestable, bullied* and the like.

Teasing and verbal duelling 149

The most frequent use of *to tease* in texts not dealing either with juveniles or romance, however, seems to be where a speaker *displays* an emotion or opinions which somehow threaten or criticize or belittle the hearer(s) but where the threat or criticism is somehow hedged or understated:

(12)   he **teases** but will not humiliate or patronise;

(Newspapers)

and more especially still, where the attack is meant as less than fully serious, is performed in play frame:

(13)   indulging himself with a stream of long throws to the left touchline, and **teasing** the crowd by losing his balance on the goal line;

(Newspapers)

(14)   Yet it all sped by so quickly in a welter of laughter and **teasing**.

(Newspapers)

We might note that the revelation on the part of the teaser that their attack is non-serious is often delayed. In such cases the teasing act once again embodies a distinction between present and future states. This is made explicit in the conventionalized collocations *only teasing* and *just teasing*:

(15)   '[...] Men don't like that. Especially hearing about other men. It's natural. I wouldn't want you to tell me about your love affairs.'
'Wouldn't you?' I said. 'I was just going to tell you about my love affairs.'
'Were you truly?' she said with a flattering amount of alarm in her voice.
'I'm **just teasing**,' I said.
'Good,' she said. 'I don't want you to have any women in your life except me.'

(BNC)

Finally, in the following somewhat sarcastic example, note how *only teasing* explicitly coheres with the negation of *serious designs*:

(16)   It seems to be readily accepted among more than pacifists, Arabists, anti-semites and anti-Americans that Saddam has been **only teasing**. No expert, it is said, supposes that he has serious designs on Kuwait or other Gulf oil states.

(Newspapers)

A tease, then, in terms of the laughter-talk theories developed in this work, is a face-threatening act performed (apparently) in non-*bona-fide* mode. It is non-*bona fide* because it violates the maxim of sincerity. It is insincere in that it is (supposedly) not meant to really threaten H's face. It is (apparently) a fictional attack. Typically, but not necessarily, the 'victim' will be a single individual and the tease will take place before an audience. Sometimes, especially in high-risk situations (such as, for example, flirting with a stranger or in the hospital discourse discussed earlier, where misfiring could well lead to breakdown of the lines of communication), teasing will be accompanied by clear, unequivocal paralinguistic indications of play frame, for example, exaggerated intonation, smile or laugh voice, winking. However, in lower risk and more sophisticated talk, there may well be an almost complete absence of play mode signals, this absence actually being part of the game. In such cases, the non-*bona-fide* nature of the act has to be recovered solely by working through its contextual implicatures. In the briefings, in fact, a sort of deadpan tease was quite frequent.

Such a definition enables us to distinguish teasing from, first, serious, *bona fide* face attacks such as simple insults and, second, ridicule, defined as an insulting attack in play frame where there is no evidence that the speaker has any regard for the hearer's face or, indeed, where the speaker is deliberately attempting to aggressively compromise such face.

5.2 Who teases whom

5.2.1 Teasing absent parties

We can now turn our attention to examples of teasing in the briefings corpora, both *Dems* and *Reps*.

Boxer and Cortés-Conde (1997) make a distinction between teasing directed against an absent third party, which they see as 'bonding' or affiliating, and teasing of a present party which can be either bonding or 'biting'. The main third party butts here are the President (targeted by the press) and occasionally the opposition party (by the podium). In the latter case, Boxer and Cortés-Conde's (1997) prediction of bonding function seems to be fulfilled. We have already seen an example (Chapter 3) of a Democrat podium teasing the Republicans:

(17) MR. MCCURRY: Gingrich didn't vote for George Bush's program, and Armey didn't vote for it, and DeLay didn't vote it, and Kasich didn't vote for it. They opposed it. They said it would ruin the economy. And they said the same thing about Bill Clinton's program in 1993. John Kasich went so far to say if it worked he'd turn himself into a Democrat. And we've got the DNC sending him a membership application now. (Laughter)

and there are a couple more in the next chapter. Here is a Republican reciprocation:

(18) Q: Well, if the Democrats are moving towards the President, why wouldn't – they're being so accommodating, why wouldn't the President move a little bit towards them?
MR. FLEISCHER: They may keep moving. (Laughter)

which, we may notice in passing, has the added effect of avoiding the question.[2] There appears to be at least some audience alignment with the podium given the laughter which ensues. As Tholander and Aronsson point out, 'the most common aligning device is probably laughter' (2002: 584). Nor does anyone make a verbal move to the victims' defence.

When the object of a press tease is the President, the upshot is rarely to bond the two parties present, in contrast to the Boxer and Cortés-Conde prediction.

Teasing and verbal duelling 151

Teasing or mocking the President is highly face-threatening for the podium and, predictably, usually provokes either a spirited defence or at least a dampening one. We shall examine other occasions where the podium leaps to the defence of his masters in the section on cynicism and on responses to teasing.

On rare and special occasions only does the podium align with a teasing attack (in this case, a mildly sarcastic one) on his political masters (Bono is the *nom de plume* of the socially committed rock singer Paul Hewson):

(19) Q: Ari, we saw Bono coming in. What's his role in the aid announcement?
MR. FLEISCHER: Well, Bono has been a real proponent around the world of helping developing nations to achieve growth. The President's staff spoke with Bono in the formulation of the policy the President is making today. [...]
Q: They don't just think it's cool to hang out with him?
MR. FLEISCHER: You, too, think that? (Laughter)

The journalist's cynical comment on the President's staff is met by a skilful piece of play-acting. The response can superficially be read either as affiliating with the questioner ('I think that too') or as ingenuously asking whether this is the journalist's opinion ('I've heard some other people say the same but it would never have occurred to me'). But it contains a kind of double-bluff, the exaggerated intonation used by the podium is a signal not to take his ingenuity seriously, implying 'well, of course I think that too but I'm not allowed to say so'. The play frame allows what we might call 'strategic ambivalence' and the podium cannot be called to account for helping poke fun at his employers.

5.2.2 Teasing those in the room

Turning to teases enacted upon parties who are present, there is the occasional dig by one journalist at another. There is a certain degree of competition for time and the floor among the assembled journalists which can result in tension which needs defusing:

(20) Q: Please, proceed.
Q: – sorry – the Russians aren't part of that. Sorry, Sam.
Q: No, whatever time you require. (Laughter)

Sam here adopts a hyper-polite persona as an ironic tease in which the hyperbolic 'whatever time you require' implies the other may hog the floor (and is a warning not to do so). His tease recovers the face loss inherent in ceding the question to the other journalist. In another episode, example (21), a journalist has just asked a question about a particular Senator's activities but then a second journalist asks about this Senator's mistress. The first journalist exclaims:

(21) Q: I did not put him up to that, okay? I have nothing –
MR. FLEISCHER: I think I'll leave this to the two of you to figure out. (Laughter)

Differences among the journalists can thus allow the podium to act as an arbiter *super partes*, a superiority role that Mr Fleischer in particular much savours.

By far the majority of teases however are, predictably, exchanged between the podium and the journalists in the room, usually involving the teasing of one individual by another. Only very occasionally does the podium tease the whole audience, and in such cases it is mild, deliberately comic and non-threatening:

(22) MR. MCCURRY: How many people have done their taxes? [...] Less than 10 percent. What is wrong with you people? You must not have any refunds coming to you, right? (Laughter)
Q: I owe them.
MR. MCCURRY: The front row here, they all have accountants, so they don't have that problem [...] (Laughter)

The podium can ill afford to antagonize the whole room. The narrative adopted is the in-joke of money-chasing, the 'avaricious' in-script we have met elsewhere.

5.2.3 Collaborative teasing

In their study of classroom teasing, Tholander and Aronsson (2002) found that it was quite normal for teases to be co-constructed, an aspect of teasing which they claim has been seriously underanalysed in the past. Once a teasing attack has begun, other pupils would join in, an obvious and extreme form, of course, of alignment with the teaser. The phenomenon, though much rarer, is still observable among adults in the briefings.

In the following episode, we find a journalist who joins forces with the podium:

(23) MR. FLEISCHER: [...] John Roberts, did you have a question earlier? [...]
Q: [1] No. Some of us need to ask questions, and others already have the information. Today, I already have the information. (Laughter)
MR. FLEISCHER: That's very, very impressive. Major Garrett?
Q: [2] Ari, that's what we say when we know we're not getting on the air. (Laughter)
Q: [Audience] Ooooh!
Q: [1] No, that's what we say when we had the story five weeks ago.
Q: [2] Whatever story it is.
MR. FLEISCHER: Please, carry on. (Laughter)

The podium has an ironic risposte to Mr Roberts's claim to 'have the information', adopting a superiority/judgemental role, but does not dwell on the matter and appoints the next questioner. But another journalist inserts an unsolicited teasing move which is far more cynical than anything the podium has produced. The audience's 'ooooh!' signals recognition of the severity of the face threat.

Later, we will examine episodes when targets collaborate in their own teasing.

5.3 Types of tease

There have been few attempts in the psycho- or sociolinguistic literature to categorize types of tease. In the material examined here, there seem to be three general classes of tease which we might call, respectively, the *frustration*, the *fallibility* and the *mimicry* teases. A fourth sort, the *cynicism* tease displays elements of the other three.

5.3.1 *Frustration*

The first of these, the frustration tease, that is, teasing through withholding information (for the time being at least), is exemplified in the following episodes:

(24) MR. LOCKHART: Again, let me look at the first question, and I'll come back to you.
  Q: When will you come back?
  MR. LOCKHART: Maybe next week, maybe never. (Laughter) Next, please. (Laughter)

(25) Q: How could you predict so long ago that the Clinton-Lewinsky relationship would turn out – could turn out to be very complicated, without a simple, innocent explanation?
  MR. MCCURRY: Clairvoyance. (Laughter)

Such responses, while remaining conversationally cooperative (in that they at least address the question), are deliberately uncooperative *interactionally*. In Gricean terms, they flout the maxim of quantity in being far less informative than the interlocutor requires. Moreover, they defeat the expectations of briefings talk that the podium provide at least a minimally informative answer to questions, or if he fails to do so, that he supply an explanation. Having said this, the Q-R format of institutional talk makes it a fertile ground for this kind of information-withholding frustration tease.

The audience laughter occurs, presumably, as a result of the podium's adoption of an unexpected uncooperative role, reinforced in (24) by the flippant 'Next, please' which emphasizes that the question and the questioner have been liquidated to the podium's satisfaction. That such role shifts are also so blatantly evasive augments their laughter potential. However, the uncooperative behaviour is only relatively unexpected, it is one of the podium's set roles and so such frustration responses also have the status of a running joke. The podium clearly intends these quips to cause laughter, they are generally accompanied by signals of play frame and so the audience are primed, indeed 'instructed', to laugh. Instructing the audience to laugh in this way is a relatively high risk tactic; should the audience fail to deliver, this would be taken by all as a direct affront to the speaker's face.

In politeness terms, such responses (or 'non-answers' if, following Harris (1991), we define *answer* to be a response which satisfies the questioner) carry a considerable threat to face since they imply quite explicitly a lack of attention to

154 *Teasing and verbal duelling*

the interlocutor's interests and requirements. There is a degree of debate in the literature as to whether FTAs performed indirectly, particularly in play frame, are more or less severe than an equivalent performed without play or humour (Dews and Winner 1995; Jorgenson 1996; Toplak and Katz 2000). The examples here provide evidence that, in certain circumstances (especially in front of an audience), play can exacerbate the face threat. The podium in (24) could have replied 'I can't say' but his actual reply ('Maybe next week, maybe never') carries a hint of mockery, of deliberate and wilful frustration of the questioner. However, it has to be said that these teases are frequently greeted by the audience with considerable magnanimity. The journalists, through long experience, know that the podium will often avoid answering a question. A play evasion at least keeps them amused:

(26) MR. MCCURRY: Anything else?
      Q: What was the answer?
      MR. MCCURRY: Same one I gave now.
      Q: You wouldn't repeat it for us now, would you?
      MR. MCCURRY: Nope. (Laughter)

The majority of frustration teases in these texts are concerned with time. The following follow the same format as (24):

(27) MR. LOCKHART: There's been no decision made.
      Q: When will that decision be made?
      MR. LOCKHART: When I announce it. (Laughter)
(28) MR. LOCKHART: [...] It says here we'll arrive at 1:50 a.m. Don't count on it.
      Q: And the press plane arrives?
      MR. LOCKHART: Later. (Laughter)
(29) Q: Does the President agree with Baltimore's Mayor Schmoke, who was here today and is a close friend and ally of the President, in his statement that pedophilia is not a sexual orientation but is, 'an inclination'?
      [...]
      MR. LOCKHART: I would have to look more fully at his remarks before I would render any kind of judgment.
      Q: When will you have looked so I can inquire again?
      MR. LOCKHART: I would expect it to be early winter 2001. (Laughter)

In these episodes, the comic non-information is performed by pitching the temporal precision at the wrong or unexpected – and thoroughly unhelpful – level. Moreover in (29) the phrase 'early winter 2001' (said in May, 1999) belongs to a somewhat different register than briefings responses. As well as being absurdly distant, it sounds like a phrase from political or economic prediction. The three examples of *early* {season} + future date in the *Newspapers* corpus (whose texts date from 1993) were all from these fields:

1   The indicators are that the sale [of the Government's holding in British Coal] could come in the spring or *early summer of 1994*.

2   David Lewis, finance director, said the float was pencilled in for the spring or *early summer of 1994*.
3   Lord Scott said he hoped to [...] be able to deliver a report 'in the *early spring of 1994*'.

Note how this withholding-information ('but I might tell you one day') waggery resembles the flirtatious 'present-denial-for-future-promise' type of tease discussed in the introduction to this chapter.

5.3.2 *Fallibility*

In the second of the general classes of tease, the *fallibility* type, the butt is accused of some kind of error, shortcoming or misdemeanour, either openly or, more subtly, by implication. This form of teasing is clearly closely related to shaming as defined earlier, that is, the deliberate provocation of embarrassment by accusing the victim of having failed to be, act, behave or think in accordance with the standards which an implied community supposedly sees as good or proper.

One favoured topic of mild teasing is age (it being, of course, 'good' to be young):

(30)   MR. BERGER: [...] Allen and Rossi was the act that followed the Beatles on the Ed Sullivan Show in the early 1960s – small piece of trivia.
Q: You're dating yourself.
MR. BERGER: If you're too young, ask Wolf. (Laughter)

When the butt is a woman, the tease is probably seen as more face-threatening and certainly, in the following, produces quite a stir:

(31)   MR. LOCKHART: [...] But I do understand that there are some implications 20 years down the road – I hope none of us in this room are here then. (Laughter) For the record.
Q: Helen – (Laughter)

Helen Thomas (UPI) being, at the time, the senior member of the press corps. The first round of laughter is due to the sudden insertion of the familiar and personal into the business mode, allied to a hint of the 'tough job' in-script ('I hope none of us are here then'). The second follows the ironic indication that Helen could still be around – after all, she has been around since anyone can remember (this example will be analysed further in the next chapter).

Unsurprisingly, *real* fallibility, actual errors of fact – someone committing an authentic *faux pas* (see Chapter 3) – are seized upon:

(32)   Q1:   Could you explain why there have been no consequences for Secretary Rubin for publicly criticizing the steel –
Q2:   O'Neill.
Q1:   Oh, Secretary O'Neill, thank you. (Laughter)
MR. FLEISCHER: Did you have to correct him? I was going to work with him. (Laughter)

Q1: And I was thinking I was doing so well this time. Sorry. It's President Bush, right? (Laughter)
MR. FLEISCHER: That's correct.

There are three bouts of laughter in the transcription. The first follows the questioner's mistaking a protagonist's identity (all the more serious since Secretary Rubin actually worked for the previous administration). This kind of laughter is presumably related to glitches-in-business laughter, one of the protagonists – here a journalist – is misplaying their role. There may be an element of audience embarrassment management and *schadenfreude* – the other journalists are relieved not to be the butt themselves. Any mistake on either the podium's or a journalist's part is highly likely to receive attention, usually in the form of what we might call a 'rubbing-it-in' tease. In this case, Mr Fleischer issues a mock threat-cum-promise which simultaneously plays with register: 'I was going to work with him', meaning I was going to help him make a fool of himself and keep you, the audience, amused. The expression *work with* is frequent in podium talk, especially Mr Fleischer's.[3] It means everything from cooperate with or to have contact with, for example, 'how then do we work with Iran...?'. The journalist picks up the tone – and thereby saves a little face by projecting himself as a congenial type – and adopts the game or test fantasy in-script: 'I was thinking I was doing so well'. He follows up with a touch of self-deprecating sarcasm, involving exaggeration (it might be possible to forget who the Secretary is but hardly the President).

This example is interesting in the more or less explicit reference by the podium to the potentiality of teasing to shame the butt in public. It is also an illustration of how teasing may differ from more face-threatening forms of shaming (of which more below). Actually allowing someone to make a fool of themselves, and so commit long-term damage to their own face, would probably have to be classified as something different from a tease. But the *play-threat* to do so remains in the realm of teasing.

Some fallibility teases can be quite subtle, for instance (the podium has been asked about research into child abuse):

(33) MR. LOCKHART: The White House isn't aware of the academic research that they've done. I'd need to –
Q: It was published in the American Psychological Association –
MR. LOCKHART: It's sitting right on my bedstand. (Laughter) I just quite haven't gotten to that issue yet.

The suggestion that this highly academic research is 'bedside reading' is, of course, ironic. The primary, overt implication is that it is quite the reverse, heavy-going. The deeper, interactional implication, however, is that the questioner is being unreasonable in expecting anyone to have read it in the normal course of affairs. There is a conflict of philosophies and of evaluations here. The journalist is arguing that this is important literature and so should be read. The podium's risposte is that it is obscure and you cannot expect it to be read casually.

Drew (1987) notes that many teases contain 'a considerable degree of *contrastiveness*' in that one participant produces a second, very different reading of events often, as in (33), a bathetic one, in which the research in question falls from high, important literature to tedious verbiage. In one of Drew's examples:

(34)   NANCY: All I had to do was look at a cigarette and he was out of the chair lighting it.
EMMA: They do that before and after.

'Nancy's depiction of this man's chivalrous attentiveness' contrasts with 'Emma's cynical image of men's manipulative use of considerateness only to get what they want' (Drew 1987: 232). Given this contrastiveness, much, perhaps most, of teasing can be considered bisociative in form. Although the bathetic fall in the examples (33) and (34) regards the logical, surface targets, respectively, the research in question and men's sexual behaviour, the real interactional butts (and the *point* of the teases) are, in the first case, the questioner who suggests reading it and, in the second, the supposedly ingenuous Nancy.

One of the podium's favourite fallibility teases is the 'logical' tease, a playful accusation that one's interlocutor has indulged in faulty or quirky thinking:

(35)   Q: How long will that last? Will we find out by either seeing her or not seeing her? Or will we know sometime before that?
MR. FLEISCHER: Well, that certainly is one way. (Laughter)

(36)   MR. FLEISCHER: [...] The issue is pre-recorded, pre-taped information that obviously sits in a can and is released at a timing and in a manner of Osama bin Laden's choosing. It's not as if it's a live interview that any of you all would do. I think if somebody were to have a live interview, that's not –
[...]
Q: If you were Osama bin Laden would you give a live interview right now on satellite feed – (Laughter)

In the first of these, Mr Fleischer delivers his line deadpan. There are few intonational or gestural cues, only perhaps a slight lift of an eyebrow and a particularly direct look at the target. In the second, he does not join in the laughter but delivers only a mirthless half-smile. In both cases, the laughter is not immediate but when it comes it is loud and appreciative. Among participants who pride themselves on their intelligence, the logical tease is effective because of its intellectual aura: the strength of laughter is partly glee but also a self-congratulatory signal that the laugher has recognized and understood the subtlety.

Similarly, the implication may be that the interlocutor's past behaviour or experience is somehow logically incongruous:

(37)   MR LOCKHART: [...] Congratulations to Clyde Robinson, 30 years on the job. (Applause.) Where is he? Where is he? (Applause.)
Now, the only question I have is, you work for GE and it took you 30 years to get a refrigerator back there? (Laughter) Never mind. That's all.

158 *Teasing and verbal duelling*

This has the traits of a prepared joke, rather laboriously set up in this particular case. The humour works on the seeming paradox, with a bathetic touch, of working for General Electrics, a company which makes advanced electronics equipment, and having to wait thirty years for a refrigerator. The *point* of the tease is that the butt must somehow be inept or stupid. This is quite a refinement of the mistake tease.

Related to the logical tease is the 'definitional' tease, accusing the interlocutor of faulty semantics, of misusing language:

(38) MR. FLEISCHER: Well, I'm not going to discuss with you the timing of any military actions.
Q: Not timing, but just imminent as a kind of a –
MR. FLEISCHER: The last I look up 'imminent', it had something to do with a sense of time. (Laughter)

(39) MR. FLEISCHER: Well, I think he said the word 'soon', as I was reminded today by a very knowledgeable official at the State Department, that's called 'State Department soon'.
[…]
Q: The American people thought 'soon' meant 'soon'. (Laughter)

Or the podium might pick the questioner up on forgetting the name of a new government department:

(40) Q: Yesterday there was some skepticism expressed by some legislators about the President's proposal of creating the super ministry of internal security. Is the President willing to work with these people, but –
MR. FLEISCHER: I'm sorry, what did you call it? The super ministry of internal security? Which country is this? (Laughter) You mean the Department of Homeland Security?
Q: Okay, Homeland Security –
MR. FLEISCHER: I'm sorry, I couldn't resist.

This last episode is reminiscent of register play. The questioner's phrasing – 'the super ministry of internal security' – sounds un-American to the podium, reminiscent of the language usage of some kind of foreign dictatorship. 'Homeland' does indeed sound reassuring, non-threatening and one may presume it was chosen for this very reason.

One more variation is teasing the opponent on their confusing use of language:

(41) MR. FLEISCHER: As the Secretary [Powell] said in the Rose Garden, as we are able and as it unclassifies, which clearly implies it is a classified document that is not unclassified.
Q: Say that again. (Laughter)

There is clearly a contrastive tease with a bisociative, bathetic structure. The questioner replaces the business-like with the familiar, complex language with plain and, by adopting the role of simple, regular guy, implies that the podium is guilty of gobbledegook.

Closely related to the definitional tease is the 'own petard' ploy, that is, using the interlocutor's words – the more pompous the better – against them:[4]

(42)   MR. FLEISCHER: [...] I think one of the things, as the President has said, as the nation goes through all the effects of everything from September 11th is, keep the public informed. And we've talked about this before – the best way for our nation to win this war is through the forthright sharing of information. And that's important.
Q: Well, in that spirit, can you share the evidence against bin Laden? (Laughter)

The questioner receives a broad, indulgent smile, but, of course, no further information.

Another popular fallibility tease, especially beloved of Mr Fleischer, concerns 'briefings etiquette' – someone gets accused of ignorance thereof or simply bad briefings manners:

(43)   Q: Can I have one more on the mid-East, though? Do you mind? Don't answer that. (Laughter)
MR. FLEISCHER: Kelly, you may have your ninth question.
(44)   Q: Ari, I have a follow-up. My other one, my second one, Ari –
MR. FLEISCHER: How can you follow up when I didn't answer your first question? (Laughter)
(45)   Q: I was going to ask, because I wanted to go. What –
MR. FLEISCHER: Wait a minute. You can't ask a question and then leave. (little Laughter.)
Q: Thank you, Ari.
Q: When the President was –
MR. FLEISCHER: What about your colleagues' questions? (Laughter)

The implications are either that the target is slow to understand or downright inconsiderate.

5.3.3   *Mimicry*

Mimicry is tease by imitating the interlocutor in some way. In juvenile teasing, exaggerated mimicking of an interlocutor's voice is quite common and can of course be highly face-threatening (examples in Tholander and Aronsson 2002: 571, 574). A milder kind is when one participant picks up another's use of language and teasingly plays with it:

(46)   Q: Joe, can I ask one more on the budget before we get to something dramatically different? (Laughter)
Q: How do you know it's going to be dramatically different?
MR. LOCKHART: Wait a second. I'm in a dramatic mood. (Laughter)

160   *Teasing and verbal duelling*

There is accompanying horseplay as the podium assumes a melodramatic expression.

The following tease is a little sharper:

(47)   Q: No, I don't want you to write the deal, but if those trade-offs are really excellent and the benefits to children and the American people are really terrific, better than you can imagine – (laughter)

The question contains a mocking *pseudo*-echo of podium speak. A great deal has been written on the echoic quality of much aggressive language, especially in the wake of Wilson and Sperber's (1992) echoic theory of irony (section 6.2). Generally speaking, however, in 'polite' discourse, 'pure' echo is rare, whilst pseudo-echo is more common. The questioner produces a number of hyperbolic-sounding phrases which he feels the audience might associate with podium language, piles them together in an exaggeration which produces a kind of caricature of such language. Several authors, including Drew (1987) and Grainger (2002) mention the role of exaggeration in teasing. Another tactic is to pick up on one of the victim's favourite themes:

(48)   Q: Not to ask a hypothetical question, because I know your aversion to that – (laughter) –

Mr Lockhart, in particular, has in the past made it abundantly clear he will not answer what he calls 'hypothetical' questions:

(49)   I'm not going to speculate on a hypothetical;
(50)   I'm not going to get into a situation of complex hypotheticals;
(51)   We are well into double, if not triple, hypotheticals;

and so (48) has the status of an in-joke.[5]

The mimicry tease is another bisociative form. It replaces the target's interpretation of a certain expression with quite another reading by placing it in a different context, a rereading, a reformulation which pokes fun at the original one; yet another example of bathos.

Why should mimicry of this kind be so face-threatening?[6] One reason must be that the interlocutor switches unexpectedly from discourse *ad rem* to *ad personam*, switches from dealing with what you have said to how you have said it. This both shows a bald on-record lack of care and respect on the part of the interlocutor for your opinions and beliefs and implies that what you have said is somehow trivial.

5.3.4   *Cynicism and teasing*

There is another kind of tease, in which one party implies that the other's motives are less honourable than he or she wishes the world to believe. We might call this the cynicism tease and it combines elements of the three kinds so far treated. It incorporates an accusation of fallibility – of not living up to proper standards of openness – but it also stops the other speaker in their tracks and is highly

Teasing and verbal duelling 161

frustrating. Moreover, such teases frequently contain an explicitly imitating echo:

(52)   MR. TOIV: There's a three-day trip to five states. The President's looking forward to visiting every one of them.
      Q: He's looking forward to collecting money from every one of them for the Democratic party. (Laughter)
      MR. TOIV: He's looking forward to helping some very good candidates in those states and also talking about some very important issues.

The operative feature of the questioner's tease is the ironic and bathetic transposition of the benign 'visiting' narrative to an avaricious 'collecting money' one. Laughter occurs at this unexpected change of narratives and also thanks to the skilful rhetoric of the face attack with such an openly aggressive display of cynicism. This episode is discussed further in section 5.4.3.

Accusations of cynicism are largely one-directional, they are made by the press against the podium or his clients (with the exception discussed in Chapter 3, example 36). For example:

(53)   Q: And just one other question about this. Can the President imagine a deal that would both meet his objectives and also, when it's announced, boost the stock of the tobacco companies? (Laughter) No, I mean, is that – is something that is good for the tobacco companies' bottom line also –

The laughter is partly in acknowledgement of the cleverness in juxtaposing the two impossible objectives and putting the podium in a tight spot. However, the speaker is also being cynical about the President's activities, implying not only that his motivations are political but that he is altogether sly and devious.

The podium is correspondingly annoyed and dismissive:

(54)   MR. MCCURRY: It's a wildly hypothetical question that leads to speculative activity in the market – two good reasons not to respond.

Surprisingly, perhaps, not all cynicism teases are greeted with such irritation. In fact, they often appear to be received with a certain amount of patience or *playing along* (see next section). In the following episode, the journalists have just been complaining about the lack of opportunity to question the President directly:

(55)   MR. FLEISCHER: – and I understand that you would like him to take questions in the form of a news conference. I assure you we take a look at this often, and –
      Q: And say no. (Laughter)
      MR. FLEISCHER: And say no.

and see Chapter 2 example (48). In both cases, the podium chooses not to rise to the attack, a tactic which, as we shall see, has its own merits.

In both of these episodes, the journalist intervenes to complete the other's turn, a common and very effective way of delivering a cynicism attack. Again the bisociative nature of the tease is apparent. The interruption abruptly turns down the podium's narrative, replacing, in the first case, 'we examine all questions openly' (fairness) with 'you only pretend to examine them' (hypocrisy) and in the second, 'we are careful and punctilious in our planning' with 'you are disingenuous and obsessed with spin'. But the transformation goes deeper still. The second speaker replaces the high-flown rhetoric with a much more worldly register, and she also converts the serious frame to the comic.

5.4 Reactions and responses to teasing

5.4.1 Range of reactions

We have so far concentrated on the teaser and the tease. Two important papers, on the other hand, look at how subjects react to being teased, the first in adult telephone conversations (Drew 1987), the second in early teen classroom interaction (Tholander and Aronsson 2002). Drew proposes a playful-serious continuum in the receipt of teasing, which Tholander and Aronsson combine with a defensive-offensive reaction cline. When combined, they allow us to envisage a wide range of possible reactions, including:

- *minimal response*: no direct response to the tease is apparent;
- *denials*: the victim simply disputes they were involved in the behaviour being criticized;
- *accounts*, comprising both *excuses* and *justifications*: in an *excuse* the teased 'admits that the act in question is untoward, but denies full responsibility for it; in a *justification*, the teased 'accepts responsibility for the act, but denies its deprecatory qualities' (Tholander and Aronsson 2002: 567);
- *going along* and *playing along*;
- *playful* and *serious retaliation*;
- *proactive response work*: the target tries somehow to prevent future teasing (to *inoculate* themselves).

Somewhat to his surprise, Drew finds that in his adult material most victims respond in a serious vein, in what he calls a 'po-faced' manner. In other words, minimal responses, accounts and denials comprise the lion's share of reaction types. In contrast, Tholander and Aronsson find that, in their classroom talk, where teasing is endemic and the ability to respond appropriately is a paramount skill, the situation is very different. Very rarely is a tease disregarded among these teenagers: 'the targets of teasing almost never chose to ignore the attacks' and pupils adopt a wide array of creative and refined rejoinder strategies: 'the ways in which they responded were just as varied and sophisticated as the ways in which they were attacked' (2002: 584). Moreover, offensive strategies which included both retaliation and proactive 'inoculation' against future attacks were found to be more successful in warding off criticism. Given the vital importance for teenagers of not revealing that teasing has caused hurt, there was also much more humour in their reactions both when playing along and when retaliating in teasing kind.

Teasing and verbal duelling   163

The hypothesis to be embraced here is that reaction to teasing in the briefings will fall between the two stools. The participants are, of course, adult intimates (or *pseudo*-intimates), as Drew's experimental subjects. But the interaction also takes place before an audience, which means that face is at high risk, as in the classroom situation. Commitment, then, to face preservation or enhancement, to winning or at least not being seen to lose, will presumably be higher than in a one-to-one telephone conversation.

5.4.2   How the journalists react

One special feature of briefings is that the podium has the microphone, and has the power (and duty) to nominate speakers. This makes it correspondingly more difficult for members of the audience to make their response audible or, more importantly, to make it in time before the podium, after his barb, has swiftly moved on to the next questioner. As already mentioned, a favourite tease of Mr Fleischer's, a podium who is particularly committed to winning competitive encounters, is to remind a journalist of briefings etiquette, of 'how we do things here' (a form of fallibility tease, as we saw above):

(56)   Q: Any more you can say on the progress –
        MR. FLEISCHER: Connie.
        Q: Thank you –
        MR. FLEISCHER: Kelly, didn't you have yours already? You did. (Laughter)
        Q: Other people get more than one. (Laughter)
        MR. FLEISCHER: You did. Remember, this is our orderly system. And then we come back to the front, and you ask something, and we go to – Connie. (Laughter)

The podium's first move to Kelly ('didn't you have yours already?') is delivered with exaggerated fall-rise intonation, like a teacher speaking to a refractory pupil, clearly signalling play frame and at the same time a 'superiority' role. Kelly responds at first with an account, a justification, that she only wants to be treated as others have been. It too is delivered in play mode; it is the kind of account a child might produce. In other words, Kelly temporarily plays along with Mr Fleischer's frame and the role assigned to her within it. It is interesting to observe that any single tease response can combine strategies from the Tholander and Aronsson list: here Kelly fuses an account form with playing along delivery.

Tholander and Aronsson argue that playing along is one of the more sophisticated types of response, as well as one of the most effective, in that 'the target shows that s/he is unperturbed by avoiding displaying recognition of the tease' (2002: 577). Moreover, if a malicious or potentially deeply threatening tease is *treated* as if it were merely playful, 'the target of the tease can transform a seemingly malicious attack into a humorous remark'. In this way the quality of a tease is 'partly defined dialogically (by the way it is received)' (2002: 578). Example (32) is an instance of a journalist playing along in this manner ('Sorry. It's President Bush, right?').

164   *Teasing and verbal duelling*

However, Kelly's playing along in (56) seems altogether different. Rather than being a sophisticated response, playing along can also, it would seem, be simply a default reaction when one can think of no suitable reprisal. Nor does she save herself. Her account – 'other people get more than one' – can, unfortunately for her, be read by a prickly podium such as Mr Fleischer as criticism of his floor distribution. She is thus subjected to further teasing – treated as a 'slow learner' – and, to add injury to insult, is denied the further turn she requested since the podium confirms his nomination of Connie. This latter immediately begins her question: 'Thank you. Does the massive pro-Israeli demonstration yesterday...' and Kelly has no chance to retaliate without interrupting a colleague. As we have noted, control of next speaker nomination can be a powerful weapon in face wars.

The next example involves the same protagonists and a similar kind of briefings etiquette reminder tease:

(57) Q: Week ahead?
MR. FLEISCHER: Let me give the week ahead.
Q: Can I have one more on the mid-East, though? Do you mind? Don't answer that. (Laughter)
MR. FLEISCHER: Kelly, you may have your ninth question.
Q: Okay. What can account for some feeling on the part of the Israelis, Israeli government [...]

On this occasion Kelly delivers a minimal response to the podium's exaggeration tease, that is, her 'Okay' non-committally acknowledges that she has been given the floor. Minimal responses may not seem like a particularly effective way to counter teasing but, as Tholander and Aronsson point out, since 'there is not enough information to code the response as defensive or as offensive', they are 'always ambiguous' (2002: 574). The teaser is left in doubt as to whether their attack has hit home. We might add that the butt also turns down the first speaker's play frame, which can itself be an aggressive face move (see, for instance, Chapter 3, example 20: 'I understand you like to make jokes'). In the classroom this is of little avail since teasers will tend to continue to impose their tease frame until they obtain a more informative response. In the (hopefully) more adult and restrained environment of briefings this is less of a danger. Moreover, as in this example, questioners may well desist from retaliation simply because it is more important to get the business of questioning done without distractions and without wasting their own and colleagues' time.

5.4.3   *How the podium reacts*

Turning to episodes when the podium is on the receiving end, it is generally in their interest to show they can take a good-natured quip in their stride. If the attack is not too serious and is directed against them rather than their political masters, a frequent strategy is to join in, to play along (Scott is Scott McClellan, another White House spokesperson):

(58)   [...] because the President would surely take a pay cut rather than lay off you and Scott, wouldn't he? (Laughter)
MR. FLEISCHER: You're half right. (Laughter)
(59)   Q: [1] A dodge. That's an evasion, Ari.
Q: [2] No, the evasion will be me.
MR. FLEISCHER: Do you have a question I can evade?

Sometimes the podium can even *initiate* the tease:

(60)   Q: You can fool some of the people some of the time [...]
MR. FLEISCHER: That's why I'm here.

which, of course, reinterprets Lincoln's celebrated aphorism from a warning into a double tease, of both self and his audience.[7] The advantage of such pre-emptive self-teasing is that it allows the self-teaser/butt to dictate the terms of the tease. Another instance is to be found in Chapter 3, example (28) – 'Want a little bit more of that? [...] I don't think they're going to ask that question again' – where Mr McCurry senses a tease might be in the offing and so he creates a tease which reflects as much as possible to his own credit: 'I was blustering but I only do so because it's my job ("regular guy" script) and I still managed to give you a hard time' ('tough guy' script).

Of all the podiums here, Mr Fleischer, whose persona as authority is of importance to him, is the most likely to respond with a retaliation. On some occasions with justification:

(61)   MR. FLEISCHER: The President will travel to Orlando, Florida, on Wednesday, March 21, to speak to the American College of Cardiology's annual convention. And that will be a day trip, for your planning purposes.
Q: Is Cheney going? (Laughter)
MR. FLEISCHER: Are you? (Laughter)

The tease is a cruel one since Mr Cheney had recently suffered a heart-attack. The podium's quick repartee admonishes the questioner and reminds him that he might one day be in the same need.

On other occasions, however, retaliation simply seems to be Mr Fleischer's first choice, his default reaction:

(62)   Q: All right. And another question, could you give graphic detail as to your disappointment about Turkey? (Laughter)
MR. FLEISCHER: Work with me, is there something specific you're looking for? (Laughter)
Q: I mean, just, though I understand –
MR. FLEISCHER: Would this be verbal, would this be –
Q: – smarty-pants. (Laughter)

166 *Teasing and verbal duelling*

The questioner is using a mimic tease since the podium has spoken earlier of his 'disappointment' with Turkey's lack of cooperation with US war plans. This is accompanied by another play signal, the phrase 'graphic detail', comic incongruous register insertion. The podium counter-attacks whilst, conveniently, omitting to address the question, a delicate one since Turkey was an ally of the United States at the time.

But occasionally, as we saw in Chapter 3, a podium will be caught *in flagrante delicto* with no attenuating circumstances. How does Mr Fleischer react in these circumstances?

(63) Q: Where in Northern Ireland will the two leaders meet?
 MR. FLEISCHER: Dublin.
 Q: No, no.
 MR. FLEISCHER: I'm sorry. I'm sorry. I said, 'Dublin.' I had written down Belfast and I said 'Dublin.' Belfast.
 Q: A historic development, Ari. (Laughter)
 MR. FLEISCHER: Thank you for the – I was not a geography major. (Laughter)

The audience underline his factual mistake in indicating Dublin as capital of Northern Ireland. Mr Fleischer at first responds with a rather weak account, an *excuse* in that he 'admits that the act in question is untoward' (he can hardly do otherwise), 'but denies full responsibility for it' (Tholander and Aronsson 2002: 567). One of the journalists produces a mild 'rubbing-it-in' tease, ironically complimenting the podium on his 'historic' achievement of uniting the two Irelands. Mr Fleischer is about to retaliate ('Thank you for the...') but thinks better of it and finally retreats into a slightly self-deprecatory comment.

When the issue is a very serious one, however, podiums will generally produce a non-humorous – or 'po-faced' – response:

(64) Q: You mentioned that Saddam Hussein has been in a box, a very tight box for quite a long time, but every six months or so he seems to act up. Is there any U.S. plan to try to keep him more firmly in this box?
 COLONEL CROWLEY: Again, these are expressly the kind of issues we'll consult with the Security Council in the coming days. But I think that we have maintained a tight rein on Saddam. He is not currently a threat to his neighbors. And we'll have to wait and see.

There is sarcasm in the questioner's production of a mimic tease which drags up the Colonel's previous colourful, figurative phrase 'keep...in a tight box'. Note how the podium in his response transforms the phrase in question to 'maintain a tight rein on...'.

Where we are particularly unlikely to find the podium playing along is when the attack is directed at the President, as in example (52). The President has been accused of cynical money-grasping: 'He's looking forward to collecting money from every one of them.' Mr Toiv's rather exasperated rejoinder, 'He's looking forward to helping some very good candidates in those states and also talking about some very important issues', is indeed 'po-faced' in Drew's terms, but of precisely what type is it? It has some of the features of denials and some of accounts but it is not quite either. It involves a reformulation (section 4.6.5) of the other party's version of events, and of the language they have employed. In terms of teasing types we might call it a *corrective*, a category to be added to Tholander and Aronsson's list. In a corrective response, the target does not explicitly deny or decline responsibility for the indicted behaviour but corrects the version of events given or implied in the tease. In general conversation, especially among juveniles, they are conventionally introduced by phrases such as 'for your information...', 'if you really want to know...'.

Corrective reformulations are highly contrastive. They rely for their interactional effect on emphasizing one's non-alignment with the play frame of the previous speaker, replacing it with a punctilious hyper-seriousness which – one hopes – will of itself condemn the other's levity:

(65) [...] the President is going the last mile for diplomacy. We shall see if the other nations in the Security Council are willing to entertain that last mile. We shall see.
Q: Is the last mile 10 days long?
MR. FLEISCHER: Not going – (laughter) – I'm not going to define either the duration of the last mile or the length of the last mile.

They can certainly dampen spirits and one suspects they are not always very successful in winning over an audience. In the following, the podium seems to realize that he might perhaps have been overserious and mistaken the mood of his audience:

(66) MR. FLEISCHER: [...] I cite Secretary Powell's words today. As the Secretary said in the Rose Garden, as we are able and as it unclassifies, which clearly implies it is a classified document that is not unclassified.
Q: Say that again. (Laughter)
MR. FLEISCHER: It's a classified document that is not unclassified. The Secretary said, as we are able and as it unclassifies – those are his words [...]

He at first insists, then eventually disowns the odd-sounding language.

5.4.4 Audience reaction

Another aspect of teasing which has received little attention in the literature is the role, or in Goffman's (1981) and Levinson's (1988) terms, the *participation status* of the audience of a tease. In these briefings it can vary considerably and is often a highly active one, the audience influencing the interaction very directly.

We have already noted Tholander and Aronsson's observation that laughter frequently signals audience affiliation with the teaser. Since all parties in briefings are acutely conscious of this fact, attempts are constantly made to win over this affiliation. The audience in effect is used as an arbiter, a jury. In the episode already partially discussed in section 5.3.2 as embodying a clash of logics:

(67) Q: It was published in the American Psychological Association –
MR. LOCKHART: It's sitting right on my bedstand. (Laughter) I just quite haven't gotten to that issue yet.

there is a combination of other and self tease. There is an admission of shortcoming – of not having read the work – but this is inextricably bound to the suggestion that the questioner is unreasonable in their expectations, and perhaps wearisome in their choice of reading matter. But the point is that the podium's employment of laughter-talk has the instrumental aim of encouraging the audience to accept his thesis. Amusing an audience, maybe even your interlocutor, can help win them to your side. Laughter creators are seen as both congenial but also as powerful, even dangerous (they might ridicule you) and it might well be best to side with them, a process which can include adopting their argument and reading of events. The participant role of the audience in the tease in the previous example can be described as the *beneficiary* (Partington 2003: 57–58) of the discourse, the party for whom it is ultimately designed.

But the influence the audience exerts is by no means limited to arbitration. It has the power to transform events. In the data there are several episodes in which the import of a participant's move seems unclear or ambiguous, and it is often the audience's reaction which decides which kind of event has occurred. The following are potential examples:

(68) Q: Can you give us some kind of time frame?
MR. FLEISCHER: Of course not. (Laughter)
(69) MR. FLEISCHER: And what's the name of that official?
Q: The official is unnamed. But it is –
MR. FLEISCHER: Then how do you know he's 'top'? (Laughter)
(70) MR. FLEISCHER: You're easy to read, David. (Laughter)

The laughter here is not easy to interpret. The moves it follows all appear at first sight non-humorous and to constitute rather serious face-threats. It may therefore be simply embarrassment management laughter or glee at someone's discomfiture but, in some instances at least, it may denote that the audience is treating the move as non-serious, as a play-attack.

On other occasions the audience is more active still and as a group seems almost to collaborate in the production of the discourse:

(71) Q: Mike, are you going to write a book?
MR. MCCURRY: No. Well, not immediately. I might – (laughter) My agent advised me never to say 'no.' (Laughter)

The event at this point is in interactional mode, the talk is about Mr McCurry's personal plans on retiring from the post as White House spokesperson and so the situation is already primed for laughter. Mr McCurry begins to give a serious, informative answer to the question but the audience's expectation and desire to be amused is so strong that it almost forces him to switch to play frame, which he enters with a bathetic self-tease adopting the familiar and comradely making-a-buck in-script.

Each member of the audience is also a *potential* producer as well as recipient. This is most evident in the classroom discourse where participants move back and forth between the roles of producer, recipient and beneficiary with great rapidity. In briefings too any individual in the audience can intervene to engage either the podium or another journalist (though the latter will usually mean interrupting or chipping in). What is most striking is how the audience *as a whole* is an arbiter, a client to be assuaged, kept happy and won over, and thus helps shape the nature of what is said.

5.4.5 Conclusions on reactions to teasing

The strategies that victims adopt in reaction to teasing, then, depend on various factors: judgements about the seriousness of the tease, evaluation of the seriousness of the topic, contingent considerations such as time constraints and the need to maintain politeness norms among colleagues and, of course, the personality of the victim. Not to mention individual skill in devising a suitable response and whether one fears further comeback from the adversary.

Different strategies each have their own special merits and demerits. We find very few out-and-out *denials* in these briefings, the following being the clearest case (the context is President Clinton's supposed unwillingness to take questions from the press during the Ms Lewinsky investigations):

(72) Q: Mike [...] why has the President made it a practice in recent days [...] to beat such a hasty retreat from the podium after he's made a statement? He almost knocks over people. He ran into the flag on his way out this morning. Has he become –
MR. MCCURRY: Oh, that's not true.
Q: Well, it is true.

Mr McCurry reacts to the sarcastic portrayal of a clumsy and timorous President. But the episode reveals why simple denial is rare in this context: it is unproductive. In place of denials the podium is better advised to produce reformulations-correctives which have the advantage, first of all, of sounding less puerile and, then, of presenting an alternative, more favourable version of affairs.

Minimal responses, as we have seen, have the advantage of leaving the teaser unsure of the effect of their tease and of getting the tease out of the way. It is a low-risk strategy but it has, of course, the disadvantage of not inoculating against future attacks. It is at the opposite end of the spectrum to *retaliation*, the high-risk strategy which, by engaging the teaser, risks prolonging the tease or even provoking the antagonist into some more face-threatening or even malicious behaviour (see following sections). But retaliation has the merit of potentially making the attacker think twice next time.

Somewhere in the middle are *accounts* which would seem to have the double drawback of neither putting an end to the tease nor inoculating against future teasing. Moreover, according to Tholander and Aronsson, they both acknowledge the tease and also, because they are serious responses, admit culpability: 'only a person who feels guilty of having committed a "real" transgression responds seriously to a tease and thereby reveals the felicity of it' (2002: 587). Although Drew found accounts to be common in his adult interaction, there is often an element of correction in them which place the teased party's activities in a better light:

(73) DEL: What are you doing at home?
PAUL: Sitting down watching the tube
DEL: Watching daytime stories uh?
PAUL: No I was just watching this, um, you know, one of them game shows.

(although it is a moot point whether game shows are more meritorious than fiction).

The great advantage of *playing along* with the tease is that, although the attack is acknowledged and the transgression is admitted, a signal is sent that no serious guilt is felt and so the felicity, the barb of the tease is blunted. In addition, of course, the butt can reinforce their credentials as a congenial sort with the same sense of humour as the group: playing along aligns the target with the teaser(s). It might fail to inoculate against future attacks but it makes the prospect of any malicious re-teasing somehow less satisfying. We might conclude, then, that a tease is only fully and properly effective when it is perceived and treated as such by the target as well as by the teaser and the audience.

Finally, in many circumstances, pro-active work, especially the counter-tease, is a highly effective response in that it both preserves face and helps inoculate against further attack. When overused, however, it can portray the speaker as thin-skinned and aggressive, which is why not all podiums resort to it as often as they might. It also requires a high degree of verbal skill and, if the interlocutor rises again, there is the risk of being sucked into a sort of recursive cycle of teasing (see the next section on verbal duelling).

These considerations remind us of the observations made in section 3.3.4 on the nature of face in interaction, namely that people appear to have two principal sorts of positive face: a competence and an affective face. By convincing others that we are capable and authoritative we address our competence face. We reinforce our affective face by persuading our peers that we are congenial and aspire to belong to the same in-group as them. We attempt to stress this belonging in many ways, including by teasing others, temporarily casting them in the role of outsider to accentuate the sense of solidarity and affiliation of the remaining members (in-group belonging being in sharpest focus only when there is an out-group for contrast). If the target plays along with the tease they do not entirely forfeit their group membership, although their competence (authoritative) face may well be diminished. Conversely, resistance to teasing – which might take various forms from 'over reacting' to po-facedness – may well entail a loss of affective face on the part of the teased party. The podium in particular, being most at risk of group exclusion, has to exercise careful judgement in such matters.

5.5 Verbal duelling

Generally, then, it would seem that the most effective way of responding to a tease in front of an audience is with a counter-tease, especially if it is in the same vein, that is, if one reacts with the same degree of play and aggression as the original attack. If the response is too meek, competence face may be lost, if too aggressive, congeniality face may be at risk. But if the reply is well-calibrated, all faces are preserved and no one is left smarting for revenge. For example (on Kosovar Albanian refugees; Arkansas was the President's home state):

(74) Q: Have we given any thought to where we're going to put these 20,000 –
 MR. LOCKHART: We've given a lot of thought to it, we just haven't come to a final conclusion.
 Q: – suggested that they put them in Arkansas. (Laughter)
 MR. LOCKHART: I will pass that suggestion on with your name on it. (Laughter)

Here the tease is meant for the President but, as already noted, teasing the President is also vicariously teasing his proxy, the podium. But since there is a perfect symmetry between the question and response in the second exchange pair in example (74), each comprising a mock threat, another classic tease mechanism, honour is even. This episode also indicates how, very often, if the question is met with laughter so is the response, laughter being, as it were, 'in the air'.

The next example, however, is a lesson to all would-be teasers:

(75) Q: Were you going to ever announce this, or was there some reason – (Laughter)
 MR. LEAVY: It's in the bins, back there.
 MR. LOCKHART: What do you think, guys? I think I've got them now. Should I let it go, or – (laughter) – come on, Terry, let's go find it. (Laughter).

If you are going to indulge in teasing, get your facts right. The questioner asks 'why haven't you announced...', but in a clearly sarcastic manner. Mr Leavy replies that a press release on the matter is already on the record and readily available ('in the bins'). This is obviously highly embarrassing for the questioner and the podium milks the situation.

As these examples show, successfully countering a tease with another is a powerful rhetorical ploy. As long as the second move remains within the bounds of play frame the speaker appears congenial, rhetorically skilful and has the benefit of having the last word, which, as Vuchinich points out, 'does not win a conflict but it does show that you haven't given in' (1990: 133).

Such duelling exchanges are, of course, in the interpretative framework adopted in this work, the working out of clashes of face. Consider the following:

(76) MR. FLEISCHER: Actually I haven't seen stories that said 15-percent increase each year over three years.

172 *Teasing and verbal duelling*

Q: I believe there was one in The New York Times, actually. (Laughter)

This first bout of laughter is at the podium's expense. The questioner is in fact the *New York Times* journalist who wrote the article. The hedging phraseology 'I believe...actually' is a sarcastic understatement. But the podium is not so easily bettered:

(77) MR. FLEISCHER: Yes, I think that story said 15 percent in the first year.
Q: No, I know what I wrote. (Laughter)
MR. FLEISCHER: I know what I read. (Laughter)

The journalist's one-upmanship is twice successfully faced down. The entirely reasonable argument that since I wrote the article, I know what it says, is countered by a rather more novel one – presented by the podium, however, as just as reasonable – that since I *read* the article, I also know what it says, a logic so superficially perfect (thanks to the use of a parallel and echoic phrase in the retort – 'I know what I wrote: 'I know what I read') that the journalist has little chance of producing an appropriate 'last word'. When face is under attack, rhetorical expertise is often a far more powerful tool than either logic or common sense.

As the next episode shows, the desire to have the last word can lead speakers to step beyond the bounds of play, to appear overcommitted to 'winning':

(78) MR. FLEISCHER: Bob.
Q: But wait a minute.
MR. FLEISCHER: Bob. We're going to keep moving. We're losing our audience. People are walking out. (Laughter)
Q: Well, that's not my problem. I have a question I want answered.
MR. FLEISCHER: Well, they walked out in the middle of your question. (Laughter)
Q: They wanted some other stuff. (Laughter) Anyway, what was the impetus of this 'Ask the White House'? What was the impetus; why?

The journalist in this exchange has already had several moves and Mr Fleischer decides it is time to nominate someone else (Bob). The questioner indicates that she has not finished but the podium tries to insist. He adopts a play strategy, switching to a 'performance' or 'stage' narrative ('we're losing our audience', which is delivered in a higher voice pitch accompanied by an imitation Jewish voice, accompanied by a hand gesture sweeping the room) which is, in effect, a fallibility tease combined with a joke account, that is a reason for his refusal of the journalist's request to continue. His intention is probably to hedge the threat to the hearer's face, which would have been worse had he simply said 'you have had the floor long enough'. This is therefore an instance when play seems intended to reduce the gravity of the FTA.

Journalists generally acquiesce to this kind of appeal to communal responsibility ('to keep moving'), but in this instance the journalist takes advantage of the room for manoeuvre that the indirectness and non-obligation of play mode allows the hearer to insist on her follow-up, at the same time rather aggressively refusing to respond to the play frame set by the podium. The podium realizes at this point that he cannot continue to refuse the journalist's request without turning the situation into one of direct conflict, but, at the same time, he is unwilling to submit completely. He therefore repeats his tease in a rather more personal manner ('they walked out in the middle of *your* question'). The response is delivered in an argumentative, justificatory tone but is followed by a smile, indicating play, thus allowing the speaker to get the best of both worlds: he first makes his point in serious mode and then retreats into non-serious mode, making it harder for the interlocutor to hold him to account. This leaves the journalist with a rather Pyrrhic victory, in command of the field but having suffered a loss of face. Nevertheless, having apparently won the day, there is some mollification of her aggressiveness in the next move ('they wanted some other stuff'), which we can see as negotiating a return to normal relations. Moreover, in recompense, she succeeds in obtaining the last word – reinforced by the following 'anyway', a topic-changing device which makes it difficult for the interlocutor to return to the fray should they so wish.

The second and third laughter bouts here appear to be audience embarrassment-management effects provoked by the underlying conflict, given that there appears to be little overt humour in the moves they accompany – one follows on the repetition of an earlier quip ('they walked out...'), the second on a simple self-justifying account-type rejoinder ('They wanted some other stuff').

5.6 Beyond the tease

In the last few episodes we have seen moves where the interaction gets quite aggressive. We have argued that 'teasing' involves some sort of deliberate limiting of the force of an attack to the hearer's face, that is, the teaser withholds the full weight of aggression by couching it in play frame, thus implying that some attention at least is being paid to that face. But a number of commentators have noted that the tease form can be utilized as a kind of mask for a fully fledged attack whose substance, whose perlocution, implies no care for the target's face. In Raskin's terms, an attack may pretend to be a tease – and therefore an FTA but one performed in non-*bona-fide* mode, whereas it is in actual fact meant as a *bona-fide* FTA. Brown and Levinson are still more explicit: 'there is the further exploitation of insulting someone in front of an audience, so that the audience thinks that the insult is merely such an assertion of intimacy, while the addressee (wounded by an accurate dart) is forced to accept it lightly' (1987: 229). To return to Boxer and Cortés-Conde's metaphor, a 'bite', whether in play frame or not, remains a bite, even though the audience may see it merely as a 'nip'.

Here we consider episodes which, in my view, go beyond a tease, where the fate of the hearer's face, whether or not it suffers long-term damage, appears to be of little consequence to the speaker. We will call such acts *taunts*.

174   *Teasing and verbal duelling*

Delivery is, of course, a vital consideration in distinguishing between a tease and a taunt. In one example, previously considered under bad manners teasing:

(79)   Q: I was going to ask, because I wanted to go. What –
        MR. FLEISCHER: Wait a minute. You can't ask a question and then leave. (Laughter)
        Q: Thank you, Ari.
        Q: When the President was –
        MR. FLEISCHER: What about your colleagues' questions? (Laughter)

the attack is delivered with little sign of play, and the intonation, instead, is quite aggressive. The laughter is minimal and quite nervous as though the audience is a little unsure of whether the podium is serious in this (seemingly) rather absurd accusation of thoughtlessness. The substance is a tease but the form appears to be a taunt.

By and large, most taunts occur in questioner moves, since the journalist may well not only have little real consideration for podium face but may even feel it their professional duty to occasionally attack it. Thus we find some fairly aggressive press moves, sometimes by virtue of their sheer sarcasm (candidates for important ambassadorial posts have to be vetted):

(80)   Q: Mike, Senator Thomas yesterday criticized the administration for leaving the ambassadorial post in Tokyo open for over seven months. I wonder, how long does it take to find out if Mr Foley paid Social Security for nannies?

There is a particularly belittling instance in Chapter 6, example (55): 'does it mean you were told to express no view ... ?' The questioners in such cases are far more interested in reinforcing their rhetorical arguments than in the podium's face and may well even feel that a severe threat to that face is necessary to make their points. Another good example is:

(81)   MR. LOCKHART: Well, Helen, you're now accusing me of withholding something that might be to our advantage about making peace, so I can't figure out what the charge is here.
        Q: I'm not accusing you, I'm simply asking why it was suppressed. (Laughter)

The podium's original response appears to be an effective one, it seems logically consistent. But Helen's follow up ignores the logic and instead picks up on the phrase 'you're now accusing me'. Her reply 'I'm not accusing you' manages to both imply that the podium's previous move was infantile in its self-pity and to set up a vague superiority narrative. The second part of her move then skilfully constrains the podium to reply – the adverb *simply* in 'simply asking' suggesting this is the most reasonable of requests – whilst, in the meantime, it relexicalizes the podium's 'withholding' to the more unfavourable 'suppressed'.[8] There is little doubt that the audience can delight in such blatant but skilful threats to podium face.

Helen is particularly prone to and proficient at running this fine line between tease and taunt. We have already seen her in action in example (81), as well as

Chapter 2, example (47): 'Does the President think that his hands-off policy has contributed in any way to the hopelessness and the rising violence in the Middle East? And, anticipating your answer, I have a follow-on' (Laughter). There is considerable sarcasm in 'and anticipating your answer...', which implies indirectly but unmistakably that the podium's response will be evasive or anodyne or both, because he habitually is so. Her delivery of these taunts is both playful and aggressive. She has a 'I will brook none of your nonsense' tone which deliberately breaks the rules of briefings etiquette by being exaggeratedly pugnacious. She forces the audience to treat the move as semi-serious because the alternative – treating it seriously – would introduce a note of high embarrassment. She has managed to adopt and arrogate the in-role of 'scourge of podiums', which, precisely because of its recurrence, is treated as not wholly serious, as an in-joke. Yet the undertone of aggression remains. The podium chooses not to rise to the taunt directly:

(82) MR. FLEISCHER: Why don't you just get it all out of the way, Helen? (Laughter)

which is accompanied by a broad smile. Mr Fleischer turns what could be a duel into a good-natured exchange, thus both avoiding a struggle with a skilful adversary and, as Tholander and Aronsson have it, refusing to recognize the barb or show any hurt.[9]

It is, however, extremely difficult, as distant observers, to distinguish between a tease and a taunt. First, we need to know what the participants' intentions are. Second, the audience, as we have seen, has the power to change the one into the other, irrespective of a speaker's intentions. And, of course, it is perfectly possible, as was mentioned at the beginning of this section, that a speaker means to taunt his or her victim but wishes the audience to think they are only teasing. Here we only have the linguistic trace of their interaction. It is not possible to invoke the occurrence of audience laughter as proof one way or another. Laughter occurs at teases and at taunts, and in the second case we, as analysts, cannot even be sure whether the laughter is sadistic or embarrassment management or a sign that the audience has actually (mis)taken the taunting perlocution for a tease. Much of this section, then, has to be taken as surmise.

5.7 Lester

5.7.1 The best-laid schemes...

Mr Lester Kinsolving is quite a personality and has his own particular style of asking questions, which are some of the longest and certainly some of the most entertaining in the corpora.[10] He generally begins a question with a preface of some kind, often referring to a current report:

(83) Q: Ari, the lead editorial in this morning's Washington Times is headlined, 'A War Decision.' And it contends [...]

176 *Teasing and verbal duelling*

After the introduction he will pre-announce his question, often warning that he has another, thus in effect booking a follow-up turn:

(84) And my two-part question [...]
(85) And my question is, does the President – and I have a follow-up – (laughter) does the President [...]

The first question is reasonably benign or uncontroversial, aimed at eliciting an expression of agreement or solidarity from the podium. The second question is – in Lester's cunning masterplan – designed to present the podium with an uncomfortable logical consequence of his agreement and trap him into a strong statement that coincides with Lester's conservative politics. A couple of examples will best illustrate the procedure:

(86) Q: Ari, the AP reports that they have filed a protest to Yasser Arafat's Palestinian Authority about threats to a cameraman who filmed crowds of Palestinians celebrating the attacks on the United States [...] And my two-part question. The first is, the President surely supports the AP and the Foreign Press Association in this protest, doesn't he, Ari?
MR. FLEISCHER: The President always supports the rights of a free press to operate around the world.
Q: Good. Now since it was (Laughter) – so many thousands of Arafat's Palestinians who in Nablus, Ramallah, East Jerusalem and Gaza publicly celebrated the mass murder of nearly 6,000 of our fellow Americans [...] Why does the President want anything to do with these creatures?

Note how the audience, well used to Lester's ploy and alerted by his satisfied evaluation of the podium's careful response ('Good'), laugh in anticipation of the follow-up 'sting'. The context of the next example is that Lester has his own talk-radio show. Talk radio has a general reputation in the United States of being right-wing and in this period was having a field-day over President Clinton's amorous peccadilloes:

(87) Q: When the President was in San Francisco taking questions from newspaper editors, CBS News, among others, reported that he 'bristled' at a question about talk radio. As the President's chief media advisor, can you identify any other part of the media that gives more time and space to public expression than talk radio? And I have one follow up.
MR. LOCKHART: I think the wise answer here is, no, Lester. What's your follow-up? (Laughter)
Q: The President said, the opinion of some of the talk show people is something that's way beyond my control, and happily so. Does this mean that the President is happy in the sense of being joyful or ecstatic

that he can't censor us? And do you really think many people believe he is really happy about this, Joe?
MR. LOCKHART: I have no reason to dispute the joy he expressed so openly in front of you. (Laughter) Next.

The preliminary questions are meant to lull the interlocutor into a false sense of security. In practice, they are more likely to alert the experienced podium to dangers that lie ahead:

(88) MR. LOCKHART: I think the wise answer here is, no, Lester. What's your follow-up? (Laughter)
(89) MR. LOCKHART: What's the trick here? (Laughter)

or simply bewilder him:

(90) MR. FLEISCHER: Les, I'm really not sure what you're driving at.

Such machinations make it easy for the podium to respond with teases, see examples (92) and (93) and Chapter 6, example (48). Lester's attempts to catch the podium out are sometimes seen as too crude and a little ingenuous and they have become, in effect, a standing joke. The audience often appears primed for laughter as soon as Lester is nominated to take a turn. Moreover, given this priming, the sheer outlandishness of some of his questions and in particular some of the juxtapositions in them tends to be enough to provoke laughter:

(91) Q: Ari, the Washington Post reports this morning that the Bush administration has dropped a Clinton administration action that charged the Southeastern Pennsylvania Transportation Authority with alleged civil rights violations, because 93 percent of all female applicants failed in its aerobics test, which test the Clinton people charged was overly rigorous. My question – given this commendable Bush administration decision, Ari, am I entirely wrong to presume that what you said, the President regards the best armed forces in the world means that he will not succumb to the extremist-feminist demands for females in ground combat units, will he, Ari? (Laughter)

Thus his reputation for 'bizarre questions'.

Finally, few of the audience share his very conservative views. All these factors permit the podium to evade – either by direct refusal to answer or by resorting to play mode – not only with impunity but with the approval of the assembly:

(92) Q: Ari, in view of –
MR. FLEISCHER: Only two today, Les. (Laughter)
(93) MR. FLEISCHER: So, Les. This better be good. (Laughter)

At times he is dealt with quite dismissively, rudely even:

(94) MR. FLEISCHER: Les, for a moment, I thought you had a half-serious question. (Laughter)

which treatment infects the audience, Lester's colleagues:

(95) Q: Ari, following Les, which I hoped never to do – (laughter) –

But Lester occasionally reacts against his stereotype, his scripting as butt of teasing, and he duels with the podium:

(96) MR. FLEISCHER: Les, for a moment, I thought you had a half-serious question. (Laughter)
Q: Do you think that's not serious?
MR. FLEISCHER: Let me take the first half of your question.
Q: The Committee to Protect Journalists thinks it's very serious, Ari, and I'm sure are appalled that you would make a joke out of this. But go ahead.

or he finishes his question with an effective barb:

(97) Q: Ari, there are 10 corporations, such as Aetna and Fleet Boston who are being sued for unspecified damages in black reparations, which presidential candidate Al Sharpton says would be good for America. The President does not agree with Sharpton, does he, Ari? And I know you won't evade, because that would suggest that he does. (Laughter)

This encapsulates a warning not to evade but also an accusation that the podium evades too often. And this time Lester is effective in eliciting a direct response, which surprises even him:

(98) MR. FLEISCHER: On the question of reparations [...] the President said [...] there are many West African, African nations that participated in the slave trade, and so the question quickly becomes, who should pay reparations to whom, given the tangled web that was part of our history that, of course, thank goodness, is long gone.
Q: That's not an evasion, Ari. I think that's splendid. Thank you very much.

5.7.2 *Deflecting a tease onto another party*

Having either desired or allowed himself to become a regular target, Lester is vulnerable to being used instrumentally by the podium as what we might call a present but third-party out-person. The following is a good example:

(99) Q: Can I follow up on that?
MR. FLEISCHER: We'll get there, Ed. You're in the on-deck row.
Q: I'm swinging my bat.
MR. FLEISCHER: Because of your desire, we'll go from left to right instead of right to left when we get to your row, to get to you quicker. Les, we'll have to miss you today. (Laughter) Ken.

Q: What is that?
MR. FLEISCHER: Nothing, Les. I was talking to Ed.

The podium turns down Ed's request to intervene, always a face-threatening act. To appease him, the podium promises both to come to him quicker and to sacrifice Les, another instance of a mock threat. In effect, Les is teased in order to salvage affiliation with Ed.

In the following, the podium finds Les still more useful:

(100) MR. FLEISCHER: You only get two, Les. Mr. Sanger.
Q1: All right, well, thank you for the two.
MR. FLEISCHER: I treat you like I treat everybody else.
Q1: Thank you very much.
Q2: That's not saying much. (Laughter)
MR. FLEISCHER: I treat you like I treat Les. (Laughter)

The joke-play here is quite complex. Lester has been interrupted fairly brusquely to give the floor to Mr Sanger. Whether or not it was so intended, this particularly prickly podium takes Les's 'thank you' as sarcastic and produces, in Tholander and Aronsson's terminology, an account of his face-threatening act – that he treats Les as everybody else, which is, as everyone in the room knows, untrue. A member of the audience steps in, teasing the podium with a move – 'that's not saying much' – which abruptly switches the podium's preferred narrative/role from that of fairness to lack of generosity. Mr Fleischer, in turn, quickly shifts the meanness narrative/role to one of toughness, his favourite 'hard man' role, by teasing Les, implying 'he is the regular butt of my jokes, and if he can take it so can the rest of you'. The podium thus deflects a tease aimed at him by elaborating it into a tease aimed at a third party, namely Les. No matter how mild the tease, and here it is very gentle, it still places the target outside the in-group, a position the podium generally likes to avoid. He therefore recovers his place within the group by substituting another as out-person.

5.8 General conclusions

Mention was made at the beginning of this chapter of Tholander and Aronsson's (2002) list of three principal functions of teasing which help explain why it is such common practice.

One function of teasing is to perform, to outdo one's opponent(s) by demonstrating superior verbal and intellectual skill. This is a highly valuable talent in what is essentially a debating chamber where 'winning' the arguing contest is often the aim of the exercise and where, as we have noted elsewhere, *ad hominem* attacks such as the tease can be just as rhetorically effective as any logical reasoning. This is the agonistic function of teasing. Some authors [e.g. Pilkington (1992); Holmes 1999 (1995)] are struck, almost shocked even, by the overt aggressiveness of some forms of (as White House briefings) male-dominated talk: 'the masculine style was an assertively aggressive one that proposed, opposed, competed' (Schick Case 1988: 52). The same authors tend to describe women's talk as characterized by far more conflict-*avoidance* mechanisms. However, conflict in the briefings environment is inevitable, given the different and incompatible aims and interests of the two sides and, as we have seen, two of the most combative questioners – Helen and Kelly – are, in fact, women. Conflict avoidance is not an option for the participants; it is a necessary process to be undergone in the search for a compromise version of events which will satisfy both sides. Furthermore, it would not be professional to go on-record as continually avoiding contention.

The kind of teasing and competitive banter which is endemic in this form of discourse is best viewed, not simply as the expression of aggression, but as a form of conflict *management*, whereby potential *real* conflict is diffused and defused by playing it out, by converting it into *ludic* combat. The more moments of cathartic teasing and banter, the lower the risk of genuine rage, which can be, first of all, inherently face-demeaning for a speaker since it demonstrates lack of self-control (Brown and Levinson's 'emotional leakage', particularly blameworthy behaviour in American culture) and, second, can lay the ranter vulnerable to counter-offensive, as the following exchange illustrates:

(101) Q: How can you call it a withdrawal? How can you call it a withdrawal? They've pulled out of a few small towns and they haven't pulled all the way out of any town. How the hell is it a withdrawal?
MR. FLEISCHER: With all due respect for your editorial, how can you not? It is a withdrawal from those towns.

Another well-documented function of teasing is its capacity to carry out corrective *social control*, as when adults tease children about their behaviour as an implicit way of 'redirecting children's activities or securing their obedience' (Tholander and Aronsson 2002: 559). It has thus been said that 'teasing does ideology' (Hopper 1995: 66). But it has a secondary but equally important socializing function. Eder (1991) argues that the ability to defend oneself against teasing is one of the more difficult interactional skills. Presumably, by being exposed to teasing, children learn the advanced verbal and cognitive skills required both to respond appropriately and to tease others in turn, both of which are vital elements in peer socialization (Willis 1981, cited in Tholander and Aronsson 2002: 561). Moreover, as Grainger noted, teasing can even be used to *promote* socialization artificially, to reduce social distance (re-ranking) more rapidly than would otherwise be feasible.

In these briefings a related form of the re-ranking use of humour in general and teasing in particular seems to be at work, if not in the creation of low social distance at least in maintaining it. One of the most striking features of this discourse type is the informality of the atmosphere in which the briefings are held. This is probably partly due to their routineness – they are held almost every day – and, as Brown and Levinson remark, frequency of interaction helps shrink social distance. However, frequency of interaction is no guarantee of friendship, of *liking* (or *positive affect*). Given the enormously complex bundle of inferences which accompany teasing, especially the general presumption that one only teases those one feels intimate with, it may be used semi-consciously, like the re-ranking teases in medical environments, to imply bonds which do not really exist and to suggest closeness when true intimacy is lacking. Participants may perhaps not be so well-meaning as they would like others to perceive.

A third reason why teasing occurs in multi-participant discourse such as briefings is to show affiliation. When the speaker attacks the hearer's face in public, playfully or otherwise, then any over-hearer has three possible courses: they can decide to affiliate with the speaker or affiliate with the hearer or remain neutral. Laughter implies affiliation with the speaker. Refraining from laughter may signal either affiliation with the hearer or neutrality, and the problem for the speaker is that he or she often does not know which choice the audience has made. Moreover, as Pomerantz (1984) observes, in normal interaction, speakers tend to operate on a 'with me or against me' assumption and a lack of positive feedback from an audience is liable to be taken as non-affiliation or even contrary affiliation. In any case, this is probably the speaker's safest interpretation. It is clearly evident when watching briefings that teasing attempts on the part of the podium are often accompanied by visual and vocal signals, smile and smile voice, which fade very quickly if there is no audience laughter. The audience's choice of affiliation will generally have a considerable influence over the subsequent development of the interaction.

However, it must also be said that these three functions are closely interrelated, a fact which emerges very clearly from the analysis of teasing in these briefings. The podium teases his victims, attempting to shame them or outperform them in order first of all to have 'power' over them, that is exercise social control to both ward off any antagonistic interrogation and to *impose* his agendas – the administration's versions of affairs. But he also teases single individuals in the hope of gaining the affiliation of the rest of the audience as a step to procuring their alignment with his message, thus winning them over to his agenda. The individual differences we have noted among the podiums show a different predilection for either the more aggressive imposition technique (Mr Fleischer) or the more subtle but perhaps riskier persuasion ploy (Mr Lockhart).

Finally, in addition to Tholander and Aronsson's three overarching or, we might say, *strategic* functions of teasing, it has become abundantly clear from the ongoing discussion that it also has local *tactical* uses contingent on the situation and the user's goals at a particular point in time. In other words, teasing is closely integrated into its context of use. In particular, in these briefings it is used to make argumentative points. Journalists use it to make accusations, for example, of podium evasiveness or of the administration's concern with form over substance, without fully going on-record as having lodged a complaint. In turn, the distracting nature of some kinds of teasing, especially the frustration tease, can be invaluable for the podium. And since, in common with other forms of humour, it involves a sudden bisociative switch of frame, it can be used to disorientate the adversary, always an effective ploy in competitive debate.

6 Irony and sarcasm

> ...he understands ironia, that with one eye looks two ways at once.
> (Middleton and Rowley)

> An irony is a nipping jeast, or a speech that hath the honey of pleasantness in its mouth, and a sting of rebuke in its taile.
> (E. Reyner)

6.1 Introduction

In this chapter I will consider whether a data-driven approach can shed light on some of the major controversies in linguistics, philosophy and psycholinguistics about the nature of irony and sarcasm, how they are understood and the functions they perform, as well as the fascinating, age-old question of how they relate to humour. Hitherto, these debates have largely been conducted with little recourse to 'external' data, that is, examples are either invented or selected anecdotally from literary sources on the simple basis that the researcher feels them to be instances of irony. We will first then, outline the bases of the controversies in question but then go on to see whether there might be a more objective way of identifying episodes of irony. Potential sites of irony are then examined in newspaper corpora and the briefings data, *Dems Reps* and *WHBig*, to see how and why, in real-life circumstances, speakers and writers employ it and how audiences (including victims) respond. Using evidence from corpora, a detailed description of sarcasm is attempted and possible episodes of sarcasm in the briefings are also studied, with a view to discovering how and how much it differs from irony.

6.1.1 Connections

Although there is agreement about very little else concerning these phenomena, there exists a general consensus that irony, sarcasm and satire are closely related and that all three have a strong association with humour. The general sense that they are interrelated is attested by the following entry in *Webster's*, which presumes they are near synonyms and discusses the nuances of difference among them:

> IRONY, SARCASM, SATIRE indicate mockery of something or someone. The essential feature of IRONY is the indirect presentation of a contradiction

between an action or expression and the context in which it occurs. In the figure of speech, emphasis is placed on the opposition between the literal and intended meaning of a statement; one thing is said and its opposite implied, as in the comment, 'Beautiful weather, isn't it?' made when it is raining or nasty. Ironic literature exploits, in addition to the rhetorical figure, such devices as character development, situation, and plot to stress the paradoxical nature of reality or the contrast between an ideal and actual condition, set of circumstances, etc., frequently in such a way as to stress the absurdity present in the contradiction between substance and form. [...] IRONY differs from SARCASM in greater subtlety and wit. In SARCASM ridicule or mockery is used harshly, often crudely and contemptuously, for destructive purposes. It may be used in an indirect manner, and have the form of irony, as in 'What a fine musician you turned out to be!' or it may be used in the form of a direct statement, 'You couldn't play one piece correctly if you had two assistants.' The distinctive quality of SARCASM is present in the spoken word and manifested chiefly by vocal inflection, whereas SATIRE and IRONY, arising originally as literary and rhetorical forms, are exhibited in the organization or structuring of either language or literary material.

(*Webster's*)

Strangely, the only indication here that these phenomena might be connected with humour is the use of the word *wit*. Norrick too notices that 'in much early theorizing about irony, the matter of humor rarely comes up' (2003: 1340), but this has changed:

[...] more recent work by Colston and O'Brien (2000a, 2000b), Dews *et al.*, (1995), Dews and Winner (1995), Gibbs (2000), Kreuz *et al.*, (1991) [...] shows that irony, too, can elicit laughter [...] and lead to further joking.
(2003: 1340–1341)

and the same is true for sarcasm:

Speakers do apparently share the idea that sarcasm is potentially humorous.
(Jorgensen 1996: 629)

although this, as we shall see, begs the question of whether *listeners* and *targets* also laugh at sarcastic wit.

6.2 Irony

6.2.1 Controversies: hearing echoes

In 1992, Wilson and Sperber were curious about 'how little attention has been paid, by linguists, philosophers and literary theorists, to the nature of verbal irony' (1992: 53). Since then, linguistics has seen an explosion of interest in the

184   *Irony and sarcasm*

topic, much of it inspired by or in critical response to Wilson and Sperber's own echoic mention/interpretation theory (Sperber and Wilson 1981/95, 1998, Wilson and Sperber 1992). To grossly oversimplify, two factions have formed. The first propounds, develops and disseminates the echoic theory while the second defends and refines what we might call a more traditional definition of irony as negation, contradiction or reversal of meaning. The controversy is also characterized by a certain amount of convenient misrepresentation of the other side's ideas.

Wilson and Sperber set out by asserting that what they claim to be the traditional view of irony as simple negation or 'a mode of speech in which the meaning is contrary to the words' (Dr Johnson, quoted in Wilson and Sperber 1992: 54; remember the definition given in *Webster's*: 'one thing is said and its opposite implied') is incapable of explaining a number of types of ironic utterances. They proceed to give examples. These include, first of all, *ironical understatements*, such as:

(1)   You can tell he's upset

spoken upon observing someone clearly blind with rage. This, the authors point out, means neither of the following:

(1a)   You can't tell he's upset
(1b)   You can tell he's not upset

as the traditional definition of irony, according to the authors, would suggest. Nor can such a definition, they say, handle *ironical quotations* and *interjections*:

(2)   When a man is tired of London, he is tired of life (Dr Johnson)

said in a 'rainy rush-hour traffic jam' does not indicate a desire to be out of London or to deny the thesis that being bored with London means being weary of living 'as the traditional definition suggests', but to make fun of the sentiments that gave rise to it, the vision of London it was originally intended to convey' (1992: 55). Ironical interjections – 'Ah, Tuscany in May!' exclaimed during an Italian summer storm – do not express a complete proposition and therefore cannot be true or false (i. e., they have no truth conditions); consequently they cannot be negated.

Sperber and Wilson propose, in the earliest version of their own theory, that all irony can be understood as *echoic mention*. Language which is *mentioned* is intended in a semi-technical sense in opposition to language which is *used*, a distinction they illustrate as follows:

(3)   PETER: What did Susan say?
      (a) MARY: I can't speak to you now.
      (b) MARY: 'I can't speak to you now.'

In the first version of Mary's reply, a state of affairs is being communicated, so language is used, whereas in the second it refers to, or mentions, another piece of language. When a speaker mentions some previous piece of language and, crucially for the theory, 'dissociates herself from the opinion echoed with accompanying ridicule or scorn' (1992: 75–76), then we have irony, as in:

(4) PETER: Ah the old songs are still the best.
     MARY (contemptuously): Still the best!

The authors, however, soon realized that mention was too restricted a concept to explain all irony. Reports of speech are not always exact reproductions of an original, they may be paraphrases, summaries, elaborations and so on, and therefore mention gives way, in the refined version of the theory, to the wider and more flexible concept of *interpretative resemblance*; the echo in an ironic statement now may only resemble an original statement. The requirement that critical mockery be present in the later speaker's interpretation remains. This new version is now said to be able to handle examples of ironic statements such as:

(5) Peter is quite well-read. He's even heard of Shakespeare.

where the speaker, it is claimed, is mocking a previously elaborated opinion that having heard of Shakespeare is evidence of being well-read (Sperber and Wilson 1995: 242). For these authors, then, the processing of irony involves the following three procedures:

> a recognition of the utterance as echoic;
> an identification of the source of the opinion echoed;
> a recognition that the speaker's attitude to the opinion echoed is one of rejection or dissociation.
> (Sperber and Wilson 1995: 240)

One of the most noticeable features of all Wilson and Sperber's writings on the topic is their recourse to invented examples and the absence of any authentic data, apart from a few literary quotations.

A good number of objections spring to mind. In fact, echo seems at the same time insufficient and yet too powerful to explain the phenomenon of irony. On the first count, ironically (?), echo even seems unable to deal satisfactorily with many of Sperber and Wilson's own examples. What, for instance, is the speaker supposed to be echoing in (1) with an utterance such as 'you can tell he's upset'? On the second, what precisely are the limits to echoic representation, if any? If the statement 'Peter is well-read, he's even heard of Shakespeare' is supposedly echoic of some potential utterance, opinion, viewpoint that is capable of being held by someone in the world, then any utterance containing any proposition whatsoever is echoic. In the absence of explicit mention markers ('as Oscar Wilde once said', 'as my granny used to say') – which is the normal situation – any utterance can be taken to be mentioning some previous one: how then could proper irony ever be distinguished from simple criticism, scorn or ridicule?[1]

In their 1998 paper, Sperber and Wilson attempt to address the problem of the limits of echo but with little success. They argue that some utterances in actual use are clearly non-echoic, such as when one speaker at dinner utters the phrase 'Can you pass the salt' after another has said the same thing five minutes earlier.

But this entirely misses the point. Their central claim by 1998 has become that 'it is always possible to echo general norms or universal desires' (1998: 285), but why continue to talk about echo? This watered-down version of echo, which is now far removed from either echoic *mention* or even *representation*, means nothing more than 'evoke'. That an ironic utterance *evokes, implies, calls to mind* something other than itself has always been central to traditional theories of irony, and will be elaborated on here. The question is: what precisely is evoked and how? This is not to argue that some simple ironic (or sarcastic, see below) utterances do not depend on echo (as example (4)), but echoic irony is only one subcategory of the phenomenon, and a peripheral one at that.

A further objection is that Sperber and Wilson's speculation arises from a caricature of traditional theory, which may involve a far more subtle and complex account than 'saying one thing and meaning the opposite'. Martin (1992), for one, felt it was altogether too precipitous to dispense altogether with the notion of negation: 'there is an obvious parallel between irony and negation' (1992: 83). He provides a series of examples in which it is very difficult to imagine the involvement of an original piece of language being recalled for interpretative echo. A couple will suffice here:

(6) [I sprain my ankle]: Oh great. That's nice.
(7) He would never commit a fraud, even though he's a personal friend of the Minister of Finance.

The first seems just too general to be intended as an echo, the second too idiosyncratic. Martin and Hamamoto (1998) independently develop an interesting negation theory of irony which sees irony as the result or the expression of defeated expectations. Martin claims that irony calls up alternative fictional (or 'counterfactual') worlds in which things are as they 'should' be, only for a contrast to be made with the imperfect sublunary one we actually inhabit (reminiscent of *Webster's* definition 'contrast between an ideal and actual condition'). Thus in, for instance (6), one has a rightful expectation to pass the day without spraining ankles. In another example, the statement:

(8) Our friends: always there when they need us

needs to be contrasted with a world in which our friends – as should be the case – are there when we need them. Hamamoto talks of 'a posterior re-evaluation of a certain *state of affairs*' (1998: 245). All this is a far cry from irony simply being the statement of the opposite of what is meant.

Moreover, Sperber and Wilson's theory necessarily distinguishes verbal irony from all other forms of irony: 'the echoic nature of verbal irony divides it from a range of non-echoic cases (situational irony, dramatic irony, romantic irony, irony of fate)' (Sperber and Wilson 1998: 290), given that these latter obviously do not involve echoing previous pieces of language, but rather mismatches in the knowledge states of different participants. Often, as in *Othello* or *King Lear*, it is the audience that is aware of the true nature of affairs whilst the main character blunders along under misconceptions resulting either from the workings of fate – Oedipus seeking the murderer that is himself – or from their own fatal character flaw. One of the subtlest episodes of dramatic irony is Macbeth's (albeit shaky) conviction of his own invulnerability, after the witches' assurance that 'none of woman born' shall harm him. Little does he know that his rival, Macduff, was not 'born' but 'from his mother's womb/Untimely ripp'd'. But the witches, of course, knew as much all along, whilst the audience is kept in suspense, just like Macbeth, by the mixed messages – 'beware Macduff' yet 'laugh to scorn / The power of man'.

If anything, comedy makes still more use of dramatic irony. Characters in disguises, hiding away or pretending to be dead in Molière, women dressing as men in *Twelfth Night, As You Like It* and *All's Well*, whenever there is the classic duping of a comic victim from the *Miller's Tale* to *Blackadder*: in each case, the audience is in the know, often complicitly with one or other of the protagonists, whilst someone else is in the dark. In the terms of reference adopted in this work, we would say that, in cases of dramatic irony, different participants (including the audience) are following divergent, often opposing, *narratives*, at the same point in time.[2]

Many authors feel, in contrast to Sperber and Wilson, that there is a natural relation among the various forms of irony, a feeling reflected in the discussion in the *Webster's* entry reported earlier. A theory which could contemplate such a link would have more natural explanatory power. One of the attractions of Martin's or Hamamoto's conceptual frameworks is the associations they permit between verbal and situational/dramatic irony, which both entail the interaction of alternative states of affairs (or 'worlds') in creating their effects. Hamamoto's definition could apply to both verbal and the dramatic irony in Macbeth:

> The first thing to consider is that a posterior re-evaluation of a certain state of affairs can be contrary to your prior expectations [...] Then 'cognition of irony' is defined as recognition of this discrepancy which lies between the posterior and prior cognition of some relevant event or thing.
>
> (1998: 264)

Macbeth's 'cognition if irony' is, of course, both his come-uppance and the climax of the play.

However, as we shall consider in the next line, defeated expectations is not sufficient in itself to explain irony: 'I really thought I would pass my exams but I didn't', thus articulated, would hardly rate as ironic. Something else is needed and we will try to discover the missing element in the following lines.

Moreover, there remain problems with the negation account of irony if this is expressed in terms of reversal of *meaning*, intended as conceptual or propositional or, in Hallidayan systemic-functional grammar terminology, *ideational* meaning. Negation theory cannot easily account for what we will call *true-seeming* or *verisimilar* irony, that is, when a speaker utters a statement from which they do not dissociate themselves and that appears to be a reflection of their true opinion. Here are a few examples from the literature:

(9) Mother (on entering child's room which is untidy): I love children who keep their rooms clean.
(10) America's allies – always there when they need you (see example (8)).

They include what we might call ironic puns such as:

(11) Christmas and New Year tribulations (instead of *celebrations*).

The negation theory also has problems, as Sperber and Wilson realized, in accounting for non-propositional irony, in explaining, that is, how it is possible to negate the meaning of utterances which have no propositional meaning.

Nor is it possible to relax the definition by saying that 'the speaker's meaning may be *other than* [rather then the opposite of] the literal content of the utterance' (Schaffer 1982: 15, in Attardo 2000: 814, my emphasis). This would then fail to distinguish irony from other figures, metaphor and metonymy, for instance. A detailed analysis of authentic uses in context may help shed light on and refine negation/reversal theory.

6.2.2 Controversies: one-stage or two-stages?

A second lively dispute over irony addresses the question of whether it is processed by the hearer in a one-stage or two-stage procedure. Attardo (2000: 809–813) gives a clear and at times humorous account of the debate.

The two-stage approaches can for convenience be called neo-Gricean, as many of them draw their inspiration from Grice's theory of irony (Grice 1975, 1989), which, as Attardo points out, 'is not radically different from traditional accounts' (2000: 798). This theory postulates that in processing irony the hearer first realizes that the utterance is non-literal and that the speaker cannot mean what his/her utterance appears to mean on the basis of incongruity between the utterance and its context, defined as including the set of beliefs ascribed by the hearer to the speaker. Presuming the speaker to be attempting to maintain cooperation (and not lying or delirious or mad), the hearer will, in a second phase, try to infer the speaker's intended real meaning. One obvious solution is that the speaker is wilfully violating one of the maxims, that is, of truthfulness (or 'quality'), of quantity or of relevance and intends to indicate a meaning radically opposed to the one expressed in the utterance. Grice himself seems to have felt that utterance meaning in expressions of irony was always false, or at least counter to the speaker's true beliefs, but we shall see that this is far from being generally the case. In addition, the hearer assumes that if the speaker is bothering to be non-literal he/she must also wish to convey an attitude towards some entity in the context, which might be the subject matter, some individual referred to or the hearer, or any combination of these.

To this I propose to add that normal human beings, in all probability, acquire what we might call the 'irony frame'. Socially competent hearers know that, just as they themselves frequently perform irony, others do too, and that on meeting a non-literal utterance, a hearer is *primed* (to extend the general sense outlined in Hoey 2005) to apply the irony frame and to interpret the event as an attempt at irony.

An important revision of Grice was undertaken by Giora and her associates (Giora 1995, 1997; Giora *et al.* 1998), who devise the *indirect negation* view. Whereas Grice's original theory proposes that the apparent literal meaning be first perceived but then discarded in the search for the real, intended speaker's meaning, indirect negation supposes instead that irony comprehension should involve retention of the activated literal meaning so that the comprehender may 'compute the difference' between the (usually desirable) state of affairs alluded to by the literal meaning, and the less desirable, ironicized situation. This is an important departure and something we will test against authentic examples in the course of this study. In the terms used here, we will look for evidence that hearers retain awareness of the surface, literal meaning or ironic utterances, that they keep in mind two narratives in order to compare and contrast them.

The proponents of the one-stage approach, principally Gibbs and co-workers (Gibbs and O'Brien 1991; Gibbs 1994), argue instead that hearers process irony directly in the same way as they process 'literal' meaning and that there is no need to posit a separate stage in which a first interpretation is rejected. To paraphrase the argument: hearers access ironical meaning directly because it is the most salient one. The irony frame we posited earlier is triggered immediately when one notes that features of the message are incongruous in relation to its context. Gibbs and his associates present a sizeable body of psycholinguistic laboratory-based research which, they claim, shows that subjects take no longer to process ironical sentences than their literal counterparts, evidence that the processing procedures are analogous. Unsurprisingly, Goira and colleagues also present laboratory work which shows that subjects *do* instead take longer to process irony.

Intuitively one feels that such laboratory experiments may have little relevance to the present kind of study. 'Processing' irony is not the same thing as understanding it in authentic situations outside the laboratory, and is certainly not the same thing as grasping its point. Apart from purely cognitive questions, politeness/face issues such as how to evaluate the import of the ironical utterance, what it means for the hearer personally, whether it was intended as mild or savage, how should one respond, will all need to be 'computed' when trying to appraise irony, let alone when timing the hearer's response to it (all this applies equally, *mutatis mutandis*, to sarcasm: see Appendix 2).

6.2.3 Suitability of data

One very noticeable feature of the vast majority of irony research is the limited data field it employs. Artificial examples and isolated individual instances are recycled from paper to paper, whilst the experimental work tends to expose subjects to rather simple invented examples and situations. One commendable exception is Kotthoff, who, noting how 'irony has seldom been studied in live interaction' (2003: 1392), concentrates on data from two interactive environments, conversation among intimates and television discussions. She shows how 'ironic activities are always interpreted in connection with the ongoing conversation, not as isolated acts' and how their interpretation depends on 'conversational inferencing [...] an ongoing process which works with assumptions that are continually readjusted' (2003: 1408). Those approaches which deal in invented or isolated examples would once again seem to be ignoring this vital point.

Yet another underlying methodological problem remains. In almost all studies in the field, the examples discussed, whether invented or selected, are taken for granted as being ironic for no other reason than the author feels them to be so. Any theory of irony based upon data which has not been previously validated as ironic runs the risk of being both over-subjective and circular.

6.2.4 Explicit irony

One exception to this trend is Barbe's paper on 'explicit irony markers' (1993). She examines conjuncts such as: *it is ironic that, ironically, in an ironic example of, there is a certain irony*, among others, as used by the authors of the *Letters to the Editor* section of the *Chicago Tribune* and the *Northern Star*, a student paper at Northern Illinois University.

Although she does not use the word, Barbe's analysis shows clearly that explicit irony is also explicitly bisociative. It utilizes 'duality in terms of incongruency, incompatibility, opposition etc.' (1993: 589) and is characterized by the fact that both sides of the duality are present in the text. First, a straightforward example:

(12) **It is ironic** that the majority of Quebecers favor constitutional recognition of their special and unique heritage, yet have failed and continue to fail to treat native North American Indians with any special respect due to their unique heritage.

(Chicago Tribune 9/3/1990)

In the terms adopted in this work, the writer juxtaposes two narratives:

NARRATIVE 1: Quebecers demand recognition of their own special heritage.
NARRATIVE 2: Quebecers deny recognition of the special heritage of native Americans.

linking them with *yet* and leaving the reader with the simple task of working out the contrasting relation between them. Barbe also notes that all her examples are critical of someone mentioned in one of the narratives, in other words, the purpose or point of the irony is to censure. As we shall see, the nature of the criticism can differ. She also makes an interesting distinction between strong and weak ironic statements, comparing:

(13) **It is ironic that** Fireman Alan preaches prevention of fire but sets himself on fire while smoking in bed.

(adapted from Littman and Mey 1991)

where:

NARRATIVE 1: A protagonist performs an action.
NARRATIVE 2: The same protagonist performs another (stupid) action incongruent with the first and suffers unpleasant consequences (deserved for reasons of stupidity)

with the weakly ironic:

(14) **It is ironic that** on Monday, Fireman Alan preached prevention of fire at the same time that Fireman Bob set himself on fire smoking in bed;

where

NARRATIVE 1: Protagonist A performs some action.
NARRATIVE 2: Protagonist B, who has some connection with Protagonist A performs some action incongruent with A's action and suffers unpleasant consequences.

Note too how a good part of the ironic 'weight' of the first version resides in its implying a moral judgement, an implication missing from the second. Very many observers of irony have commented on the relationship between moral – or moralistic even – judgement and irony. It clearly holds in many authentic ironic uses:

(15) There is **a certain irony** or poetic justice in what is now happening [...] France has been Iraq's biggest weapon supplier, after the Soviet Union [...] **Ironically**, now these French missiles may be fired [...] to sink French warships expected to join the international force.

(*Chicago Tribune* 10/5/1990)

This, indeed, is 'poetic justice' or 'just deserts' or 'hoist-by-his-own-petard' irony, reminiscent of the 'own-petard' teasing ploy (see section 5.3.2).

Barbe finds a good number of opposition conjuncts in her data, including *but, while, just* and *when*. However, in just as many instances, the opposition inherent in the narratives is implicit and taken for granted.

In the following sections we will adopt a similar procedure but supplement it with corpus analyses. We will look at explicit markers of irony as they are used in *WHBig* (briefings), *Ints* and *Papers*.

6.2.5 Corpus analysis

An examination of the collocational behaviour of the item *ironic* in *Papers* proved quite revealing. The largest corpus was chosen for this analysis because smaller corpora may not contain numerically significant collocates of rare words in any quantity. *WordSmith Tools* provided a list of the 220 most significant collocates. One set of collocates included (in order of significance) *commentary, say, story, reference, says, question, quotation, writing, written*, which reveals an association of irony with language, that it is largely a linguistic phenomenon. Its connection with humour was also confirmed since the list included *humour* (40), *wit* (19), *witty* (11), *comedy* (14) and *comic* (4), *laughter* (5), *laugh* (4), *smile* (10) and *funny* (8). Of interest too was the semantic group *reversal* (8), *twist* (23) and *turn* (6), clear evidence of how irony is felt to be a bisociative phenomenon.

What follow are selected sentence concordance lines illustrating *ironic* in the context of *humour/humorous*:

1   [...] and carved out a niche with colourful cocktails of **ironic** humour and outrageous kitsch such as Tie Me Up, Tie Me Down!, High Heels, and Matador.

2   [...] what appears superficially to be political correctness is, in fact, a manifestation of the British genius for **ironic** humour.
3   It is hard to convey the flavour of a volume so rich in observation, history, philosophy, political ideas and **ironic** humour.
4   He has a soft, fluty voice and a gently **ironic** sense of humour.
5   This collection of stories by a Romanian writer [...] is **ironic**, tactful and humorous

ironic in the context of *wit/witty*:

1   [...] it is Rushdie's voice: sharp, witty, **ironic** and utterly in control.
2   [...] their succinctly eclectic musical language in turn witty, **ironic** and lyrical.
3   Streetwise, witty, **ironic** and bright, The Big Breakfast has completely changed the ground rules for breakfast television [...]
4   How else could you make such dull heavy-going of Ben Jonson's mercurially witty, **ironic** satire on greed?
5   Behind the large glasses the eyes twinkled and the **ironic** wit sparkled.
6   [...] but Colette's prose, well served here by Margaret Crosland's elegant translation, is still a delight, and her **ironic** wit is well to the fore.
7   The jackets and coats [...] were a witty and **ironic** reference to the tailor's art, to be worn only by the witty and ironic.
8   The three-hour Valley Abraham is a sustained marvel of visual elegance and **ironic** wit

ironic reversal:

1   From Bangkok to Jakarta, businessmen and government officials are haunted by the spectre of a commercially-rampant China claiming large chunks of their markets. It is an **ironic** reversal of roles for the economic 'tigers' of south-east Asia.
2   Anglo-Catholic hopes that the High Court would throw out the women priests measure just before the parliamentary debate were therefore yet another **ironic** reversal of history.
3   In an **ironic** reversal of roles, hundreds of Khmer Rouge defectors are being taught the meaning of liberal democracy and human rights at a 'unification centre' near Phnom Penh.
4   The variations of that oh-so-smart school uniform are another useful indicator. In an **ironic** reversal of British expectations it is the best schools that do not have uniforms.

and *ironic twist*:

1   If anyone was able to defend the White House it was Col-Gen Achalov, who, in an **ironic** twist of history, helped the coup plotters of 1991 make plans for their own storming of the building.
2   Although regarded by white right-wingers as a leading black Communist and guerrilla fighter, Hani, at 50, had by an **ironic** twist been attacked by militant socialists of the Pan Africanist Congress for calling on them to give up the armed struggle against apartheid.

3 France's sudden willingness to embrace the idea of an independent central bank ahead of schedule is an **ironic** twist in the debate on monetary union and constitutes an important policy U-turn.
4 It would cost less to keep me at college than on various benefits; yet there seems to be less encouragement to carry on studying than to live off the state... an **ironic** twist to the Government's claims that this country needs more graduates.
5 In a supremely **ironic** twist, the French city with the highest per-capita sales of the fruity fragrance happens to be Epernay, capital of the Champagne region.

Very noticeable was the number of adverbial intensifiers found in the company of *irony* and *ironic* in the concordances, including: *deeply, particularly, especially, indeed, certainly, doubly, genuinely, bitterly* and *supremely*. Seto too (1998) lists a good many similar adverbs. Irony is closely connected to hyperbole. He argues that speakers regularly intensify the 'surface meaning' as a signal to the hearer to 'reverse the polarity' (usually from positive to negative) (1998: 244–246). A wide range of intensifying signals are used. One brief illustration he gives is a passage from Eco's *The Name of the Rose*:

(16) 'Truly this is the sweetest of theologies,' William said, with perfect humility, and I thought he was using that insidious figure of speech that rhetors call irony...

William's utterance exhibits three hyperbolic ironic signals, two lexical and one grammatical: *truly, sweet* ('a very positive degree word') and *–est* superlativization. Other possibilities include exclamation (*what lovely weather!*), focus topicalization, (*a fat lot you know*) and in speech, of course, the intensification is often intonational (Seto says 'prosodic', 1998: 248).

The next step was to examine the use of explicit irony markers by concordancing the items *irony, ironical* and *ironically* in the spoken political corpora, *WHBig* and *Ints*. Surprisingly, these words were used just nine times in the circa 6 million words of briefings but also nine times in the 250,000 words of the interviews. Since these are fairly erudite words, this disproportion probably reflects the greater formality of the interviews.

The clearest and most immediate observation was that the explicit irony markers in such structures are not simply metalinguistic flags, noting and bringing to the readers' attention some ironic potential pre-existing in the discourse at some particular point. Instead, and far more creatively, they are rhetorical structures and are organized purposefully by an author to construct an argument with a specific critical message. First of all, explicitly marked irony can be employed to accuse a person or group of people of having contradicted themselves, either wilfully or otherwise. When the implication is of deliberate self-contradiction, there is generally an ulterior imputation of dishonesty, double-dealing or deceit, sometimes openly expressed:

(17) Q: [...] You cited two precedents: one, the Kosovo situation and the other, the second is Desert Fox. Both of those were actions taken under the Clinton administration. The President, going back to the campaign,

was very critical and even disdainful of the foreign policy of that administration. Is that not somewhat **ironic** and even a little *hypocritical* that you're citing –

(18) Q: Ari, can I go back to the United Nations sanctions question, and I guess follow up on Bill's question about the French role, especially the Russian role. These are countries that fought sanctions in the past, and now seem to want to keep them. Do you not see something, at least **ironic**, and maybe *cynical*, about this?

The first of these can be paraphrased in terms of a pair of allegedly conflicting narratives:

N1: The President, before he came to office, said military intervention was bad.
N2: The President is now saying military intervention is good.

In other words, he has reversed his own *evaluation* (see section 6.2.6) to suit his purposes. But these utterances also, of course, have a strategic discursive or rhetorical function, in other words, a *point* (the term is borrowed from Labov 1972), which here is to accuse the President of inconsistency or even double standards.

The second example, (18), can be similarly analysed into contrasting narratives:

N1: The French and Russians first fought sanctions.
N2: They now support them.

They too have reversed an evaluation (they first said sanctions were *bad*, now they are saying they are *good*), and once more the point of the utterance is to accuse them of duplicity.

At other times, whether the contradiction was deliberate is not explicitly revealed:

(19) MR. FLEISCHER: Well, there is a prohibition in law that stops the Department of Transportation from fully reviewing this report. It's an **irony** that Congress is asking for a National Academy of Sciences study on CAFE standards, but then they prohibit the administration from reviewing that study in its entirety.

Nor is the point of the irony explicit. It is left to the hearer to work out what the charge is. Is the Congress guilty of underhandedness or just stupidity?

On other occasions, *irony/ironic* appears in the reply to a question and is used to imply that the latter contains unfair allegations or presuppositions:

(20) Q: [...] what does he say to his critics [...] who say that the government has succumbed to protectionist pressures [...]?
MR. FLEISCHER: I think that's kind of an **ironic** statement for people to make, given the fact that this is one of the most free trading Presidents we've seen.

(21) DAVID FROST: What about what Gordon Brown said yesterday [...] that state schools provide 67 per cent of suitably qualified leaders but only 52 per cent of places at Britain's five leading universities?

JOHN STEIN: I think that's incredibly **ironic** because I pointed that out in a seminar in the House of Commons three years ago [...] the steps that we were taking in Oxford to widen access [...]

In these cases too evaluations are reversed. The President is no protectionist (bad), he's a free-trader (good). We are not elitist (bad), we are widening access for the less well-off to the top Universities (good). The point or purpose here of the rhetorical figure is to defend one's actions and to make veiled charges of unfairness on the part of the accuser. Note, too, the presence of intensifying elements *one of the most* and *incredibly*. We need to stress once more that explicit irony is not just a way of pointing out some pre-existing irony in a certain situation. Instead, the ironist adopts a particular stance, marshals particular information and organizes it in a particular way, highlighting contrast and often intensifying elements of the context, so as to – borrowing parlance from CA – '*do* criticism' of the object of his or her attention (see Appendix 3).

6.2.6 Evaluation

Evaluation is here intended in the sense defined by Hunston as 'the indication that something is good or bad' (2004: 157). Evaluation theory is highly complex in detail and covers much of the same ground as other concepts in the literature such as *modality* – especially *attitude* – (Halliday 1994), *appraisal* (Martin 2000) and *stance* (Biber et al. 1999; Conrad and Biber 2000). Hunston's elaboration has a number of advantages for the present study. First of all, she concentrates on naturally occurring texts. Second, much of her work takes place within the environment of Corpus Linguistics, for example, she uses corpus evidence to illustrate how many more words and phrases carry good or bad evaluations than is generally thought. Finally, she never loses sight of the basic duality underlying evaluation: that entities, behaviours, people and so on, can be good or bad to varying degrees, but that evaluation is fundamentally a two-term system.

Evaluation can be expressed overtly or covertly. Overt markers can be (i) lexical: *splendid, untrue, happily, unfortunately, success, failure, win, lose* or (ii) grammatical, for example, comparatives, the use of past tense to indicate remoteness, modals of all kinds or (iii) textual, for example, final paragraphs of newspaper editorials tend to indicate favoured solutions to problems proposed in the previous parts of the text (Morley 2004). However, evaluation can also be implicit or 'conceptual', with no obvious linguistic clues, exploiting the audience's ability to recognize a good – or bad – thing when they see it. Hunston argues, for instance, that what is good or bad is frequently construed in terms of goal achievement, and so all the actions in a narrative are meant to be evaluated in reference to an explicit or implicit goal (such as, say, 'survival' or 'getting the girl/boy'). Irony exploits all these forms of evaluation. It makes use of explicit indicators, principally intensifiers of various kinds, but the very appearance of irony generally announces to the audience that something is going to be evaluated, as a rule very negatively.

Although rarely expressed in such a way, evaluation can be seen as a fundamental socio-biological or ethological impulse. In evolutionary terms, it is of extreme importance for an organism to judge whether an incoming stimulus, a change in its environment, is likely to bode well or ill (and of course *how* well or ill) because such evaluations are the basis for action, of the decision whether to flee or fight. Indifference can set in at a later moment, but the initial process of evaluation is bi-dimensional: is it dangerous? (yes = bad, no = good) can I eat it? (yes = good, no = bad).

Other forms of appraisal are, in origin, largely instrumental to good-bad evaluation because it is only this latter which informs decision-making directly. For instance, the assessment of how likely or how true an event is, which subsumes a large proportion of modality (probability, ability, certainty, doubt etc.), is only important in phylogenetic terms if the event itself is of survival relevance, that is, is beneficial or harmful to the organism. The degree of *truth* or *certainty* which can be attributed to the report of, say, a new food source two days' journey away only really matters, in evolutionary survival terms, because a new food source is intrinsically and a priori evaluated as a good thing. Judgements on how *necessary* an action is are, still more transparently, factors in deciding whether to commit oneself to action which will bring some benefit. In short, human (and animal) perception is decision-driven and decisions are dual: one can either do or not do something on the basis of a prior evaluation of global advantage or disadvantage.

It might be argued that evaluation is too individualistic, too solipsistic to form the basis of a theory of language use. If evaluation is personal judgement, why do speakers communicate their evaluative opinions so incessantly? A full treatment of the social functions of evaluation and therefore of language is beyond the scope of this work. But signalling one's evaluation has two major functions. First of all, it expresses group belonging by (seemingly) offering a potential service to the group (it is argued in the final part of this work that laughter itself in its origins probably had this very same group-serving function) by warning of bad things and advertising good ones. Moreover, it can assure an audience that the speaker/writer shares its same value system. In this way it helps 'to construct and maintain relations between the speaker or writer and hearer or reader' (Thompson and Hunston 2000: 6). But second, it can be used to direct, control and even manipulate the behaviour of others, generally to the advantage of the individual performing the evaluation. Evaluation is the engine of persuasion. It tries to convince an audience of what should be seen as right and proper and what not and that therefore the audience should conduct itself in a manner appropriate to the goal of achieving the former and eschewing the latter. Thus, as well as reflect, it can impose, overtly or covertly, crudely or subtly, a value system. The highly evaluative nature of irony marks it out as just such a tool for persuasion, and it is no surprise that it is particularly common, as we have seen, in argumentative texts such as newspapers or political debate.

6.2.7 The evaluator

Having isolated reversal of evaluation as a key element in irony, it becomes necessary to determine who is projected by the speaker as performing the evaluation, in other words, who is said to be the 'principal' (Goffman 1981) or the 'responsible' or 'motivator' (Levinson 1988) of the evaluation, that is, the supposed evaluator. In (16), (17) and (18), the questioners attribute the (contradictory) evaluations to another party; the President, foreigners and Congress respectively are projected as the evaluators. Very often, however, the speaker takes responsibility for the evaluation:

(22) Because **ironically** although the, the Euro is the subject about which people get most neurotic in British politics at the moment, the fact is we all talk about wait and see, I and people in Britain and Europe say we're waiting until the economic conditions come right and then we'll have a referendum [...]

This is analysable as:

N1: [I assert that] people (*we*) 'get neurotic' about – that is, there is a lot of argument regarding – Britain joining the Euro.
N2: [I assert that] people (*we*) are in basic agreement that the correct policy is to wait and see.

Presumably the *we* here is exclusive; the speaker is not criticizing himself. The contrast in evaluation is quite subtle and evokes an implied value system underlying the discourse. In the wide world, we are meant to understand, argument (in N1) is generally to be considered a bad thing, whilst agreement (in N2) is a good thing. We will meet other cases of these implicit value systems at work in irony.

The episodes seen so far would seem to be instances of Barbe's strong irony, given that the evaluators in each case are the same person or group in both narratives, as are the narrative protagonists (for example, Congress in example (19) or *we* in example (22)). However, the data throws up a number of cases of varying degrees of weaker irony, for instance (the context is the 1999 Seattle protests against the World Trade Organization):

(23) CLARE SHORT: [...] So the [protesters'] broad intent was right but it was very misinformed [...] whereas actually it was the most democratic forum we've ever had for trade negotiations... **ironically**.

in which:

N1: People protested against the forum (they evaluated it as bad).
N2: (I assert that) it was the most democratic forum we have had (I evaluate it as good).

If the projected evaluators are different, can the relationship between the narratives still be described as ironic? This is in fact an example of what we might call *paradoxical* irony, in which the speaker suggests that, *of all* the forums possible, they had to protest against *this one*. The current forum is assessed as good, the others as deficient by comparison. A similar but specular instance of this sort of irony occurs in a briefings question:

(24)   Can I just ask you, is it not true that the average – and even this year's or next year's projected annual growth rate – is higher for every year annually for the next 10 years than an economist would expect growth to be this year? So, isn't it **ironic** when you're talking about conservative projections that the year you want to pass this budget, you're going to have anemic economic growth, more anemic than any year your conservative estimates project for the next 10 years?

This complicated question (in fact, the podium's reply opens with 'I'm not sure I understand your question...') can be glossed as: *of all* the years you could have passed this budget, you have to choose *this*, the one with the lowest projected economic growth. This year is evaluated as bad, the others good by comparison.

The point of paradoxical irony seems generally to be to criticize some protagonist/evaluator, at least in these discourse types, but there is sometimes an additional sense of wryness, of irony of fate, of it being a funny old world.

There are other cases of weaker irony in the data of various types. First:

(25)   What **irony** that Gordon Brown, the Cabinet colleague Mandelson gripes most about, should be the man poised to deliver the next election for Blair.

This seems to express:

N1: Mr Mandelson criticizes Gordon Brown. (Mr Mandelson evaluates Mr Brown negatively).
N2: Mr Brown is the man who will add to Mr Blair's success. (I assert that, for Mr Blair, Mr Brown is a good thing).

Since there is a mismatch in evaluators, the irony can only be interpreted by importing the extra-textual knowledge that Mr Blair and Mr Mandelson are very close allies.

On occasion, any real irony is very faint indeed:

(26)   [...] could I just say how saddened I was to hear of the, yesterday, of the death of my good friend and colleague Bernie Grant who was someone who'd always spoken up for Londoners [...] always said what he thought and **ironically** I was supposed to be appearing on a platform with him this afternoon.

There hardly seems to be a contrast at all here, and a better choice of word might well have been *coincidentally*, but *ironically*, being more erudite, adds gravitas to a sad topic. The point remains that just calling a situation 'ironic' does not always necessarily make it so.

At the beginning of this discussion, we mentioned that normally in explicit irony the two narratives are present to some extent in the text. This is perhaps an oversimplification. We have seen how it is often necessary for the reader to perform considerable inferencing work to recover one or other of the narratives and to understand how they interrelate. It might be more precise to say that the reader is meant to construe both narratives using, first, the immediate co-text around the explicit irony signal, second, the wider context the irony is contained in and, third, his or her knowledge of the world. Thus some explicit irony is perhaps more similar to implicit irony than we might think. Consider the following:

(27) 'The [Conservative] party overwhelmingly selects white, heterosexual, middle-aged, male, professional people as its Parliamentary candidates, and the people doing the selecting are likely to be female and more than 50,' he says. 'It's always been the great **irony** that it's women who select the men and who say to the women "What will your husband do if you're not there to make his dinner?"[...] This is something we have to deal with.'

There is a complex interplay of evaluations enacted in this piece; evaluations seem to be embedded within other evaluations. The immediate narratives might be, first, that Conservative selectors disfavour women as candidates and, second, that the selectors themselves are women. This is presented as a paradoxical irony: the reader has to avail him/herself of some general implied expectation such as 'one might normally expect people to elect other people who are similar to themselves'. As we observed earlier, Martin describes how irony recalls what he terms 'counterfactual worlds of expectation' (1992: 83–89), how it often depends upon an imagined prior expectation being defeated or disappointed. The reversal of expectation is clearly signalled by the marked grammatical-informational structure 'it's the women who select the men' (when you might have expected it to be the men). But there is also an underlying unfavourable evaluation. Indeed, the last phrase signals explicitly the situation as a 'problem': the writer is presenting the situation not just as paradoxical but perverse. But not only is the selection procedure, that is, the evaluations performed by the women, evaluated badly, with the speaker reversing their evaluation (choosing women becoming a good thing), but so are the women themselves. Finally, since the speaker is the chairman of the political party in question, and therefore in a position to remedy things, there may even be an implicit unfavourable evaluation of the speaker on the part of the author of the article.

6.2.8 Conclusions on explicit irony

This kind of irony then is explicit not only in being introduced by an unequivocal signal of the speaker/writer's intention to be ironic but also in being overtly bisociative. The two narratives are present in the text, with very few exceptions where the speaker/writer presumably feels the other one to be so obvious it would be tiresome to spell it out.

The hearer/reader is told quite openly that there is a discrepancy between the two narratives. Is she or he left, then, with any more work to do? First of all, they must infer the point of the rhetorical exercise. It is always critical or censorious, at least in all the examples we have examined, but who is being criticized and for what? Sometimes the nature of the criticism is stressed, as in (17) and (18), but more generally it is left to the hearer/reader to decide whether the offence is deceit, injustice or stupidity. It must not be forgotten that this form of ironic criticism is, superficially at least, indirect. This is, in fact, the very essence of the rhetorical effect of using a form with no personal subject as actor: *it* is ironic that..., *there* is an irony in,... Ironically.... The subject is not fingered for blame entirely openly, we are told instead that a state of affairs happens to exist. The degree of blame and the level to which it is hidden can vary considerably, as we have seen. In (18) the French and Russians are obviously hardened reprobates, but in other cases further linguistic signals are required to assist us. The negative connotation of *gripes* in (25) informs us that it is Mandelson rather than Blair or just fate who is behaving badly. In (27) we might at first feel sorry for the misguided Conservative women who favour male candidates, until their wrongheadedness is compounded (by the writer, of course) by an indication of the kind of question they are supposed to ask the female competitors. This very indirectness makes these formulae a useful tool when it is prudent to be polite in answering criticism and one's critics as seen in (22) or when it is politic not to be too harsh on someone, such as the misguided demonstrators in (23).

Then again, however, given the perversity of human nature, the veiledness, the indirectness inherent in ironic evaluation can be exploited rhetorically. Sometimes subtle criticism can hit harder than cruder, more open kinds. Episode (19) might qualify as such a case.

Explicit irony of the kind we have studied here makes use of rhetorical figures of speech which show very clearly how irony is not independent of the ironist, how it is the speaker/writer who creates the ironic relationship between the two narratives in order to formulate a (critical) argument. Sometimes in a rather laborious or suspect manner. An instructive example is the following. The speaker has hinted that her associates in the self-appointed 'Countryside Alliance' would be prepared to break the law in support of their protest against a proposed ban on fox-hunting:

(28) JONATHAN DIMBLEBY: [...] just very briefly one thing you've said in the past that if a ban went ahead you and your family might find yourselves in prison. Does that mean that you are ready to defy the law if it goes against you?
ANSWER: No I am not ready to defy the law and I don't urge anybody else to do so and nor does the countryside alliance at all, but it is an **irony** that people who have lived totally law abiding lives and want to go on doing so are being pushed by people like Tony Banks into contempt for the law and that would be a tragedy.

The argument being indirectly constructed by the interviewee is that if one breaks the law in support of one's own ideas, it is the fault of people with opposing ideas, and who have the power to make the laws. The contrast in the two narratives is between the good, the righteous 'we, who are law abiding' (and yet might well break the law) and the wicked 'Tony Banks, who is pushing us into contempt for the law'. But the (largely middle-class) Countryside Alliance avoids open declaration of criminal intent by using the impersonalized and responsibility-shifting explicit irony structure: *it is an irony that*.

Looking at irony using only invented or decontextualized examples, then, has led many authors to underestimate such aspects. Those schools of thought which emphasize the echoic aspects of irony seem consequently to miss its creative impetus, its essentially imaginative, even ingenious raison d'être.

6.2.9 Reversal of evaluation

The essential question then is the following: what is the precise nature of the relationship between the two narratives which compose an ironic figure? From the evidence accumulated so far, an implied reversal of the evaluation is extremely frequent and appears to be a dominant factor. The two parts to an event, situation, piece of behaviour are evaluated by someone positively in one of the narratives, negatively in the other, either by the same someone or another party. Ironies consisting of simple reversal of propositional or ideational meaning may well occur, but when they do, one suspects they will be used to support other kinds of interpersonal effects, face-work in particular (see example (34)). But in general speakers rarely go to the trouble of using a complex rhetorical technique, perversely saying the opposite of what they really mean, unless there is a pay-off of some kind. Irony, like all rhetoric, will tend to fulfil interpersonal as well as ideational functions, and evaluative meaning – expressing, projecting or imposing the view that something is either good or bad – is one of the principal ways speakers combine the ideational and the interpersonal functions in communication.

However, reversal of evaluation by itself is too powerful a definition. The reversal must be signalled as marked in some way, as being a discrepancy which is out of the ordinary and therefore worthy of note, debate or scandal. As has been noted, this reversal and contrast is often painstakingly emphasized, grammatically, lexically and phonologically. It is not sufficient to say, for example, '{A asserts that} X did well but {B asserts that} Y did badly' (where A and B may or may not be the same party). The contrast in evaluation is intensified, especially when protagonists of the two narratives are different parties or when in actual fact the contrast runs the risk of appearing a little weak, and has to be expressed as 'it is ironic that, whereas X did extraordinarily well, Y did remarkably badly':

(29) **Ironically**, whereas Agassi *confounded the sceptics* by *slipping through with little cause for alarm*, the No. 3 seed Stefan Edberg had a *monumental struggle* with a Canadian qualifier, Greg Rusedski [...]
(EdReps)

(30) The *cruellest* **irony** is that while publishers *turn up their noses* at the thought of Lamont's bitter reminiscences, the diaries of another former Conservative minister, Alan Clark, are about to become *the best-selling* political memoirs *for decades*.

(*Papers*)

Note the liberal sprinkling of emphasizing expressions (highlighted). These two constructions have the very openly bisociative form whereby the relationship is introduced by *ironic/irony/ironically* followed by a contrastive conjunction *while/whilst/whereas*. This appears to be a fairly common structure, at least in newspaper prose, given that *Papers* contains fifty-seven instances. It needs also to be said that the ironic contrast in (29) has been prepared earlier in the opening paragraph of the article:

(31) Suggestions that André Agassi's reign as Wimbledon champion would be terminated on the opening Centre Court session yesterday [...] proved to be unfounded

(*EdReps*)

which sets up a contrast between Agassi's success and a prior 'straw man' expectation ('suggestions') expressed by unnamed critics (for 'straw man' rhetoric in newspapers, see Morley forthcoming).

Similarly, as we have already mentioned, simple defeat of positive expectations is not a sufficient condition for irony. Once more it has to be stressed that irony does not somehow exist in a situation but has to be construed by the ironist. As regards the example we used earlier: 'I really thought I would pass my exams but I didn't' is not, as it stands, ironic. Expressed in terms of its underlying narratives this would be:

N1: I worked very hard for this exam thus having a reasonable expectation of passing
N2: I didn't pass

which is just a hard luck story. Irony can be construed into the situation by presenting it as a paradox along the following lines: 'I failed my exam. *The irony is* I worked harder for this one than all the others put together', in which:

N1: I didn't work hard for other exams but passed.
N2: I worked very hard for this exam (thus having a reasonable expectation of passing) but didn't pass.

The relation between the two narratives is now inversion and involves a combination of paradoxical irony and irony of fate.

We have, of course, met the bisociative mechanism of evaluation reversal before, in Chapter 1, where it was seen to be one of the most important logical mechanisms in jokes. This may be one of the reasons why much irony is felt to have something in common with humour (though not generally explicit irony). It might be noted in passing that advertising also exploits evaluation reversal to create both surprise and humour.[3] Moreover, irony is often used with a moral or moralistic purpose – to pass judgement on someone or something – and thus the reversal is from proper to improper (to point out the wrongfulness of the latter: consider Barbe's Fireman Alan example, or the betrayal script of many ironies, see Appendix 3), a mechanism we saw was also the basis of a vast array of joke types (although whether jokes also have a moral purpose is a monumental moot point). We have also noted how much of modern linguistic thinking considers the evaluation function to be extremely pervasive and central to language use, to which we might add, to all human cognition.

Moreover, it is this shared dependence on the sudden reversal ploy which explains why irony and humour have in common the element of surprise. In espousing evaluation reversal plus hyperbole as the main ingredients of irony we begin to comprehend why it is so popular. It enables speakers/writers to be – or to project themselves as – interesting and dramatic by springing a surprise upon the hearer/reader. Irony allows one to be both suspenseful and sententious. It says: Someone (you – me – a third party – the world) evaluated things in such a way. Let me tell you this: they were really in quite a different way altogether.

6.2.10 *'Implicit' irony*

Explicit irony seems rarely to be linked to laughter-talk. However, we can now turn our attention to implicit irony, that is, irony which is not signalled by explicit lexical irony markers of the type we have been studying, and this kind of irony frequently is. We have already seen how often the word collocates with items from the semantic sets of laughter, wit and humour. Moreover, Kotthoff demonstrates how often ironic comments are followed by laughter in both conversation and more structured television debates. This kind of irony – the kind normally intended when talking of verbal irony – is also implicit in that only one of the narratives is present in the text (the *dictum*), whilst the other (the *implicatum*) remains unspoken and has to be reconstructed by the audience.

As we have already noted, in almost all studies of implicit irony, episodes are taken for granted as being ironic for no other reason than that the author feels them to be so. Here we have already defined irony, through examination of the use of the term in authentic discourse, as involving evaluation reversal, and it is therefore contended that candidate sites of implicit irony can be identified with some degree of objectivity in interactive discourse by localizing laughter episodes where speakers employ some form of reversal. These episodes, as we saw in section 6.2.5, might well be accompanied and signalled by some kind of lexical or grammatical intensifier, some of which can be sought using the concordancer (for instance, *-ly* intensifying adverbs such as *really* or *-est* superlatives).

Several examples of very straightforward ironic reversal were apparent, including:

(32) MR. BERGER: I wish I had the clip. This is actually in the Iraqi news service, which does show that the American journalistic profession is

204   *Irony and sarcasm*

> superior to the Iraqi journalistic profession. (Laughter) And it also attacked Buddy – (laughter) – and I think you can attack the President, but it's indefensible to attack Buddy

in which the President's pet labrador, Buddy, is playfully evaluated as more important than the President (note the emphatic *does show* and *indefensible*). In the following:

(33)   Q: Joe, was the President pleased or saddened that his good friend, Mayor Schmoke, and the Baltimore Orioles participated in that "glory to Comrade Fidel" rally thinly disguised as a baseball game, and denounced by so many free Cubans? And I have one follow-up. (Laughter)
MR. LOCKHART: I can't wait. (Laughter)

the ironic enthusiasm (good) of the dictum of the podium response ('I can't wait') implies an expectation that the follow-up will be just as tiresome (bad) as the original question. The laughter is probably also partly a result of the podium's evocation of the tough job in-script. In:

(34)   Q: Ari?
MR. FLEISCHER: Les, it's not your moment yet. Let me come to you. A new approach. (Laughter)

'going round the room' giving each journalist a move in turn is, of course, the *old* approach. This, at first sight, might appear to be simple ideational reversal with no evaluation being expressed. However, behind the seeming information-provision lies the interpersonal face-work message: 'were it really a new approach, your behaviour would be excusable, but since it's the same old way, you are either a slow learner or a troublemaker'.

By far the majority of episodes, however, turned out in actual practice to be more complex and sophisticated. Take, for example:

(35)   MR. LOCKHART: [...] But I do understand that there are some implications 20 years down the road – I hope none of us in this room are here then. (Laughter) For the record.
Q: Helen – (Laughter)
MR. LOCKHART: Wolf, that was uncalled for. You should leave.
Q: God willing, she'll still be here.

This naming of Helen, the oldest member, by Wolf (Wolf Blitzer, *CNN*, no stripling himself) is deliberately ambiguous: it could be ironic, a statement that Helen will still be here, implying she certainly will not be, or it could be non-ironic, meaning good old Helen has been here for as long as anyone can remember and will outlast us all. Mr Lockhart interprets it as having the first of these meanings and good-humouredly admonishes him. Wolf retorts that he meant the second of the two. His utterance was, of course, potentially face-threatening for Helen. The indirectness of irony, like other indirectnesses, is often used to perform face threats which, if need be, can be denied.

Not dissimilar in its ambiguity is the following:

(36)   MR. TOIV: Joe, we're not ready to announce Texas.
        MR. LOCKHART: OK (Laughter) [...]
        MR. TOIV: We don't have any specifics.
        MR. LOCKHART: Gotcha. (Laughter) Okay. Everything I just said about Texas – strike. That was off the record. (Laughter) Got it back there? Off the record. Okay, now, that's all I have.
        Q: Tell your C-SPAN viewers as well.
        MR. LOCKHART: Yes. (Laughter) To my C-SPAN viewers: those of you who don't like me, please stop writing. (Laughter) I am very thin-skinned, and it really gets to me. (Laughter) Guarantees about 300 next week. (Laughter)

Mr Lockhart is able to 'mean' both the dictum and the implicatum inherent in his 'I am very thin-skinned' and to milk the rewards of both senses ('I'm a sensitive soul' and 'I couldn't care less about criticism'). Much of the laughter which accompanies ironic utterances seems to be in recognition and remuneration of a speaker's rhetorical skill. Similarly, Mr Berger's riposte to Helen (see Chapter 2, example 48):

(37)   MR. BERGER: [...]You know deadlines are a double-edged sword. On the one hand, deadlines provide a –
        Q: Selling point. (Laughter)
        MR. BERGER: No. That's more cynical than I know you mean to be, Helen. (Laughter)

a 'backhanded compliment' in lay terms, allows the speaker effectively to say 'you aren't a cynic' while implying that 'you are a cynic', with little danger of being called to account. As Brown and Levinson put it:

> Given the vulnerability of mutual knowledge (the difficulty of 'knowing what is inside someone's head'), and the non-recoverability of intonational or kinesic clues, even fairly blatant indirectness may be defensible as innocent – a speaker could protest that he didn't mean an irony in a sarcastic way, for example. S and H could both go away from the interaction 'knowing' in their hearts that it really was sarcastic, but because face (as the word implies) is largely a matter of surface appearances, S may well get away with his Face-Threatening-Act.
>
> (1978: 217)

The speaker is more likely to get away with the FTA if the linguistic packaging is rhetorically skilful, as here. The audience laughter, Mr Berger's 'reward', seems to suggest they recognize what is going on *under* the surface of discourse.

206 *Irony and sarcasm*

Questions too, of course, can be ironical:

(38)   Q1: [...] with uncertain goals, without prior consultations with Congress. His question – his question is, so just what was it that he was opposed to in Vietnam?
       Q2: Could you repeat the question? (Laughter)

In the first move, the notorious Lester has launched into a lengthy diatribe contrasting President Clinton's youthful opposition to war in Vietnam with his current intention to use force in the Balkans. The implicatum of the other journalist's quip (Q2) is that the last thing we want is to hear such a long, tendentious and outdated question again. The point, of course, is a rather sarcastic face attack on the previous speaker which again is entirely deniable: the speaker, if challenged, can claim that since the question was rather long but interesting, it needs repeating (appealing to the dictum).

6.2.11   Lose it or use it? Grice or Giora

At this point we are in a position to readdress the controversy outlined in section 6.2.2 over whether the audience, the hearers and potential victims, discard the dictum, or the 'literal' or surface version of the ironical utterance as a prelude to discovering the implicatum or hidden meaning, as Grice would have it, or whether they keep it and retain both accounts (narratives in our terms) in order to 'compute' or assess the distance and distinction between them, as Giora and her associates have stressed.

The main finding in Kotthof's excellent research into authentic irony episodes in dinner conversations and television debates was that speakers can respond to an ironic remark by addressing either the dictum or the implicatum. At dinner, friends tend predominantly to choose the former (twenty-six responses to the said, only four to the meant), whereas the opposite is the case in the serious debates (only one to the said and fourteen to the meant). We can interpret these results as follows. In a serious discourse context, an ironic remark usually entails an interpersonal face attack against which the victim feels the need to defend him/herself in order to preserve what we have called in Chapter 5, their competence face. Thus in one of Kotthoff's examples, in a debate on the joys and dangers of motorbiking, the moderator, whose favour leans towards the critics, is invited by Theo, one of the bikers, to try the experience (translated from the German by Kotthoff, light editing by myself):

(39)   THEO: [...] do take a trip in the summer, now we're having the summer club
       MOD: yes, I do not intend to live until retirement (laughter voice)
       THEO: but I beg your pardon, look here, I really am not crazy either.
       (2003: 1401)

Theo's response to the moderator's sarcastic irony is at implicatum level. In a non-friendly, competitive environment such as this, if the hearer/victim of sarcasm should fail to address what is meant they run two risks. First of all, the accusation behind the remark passes unchallenged and, second, the butt can be perceived as failing to garner the irony and so appear stupid or naïve, with all the extra loss of face that this entails.

Among friends, on the other hand, hearers/victims tend to play along with the irony (to 'frame-adopt') and, in the terms adopted in the current work, act out the fantasy narrative/persona that the ironic remark constructs for and around them, for example:

(40) MARIA: You are having such a rich social life lately
DAVID: a lot, a lot is going on lately, because I have taken the initiative now.
(Kotthoff 2003: 1395)

David is known by all present to be a man who likes his peace and quiet and loathes most social gatherings. He enters the play frame and accepts the fantasy role assigned to him by Maria as enjoying life as a socialite and later in the conversation even notches up the irony by suggesting that all present fly off together to the Caribbean when everyone knows he vehemently objects to air travel. In relaxed friendly circumstances, a speaker who responds to the meant rather than to the said risks killing the joke and appearing to lack a sense of humour. This would entail forfeiting affective face, the kind of face which is generally at least as much in play in social situations as competence face (3.3.4).

These observations seem to prove that speakers far from forgetting or 'discarding' the surface narrative of irony will often exploit it to great effect. We have seen still further evidence in the episodes from the briefings earlier, where speakers are seen to actually play with the two narratives to the point even of maintaining commitment to both at the same time. In order to do so they must be able to rely on the audience's simultaneous awareness of both narratives. Wolf can make a sarcastic remark and yet deny that there was ever a second narrative intended (35). Mr Berger both says and does not say that Helen is a cynic (37). Mr Lockhart too lays claim to delicate feelings and at the same time mocks his own claim (36). There can be no doubt that Giora's argument (that hearers retain both narratives) can draw much comfort from such analyses of strategic uses of irony in real-life situations. We might, in fact, go further and suggest that more work needs to be done on how the narratives are not simply retained but on how their potential interplay is used to advantage, both by speakers and hearers of the irony.

6.2.12 Verisimilar ironies: litotes

As we have seen, a good part of the debate raging over irony has focussed on the phenomenon of ironic utterances in which speakers, rather than saying the opposite of what they intend, seem to say something that corresponds to 'the facts', to their apparent beliefs, or to the way things really are to the best of their knowledge. We decided to call this quite common variety of irony, 'true-seeming' or 'verisimilar'. How does the reversal of evaluation theory as expounded here explain such forms?

208   *Irony and sarcasm*

There are several intriguing instances, for example:

(41)   Q: [...] I wonder if you could comment on that difference in his position.
       MR. MCCURRY: His constitutional thinking has undergone quite an evolution in the time. (Laughter)
(42)   Q: Mike, why do you think the President is not watching this very closely? Isn't he very interested in what comes out –
       MR. MCCURRY: He's not very intellectually stimulated by the debate on the Republican side. (Laughter)

In the first, the Democratic podium is sincerely critical of the inconsistency of a Republican, whilst in the second he truly means to say the Republican debate is unengaging. However, they are also clearly examples of understatement: they remind us of Sperber and Wilson's example:

(1)   You can tell he's upset

uttered upon seeing someone in a violent temper. In (41) the dictum 'undergone quite an evolution' implies 'has performed a complete u-turn', 'his thinking is in utter contradiction with itself', whilst in (42) 'is not very intellectually stimulated' implies 'is totally uninterested in'.

How, then, can understatement be ironic? It will be recalled that we have defined irony as involving in the majority of cases a reversal of evaluation on the part of some adjudicator, either the speaker themselves or some participant in the narratives. In understatement or *litotic* irony, the evaluator evaluates an entity as *little* to imply the opposite, that it is in reality *a lot*. Thus, as we saw, the modest 'evolution' is really a thorough revolution; 'not very stimulated' is really downright bored.

The comic effect is often heightened by stylistic choices: note *stimulated* in (42). The most effective and elegant use of litotic irony in the corpus is the following (the context is a question on how the podium feels to learn that his retirement is a big news story):

(43)   MR. MCCURRY: [...] we come and go, but we didn't get elected to be anything. And I will certainly enjoy whatever notoriety I have, and I will certainly use it to the good fortune of my family in the future. (Laughter)

The speaker has slipped into self-parody (section 2.5 and 2.6), using a stilted diplomatic speech-style, and so the register he employs contains understatement. By the rule of ironic reversal, then, in underemphasizing the dictum narrative in this way, he manages to imply an opposing one in some kind of emphatic colloquial register, something along the lines that he will flog his fame for all it is financially worth.

Thus the reversal of evaluation theory seems to deal rather well with litotic irony, often considered a difficult or borderline type of irony and much discussed in the literature. It simply states:

N1: Someone understates a value; evaluates something as a little.
N2: Someone emphasizes a value; evaluates something as a lot.

in close analogy to other more common forms of evaluation reversal irony.

In practice, judging from the briefings, speakers also exploit litotic irony in complex ways to achieve particular rhetorical effects. Consider the following (discussed in the previous chapter as a tease):

(44) Q: Joe, have you read the reports that Yugoslavian TV and movie theaters are showing reruns of the movie 'Wag the Dog'?
MR. LOCKHART: I saw that on television.
Q: Do you believe it?
MR. LOCKHART: Do I believe it? Yes. I mean, I believe what I see on television some days. (Laughter)

Mr Lockhart's final turn here recalls and relies on the folk phrase 'Don't believe everything you see on television'. It is another example of irony ambiguity through indirectness. The speaker means to say something like: 'Yes, I believe it since I have no impelling reason to disbelieve what ought to be a truth-telling medium'. But this is an *uninteresting* way to answer and so he employs litotic irony, saying 'some days' to imply 'most of the time'. Contemporaneously, he manages to adopt an in-group persona of cynic much appreciated by this particular audience. It must also be noted that his answer is also mildly sarcastic, given his audience partly consists of TV reporters.

In another episode (on President Clinton's peccadilloes):

(45) Q: Billy Graham has said that he forgives the President and anything the President may have done.
MR. MCCURRY: Well, that's encouraging. (Laughter)

The irony at first sight seems fairly normal. The famed preacher Billy Graham's opinions are evaluated in the dictum as important but with the opposite implication. However, the speaker does not use the hyperbole we have so often seen. Rather than saying 'that's magnificent', he uses the milder 'encouraging'. In other words, there is a mixture of normal irony and understatement at work here. The effect is that the unfavourable evaluation in the implicatum is also less extreme since the speaker presumably wants to avoid appearing to deride the popular preacher. It would seem that the stronger the approval/disapproval in the apparent narrative, the stronger the disapproval/approval in the other. All this lends considerable weight to Seto's ideas on reversal of polarity (1998), to which we may add the rider that there is an implicit rule which tells the hearer 'if the dictum is not extreme, do not overcharge the reversed evaluation'.

Litotes in irony is, in fact, simply the mirror of a much more common procedure, hyperbole in irony. It has been noted how often irony involves exaggeration. In the following couple of episodes from the briefings, someone says *a lot* to mean *a little*:

(46) Q: Please, proceed.
Q: – sorry – the Russians aren't part of that. Sorry, Sam.
Q: No, whatever time you require. (Laughter)
(47) Q: [...] Joe, how do you respond to those who say this is part of an effort to drive down Giuliani's numbers?

>   MR. LOCKHART: I'd say that the fact that we've been doing this for six years shows amazing, amazing preplanning on the part of lawyers at the Justice Department. (Laughter)

The first has already been discussed in the previous chapter as an ironic form of tease. It is a polite but ironic warning to the other to be brief. The overstatement in (47), highly charged with the repeated intensifier ('amazing, amazing'), evaluates the matter in hand extremely highly in order to imply that the accusation is to be evaluated as impossible, unfounded and even ridiculous. The higher the apparent appraisal the lower the intended one. Hyperbole in irony, of course, generally overlaps with good-bad evaluation reversal, given that exaggeration is normally projected as inherently bad: it would not go down well, for example, if the journalist in (46) really did take all the time in the world.

6.2.13 Other 'difficult cases' of irony

Understatement irony was one of the 'difficult' cases which the traditional theory of irony as *ideational meaning* negation was supposed to be unable to handle. It seems to be explained quite satisfactorily by positing reversal of *evaluative meaning*. Can this latter also handle other forms of irony cited in the literature as problematical?

Another kind of verisimilar irony is that in which some version of what the speaker believes is actually stated but with some degree of indirectness. One example discussed in several papers (Kaufer 1981: 501; Martin 1992: 86; Attardo 2000: 798), namely:

(10) America's allies – always there when they need you

does not imply that they are *not* there when they need you, but depends upon the reversal of the favourable evaluation of what the role of allies/friends should be, casting these specific allies in a negative light. This particular example is undoubtedly 'echoic' in the sense that its interpretation depends on the hearer's awareness of the adage 'friends are always there when you need them' and its favourable connotations. But other examples are not. Another much-debated instance (Gibbs and O'Brien 1991; Hamamoto 1998; Sperber and Wilson 1998) is:

(9) Mother (on entering child's room which is untidy): I love children who keep their rooms clean.

The mother is clearly not saying the opposite of what she means *ideationally*, that is, either 'I hate children who keep their rooms clean' or 'I love children whose rooms are untidy'. But the notion of *evaluation* reversal would predict quite simply that she is evaluating the scene in a contrary fashion and is implying (confidently assuming that the child will work out the import via the application of the same implicatures she is using) 'I *don't like* children (that is, *you*) who have untidy rooms'.

The briefings corpus offers the following:

(48) Q: Mike, the transcript records your very careful –
MR. MCCURRY: When you need a good, bizarre question, boy, I tell you, it's really helpful to have Lester Kinsolving. (Laughter)

The speaker is both expressing what he feels to be a truth, that Lester can be relied upon to provide off-the-wall questions (unfavourable evaluation), but he is also evoking a second script-like narrative of the kind: 'it is good to have X around when one requires something *useful*' (favourable evaluation).

Ironical questions are often cited as difficult cases, indeed are sometimes felt to be a test for any theory of irony, for instance:

(49)   Do you have to make that noise while you are eating?

(McDonald 1999: 488)

Once again the bisociative evaluation reversal theory would seem to account well for such cases. The speaker creates two narratives of the type:

N1 (dictum): (I ask you whether) you evaluate that noise as necessary. (i.e. as good)
N2 (implicatum): I evaluate it as unnecessary and indeed irksome. (i.e. as bad)

In the briefings we find a number of similar rhetorical questions, such as:

(50)   Q: If you were Osama bin Laden would you give a live interview right now on satellite feed – (Laughter)
       MR. FLEISCHER: Connie.

Note how the podium ignores the question and the questioner. These seem to contrast two narratives of the type:

N1 (dictum): (I ask you whether) you evaluate [this stupidity] as good.
N2 (implicatum): I evaluate it as self-evidently bad.

where the *point* is to suggest that the interlocutor must be stupid or naïve or incompetent.

McDonald also includes excessive politeness among challenging cases:

(51)   Oh I do beg your pardon, o exalted one!

(McDonald 1999: 488)

These seem to fall into the category already discussed of hyperbolic irony, and the subject is apparently evaluated most highly to mockingly imply the opposite.

Finally, apart from ironical understatement, Sperber and Wilson criticize traditional negation theory and advance their proposal of echoic mention/interpretation theory on the grounds that only the latter can elucidate ironical quotation and ironical interjection. Leaving aside the self-fulfilling circularity of supporting a theory of irony as echo on quotation data, we can safely conflate the two, and instances such as:

(2)   QUOTATION: When a man is tired of London, he is tired of life. (said in a metropolitan downpour)
(52)   INTERJECTION: Ah Tuscany in May! (said in an Italian rainstorm)

(Sperber and Wilson 1992: 55)

212 *Irony and sarcasm*

can be seen as drawing their effect from reversing the evaluation conveyed, in the first case, by the original version of the quotation and, in the second, by the unmarked version of the interjection.

6.3 Sarcasm

6.3.1 Sarcasm and irony: the same or different?

There is, writes Attardo, 'no consensus on whether sarcasm and irony are essentially the same thing, with superficial differences, or if they differ significantly' (2000: 795). Attardo himself favours the first of these positions, with the specification that 'sarcasm is an overtly aggressive type of irony, with clearer marker/cues and a clear target' (2000: 795, presumably clearer cues than implicit irony – explicit irony having the clearest markers of all). He nevertheless outlines the opinions of those who attempt to distinguish the two. Haiman (1990, 1998) believes that irony does not necessarily require the intention of the speaker, whereas sarcasm must be deliberate. There is such a thing as situational and/or dramatic irony, whilst sarcasm is strictly a verbal, usually spoken, phenomenon.

It might be useful to look at what dictionaries say. The *OED* reminds us that sarcasm derives from the Greek word σαρκάζειν, 'to tear flesh'. It does not include the word *irony* in its definition – 'A sharp, bitter, or cutting expression or remark; a bitter gibe or taunt' – but several of the quotation examples do:

> **1579** E.K. in *Spenser's Sheph. Cal.* Oct., Glosse, Tom piper, an ironicall Sarcasmus, spoken in derision of these rude wits [...]
> **1605** J. Dove *Confut. Atheism* 38 He called the other Gods so, by a figure called *Ironia*, or *Sarcasmus*.
> **1690** C. Nesse *Hist. & Myst. O. & N. Test.* I. 234 No lye, but an irony...a witty way of speaking?...such sarcasms as Elijah used.
> **1725** Blackwall *Introd. Class.* (ed. 3) 179 When a dying or dead Person is insulted with Scoffs and ironical Tartness 'tis usually call'd a Sarcasm.

We might recall how *Webster's* compares the two:

> IRONY differs from SARCASM in greater subtlety and wit. In SARCASM ridicule or mockery is used harshly, often crudely and contemptuously, for destructive purposes. It may be used in an indirect manner, and have the form of irony, as in 'What a fine musician you turned out to be!', or it may be used in the form of a direct statement, 'You couldn't play one piece correctly if you had two assistants.' The distinctive quality of SARCASM is present in the spoken word and manifested chiefly by vocal inflection, whereas SATIRE and IRONY, arising originally as literary and rhetorical forms, are exhibited in the organization or structuring of either language or literary material.

(Webster's)

Irony and sarcasm

What does the corpus data say? First of all, unsurprisingly, there is no evidence of explicit sarcasm markers analogous to *it is ironic that* or *ironically* and so on, in other words, there were no instances in any corpora of *it was sarcastic that* or *sarcastically* used as a disjunct. In recompense, there is a very good number of items such as [Human actor] *said/asked/enquired sarcastically*. This underlines the verbal and deliberate nature of the phenomemon; there is no such thing as 'situational' or 'dramatic' sarcasm.

There was some evidence that writers feel sarcasm and irony to be different, for instance:

(53)   But the tone of the book as a whole is more sarcastic than ironic. At times, Williams seems bent on being as offensive about Islam as possible without bringing down a fatwah on his head.

(Papers)

(54)   Jane Austen's infant stories show her sarcasm before life ripened it into irony.

(Papers)

The first of these lends weight to Attardo and *Webster's* claim that sarcasm is especially acute and aggressive in its criticism, the second to the latter's observation that irony is seen as more artistically valid than satire.

The collocational evidence in *Papers* shows, first of all, how *sarcasm/sarcastic* is often perceived as aggressive or face-threatening, in the terms we have adopted in this work. The collocates include:

aggressive, intimidating, belittling, bitter, brutal, cynical, hostile, piercing, sneering, stingingly.

It is also seemingly deemed to be direct, unsubtle, unsophisticated:

elephantine, heavy, loud, lumbering, ponderous, unremitting;

although there are several exceptions:

clever, genially, splendidly.

This apparent split personality of sarcasm gives food for thought. It can at times also be toned down:

mild, soft, suave;

whilst it is no surprise to learn that it is frequently associated with humour:

humour (8), *laugh/laughter* (4), *smile* (3), *wit/witty* (3) and *jokes* (3).

6.3.2 Sarcasm in the briefings

Given that phrase markers of sarcasm do not exist, we cannot replicate the work described earlier on explicit irony. How, then, is it possible to locate instances of sarcastic usage without relying entirely on observer intuition? We have already considered the collocational evidence that sarcasm is often seen as particularly face-threatening. In addition, *Webster's* definition of sarcasm included ridicule and mockery. One form of mockery, as we have seen, is reformulation, defined as repeating back to a speaker some version of his/her previous utterance. Reformulation, as we have seen, can be highly face-threatening and so laughter episodes in which one speaker appears to reformulate another speaker's move may be prime candidates for sites of sarcasm: see Chapter 5, example (52) and also:

(55) Q: Barry, let me ask you this. When you say that you have no view of the possible testimony of Monica Lewinsky, does that mean that in the daily meetings that you attend at the higher levels in the White House, no view was expressed of her coming testimony? Or does it mean that you were told to express no view of her testimony? (Laughter)

The podium's words are repeated back with reversal of evaluation at the end, which is clearly designed to attack the podium's face. The speaker recalls an earlier podium statement of having 'no view' on the matter, but the journalist evaluates both the statement and the podium's face very negatively indeed.

In the following episode the reformulation is a little less obvious:

(56) MR. MCCURRY: [...] the problem with it is it might erase our very good surplus event today. The American people have a surplus and we're entitled to enjoy it today.
Q: Story of the year. Day, I mean. (Laughter)

The journalist coins the phrase 'story of the year' based on 'story of the day', a phrase the podium often uses. The speaker then goes on to produce the original source phrase too, in order to make the reference clear. The fact that the podium is the source is not stated openly but the audience recognizes the reformulation of the *kind* of language he uses and delight in the face attack. The evaluation of 'story of the day' and 'story of the year' are reversed, the first usually being good news, whilst the second is mocking. The point is to imply that the podium is tiresome in his repetition of the financial surplus story.

Not all reformulation, however, appears particularly threatening:

(57) MR. MCCURRY: [...] that after hearing for years and years about deficits, we now have a surplus, as of midnight tonight, as of the end of this fiscal year.
Q: Why can't there be two stories? (Laughter)
MR. MCCURRY: Looking back over the last eight months, I would have been happy to have had two stories. (Laughter)

The podium is complaining about the press's obsession with the Clinton-Lewinsky affair. The podium ironically reverses the journalist's narrative – I'm not avoiding two stories, I welcome them – but the tone appears more rueful than aggressive, evoking as it does an in-group script of 'tough job'. The effect seems to be teasing of a rather bonding kind (Boxer and Cortés-Conde 1997) since the evoking of in-scripts/in-personae/in-language stresses group belonging. We are reminded that corpus evidence suggests that sarcasm can be adjudged 'mild', even 'suave'. Such occasional favourable perceptions of sarcasm may then, in general, be due to the possibility of combining it with positive face-work and in-group teasing. Another interesting episode is the following (the context is the announcement of the retirement of Amy Weiss, a member of the White House staff: Mr Leavy is also a member of the staff and an occasional podium. We are in full interactional mode):

(58) MR. LOCKHART: [...] It's Amy Weiss's last day here at the White House.
Q: Awwwww.
Q: We were hoping it would be Leavy. (Laughter)
MR. LOCKHART: That remark was completely uncalled for. Who said it? (Laughter)

There can be little doubt about the weight of the face attack on Mr Leavy, but we are reminded that:

> The irony of irony is that an extreme insult is less insulting than a mild insult, since the former is less likely to be taken literally and more probably cognitively restructured as 'He's only joking'.
>
> (La Fave and Mannell 1976: 121)

The podium certainly takes it as a joke and playfully joins in by feigning mock offence.

6.3.3 Sperber and Wilson: echoic irony or echoic sarcasm?

It might be remarked that the kind of reformulation observed here is a kind of 'echo', an observation which becomes particularly interesting in relation to Sperber and Wilson's theory of irony. It will be recalled that they claim all irony is echoic mention/interpretation of some previous utterance, thought, belief etc. An examination of the examples of irony they devise, especially in the Sperber and Wilson (1995: 237–245) elaboration, reveals that they are almost all instances of sarcasm, for example:

(5) Peter is quite well-read. He's even heard of Shakespeare.

(1995: 242)

and:

(59) PETER: It's a lovely day for a picnic.
[They go for a picnic and it rains.]
MARY (sarcastically): It's a lovely day for a picnic indeed.

(1992: 239)

These examples seem to fit the sarcasm bill quite nicely: they are 'overtly aggressive' and have a 'clear victim'. We might well surmise that, in concentrating on sarcasm, which often functions by a relatively straightforward mocking reformulation of a victim's utterance, Sperber and Wilson overestimated the importance of echoic mention to the phenomenon of irony in general. It also reminds us of the dangers inherent in devising one's own examples to suit one's own theory of any linguistic phenomenon, without taking the further step, if possible, of testing it against authentic data.

6.3.4 Conclusions on sarcasm

The 'duality' of sarcasm

The question remains of the apparent duality inherent in the general concept of sarcasm: it can be seen as both funny and hurtful, it can be both lumbering and sparkling, loud yet suave. Some light is thrown on the question by the psycholinguistic research of Jorgensen (1996) and Toplak and Katz (2000). These were studies in which informants were asked to evaluate their reactions to sarcasm from three different viewpoints, that of speaker, of the victim and of the overhearer or audience, in order to ascertain whether there are any differences in the ways sarcastic moves are perceived and assessed by the three parties involved. More technically, they aimed to discover whether there are any mismatches between the illocutionary intent of a sarcastic speaker and the perlocutionary effects of a sarcastic speech act as experienced by the other two parties.

First, we have already observed how sarcasm can potentially play a bonding role, and this accounts in part for some of its occasional positive appraisal. Things, however, may be more complex than this suggests. Toplak and Katz found that third parties, on hearing sarcasm used, assumed the relationship was closer than either speaker or butt necessarily felt it to be. The bonding potential of sarcasm might be overestimated by outside observers.

The weight of the face-threat performed by a sarcastic remark was also found to be perceived differently by speaker and victim. In general, the experimental informants when in speaker role unsurprisingly judged their sarcastic performance in more positive ways, as skilful and adroit. Moreover, from the speaker's point of view it was seen merely as an outlet of aggression, whereas the victim felt it to be a particularly drastic form of criticism, more drastic than criticism performed directly. Both Jorgenson and Toplak and Katz also speculate that such effects may well be exacerbated when sarcasm is performed before an audience (as in the briefings). This would go some way to explaining why sarcasm is seen as *piercing* and *ponderous*, if you are the victim, but *suave* and *genial* if you happen to be the author.

Sarcasm v. irony revisited

Nevertheless, on the whole, sarcasm is judged negatively, it has far more unfavourable collocates than favourable ones. The reverse is the case for the collocates of irony: looking at the concordances of the item in section 6.2.5 we find a good number of elegant or erudite words and expressions, including *genius for, tactful, lyrical, mercurially, art, elegance* and *colourful cocktails*. The explanation is the one outlined in the previous paragraph, that is, some critical remark may be described, may be characterized, as *ironic* by the speaker but as *sarcastic* by the victim. We can conclude that 'the distinctions between irony and sarcasm are as likely to be pragmatic and discoursal as semantic' (John Morley, personal communication). We are reminded of the *Washington Post*'s playful definition of the word 'sar*chasm*' as 'the gulf between the author of sarcastic wit and the person who doesn't get it'.

Evidence from the *Papers* corpus lends support to this view. Speakers appear to have no problem in assigning *ironical* speech acts to themselves. A concordance of *I* within five words to the left of *irony/ironical* produces seven instances of *I find it ironic*, as well as:

1 ...how can I put it in an ironic way...?
2 I wrote up a heavily ironic story for the Observer.
3 Even the sublime Guardian (I speak ironically, not complacently)...
4 I reflect, not without irony, that I have probably enjoyed it more than him.

It is seen as sophisticated to *be* ironic. And, as the following show:

5 I relished the irony, unfortunately lost on this audience...
6 I explained that a grammatical error, in my previous week's column, was deliberate because I was being ironic. And I went on to say that there will always be someone who takes irony literally.

it is just as clever to *perceive* it, especially when others fail to. As we might imagine, people are less eager to own up to sarcasm and when they do so there is often a note of apology:

7 'I look laconic and I have a sarcastic way,' he says, adding that it is all a front. 'I'm the original duck. Calm on the outside. Paddling like hell underneath.'

in other words, I may appear sarcastic but that is not the real me. Similarly:

8 As I was feeling so low, the remarks I made were sarcastic and caustic. To my amazement they brought the house down and the germ of a comedy act was born.

Ironically, as it were, on the very evening I was feeling my lowest and sarcasm got the better of me, I was embraced by success.

The link then between verbal irony and sarcasm is undoubtedly very close but, to conclude, we must recall that the term *irony* has an illustrious literary history and is celebrated for its elegance,[4] whilst its less fortunate sibling, *sarcasm*, has a more chequered reputation and is more often than not disowned by polite society. In consequence, irony tends to reside in the mouth of the speaker, sarcasm in the ear of the unfortunate victim.

6.4 Conclusions

In this chapter, we have examined the use of irony and sarcasm in communicative contexts in the hope of discovering how they work, how they are comprehended and the functions they serve, as well as the nature of the relation that exists between the two. We have seen in particular that irony is not a single, uniform phenomenon but can be explicit or implicit in form, humorous or non-humorous (explicit irony is rarely, if ever, humorous in intent) and can have different degrees of strength (see below). Nevertheless, we have tried to ascertain what these different types have in common.

We began by discussing some of the current issues in the literature on these topics, particularly the controversies surrounding the echoic versus negation theories, the one-stage versus two-stage processing conjectures and the question of whether surface meaning is rejected or retained.

In an attempt to reach a more objective criterion for selecting ironic data than is generally applied, we began with instances of explicit irony, that is, episodes containing an explicit lexical marker of irony: *ironically, it is especially ironic that*, and so on. Applying some of the lessons learned, we went on to look at instances of, first of all, implicit irony and then sarcasm in the briefings, paying particular attention to 'difficult' cases, that is, uses of irony/sarcasm which are not well explained by some of the pre-existing theories.

The analyses showed how irony is a bisociative phenomenon in which the speaker constructs a pair of narratives, both of which are more or less present in the text in explicit irony, whereas in the implicit type only one is apparent and the other is implied. At first sight it might seem that only implicit irony actually performs an operation, whilst the explicit sort merely points out the irony pre-existing in a particular situation. This, however, is far from the case, as we saw in the examples from authentic discourse; both forms can be used strategically and creatively to execute criticism. Both forms can also misfire; simply explicitly labelling some relation 'ironic' does not necessarily make it so, whilst attempts at implicit irony can fall flat if they are not perceived as such.

The two narratives at work in an ironical utterance are portrayed by the author as being in sharp contrast and the hypothesis which has arisen out of the examination of data conducted here is that the principal mechanism of contrast employed is reversal of evaluation. In other words, the evaluation expressed or implied in the first narrative is suddenly and radically overturned in the second. Evaluation is to be intended in the dualistic sense developed by Hunston that an entity is pronounced to be either good, favourable, pleasant or propitious for some party or is projected as bad, unfavourable, unpleasant and so on. Often irony has a moral or moralistic overtone and thus the reversal frequently involves the interchange of propriety and impropriety. In the variant case of what we have termed litotic irony, the evaluation reversal works instead by projecting an entity as *minor, small, only a little*, whilst implying that in reality it is *large, a lot*, usually in fact *too much*.

Sharing the mechanisms of bisociation and evaluation reversal explains why irony and humour are felt to have something in common. As Attardo notes, 'the functions of humor and irony seem to be largely overlapping' (2001a: 174). He lists 'retractability' (humorous or ironic intent can sometimes be denied), social

Irony and sarcasm 219

management (in and out-group marking), mental dexterity and politeness. Moreover, many jokes, as we saw in Chapter 1, depend on the interplay of propriety and impropriety. However, since both humour and irony have so many functions, a certain overlap is not surprising. The fact that they exploit similar mechanisms, on the other hand, does account in particular for the sense that irony is often somehow perceived as comic.

The notion of reversal of evaluative meaning is able to handle precisely those objections raised by Sperber and Wilson to theories of negation or reversal of propositional meaning. Negation of propositional meaning converts a statement such as 'John is a genius' into 'John is not a genius'. Reversal of evaluative meaning is more pragmatically flexible, and in this case would convert *genius* into *idiot*, which is what such utterances are normally used to mean. We have seen in practice in the data how the strength of the evaluation in the dictum is reflected by the strength of opposite polarity in the implicatum.

In addition, evaluation reversal can explain verisimilar irony, where a speaker does not dissociate from the thought expressed in the dictum ('His thinking has undergone quite an evolution') and it copes quite adequately with ironic questions and interjections, which have no propositional content. Utterances can have meanings other than propositions, including and especially evaluative meaning.

As Barbe also discovered, there are differences in the strength of irony constructions, and also, we might add, in their 'success', in the sense of well-formedness. This is a complex issue and there are a number of potential well- and less well-formed types. If a protagonist says something containing evaluation E in one narrative and deliberately and wilfully says, believes or commits ¬E in the other, we have a well-formed hypocrisy, duplicity and/or betrayal irony (the symbol ¬ is used in logic to indicate negation. Here, by ¬E, I wish to indicate reversal of evaluation). If a protagonist says or does E in one narrative and then inadvertently commits ¬E in the other, we tend to have a stupidity irony. If a protagonist believes E but in the second narrative someone else or events conspire to show that things are in reality ¬E, then we tend to have either a tragic or a comic dupe irony. Littman and Mey (1991) talk of a kind of 'thwarted plans' irony template, in which someone, despite acting rightly and properly, nevertheless suffers unpleasant consequences of their plans. Weaker or less successful or less well-formed ironies occur in at least three cases. First, when one protagonist commits E and another protagonist somehow associated with her/him commits or is involved in ¬E. Second, where there appears to be not a radical reversal but only a divergence between the two narratives, for instance (28) where A wishes to do one thing, B wishes something different. Third, where there is only a time relation between the two narratives, in other words, a coincidence, a 'just when' type of irony, as in (26) where a protagonist dies just when another was supposed to appear on the same platform as him. We saw a similar example in the briefings in Chapter 2, at the end of example (6), when Mr McCurry, on his retirement, has been asked what his best and worst moments as podium have been (my emphasis):

(60) [...] Actually – the worst moments and the ones that I've struggled with, *ironically*, we touched on today, and that's the tragedy in the Balkans [...]

Here, too, *ironically* only really means 'coincidentally'.

A question which has received far less attention than its due in the literature is the fact that irony in use always has a *point*. This fact is entirely in consequence of irony's association with evaluation, as Hunston and Thompson assert:

> Evaluation which both organizes the discourse and indicates its significance might be said to tell the reader the 'point' of the discourse.
>
> (2000: 12)

We have seen a number of different sorts of points to ironical utterances: they can be vehicles for accusations of varying degrees of directness, of cynicism, hypocrisy, double-standards, betrayal and inconstancy.

Herein lies yet another controversy surrounding irony. Is the point always in some way critical or at least, in the case of irony of fate, negative, as Grice, Sperber and Wilson and others claim? Or is *asteism*, that is praise by apparent blame, also a subset of irony, as Attardo (2000) avers and of which he gives the following example?

(61) These American cars which break down after 100,000 miles!

We have already discussed (Chapter 2) one example of asteism from the briefings (my emphasis) '[we shall persuade Congress to accept our nomination of Governor Weld by hard work] and by the overall superior record and qualifications of the nominee – *save his summa cum laude degree from Harvard*' (Laughter). Whether we include asteism under the heading of irony, or call it reverse irony or something else altogether seems to be a question of definitional choice. It may well be more frequent than generally thought, especially in informal talk, and more work needs to be done on the phenomenon.[5] Nevertheless, criticism remains the main point of irony, and certainly of sarcasm. Kotthoff (2003) claims that irony among friends is used as much to bond as to bite, and we have seen in the briefings data too how it can strengthen in-group feeling. However, I contend that these effects are exploitations of its main critical function: it bonds by saying, look, I might disparage and fault-find, but trust me enough to know I do not really mean what I'm saying.

Which brings us to the fundamental question of what the main discourse functions of irony might be. Why do speakers employ it and with such regularity – why do they not simply limit themselves to direct criticism? Sperber and Wilson, in their critique of the standard non-echoic approach negation theory, make the following requirement:

> it would then have to be explained how the practice of saying one thing and meaning the opposite could have arisen spontaneously in culture after culture; how children acquire it; [...] why it lends itself to blame-by-praise more easily than praise-by-blame.
>
> (1998: 290)

The observations we have made in this chapter suggest a number of ready responses. Given the pervasiveness of evaluation, playing with evaluation for rhetorical effect does not seem at all strange or unforeseeable. More in particular, speakers use irony to be interesting, incisive, dramatic and memorable. This may simply be performed for the purposes of self-display but Brown and Levinson also include 'making a good story' among the strategies of positive politeness. A speaker, they say, can 'communicate to H[earer] that he shares some of his wants' by intensifying 'the interest of his own contributions to the conversation' (1987: 106). Laughter is often the reward for the verbal sophistication that irony is perceived as displaying. Allied to this is the intricate face-work it allows speakers to indulge in. Irony and sarcasm, as we have seen on many occasions here, permit speakers to perform face moves indirectly. Indirectness is fundamental to politeness theory which therefore actively predicts that irony should arise in culture after culture. Indirectness has a whole range of interpersonal functions, and it should therefore come as no surprise that such an obvious form of indirectness as irony – evaluation reversal – should appear across human cultures and be acquired as a skill by normal children.

Finally, we conclude by addressing the controversies outlined in the first part of the chapter. We have already raised a good number of objections to echoic theory, which, we will recall, lays down a three-part processing procedure

> a recognition of the utterance as echoic;
> an identification of the source of the opinion echoed;
> a recognition that the speaker's attitude to the opinion echoed is one of rejection or dissociation.
>
> (Sperber and Wilson 1995: 240)

These reservations can be summarized briefly. We have met far too many episodes in which no source was discernible or could ever be discerned. As Attardo points out: 'the echoic mention theory involves some extra steps (labelling the utterance echoic and looking for a source) which are unnecessary' (2000: 807) since, as we have seen, simple contextual inappropriateness is usually enough to trigger the audience's awareness of irony, what we have termed here their 'irony frame'.

Echoic theory also, as its authors readily admit, cannot handle non-ostensive or non-deliberate irony. Echo presupposes deliberateness, choosing a previous piece of language to use in mockery. But non-deliberate irony abounds and presents no problem to reversal theory: in such cases it is simply the hearer who perceives a double narrative that a speaker did not intend. Echo theory also fails to connect verbal irony to other non-ostensive forms such as dramatic or situational irony (section 6.2.1). Reversal theory links them quite satisfactorily.

The most damning criticism of all, however, is the last. There is no doubt that cases of echoic irony exist, especially echoic sarcasm, but echo-plus-disapproval/ rejection is easily subsumed as a subcategory of a larger phenomenon by evaluation reversal theory. To reduce *all* irony to mere mocking echo is to turn one's back on the richness, the power, the elegance, the variety and the sheer creativity that the use of this figure entails. We might recall some of the rich positive associations we found the word to have in *Papers*. Irony does not echo but evokes and invents. Martin talks of 'other worlds', we content ourselves with 'alternative narratives'. Irony does not simply hold up a mirror to some folly or vice or accident of fate – it shapes it, construes it, warps and exaggerates it for the sake of a speaker's argument.

Turning now to the second controversy: is irony processed in one stage or two, and is the apparent meaning discarded or retained in order to arrive at the real one? Taking the second part first, we have seen both how hearers can choose to respond either to the dictum or the implicatum and how speakers readily presume their audience will not only retain but engage with both meanings.

As for the first, the one or two-stages question, we have observed how the understanding of irony, like the understanding of most utterances in context, especially those in any way indirect, comprises several stages. We might surmise that the procedure is something like the following. We 'access' salient meaning first (by definition first – this is what makes it salient). This is not necessarily the literal sense but could be the ironical one because our irony-recognition frame may be alerted by some incongruity between the message and its context. But as is usual with incoming information, we generally go on to ask ourselves what other meanings the utterance might have. We ponder: what are the speaker's intentions? What evaluation is the speaker expressing with regard both to their message, to themselves and to the audience? What does the utterance and the speaker's evaluation mean for my face? How should I best respond to protect my face and influence the communicative situation to my advantage?

In this regard, undoubtedly one of the most interesting experimental studies in the area is McDonald's (1999) research into the reaction to irony/sarcasm on the part of patients with traumatic brain injury (TBI). She found that 'brain-injured subjects who have no difficulty with literal comments were frequently stymied by the same comments meant sarcastically [which] suggests that such nonliteral comments have a special status and require additional cognitive processing'. She also discovered that 'inferencing about mental states' – about what the speaker knows, what knowledge is shared, the relationship among participants, in other words, all the information which permits us to adopt the point of view and understand the intentions of other speakers – caused far more difficulty than inferences 'about the (counter)factual claims' (1999: 499). In other words, such patients are unable to conduct the best-guess inferencing, the construction of mental models from the context of situation which is vital to 'getting' the irony (and much humour, of course, as we saw in section 1.2.6). Thus, at least in these cases, it is assessing the affective, evaluative and face relevance of the ironic move which causes problems and takes up the time.

McDonald's work thus lends considerable weight to a multistage theory of irony understanding and reminds us how purely cognitive approaches which ignore the interpersonal aspects are unlikely to reveal too many of the mysteries of a phenomenon as ingenious – and as devious – as irony.

6.5 Postscript: a bout of irony

From a lexicological point of view, it is somewhat singular that the term *bout* has been very widely adopted in the field of laughter studies, in competition with *episode* (in this work the two are used interchangeably), to indicate a single instance of laughter. Corpus evidence (from *5mil* and *Papers*) shows how *a bout of* and *bouts of* have a highly unfavourable semantic prosody, that is, show a very marked tendency to co-occur with highly unpleasant entities. These include diseases: *a bout of pneumonia/tonsillitis/morning sickness*, along with a mixed bag of other unpleasantries: *arrogance, childish petulance, drought* and *manhandling*.

However, among its co-occurring items we stumble upon the occasional *prima facie* favourable one, for example, *these bouts of drama-therapy*. However, a close look at the wider co-text:

1   As well as feeling unrealistic, these bouts of drama-therapy come across as too pat a way of showing how easy it would be to lapse into the old power relations [...]

shows how the writer is using the negativity of *bouts* to be ironic about the drama-therapy sessions in question, that is, to reverse or undermine the favourable evaluation. As we have noted throughout this chapter, irony consists in just such overturning of the polarity of evaluation.

Such is the priming for unfavourable prosody and potential for irony of *bout(s) of* that its mere appearance seems often to be enough to instruct the text receiver how to evaluate the phrase it appears in:

2   Dick's latest bout of culinary angst coincides with the strawberry season.
3   John Major arrives for his annual bout of bagpipes and charades.
4   Iraq's latest bout of defiance and probing of grey areas of UN resolutions...

and it certainly serves to bolster any underlying unfavourable evaluation lurking elsewhere in the co-text (in italics):

5   The *catch* is the price of this bout of champagne socialism...
6   The prospect of another bout of cohabitation with an exultant conservative majority must *dismay* him.

This sort of what we might call 'collocational irony' was first noted by Louw (1993), who quotes an example from *Small World* by David Lodge:

The modern conference resembles the pilgrimage of medieval Christendom in that it allows the participants to indulge themselves in all the pleasures and diversions of travel while apparently bent on self-improvement.

He shows, through evidence from the *Cobuild* corpus, that *bent on* usually collocates with pretty unpleasant items – *bent on destroying/harrying/mayhem*.

And so, by reversing the evaluative prosody of *bent on* in making it collocate with the evidently favourable *self-improvement*, Lodge is searching for an ironic effect at the expense of academics. He also argues that writers can also diverge from a prosody by accident, in which case the reader may detect a difference between what the writer is apparently saying and what he/she really believes. One wonders, then, just how researchers into laughter who have adopted 'bout' actually view their object of research. Pathological laughter exists, of course, but surely in general it is a jolly good thing.

7 General conclusions

A number of research questions were posed at the end of the Introduction (section I.9). To evaluate the extent to which these questions have been treated, we need to effect a rapid summary of the observations and findings obtained thus far.

7.1 Overview

In the Introduction we introduced the concept of laughter-talk and conducted a rapid review of past linguistic research into laughter in discourse. The main purpose of this book was to examine the linguistic context around laughter episodes in authentic discourse, in the attempt to discover what precisely provokes laughter. Although well-aware that humour and laughter are by no means coextensive, we resolved that one of our aims in this work would be to consider how they might interact.

In Chapter 1 we examined the most influential of current cognitive theories – or family of theories – regarding humour, namely, bisociation, the clash of two habitually 'incompatible' or 'incongruous' frames of reference (Koestler 1964). As Ritchie (2004) points out, almost all current cognitive explanations of humour derive to some degree or other from the bisociative theory of the clash of incongruities.

Koestler's ideas were revisited, particularly as regards *joke humour*, the area for which he intended them. A critical appraisal was also conducted of the bisociative Semantic Script Theory of (joke) Humour. This appraisal necessitated an examination of Script Theory itself, a script being defined as a coherent set of facts and rules associated with a particular situation, which the mind has assimilated through learning. Raskin's theory contends that jokes entail the sudden movement from one script to another. Here, however, it was contended that many jokes function in a somewhat more complex manner. It was proposed that human cognition relies on two general principles, namely, script recall and inferencing. Many jokes seem to make use of, not scripts, but best-guess mental models constructed through inferencing, and so exploit the possibility of shifting not just from one script to another but from the one cognitive mechanism to the other. I proposed the superordinate term *narrative* to include both script-based and inference-based sequences of events. We noted how, in the modern linguistic theory of lexicogrammar, the processing of language is described as employing two general principles, the phraseological and the open-choice, closely analogous to script recall and inferencing respectively.

It was seen, however, that sudden narrative shift alone is not a sufficient condition for humour. The nature of the relationship between narratives is of paramount importance. In other words, as Glenn asks, what do writers mean by incompatibility between narratives and what kinds of incongruity – and ways of presenting it – are funny? We attempted a partial answer to such questions using both formal concepts, such as evaluation and reversal of evaluation, and more pragmatic cultural-moral ones, especially (im-)propriety.

Bisociation, then, is often invoked to explain joke humour. In Chapter 2 we considered whether bisociative narrative shift can also help explain *laughter-talk* in *spontaneous discourse*. By examining the corpus data, evidence was uncovered of several kinds of sudden and deliberate shifts by speakers which precede outbursts of laughter. These include, first of all, shifts of *mode*, from the transactional (where attention is paid to doing the business of briefings) to the interactional (where attention is focused on personal social interaction), which facilitates a transition into play frame. They also comprehend shifts of *narrative* and of *persona*, generally entailing the sudden adoption of fantasy narratives/personae. And they include shifts of linguistic *register*, both 'downwards', traditionally recognized as a method of achieving comic bathos, but also, and less expectedly, 'upwards', a process which we define as 'upgrading' and which is often used for parody, including self-parody. It is concluded that something very akin to bisociation plays a vital part in spontaneous non-joke-based conversational laughter-talk. It is also clear that, as predicted by the narrative shift theory outlined in the previous chapter, inferencing and not just script recall has to be employed by listeners in interpreting fantasy narratives and personae.

However, we also unearthed intriguing evidence that bisociation in authentic discourse is no idle phenomenon, no end in itself as it sometimes appears to be in joke research. On the contrary, these sudden transitions of narrative, with their accompanying switches of role and language are very frequently performed for a precise rhetorical purpose (where, by *rhetoric*, we intend the art of persuasion). Participants adopt fantasy narratives and roles which favour their side of an argument, which help to project their professed view of the world and which reflect well on themselves and their clients. It also became clear that different participants espouse different strategies.

In Chapter 2 we began to see how laughter-talk contributes to the construction of identity within the group and in Chapter 3 we continued to examine its social aspects through an examination of the data. The framework of social relations embraced draws heavily upon Brown and Levinson's Politeness theory, especially their definition of positive and negative face. We examined first of all the different kinds of face on display and at risk in a professional but informal environment such as briefings. Of special interest is the relationship between *facework* and the notion of in-group and out-group. Numerous examples were uncovered of the way speakers use laughter-talk to imply their own belonging to the group and, often, at the same time, to manoeuvre their argumentative adversary into the role of 'out-person'. The employment of *asides*, that is, explicit references to briefings business and in-group shared knowledge, was a frequent means of claiming common ground and a regular site of recognition laughter. We reflected too on the effect of the presence of an audience on facework, especially given that briefings are followed by quite a variety: the people in the room, the TV audience, the podium's political masters and journalist colleagues who observe proceedings at a distance, not to mention 'foreign powers'.

One of the most frequent sites of laughter is subsequent upon some form of *hitches and glitches* in the performance of briefings business. Laughter is closely bound up, in social situations, with the management of embarrassment, real and potential. From the evidence here, it would seem in particular to be used to signal that some action, some behaviour is being perceived as unusual and untypical. People laugh at what they find surprising but then adjudge to be non-threatening. People laugh at their own mistakes, shortcomings or *faux pas* to imply that these do not represent their normal behaviour whilst the audible and visual signalling intrinsic to laughter tells others that there is nothing to worry about. Goffman (1981) argues that laughter in such cases is a form of *remedial* work, negotiating the return to normality. Laughing at other's shortcomings, however, is more complex. At times, it can express affiliation, signalling that the hearers too recognize this is not your normal behaviour (laughing *with*). At others, of course, it expresses the opposite (laughing *at*), and can be deeply face-threatening.

We saw too how it was necessary to take into account at least two sorts of face when examining institutional talk, that is, *competence face* and *affective face*. We noted how speakers attempt to remedy the loss of one by seeking to bolster the other.

In Chapter 4 we returned to the theme of bisociation as it relates to puns and *wordplay* or *phraseplay*. The pun was defined as a bisociative play between two stretches of discourse which are phonologically similar but different in meaning.

In defining wordplay and attempting to answer the question of whether linguistics can help define its *quality*, that is, the difference between a good pun and a bad one, we drew on the concepts of *delexicalization* (Sinclair 1991) and *relexicalization* (Partington 1998) as developed in the field of Corpus Linguistics. In Chapter 1 we examined studies which claimed that the collocational or phraseological tendency was the default way of interpreting stretches of discourse, whereby the stretch is taken as a single unit but, should this fail (in the sense of failing to explain the text), hearers retain the option of applying the open-choice principle of treating a stretch as a composite of smaller parts. It is always possible to treat even tightly idiomatic phrases as if they were capable of analysis into smaller units. This enforced reinterpretation of whole units of linguistic schemata into smaller analytical elements is the mechanism driving much bisociative phraseplay.

We went on to examine the wordplay and phraseplay in two sets of data, newspaper headlines and the briefings. From the first, we were able to construct a taxonomy of the mechanisms used by headline writers, namely, *substitution, abbreviation, insertion* and *rephrasing*. We also considered the psychological mechanisms readers must use to detect the bisociation and link the new phraseology

228 General conclusions

they find on the page to the 'original' versions stored in the brain. Again, concepts developed in Corpus Linguistics were useful. In sum, there seem to be two distinct cognitive mechanisms of which hearers avail themselves: the recognition of phrase structure and co-occurring-item recall.

In examining the second data set, the briefings, we considered Norrick's argument (1993, 2003) that punning, in contrast to other forms of humour, anecdotes for instance, is always, as he puts it, *disruptive* of conversation. However, a good number of episodes were unearthed in the briefings where wordplay is only apparently disruptive of discourse argumentation and, in reality, is used strategically to advance it.

In Chapter 5 we returned to the themes of facework and how speakers manoeuvre themselves and others in terms of the in/out group. The data presents many examples of what appears to be laughter occasioned by teases and verbal duels.

Using corpus data as evidence, *teasing* was defined, in terms of the laughter-talk theories developed here, as a face-threatening act performed (apparently) in non-*bona-fide* mode. It is non-*bona fide* because it violates the maxim of sincerity; it is insincere in that it is (supposedly) not meant to really threaten the hearer's face. It appears to be a fictional attack, though this appearance can in practice be deceptive and may veil more aggressive intentions. We went on to examine who teases whom, when and for what reason. From the data, we hazarded a typology of teasing. There seem to be three general classes of tease which might be called, respectively, the *frustration*, the *fallibility* and the *mimicry* teases. A fourth sort, the *cynicism* tease, displays elements of the other three. We then examined the various strategies of response to teasing which victims can employ – from ignoring, through playing along to counter-attack or verbal duelling – together with the relative merits and demerits they seem to display in practice. The typology of responses and preferences displayed by the participants in this particular discourse type was different from that found in other studies (especially Drew 1987; Tholander and Aronsson 2002), suggesting that contextual features such as the presence or otherwise of an audience and the age and roles of participants are very influential. We noted how bisociation plays a part in teasing, given that many teases contain a considerable degree of contrastiveness, where the teaser seizes upon a previous speaker's utterance and produces a different, less favourable evaluative reading, usually to imply how naïve or credulous he or she was to believe what they did.

There is much evidence, from corpora and from literature in the field, that both language users and analysts feel there is a natural link between *sarcasm* and *irony*, and that both are often associated with humour. In Chapter 6 we examined the use of irony and sarcasm using contextualized data from newspapers and interactive data from the briefings corpus.

We began by examining speakers' and writers' uses of what Barbe (1993) calls 'explicit irony markers', such as *it is ironic that, ironically, in an ironic example of, there is a certain irony*, in order to discover what speakers instinctively feel irony to involve and how they use critical (and defensive) irony for strategic argumentative effect.

The principal mechanism of irony was adjudged to be bisociative, because it juxtaposes two narratives, one of which reverses the meaning – the *evaluative* meaning – expressed in the other. In explicit irony both narratives are present in the text, whilst in implicit irony one of the narratives is apparent in the text (*dictum*) and the other is implied (*implicatum*). Having already defined irony as involving evaluation reversal, it was contended that candidate sites of implicit irony can be identified with a degree of objectivity in interactive discourse by localizing laughter episodes where speakers employ some form of reversal, especially when this is highlighted by tokens of intensification (Seto 1998). The analysis of such sites shows how closely irony and its close relative sarcasm are bound up both with facework and with strategic argumentation.

As regards two of the current controversies in irony studies, we found, first of all, much evidence of how irony, rather than being 'echoic' of previous utterances or viewpoints (Sperber and Wilson 1981, 1995, 1988), is used 'proactively' and creatively to argue one's own case and tactically construe the arguments of one's interlocutor. Many instances were also found in the data where participants – both speakers and hearers – play with both the dictum and implicatum of an ironic utterance, lending support to those who argue that, far from the surface meaning being 'abandoned' in favour of the second, it is preserved and that the meanings coexist (Giora 1995; Giora *et al.* 1998).

7.2 Appraisal of observations and findings

First of all, then, I hope to have given some indication of the utility of a corpus-based approach to the study of a complex psychological and sociological phenomenon such as the role of laughter-talk in interaction. The integration of quantitative and qualitative analyses encouraged by Corpus-Assisted Discourse Studies methodology provides insights which can be tested against the data, whilst the very act of testing provides new insights to be pursued.

We have seen much evidence that laughter is not simply a response to incoming stimuli but that, as Glenn would have it, people 'do' laughter, laughter helps participants to 'do' talk and laughter 'does' the participants (2003: 3). It plays an essential role in building and expressing affiliation, alignment, identity and relationships.

We have learned too that laughter-talk is far from being a luxury or a pastime or a 'diversion' in either sense of the word. It is integral to many of the rhetorical strategies speakers use to construct identity through talk and to make their case in a competitive, argumentative environment.

It seems, moreover, that bisociation plays an important role in laughter-talk well beyond joke humour and wordplay, the areas in which it has generally been contemplated. The rapid and unexpected shift from one language mode, frame, narrative or register to another is a valuable key to understanding the cognitive processes underlying much *conversational* laughter-talk. Irony and sarcasm, frequently associated with wit and laughter, rely on the bisociative contrast between what is said and what is implied, whilst even much teasing involves a second speaker producing a contrasting variation of a first speaker's utterance.

7.2.1 Bisociative shift and evaluation reversal

What gradually became very clear during the course of this work was the strong association between the bisociative shift and the socio-psychological mechanism of reversal of evaluation. In jokes, this tended to take the form of the replacement of the proper with the improper, that is, the exchange of a socially and morally acceptable narrative with some improper version of the same. This frequently involved the *reinterpretation* of a value, that is, what is normally seen as bad is construed as good by some protagonist in a particular circumstance in the joke [fuel shortages (section 1.3.7, example 22), nun and rape (section 1.3.7, example 26)]. Reversal of evaluation was also seen as the driving force of ironical utterances; speakers use irony to indicate that what has been or might be evaluated by themselves or someone else as favourable is really to be seen as unfavourable. This is then used as the basis to make all sorts of other local strategic arguments, including facework ploys, usually to ridicule those who are projected as espousing the original evaluation. This face-attack is still clearer in contrastive teasing or taunting, where another speaker's opinions are directly contrasted with a 'superior' viewpoint with varying degrees of derision.

7.2.2 The 'quality' of laughter-talk

One of the thorniest questions in humour studies is the quality of verbal humour, that is, what makes an utterance more or less amusing? In a data-based, observational, 'outsider' study such as the present one, where any information on inner feelings is indirect at best, we are not justified in passing judgement on what participants find particularly funny. What we can do, however, is ascertain from an analysis of the data what the likely sites of laughter are, that is, the contexts where laughter frequently occurs. The visual and audio data, where available, indicates the loudness and length of laughter bouts.

First, the *unexpectedness* of the bisociative shift plays a part. In the briefings, the more outlandish the fantasy narrative, by and large, the 'better' the laugh it provoked: see Chapter 2 (example 9: the spy with the listening device in his teeth). Indeed, colourful language, that is, unexpected imagery, even by itself is enough to raise a laugh (see section 2.7).

The counterpart in joke humour is the sheer intellectual delight felt at inventive narrative juxtapositions, the yoking of the previously unimagined. Unexpectedness can be context-dependent and many jokes will spend considerable time leading the listener astray before the narrative-switch or backtrack trigger is pulled.

Second, where we find *combinations* of shifts we are likely to find laughter. In conversational laughter-talk, we saw how participants, having passed from transactional to interactional mode and entered into play frame, switch into a fantasy narrative and very frequently also adopt a new register, frequently reinforced by bathos or upgrading.

Correspondingly, much joke humour also relies on register shift. The humorous writings of Woody Allen, for instance, depend upon it almost exclusively.[1]

Third, in the type of laughter-talk which involves a bisociative evaluation reversal, the nature and strength of the value being played with for the particular target social group, in other words the in-group value system, acts as a context or framework within which the potential humour is interpreted, and perhaps magnified or otherwise. In the briefings, references to 'in-values' such as 'earning an honest buck', 'tough questioning', 'being a regular guy' and suchlike are very common laughter sites.

Value-dependence is equally significant in joke humour. In the world of Freud's Jewish jokes, marriage-brokering had an importance lost on us today and jokes about it have lost much of their appeal. Similarly, many of us no longer find jokes about female sexual availability or male homosexuality to be particularly hilarious (although I was depressed to find, on a recent trip to the United Kingdom, how much television 'humour' still seemed to rely on such material).

Last, in-group knowledge, 'privileged' information, as it were, especially about people and their doings, acts as a similar contextualizing and magnifying lens. In the briefings we have discussed references to participant's age ('If you're too young, ask Wolf'), role ('but I'd suggest you give Jim Kennedy a call, who's a vastly under-used person here' Laughter), personality ('No, that's more cynical than I know you mean to be') and so on. This is also, of course, an extremely vital component to situation comedy, where one needs to know the *dramatis personae* intimately to get the full benefit of any humour.

We hypothesized at the outset of this work that, in order to understand laughter-talk, it would be necessary to adopt a model which encompassed, first, a theory of cognition as it relates to humour (bisociation), second, a theory of human social interaction (politeness) and, third, a theory of language production and reception (lexicogrammer). It is hoped that this prolonged examination has shed a little light on how these aspects of the model interrelate. To conclude, we might allow ourselves a final speculation on how the connections between bisociation and facework might have arisen.

7.3 Speculation on the evolution of laughter: bisociation and facework entwined

The three main theories, in historical terms, which have been devised to explain *humorous* laughter are, famously, the aggression or superiority theory, the incongruity theory and the theory of emotional relief. As Glenn notes, all these theories tend, erroneously, to conflate humour and laughter, to presume that 'finding something funny leads necessarily to laughing' and that 'laughing is - necessarily provoked (only) by finding something funny' (2003: 18–19). Moreover, these theories are often discussed in terms of 'origins', in other words, they assume that laughter 'originally arose' to fulfil one of these functions. It is misleading to talk of the definitive evolutionary 'origins' of laughter (just as we cannot talk of the 'original meaning' of words): do we mean, for instance, its origins in man, in primates or in animals in general? Bearing these caveats in mind, we might draw a rapid outline of each of the theories (for fuller treatments, see Attardo 1994; Provine 2000; Glenn 2003).

232 General conclusions

The aggression/superiority theory (or hostility, disparagement, triumph, derision: Attardo 1994: 47) maintains that people laugh 'when comparing themselves to others and finding themselves stronger, more successful, or at some advantage' (Glenn 2003: 19).[2] In the origins fallacy, then, laughter 'arose' as a cry of victory over a vanquished foe: 'the single source from which all modern forms of wit and humor developed is *the roar of triumph in an ancient jungle duel*' (Rapp 1951: 21). Aristotle was an early exponent of the aggression/superiority school and maintained that we laugh at deformity, both physical and moral. Koestler notes: 'The princes of the Renaissance collected midgets, hunchbacks, monsters, and Blackamoors for their merriment' (Koestler 1964: 75).[3] In modern times Bergson and, most recently, Billig (2005) argue that laughter is often derision and used as a social corrective.

We have seen plenty of aggression at play in the briefings. But the aggression theory by itself fails to explain precisely *why* we should laugh at that we feel superior to, or under what circumstances (there are all sorts of things we might feel superior to but do not normally find risible, from ticket machines, through spiders to, as Koestler reminds us, dead bodies). The politeness/face framework we have been employing in this work has proved to be helpful in addressing these questions. In particular, laughing at what is perceived as inferior serves our personal face needs, bolstering our positive face and expressing our in-group belonging. Moreover, from the studies here and elsewhere, we have seen how laughter not only *expresses* superiority, it is very often an attempt to *create* it, to reify it, to construe one party as superior to its adversary.

Incongruity theory has already been much discussed in this book in the guise of bisociation. We reached the conclusion that incongruity certainly contributes to many forms of laughter-talk but by itself its explanatory power is insufficient and the term itself needs close definitional attention. Again laughter needs to be studied in authentic social contexts to discover what kinds of incongruity evoke it and the circumstances in which it contributes to humour.

Relief (or release) theories maintain that 'humor releases tensions, psychic energy, or that humor releases one from inhibitions, conventions and laws' (Attardo 1964: 50). A modern version argues that *laughter* (rather than humour) bestows various physiological benefits by releasing pent-up mental and physical stress. The major shortcoming of relief theory is its solipsism. We seem once again to concentrate on the single individual's reaction to a stimulus and ignore the active and strategic aspects, the fact that people *do* things consciously and semi-consciously with laughter-talk.

None of these three theories 'has gained widespread acceptance as a general explanation of the humor response' (Glenn 2003: 22). However, the three are not incompatible and, combined, they offer considerable insight into what we laugh at and what we find funny. We argue tentatively here that the ways in which they combine can be seen in how bisociation and facework interact.

We have stressed that laughter has no single origin. What we are entitled to say, however, is that laughter, in some phase of primate development, evolved as a signal to others. The main arguments for laughter developing at some stage as a signal rather than a simple reaction to a stimulus are that, first of all, its major characteristic is its being visually and audibly 'noisy', second, that we laugh thirty times more often in company than alone (Provine 2000: 45) and, third, as we hope to have shown here, that signalling is still its main function today. What it actually signalled in earlier times is a matter of speculation, but perhaps, at one stage of its evolution at least, it operated as follows.

One of the principal functions of the entity we call the mind is to register changes in the environment of the host organism and then to assess the relevance of the change, most particularly whether it carries a threat. Any registered change causes the organism to adopt a state of alertness (one sees this vividly in pets). It would be of great value to a group of social animals to develop a means of communicating to members that the new stimulus is either truly threatening or is in fact innocuous and therefore that normal business can be resumed. Man (or some ancestor) is a social organism, and so laughter – or its prototype – may well have been employed at one stage as a signal to others in the social group that the change which was registered was in fact non-threatening, the danger is over, we can relax. This interpretation goes back at least as far as Hayworth (1928). Laughter in play, especially play-fighting is, of course, used principally to signal this lack of threat (including in hospital patient-doctor and patient-nurse relations Ragan 1990; Grainger 2002) and Provine argues that laughter as we know it today, with the particularly energetic breathing patterns developed during the rough-and-tumble of physical play – 'the vowellike "ha-ha-ha"s that parse the outward breath in modern laughter is one step removed from the archetypal huffing and puffing that signalled laughter and play in our ancient ancestors' (2000: 97). Glenn (2003: 18), in turn, mentions a series of studies which shows that laughter itself calms and relaxes the organism by encouraging the release of endorphins in the brain. In ontogenetic terms, many analysts have observed the appearance of laughter-like behaviour even in the youngest of babies on the appearance of the mother. Maternal absence is a source of varying degrees of tension, while her reappearance removes the tension and causes the 'small euphoria' which is then signalled to the mother by smiling and gurgling. This, in turn, in evolutionary terms is a valuable reassurance for her, as well as an emotional inducement to pay the child attention.

Thus we might hypothesize that laughter today is associated with the relief of tension and also, more sophisticatedly, with the *management* of social tension as follows. Many of the changes our social animal registers will be caused by other members of the group – other people, in short, are a major source of tension. Politeness theory, in fact, predicts that we are in a constant state of alertness and tension over the status of our face. And laughter is quite evidently bound up with social-group tension management in lots of different ways. The continuous giggling and twittering of friends is expressing 'we feel comfortable with each other'. When strangers meet socially, laughter generally occurs with the utmost frequency. This kind of laughter is normally described as a reaction to embarrassment but here once again the signalling function of laughter is paramount. Participants indicate that they are enjoying the others' company and do not feel threatened by them, even though, thanks to the social tension, they might actually be feeling very little genuine internal hilarity. The self-laughter that accompanies some 'minor' inappropriateness of behaviour (hitches and glitches) signals to others 'this was a potentially dangerous/tense occurrence for me and is not my normal behaviour, but the fact that I'm laughing means that I feel no tension and so nothing much has happened, I can assure you'.

The notion that laughter registers and communicates the recognition of change and the unusual and, especially, that some behaviour has been perceived as improper, also has the merit of linking rather elegantly the laughter-talk we have observed here with some forms of non-verbally inspired laughter. A simple experiment on the sense of balance broadcast on the BBC (4 August 2003) required subjects to try standing on one leg whilst keeping their eyes shut. Their vain attempts to maintain balance were invariably accompanied by grinning, giggles and laughter-talk imprecations at the revelation of their own surprising ineptitude, that is, their physically inappropriate behaviour in such mundane circumstances. Most importantly, they were exhibiting before an audience and their audible laughter was meant to signal how odd they were finding their own behaviour, that they were, of course, not normally so clumsy and deficient. We laugh at the unexpected and inappropriate, then, but with a couple of riders – usually when there is an audience and only when the situation is mildly but not seriously threatening. In the experiment described above there is of course some slight threat to self-esteem and face. However, if something unexpected occurs that we feel truly threatened by, laughter is highly unlikely (except perhaps the kind of 'nervous', mirthless laughter that is a result of confusion of mental stimuli).

To continue, laughter, precisely because it developed as a signal which was offering a valuable service to the group, also has the considerable side-effect of stressing group belonging. As we have seen throughout this work, in fact, this expression of group affiliation is one of its main signalling functions today. After noise, probably the second most noticeable feature of laughter is its collegiality; laughing together creates group-feeling. But, of course, one of the most common ways of reinforcing the in-group's sense of solidarity is by laughing *at* another party, and so laughter commonly signals and stresses that party's alienation. This begins to explain the aggressive use of laughter, helps accounts for the derision of Koestler's midgets, hunchbacks and monsters and tells us why a wide variety of communities invent 'outsider' jokes – Polish, Carabinieri, Kerrymen and so on. Laughter may well have had other aggression-expression functions, but they certainly coalesce with the out-group casting use apparent in the kind of facework we have seen in this book.

But the twists and turns do not end here. Normally, we can only signal things we have previously registered and/or recognized (unless, of course, we are deceitful, conniving hypocrites – in other words, human beings). This implies that, in signalling S, one also signals that one has previously registered/recognized phenomenon P. Most simply, laughing to express my solidarity with the in-group expresses that I wish to belong to that group and also that I share its values. Sometimes this signalling of having recognized P can reveal more about the signaller either than she or he realizes or would wish to have others know. For instance, if I laugh to communicate that a certain danger is over, this shows that I considered that phenomenon dangerous. Others might not see it the same way and this gives an insight into my views and preoccupations, perhaps even my personality. Similarly, those who laugh at jokes about gays, nuns or Jews are saying something about themselves ('there is nothing in which people more betray their character' says Goethe, 'than what they laugh at'). Giggling too much on meeting someone one finds attractive (revealing high levels of tension) could well signal this attraction before one is ready to do so.

On the other hand, signalling can be used pro-positively, strategically, to further one's own interests. Human beings can lie and dissemble and deceive, they don't always signal what they really feel and can use biological signals to advantage; perhaps the clearest and most consistent example is self-deprecatory laughter. Much of this book deals with such intentional strategic signalling, of course, since the lion's share of the laughter treated here is taking place in an argumentative and competitive arena.

Most writers agree that laughter predates speech, but a crucial moment arrives when our social animals evolve language and verbal humour becomes possible. The signalling of recognition is obviously a vital consideration here too. What happens when we laugh in response to what another person has *said*? The mind scans the linguistic input, just like any other external stimulus and, as we noted earlier, it is most sensitive to changes, because change is likely to be significant. If we encounter an abrupt shift, a second narrative of some description, a switch of style or register or some such, the mind grows alert and begins to assess its significance for the organism. First of all, does it threaten my face (Politeness theory predicts that this is a dominant consideration in all human interaction)? Then, was it intended deliberately or was it a slip, a mishap, a *faux pas*, and if the latter, do I want to use it to attack the speaker's face? If it was deliberate, was it intended to provoke laughter? If I decide it is non-face-threatening and deliberate, I can *relax* and start working out, often by comparing the linguistic trace with features of context, how and why it was intended to provoke laughter. If I get it, I laugh to signal, first and foremost, that I have recognized the bisociative laughter-talk, otherwise I risk losing competence face (I show that I'm stupid, or if it's a dirty joke, that I am naïve, which is worse). Given the social-belonging valence of laughter we have stressed, I may also laugh to signal appreciation, thus bolstering my affective face – have a sense of fun and also share the speaker's and the implied group's values. Consider, by the way, how difficult it is to separate recognition and appreciation in practice. Sometimes, if the hearer fails to signal their recognition by laughing, the producer of the laughter-talk will laugh first as an intimation to the hearer to inspect the message more closely. If the latter insists on not laughing, the producer may accuse him/her of dim-wittedness when the failure to laugh may instead have been meant as a sign of non-appreciation.

To summarize: relief after tension, aggression and its management and the detection of incongruity all play a role in the laughter activities of the worlds treated in this book. More specifically, the relationship between the cognitive (bisociation) and anthropo-sociological (politeness/face theory) in laughter-talk is as follows.

The bisociative shift, whether it be realized in the sudden change of narrative in a joke, or in the introduction of a fantasy narrative in conversation which tests the hearer's understanding and sophistication, or in unexpectedly slipping on a banana skin and its social equivalents – *faux pas*, slips of the tongue, forgetting one's lines and so on, or in sarcasm or contrastive teasing, is a potential site of tension.

Politeness is an all-encompassing theory which describes aggression and tension-management in human social interaction. Politeness theory by itself cannot explain the quality of mirth, the real belly-laugh – such explanations, as we saw, need to be sought in the types of bisociative mechanisms used and the value systems of groups – but it does help to explain why speakers engage in laughter-talk: in order to bolster their affective face within a group, to attack the face of others and to regulate the group values in ways congenial to them. These activities may all be indulged in for professional reasons as well as purely socially strategic ones in institutional discourse communities like that of the briefings.

A final word. What makes people laugh (along with the different but related question of what people find funny) is one of the great anthropological, psychological and metaphysical human questions. Writers on the topic have propounded their favourite theories and their pet prejudices and I, following the time-honoured tradition, have done the same.

The modern consensus is that no single factor can suffice to explain laughter-talk. As we have seen, it is quite typical to find a number of factors at play in any single episode. To complicate matters further, different people laugh at different things, even the same individual will laugh at different things at different times depending on, *inter alia*, our mood, who we are with, what has been said so far and what we wish to communicate to those around us. Laughter, as is well-known, is highly context-dependent.

This being so, it would seem reasonable that the future study of verbal laughter should attend to attested instances in context, that is, in authentic situations, using, where relevant, data-analysis technology and techniques similar to those outlined here. This will allow us to study laughter in as wide a variety as possible of different contexts. The present study has limited itself to certain types of political interaction. It is hoped, however, that this work can serve as a guide, a progenitrix, or a harbinger at least, of further data-based studies of laughter-talk.

Appendix 1
Visual puns and verbal-visual puns

In Chapter 4, a distinction is made between the exact pun, where two sound sequences are called into play which are *identical*, and the near pun, in which two sequences are involved which *resemble* each other either phonologically or, in texts primarily meant to be read, visually. It is argued that this theoretical treatment of punning has the advantage of enabling us to draw a clear analogy with *visual puns*, which are also based on resemblance. 'A visual pun is made when someone notices that two different things have a similar appearance, and constructs a picture making this similarity evident' (Hughes and Hammond in Redfern 1984: 143). Thus, it is contended, a visual pun can be expressed as a situation comprising $A_1(M_1)$, $A_2(M_2)$ where $A_1 \approx A_2$ (A = appearance, M = meaning). This is analogous to the relation we proposed for the near pun, namely, $SS_1(M_1)$, $SS_2(M_2)$ where $SS_1 \approx SS_2$ (SS = sound sequence and M = meaning).

This similarity of mechanism probably explains why it is possible to mix verbal and visual puns. There exists, in fact, a fairly common hybrid or perhaps combinatory form which we might call the verbal-visual pun. An Italian supermarket chain ran a series of poster ads depicting foodstuffs 'dressed' as famous people, with captions. A roll of bread (*pane*) in Egyptian headgear was *TutanPanem*, a radish (*rapanello*) wearing a Renaissance felt hat was *Rapanello Sanzio* (i.e. Raffaello Sanzio or Rafael) and a clove of garlic (*aglio*) and a jar of oil (*olio*) wearing bowler hats were *Stanlio e Oglio* (the Italian names for Stanley [Laurel] and Oliver [Hardy]). We might note in passing that such extreme juxtapositions or amalgamations (an artist with a vegetable, and so on) also have something in common with the verbal simile which consists of 'a comparison statement involving two *unlike* things' (Miller 1993: 373, my emphasis).

These alimentary examples, being simply advertising, do not have the evaluative force generally conveyed by similes (Miller 1993; Partington 2006) but many visual puns do. During the 1997 United Kingdom election campaign, the Labour Party produced a poster depicting a Janus-like John Major, then Prime Minister and leader of the rival Conservatives, his head looking both ways at once, clearly a visual reference to the verbal phrase *two-faced*. Both the visual play and the unfavourable evaluation were by reinforced the slogan: '[Major said in] "1992: Tax cuts year on year": 22 tax rises since 1992'.

Appendix 1

Many of the celebrated cartoons of Larson ('The Far Side') – which have received some attention in humour literature (Paolillo 1998; Attardo *et al.* 2002) – are based on the verbal-visual pun. A very simple example (Paolillo 1998: 281):

(1) A bearded painter with a paint-splattered smock is putting the finishing touches on a painting of a stern-looking armored knight resting his foot on a child's wagon. The painter is startled by a page who bursts in asking: 'So, André! The king wants to know how you're coming with "St. George and the Dragon"'.

Slightly more complex is the following (Paolillo 1998: 287):

(2) A surfer on the beach runs directly toward the surf, bearing his surfboard over his head; a sea monster runs directly out of the surf bearing a truck over his head. A look of alarmed surprise crosses the surfer's face.

Part of the effect here stems from the reworking of the phrase *monster wave* which is relexicalized from its usual sense of 'monster *of* a wave' (the surfer's dream) to 'monster *in* a wave' (more of a nightmare). This kind of relexicalization is entirely analogous to that described in Chapter 4 which occur in verbal puns like Freud's 'Did you take a bath?' joke, among others (section 4.3.3).

A final example is the following (Paolillo 1998: 287):

(3) A hunched, balding man enters a store whose window-sign reads 'Unnatural Foods.'

This kind of verbal-visual pun offers still more evidence, if any were needed, that jokes do not always entail the switch from one set *script* to another. As argued in Chapter 1, many jokes entail the replacement of a set script with a second state of affairs which is novel and unpredictable. It is unlikely that many readers/viewers possessed scripts of 'St George and the wagon', 'monster in a wave' and 'unnatural foods' before encountering Larson's cartoons. In fact, the very effect of (3) relies on the absence from most people's mental lexicon of the antonym of 'natural foods'.

Appendix 2
Levels of sarcasm

From *I am Charlotte Simmons* by Tom Wolfe, pp. 133–134.

They chattered away. Charlotte tried to tune out, but she heard Erica saying, 'That's not Sarc Three, Bev, that's only Sarc Two. I mean, it's almost as obvious as Sarc One. I can't believe they let you out of Groton without passing Sarc. Sarc One is when I look at you and I say, "Ohmygod, a *cerise shirt*. Cerise is such an *in color* this year." That's just ordinary intentionally obvious sarcasm. Okay?'

'You really don't like this shirt, do you?' said Beverly.

'Oh, please give me a fucking break, Bev! I'm just giving you an example. I'm trying to enlighten you, and you – touchy, touchy, touchy. Now...in Sarc Two you say the same thing, only in a sympathetic voice that sounds like totally sincere. "Oh, wow, Bev, I love that color. *Cerise*. That's like so-o-o-o cool. *Umhhh*...no wonder it's so like... *in* this year." By the time you get to the "so *in* this year," your voice is so dripping with so much syrup and like...sincerity, it finally dawns on the other person that she's getting fucked over. What you've really been saying is that you *don't* love the color, you *don't* think it's cool, and it's *not* "in" this year. It's the delay in the dawning on her that makes it hurt. Okay?'

'And you're sure you're just being nice and giving me an example?' said Beverly.

'I'm sure you're going bitchcakes on me, be-atch. That's what I'm sure of. If you don't cool it, I'm not going to explain Sarc Three to you,'

Silence.

'Okay. In Sarc Three you make the delay even longer, so it *really* hurts when she finally gets it. We've got the same situation. The girl's getting ready to go out, and she has on this cerise shirt. She thinks it's really sexy, a real turn-on, and she's gonna score big-time. You start off sounding straight – you know, flattering, but not laying it on too thick. You're like, "Wow, Bev, I love that *shirt*. Where'd you get it? How perfect is *that*? It's so *versatile*. It'll be perfect for job interviews, and it'll be perfect for community service."'

The very thought made Erica laugh.

Appendix 3
Irony and popular historiography

It is not difficult to illustrate the subjectivity and creativity of explicit irony and the way it constructs arguments. One common accusation expressed by ironic bisociation, for example, is betrayal and ingratitude:

(1) It is **ironic** that the subtle but hard-headed marketing skills of an auctioneer are likely to bring record prices for works by artists who deserted him.

(Newspapers)

The first narrative in such a scenario is that party A does something of benefit for party B whilst in the second narrative party B commits an act to the detriment of A, in episode (1), 'desertion'. But betrayal is often a question of whose perspective is taken. If we take historiography as our discourse type, a number of modern popular historians seem to revel in uncovering 'ironies' in history. Here is Schama (2000):[1]

(2) It was because Henry II was so determined that his writ should run supreme that he failed to avoid a collision with the Church. This was particularly **ironic** since, at the beginning of his reign, it was the Church who supplied him with the literate and numerate personnel who staffed the Chancellory and who initiated Henry into the complicated mysteries of English government.

This was hardly 'ironic' from the Church's point of view. It was simple, unadulterated ingratitude. But the tables were later turned:

(3) [When Becket opposed Henry's plans for a tax on the nobles and clergy alike] Henry saw with stunned disbelief that a mysterious transformation had taken place in his friend. That Becket had been, as he often reminded him, raised from the ranks of commoners by his special favour and now was repaying him with presumptuous opposition only added to his rage.

---

1 Audiobook version.

From the King's viewpoint Becket is monstrously ungrateful. It would not be difficult to rewrite the tale from an observer's standpoint with an irony marker:

(4) [Rewrite] The **irony** was that, having been raised from the ranks of commoners by Henry's special favour, Becket was now doing all he could to thwart the King's plans to tax [...]

Note my insertion of the intensifying *all he could* and *thwart*.

We have also seen how misjudgement, especially where evaluated as culpable, can be expressed with an irony marker. Consider:

(5) And by no means all the clergy rallied to Becket's support. The Bishops of London and York, Gilbert Foliat and Roger of Pont l'Évêque, remained bitter enemies and believed that Becket's own vanity and egomania had needlessly destroyed a reasonable and pragmatic working relationship with the monarchy and **had actually made it harder, not easier**, to secure the proper liberties of the Church.

which, already containing strong and overt signals of reversed evaluation (highlighted), namely, the reversal of Becket's appraisal and expectations, could easily be rephrased with an explicit irony marker:

(6) [Rewrite] The **irony** was that all Becket's efforts, thanks to his vanity and egomania, **actually** made it **harder, not easier**, to secure the proper liberties of the Church.

For Schama there is also often irony when traditional roles are reversed:

(7) In one of the **greatest ironies** of British history, the traditional positions of parliamentarians and monarchists were now **reversed.**

Note once again the hyperbole. But, at times, any reversal is hard to glean:

(8) In one of the more unnoticed **ironies** of Anjevin British history, the Anjevin colonization of Ireland began as an answer to the *Welsh* problem.

a rather weak irony which leaves one to wonder what contrast lies between the Welsh and Irish 'problems', other than their being simply different.

But perhaps the best illustration of all of how the ironic relation is manufactured rather than natural and depends on who is doing the observing is the following, from Ferguson this time, on the American Revolution:

(9) **The irony is**, that having won their independence in the name of Liberty, the American colonists went on to perpetuate slavery in the southern states [...] By contrast, within a few decades of having lost the American colonies, the British abolished, first the slave trade, and then slavery itself, throughout their Empire. From the point of view of most African Americans, American Independence postponed emancipation by at least a generation.

(2004: 100–101)

For the African-American slaves themselves this 'contrast' was hardly ironic; it was nothing less than a tragedy.

Notes

Introduction: laughter-talk – research questions and methods

1 Available online respectively at: www.whitehouse.gov/news/briefings/ and www.C-Span.org
2 Available online at http: www.writerswrite.com/journal/apr99/nonf4.htm
3 Grotjahn (1987: 59–60) describes eight possible research paradigms, realized by combining the following variables: (1) data collection procedure (experimental v. exploratory design); (2) the form of the data (quantitative v. qualitative); and (3) the method of analysis (statistical v. interpretative). In this way, two 'pure' paradigms are obtained (analytical-nomological and exploratory-interpretative) and six 'mixed' forms according to the particular combination of components (e.g. *exploratory-quantitative-interpretative*, entailing a non-experimental design, quantitative data and interpretative analysis; or *exploratory-qualitative-statistical*, entailing a non-experimental design, qualitative data and statistical analysis).
4 *MicroConcord* can be downloaded without charge from: http://www.liv.ac.uk/~ms2928/software/. *WordSmith Tools* can be purchased online from: http://www.lexically.net/wordsmith/

1 Joke humour theory and language principles

1 Although the term *bisociation* is coined by Koestler, the concepts it is used to indicate go back at least to the time of the German Romantics, Kant and Hegel. As a native speaker of German, Koestler was certainly aware of this philosophical tradition (see Koestler 1964: 150–151).
2 Perhaps simply because processes of long-term memorization are difficult to observe, whilst understanding is more easily detected and tested.
3 All lexical items 'are ambiguous, vague or unspecified if they are not taken in context' (Attardo 1994: 133). See sections 4.2 and 4.3 on puns and relexicalization for a discussion of lexical ambiguity.
4 As possible exceptions, Schank and Abelson cite ritual scripts such as $PRAYER or emotional/behavioural reaction scripts such as $JILTED LOVER.
5 'Scripts allow for new references to objects within them just as if these objects had been previously mentioned; objects within a script may take "the" without explicit introduction because the script itself has already implicitly introduced them.' (Schank and Abelson 1977: 41).
6 Brown and Yule mention Heidegger's often quoted question of how the word *hammer* can have meaning to someone who has never seen a hammer used.
7 It may be more script-like in Catholic cultures. In Italy for instance people celebrate both a birthday and an 'onomastico', the day of the saint whose name they happen to have. Sometimes the two will coincide.

2 Laughter in running discourse: shifts of mode, narrative, role and register

1 Some *deadly* serious activities: 'In *Hamlet*, for example, the stage direction "they play" precedes the duel between Hamlet and Laertes which leads to the death of both. [Act V, ii, 295]' (Cook 2000: 111).

3 Face-work and the in-group

1 Using the PIXI comparative corpora (Gavioli and Mansfield eds 1990).
2 For example:

> Q: May I follow up on that? [...] When America was struck on the 11th, the first call I think we got from a foreign leader was President Putin. Why hasn't President Bush called President Putin immediately after a significant terrorist event in his country?
> MR. FLEISCHER: He did, Ron. President Bush called President Putin immediately upon the taking of the hostages and offered America's support [...] So he indeed did.
> Q: Okay, sorry about that. Did the President or have any of his people asked [...]

Note the close association presumed between the podium and the President by the questioner who apologizes to the former for misjudging the latter.

3 A *ballpark figure* is a rough estimate, usually of cost. *My dime* is my turn at talk. *Soft money* refers to corporate and private donations to political parties.
4 Nevertheless, concordancing shows that journalists frequently begin a question move either with an apology, for example, in *Reps*, *sorry* introduces a question thirty-six times, or with a request for permission, the favourite being *if I may* (thirty-eight occurrences in *Reps*, e.g. 'If I may combine two questions [...]', 'One last thing, if I may.'). The main addressee of the apologies, however, seems to be the other journalists rather than the podium and they are generally produced when the individual fears being seen to be taking more time than a single turn would allow, because s/he wants to follow up, ask an extra question, ask a particularly long question, all of which mean weightier imposition on hearers' face. When, on the other hand, it is the podium's turn which is too long, an apology is also often felt to be required but it is not always accepted with grace:

> MR. BERGER: First of all, if I answer any more questions I'll be accused of going on too long.
> Q: You're going on half as long as the President did. (Laughter)

When the podium's answer is long and, especially, when it is partisan, he might comment on the fact himself:

> MR. MCCURRY: [after a long diatribe on how Mr Clinton's prevarications are different from Mr Nixon's]
> He misused the FBI, the Secret Service to conduct unlawful wiretapping of American citizens. He maintained a secret unit in the White House to violate the constitutional rights of citizens and refused to provide information in a timely way to Congress, in contempt of Congress. So there's no parallel whatsoever [...] Little history lesson. (Laughter)

The coda – 'little history lesson' – serves as an indirect apology for making such demands on his audience's time and attention.

5 The word *classified* occurs seventy-five times in *Reps1*, the subcorpora of briefings held around September 11th 2001, compared to just once in *Reps0*, held six months before, and eight times in *Reps2*, held six months after.

244 *Notes*

4 Wordplay, phraseplay and relexicalization

1 'What, said in whatever words, is nevertheless funny, it is contained in the thing; what loses its saltiness if the words are changed, has all the funniness in the words [...] because after changing the words they cannot retain the same funniness, should be considered to rely not in the thing but in the words' (Cicero *De Oratore*, quoted in Attardo 1994: 28).
2 Koestler's example of the latter: 'The super-ego is that part of the personality which is soluble in alcohol' (1964: 66).
3 Acknowledgements to the website http://www.fun-with-words.com for a number of the examples.
4 From Bill Bryson's *Notes from a Small Island*.
5 In Italy, where the pun works even better (*Domenicani – Domine cani*), legend has it that the Dominicans actually called themselves 'i levrieri di Dio', God's greyhounds, quick to give chase to heresy in the name of the true faith.
6 *Amphibology*: 'ambiguity of speech, esp. from uncertainty of the grammatical construction rather than the meaning of the words, as in *The Duke yet lives that Henry shall depose*' (*Webster's*).
7 Supposedly at the sight of English children for sale in the slave-market. This is the pithy popular version. Bede has a far more long-winded rendition in his *Historia Ecclesiastica Gentis Anglorum*: 'Responsum est, quod Angli vocarentur. At ille: "Bene" inquit; "nam et angelicam habent faciem, et tales angelorum in caelis decet esse coherides."' (He was told that they were called Angles. 'It is fitting', said he, 'because they have the face of an angel and such as these must be the heirs of the angels in heaven.')
8 Who are many, at least in Britain, where this kind of wordplay inspired a long-running radio programme called *My Word*.
9 The same relation is often noted between the two terms in metaphors and similes, for example, in Burns's 'my love is like a red, red rose', love is abstract, while a rose is tangible.
10 Originally from P.G. Wodehouse : 'I could see that, if not actually disgruntled, he was far from being gruntled' (*The Code of the Woosters*).
11 But by no means the only kind:

> *No bones about it*: ART/Andrew Graham-Dixon comes face to face with death at the Victoria and Albert's new exhibition of funereal art
> *Make no bones about it* = There can be no doubt on the matter.
> The idiom makes it as the title simply because it contains the word *bones*.

12 A Web search of *beaten by the bell* + *boxing* threw up the obituary of a local boxer, which ends rather poignantly: 'Bertie Smith Ingram fought his last round 20th May 1997. Beaten by the bell.'

5 Teasing and verbal duelling

1 Tholander and Aronsson actually use the word *alignment* (2002: 561). Here, as explained in the Introduction, I wish to keep a distinction between *affiliation*, which describes a speaker's solidarity with other people, and *alignment* which denotes a speaker's agreement with another speaker's message, opinion or evaluation.
2 The corpus evidence suggests that Mr Fleischer is less likely to attack the opposition party than his Democrat predecessors. It was a policy decision on the part of the first Bush administration to stress common ground with their opponents in a spirit of 'bipartisan' relations. There are 164 occurrences of *bipartisan* in *Reps* (0.260 per thousand words), a mere 20 in *Dems* (0.08 ptw). The phrase *Democrats and Repubicans* appears 43 times in *Reps* (0.172 ptw), only 4 times in *Dems* (0.016 ptw). The explanation for

this magnanimity is, first of all, the closeness of the 2000 election result and then, after September 11th, the supposed need to put petty party differences aside in times of national crisis.
3 It appears 36 times in *Dems*, 89 times in *Reps1* and *Reps2*.
4 That is, 'hoist with his own petard' (originally from Hamlet). Bergson [2003 (1900)] includes *inversion* – the robber robbed, the moralist shamed – as one of the basic techniques of the comic.
5 Elsewhere I noted that: 'surprisingly, this technique seems to be fairly effective in deflecting questions' (Partington 2003: 241). So much so that, after Mr Lockhart, Mr Fleischer also adopts it. My own opinion is that reflection upon potential future developments is one of the most fundamental elements of political debate and it is very odd that journalists do not insist that 'hypothetical speculation' is fair game.
6 The first meaning of *mimic* (v) in the O.E.D. is 'To ridicule by imitating or copying'.
7 'You can fool some of the people all of the time, and all of the people some of the time, but you can't fool all of the people all of the time.' (attributed to Abraham Lincoln).
8 *Simply* is an extremely interesting discourse item. Biber *et al.* talk of 'restrictive adverbs' (*just*, *only*, *simply* etc.) which are 'used to focus on the part of the clause for which the truth value of the proposition is most important' (1999: 798). *Simply* is also used to express stance (i.e. instructs the listener how to interpret the speaker's utterance, in this episode, her utter reasonableness). In both *Dems* and *Reps* it is also used contrastively, usually in divergence from something the previous speaker has asserted or implied:

> Q: Is that a veiled threat to cancel the trip?
> MR MCCURRY: That's just simply a statement of what it is

When used by a questioner, it frequently invites the interlocutor to deny or confirm an allegation or settle some doubt or other (it thus anticipates a contrastive response):

> Q: Is the United States simply not willing to accept casualties to save Kosovars?

Both contrastive and denial-invitation functions can be explicitly conflated:

> Q: But was the original 18 months simply over-optimistic, or was it reasonable [...]?

9 In his seminal treatment of *footing*, the participant roles we adopt as speakers or are projected into by others, Goffman (1981: 14–15) discusses an episode which occurred in 1973 during an informal presidential-press get-together. Goffman uses it to highlight how a powerful speaker can impose on a less powerful female participant a footing which is both domestic and sexual, regardless of the professional context:

> WASHINGTON [UPI] – President Nixon, a gentleman of the old school, teased a newspaper woman yesterday about wearing slacks to the White House and made it clear that he prefers dresses on women.
> After a bill-signing ceremony in the Oval Office, the President stood up from his desk and in a teasing voice said to UPI's Helen Thomas: 'Helen, are you still wearing slacks? [...] This is not said in an uncomplimentary way, but slacks can do something for some people and some it can't.' He hastened to add, 'but I think you do very well. Turn around.'
> [...] Miss Thomas did a pirouette for the President [...]
> Nixon asked Miss Thomas how her husband, Douglas Cornell, liked her wearing pants outfits.

> 'He doesn't mind,' she replied.
> 'Do they cost less than gowns?'
> 'No,' said Miss Thomas.
> 'Then change,' commanded the President with a wide grin as other reporters and cameramen roared with laughter.

The victim of this humiliating 'tease', as the article calls it, is none other than the Helen we meet so often in this chapter. Small wonder she is unwilling to take any nonsense from the podiums in later times.

10 His website – http://www.leskinsolving.com/ – describes him thus:

> Les Kinsolving is the nation's un-labeled talk show host! Just when you think he's conservative, he's liberal. And just when you think he's liberal, he's in the center! From proud, vociferous patriot to opinionated social commentator to winsome, mischievous devil's advocate, Les keeps audiences on their listening toes!

Be this as it may, in his previous incarnation as a print journalist, he was twice nominated for the Pulitzer prize.

6 Irony and sarcasm

1 Attardo adds the point that echo, in theory, can be infinitely regressive. 'One may echo no-one in particular, but merely an hypothetical speaker. It follows that if one utters any sentence, one may be mentioning/echoing another utterance. This leads obviously to an infinite regression; how does H know that S is not mentioning someone else's mention of an utterance?' (2000: 805).

2 Dramatic irony in itself, then, is neither necessarily humorous nor tragic. It rather implies an underlying vision, a meta-commentary, of the human condition: Man as plaything of the Gods or of fate or of his own shortcomings. Whether this condition is presented by an author as tragic or comic or something in between depends largely on two factors: the degree of sympathy we feel for the protagonist and how things turn out. Oedipus is entirely tragic, because we feel for him and he ends badly. Viola's story is not tragic: her entreating Olivia to give her affection to Orsini when she loves him herself plucks at the heartstrings for a while but she eventually gets her man. Tartuffe is comic: we laugh even though he comes to grief because we were never meant to like him in the first place.

3 British Petroleum produced a magazine advert illustrated with a collection of rather unpleasant-looking marine worms, with the caption 'If one was missing, we'd shriek'. The small text then explained how they are particularly sensitive to pollution and so a responsible oil company like ours pays great attention to variations in their population size. (Goddard 2002: 44)

4 We might recall Ahl's comment that 'Europeans [...] are trained to admire irony but to disapprove of puns' (1988: 21).

5 For an interesting discussion, see: http://itre.cis.upenn.edu/~myl/languagelog/archives/000060.html

7 General conclusions

1 Attardo (1994) quotes the following:

> He was creating an Ethics, based on his theory that 'good and just behavior is not only more moral but could be done by phone'. Also, he was halfway through a new study of semantics, proving (as he so violently insisted) that sentence structure is innate but that whining is acquired.
>
> (Allen 1997: 300)

The passage is from *Remembering Needleman*, where the effect is created by a continual bathetic interchange between the memories of a philosopher and banal everyday life ('Authentic Being, reasoned Needleman, could only be achieved at weekends and even then it required the borrowing of a car' 1997: 301). Similarly, in another short story, *The Whore of Mensa*, there is the interchange between a Chandler-parody

narrative-register and that of a visit to a bordello. Allen's writing style is so relentlessly bathetic it can become quite tiresome.
2 As noted in Marriott Edgar's notorious *Albert and the Lion*:

> There's a famous seaside place called Blackpool,
> That's noted for fresh air and fun,
> And Mr and Mrs Ramsbottom
> Went there with young Albert, their son [...]
> They didn't think much of the Ocean;
> The waves they were fiddlin' and small,
> There was no wrecks and nobody drownded,
> Fact, nothing to laugh at at all.

   The superiority theory probably goes a long way to explaining why people go to such lengths to *seek out* humorous entertainments. They can boost our self esteem by assuring us there are some more stupid than ourselves and provide a sense of reassurance that there are those less fortunate than ourselves.
3 Koestler claims that no decent *modern* human being would laugh at physical deformity or someone's race. Before wallowing in historical smugness, we might recall how many modern comic routines involve ridiculing foreign accents and that British literature from Shakespeare to J.K. Rowling uses lower-class accents as a source of humour.

Bibliography

Ahl, F. (1988) 'Ars est caelare artem (art in puns and anagrams engraved)', in J. Culler (ed.) *On Puns: The Foundation of Letters*. Oxford: Blackwell, pp. 17–43.

Allen, W. (1997) *Complete Prose*. London: Picador.

Anderson, R., Pichert, J., Goetz, E., Schallert, D., Stevens, K. and Trollip, S. (1976) 'Instantiation in general terms', *Journal of Verbal Learning and Verbal Behavior*, 15: 667–679.

Attardo, S. (1994) *Linguistic Theories of Humor*. New York: Mouton.

—— (2000) 'Irony as relevant inappropriateness', *Journal of Pragmatics*, 32(6): 793–826.

—— (2001a) 'Humor and irony in interaction: from mode adoption to failure of detection', in L. Anolli, R. Ciceri and G. Riva (eds) *Say not to Say: New Perspectives on Miscommunication*. Amsterdam: IOS Press, pp. 166–185.

—— (2001b) *Humorous Texts: A Semantic and Pragmatic Analysis*. Berlin: Mouton de Gruyter.

—— (2003) 'Introduction: the pragmatics of humor', *Journal of Pragmatics*, 35(9): 1287–1294.

Attardo, S. and Raskin, V. (1991) Script theory revis(it)ed: joke similarity and joke representation model, *Humor: International Journal of Humor Research*, 4(3–4): 293–348.

Attardo, S., Hempelmann, C. and DiMaio, S. (2002) 'Script oppositions and logical mechanisms: modeling incongruities and their resolutions', *Humor: International Journal of Humor Research*, 15(1): 3–46.

Bachorowski, J., Smoski, M. and Owren, M. (2001) 'The acoustic features of human laughter', *Journal of the Acoustical Society of America*, 110: 1581–1597.

Baker, M. and McCarthy, M. (1990) Multi-word units and things like that, unpublished research paper, Birmingham: University of Birmingham.

Baldry, A. (ed.) (2000) *Multimodality and Multimediality in the Distance Learning Age*. Campobasso: Palladino.

Barbe, K. (1993) ' "Isn't it ironic that…" explicit irony markers', *Journal of Pragmatics*, 20: 579–590.

Barlow, M. (1996) 'Corpora for theory and practice', *International Journal of Corpus Linguistics*, 1(1): 1–37.

Barlow, M. and Kemmer, S. (1994) 'A schema-based approach to grammatical description', in S. Lima, R. Corrigan and G. Iverson (eds) *The Reality of Linguistic Rules*. Amsterdam and Philadelphia: Benjamins, pp. 19–42.

Bartlett, F. (1932) *Remembering*. Cambridge: Cambridge University Press.

Bibliography 249

Bateson, G. (1955) 'A theory of play and fantasy', in G. Bateson (1972) *Steps to an Ecology of Mind*. New York: Ballantine, pp. 177–193.

Berger, A. (1987) 'Humor: an introduction', *American Behavioral Scientist*, 30(3): 6–15.

Bergmann, J. (1992) 'Veiled morality: notes on discretion in psychiatry', in P. Drew and J. Heritage (eds) *Talk at Work*. Cambridge: Cambridge University Press, pp. 137–162.

Bergson, H. (2003) *Laughter: An Essay on the Meaning of the Comic*. Online. Available through the Gutenberg Project, release #4352 <http://www.gutenberg.org/dirs/etextø3/laemcløtxt> (accessed 19 April 2004) [Original title (1900) *Le Rire: Essai sur la signification du comique*, Paris: Revue de Paris].

Best, A. (1996) Political interviewing on the BBC Radio Four 'Today' programme: A pragmatic analysis of the controversial Anna Ford/Kenneth Clarke interview, MSC dissertation, Birmingham: University of Aston. Online. Available HTTP: http://www.les.aston.ac.uk/lsu/diss (accessed 27 Febuary 2002).

Biber, D. (1988) *Variation across Speech and Writing*. Cambridge: Cambridge University Press.

—— (1995) *Dimensions of Register Variation: A Cross-linguistic Comparison*. Cambridge: Cambridge University Press.

Biber, D., Conrad, S. and Reppen, R. (1998) *Corpus Linguistics: Investigating Language Structure and Use*. Cambridge: Cambridge University Press.

Biber, D., Johansson, S., Leech, G., Conrad, S. and Finegan, E. (1999) *Longman Grammar of Spoken and Written English*. London: Longman.

Billig, M. (2005) *Laughter and Ridicule: Towards a Social Critique of Humour*. London: Sage.

Bills, L. (2000) 'Politeness in teacher-student dialogue in mathematics: a socio-linguistic analysis', *For the Learning of Mathematics*, 20: 40–47.

Bolinger, D. (1972) *Degree Words*. The Hague: Mouton.

Boxer, D. and Cortés-Conde, F. (1997) 'From bonding to biting: conversational joking and identity display', *Journal of Pragmatics*, 27: 275–294.

Brandreth, G. (1982). *Wordplay*. London: Severn House.

Brown, G. and Yule, G. (1983) *Discourse Analysis*. Cambridge: Cambridge University Press.

Brown, P. and Levinson, S. (1978) 'Universals in language usage: politeness phenomena', in E.N. Goody (ed.) *Questions and Politeness*. Cambridge: Cambridge University Press, pp. 56–289.

—— (1987) *Politeness: Some Universals in Language Use*. Cambridge: Cambridge University Press.

Bryman, A. and Burgess, R. (eds) (1994) *Analyzing Qualitative Data*. London: Routledge.

Charniak, E. (1979) 'Ms. Malaprop, a language comprehension program', in D. Metzing (ed.) *Frame Conceptions and Text Understanding*. Berlin: de Gruyter, pp. 62–78.

Cherry, R. (1988) 'Politeness in written persuasion', *Journal of Pragmatics*, 12(1): 63–82.

Clayman, S. (1992a) 'Caveat orator: audience disaffiliation in the 1988 presidential debates', *Quarterly Journal of Speech*, 78: 33–60.

—— (1992b) 'Footing in the achievement of neutrality: the case of news-interview discourse', in P. Drew, and J. Heritage (eds) *Talk at Work*. Cambridge: Cambridge University Press, pp. 163–198.

Cockcroft, R. and Cockcroft, S. (1992) *Persuading People: An Introduction to Rhetoric*. London: Macmillan.

Bibliography

Colston, H. and O'Brien, J. (2000) 'Contrast and pragmatics in figurative language: anything understatement can do, irony can do better', *Journal of Pragmatics*, 32: 1557–1583.
Cook, G. (1989) *Discourse*. Oxford: Oxford University Press.
—— (2000) *Language Play, Language Learning*. Oxford: Oxford University Press.
Crick, F. (1979) 'Thinking about the brain', *Scientific American*, 9: 218–232.
Dews, S. and Winner, E. (1995) 'Muting the meaning: a social function of irony', *Metaphor and Symbolic Activity*, 10(1): 3–19.
Dews, S., Kaplan, J. and Winner, E. (1995) 'Why not say it directly? The social functions of irony', *Discourse Processes*, 19: 347–367.
Drew, P. (1987) 'Po-faced receipts of teases', *Linguistics*, 25: 219–253.
Drew, P. and Heritage, J. (eds) (1992) *Talk at Work*. Cambridge: Cambridge University Press.
Eder, D. (1991) 'The role of teasing in adolescent peer group culture', in S. Cahill (ed.) *Sociological Studies of Child Development*. Greenwich: JAI Press, pp. 181–197.
Fairclough, N. (1989) *Language and Power*. London: Longman.
Ferguson, N. (2004) *Empire: How Britain Made the Modern World*. London: Penguin.
Foot, H. (1996) 'Humour and laughter', in O. Hargie (ed.) *Handbook of Communication Skills*, 2nd edn. London: Routledge, pp. 259–288.
Freud, S. (1960) *Jokes and Their Relation to the Unconscious*. New York: Norton.
Fry, W. (1963) *Sweet Madness*. Palo Alto: Pacific.
Galtung, J. and Ruge, M. (1981) 'Structuring and selecting news', in S. Cohen and J. Young (eds) *The Manufacture of News: Social Problems, Deviance and the Mass Media*, 2nd edn. London: Constable, pp. 52–63.
Gavioli, L. (1995) 'Turn-initial versus turn-final laughter: two techniques for initiating remedy in English/Italian bookshop service encounters', *Discourse Processes*, 19: 369–384.
Gavioli, L. and Mansfield, G. (eds) (1990) *The Pixi Corpora: Bookshop Encounters in English and Italian*. Bologna: CLUEB.
Gibbs, R. (1994) *The Poetics of Mind*. Cambridge: Cambridge University Press.
—— (2000) 'Irony in talk among friends', *Metaphor and Symbol*, 15: 5–27.
Gibbs, R. and O' Brien, J. (1991) 'Psychological aspects of irony understanding', *Journal of Pragmatics*, 16(6): 523–530.
Giora, R. (1995) 'On irony and negation', *Discourse Processes*, 19: 239–264.
—— (1997) 'Understanding figurative and literal language: the graded salience hypothesis', *Cognitive Linguistics*, 7: 183–206.
Giora, R., Fein, O. and Schwartz, T. (1998) 'Irony: graded salience and indirect negation', *Metaphor and Symbol*, 13(2): 83–101.
Glenn, P. (1987) Laugh and the world laughs with you: shared laughter sequencing in conversation, unpublished PhD dissertation, Austin: University of Texas.
—— (2003) *Laughter in Interaction*. Cambridge: Cambridge University Press.
Goddard, A. (2002) *The Language of Advertising*. London: Routledge.
Goffman, E. (1967) *Interaction Ritual: Essays on Face to Face Behavior*. New York: Doubleday.
—— (1981) *Forms of Talk*. Oxford: Blackwell.
Grainger, K. (2002) Politeness or impoliteness: verbal play on the hospital ward, *Working Papers on the Web*, Sheffield Hallam University. Online. Available: www.shu.ac.uk/wpw/politeness/grainger.htm.
Greatbatch, D. and Clark, T. (2003) 'Humour and laughter in the public lectures of management gurus', *Human Relations*, 56: 1515–1544.

Grice, H. (1975) 'Logic and conversation', in P. Cole and J. Morgan (eds) *Syntax and Semantics: Speech acts*, vol. 3. New York: Academic, pp. 41–58.

Grotjahn, R. (1987) 'On the methodological basis of introspective methods', in C. Faersch and G. Kasper (eds) *Introspection in Second Language Research*. Clevedon Avon, England: Multilingual Matters, pp. 54–81.

Haarman, L., Morley, J. and Partington, A. (2002) 'Habeas corpus: methodological reflections on the creation and use of a specialised corpus', in C. Gagliardi (ed.) *Quantity and Quality in English Linguistic Research: Some Issues*. Pescara: Libreria dell'Università Editrice, pp. 55–119.

Habermas, J. (1984) *The Theory of Communicative Action*, vol. 1: *Reason and the Rationalisation of Society*. London: Heineman.

Haiman, J. (1990) 'Sarcasm as theatre', *Cognitive Linguistics*, 1(2): 181–205.

—— (1998) *Talk is Cheap: Sarcasm, Alienation and the Evolution of Language*. Oxford: Oxford University Press.

Halliday, M. (1978) *Language as Social Semiotic: The Social Interpretation of Language and Meaning*. London: Edward Arnold.

—— (1994) *An Introduction to Functional Grammar*, 2nd edn. London: Edward Arnold.

Hamamoto, H. (1998) 'Irony from a cognitive perspective', in R. Carston and S. Uchida (eds) *Relevance Theory: Applications and Implications*. Amsterdam and Philadelphia: Benjamins, pp. 257–270.

Harris, S. (1991) 'Evasive action: how politicians respond to questions in political interviews', in P. Scannell (ed.) *Broadcast Talk*. London: Sage, pp. 76–99.

—— (1995) 'Pragmatics and Power', *Journal of Pragmatics*, 23(2): 117–135.

—— (2001) 'Being politically impolite: extending politeness theory to adversarial political discourse', *Discourse and Society*, 12(4): 451–472.

Hasan, R. and Halliday, M. (1989) *Language, Context, and Text: Aspects of Language in a Social-semiotic Perspective*, 2nd edn. Oxford: Oxford University Press.

Hayworth, D. (1928) 'The social origin and function of laughter', *Psychological Review*, 35: 367–384.

Heritage, J. and Greatbatch, D. (1991) 'On the institutional character of institutional talk: the case of news interviews', in D. Boden and D. Zimmerman (eds) *Talk and Social Structure*. Cambridge: Polity Press, pp. 93–137.

Hoey, M. (1983) *On the Surface of Discourse*. London: George Allen and Unwin.

—— (2005) *Lexical Priming: A New Theory of Words and Language*. London: Routledge.

Holmes, J. (1995) *Women, Men and Politeness*. London: Longman.

—— (1999) 'Women, men and politeness: agreeable and disagreeable responses', in A. Jaworski and N. Coupland (eds) *The Discourse Reader*. London: Routledge, pp. 336–345.

Holtgraves, T. (1997) 'Yes, but... positive politeness in conversation arguments', *Journal of Language and Social Psychology*, 16(2): 222–239.

Hopper, R. (1995) 'Episode trajectory in conversational play', in P. ten Have and G. Psathas (eds) *Situated Order: Studies in the Social Organization of Talk and Embodied Activities*. Washington, DC: University Press of America, pp. 57–71.

Huizinga, J. (1949) *Homo Ludens*. London: Routledge and Kegan Paul.

Hunston, S. (2004) 'Counting the uncountable: problems of identifying evaluation in a text and in a corpus', in A. Partington, J. Morley and L. Haarman (eds) *Corpora and Discourse*. Bern: Peter Lang, pp. 157–188.

Hunston, S. and Thompson, G. (eds) (2000) *Evaluation in Text*. Oxford: Oxford University Press.

252 Bibliography

Hymes, D. (1971) 'On Communicative Competence', Philadelphia: University of Pennsylvania Press; reprinted in J. Pride and J. Holmes (eds) (1972) *Sociolinguistics*. Harmondsworth: Penguin, pp. 269–293.

Jaworski, A. and Coupland, N. (1999) *The Discourse Reader*. London: Routledge.

Jefferson, G. (1979) 'A technique for inviting laughter and its subsequent acceptance declination', in G. Psathas (ed.) *Everyday Language: Studies in Ethnomethodology*. New York: Irvington, pp. 79–96.

—— (1984) 'On the organization of laughter in talk about troubles', in J. Maxwell, J. Atkinson and J. Heritage (eds) *Structures of Social Action: Studies in Conversation Analysis*. Cambridge: Cambridge University Press, pp. 346–369.

—— (1985) 'An exercise in the transcription and analysis of laughter', in T. van Dijk (ed.) *Handbook of Discourse Analysis*, vol. 3. London: Academic Press, pp. 25–34.

Jefferson, G., Sacks, H. and Schegloff, E. (1987) 'Notes on laughter in the pursuit of intimacy', in G. Button and J. Lee (eds) *Talk and Social Organisation*. Clevedon: Multilingual Matters, pp. 152–205.

Johnson-Laird, P. (1981a) 'Mental models of meaning', in A. Joshi, I. Sag and B. Webber (eds) *Elements of Discourse Understanding*. Cambridge: Cambridge University Press, pp. 106–126.

—— (1981b) 'Comprehension as the construction of mental models', *Philosophical Transactions of the Royal Society, Series B*, 295: 353–374.

—— (1983) *Mental Models*. Cambridge: Cambridge University Press.

Jorgensen, J. (1996) 'The functions of sarcastic irony in speech', *Journal of Pragmatics*, 26(5): 613–634.

Jucker, A. (1986) *News Interviews: A Pragmalinguistic Analysis*. Amsterdam and Philadelphia: Benjamins.

Kasper, G. (1990) 'Linguistic politeness: current research issues', *Journal of Pragmatics*, 14(2): 193–218.

Koestler, A. (1964) *The Act of Creation*. London: Hutchinson.

Kotthoff, H. (2003) 'Responding to irony in different contexts: on cognition in conversation', *Journal of Pragmatics*, 35(9): 1387–1411.

Kreuz, R., Long, D. and Church, M. (1991) 'On being ironic: pragmatic and mnemonic implications', *Metaphor and Symbolic Activity*, 6(3): 149–162.

Labov, W. (1972) *Language in the Inner City*. Philadelphia: University of Pennsylvania Press.

Labov, W. and Fanshel, D. (1977). *Therapeutic Discourse*. New York: Academic Press.

Ladefoged, P. (1972) 'Phonetic prerequisites for a distinctive feature theory', in A. Valdman (ed.) *Papers in Linguistics in Memory of Pierre Delattre*. The Hague: Mouton, pp. 273–286.

La Fave, L. and Mannell, R. (1976) 'Does ethnic humor serve prejudice?', *Journal of Communication*, 26(3): 116–123.

Lakoff, R. (1989) 'The limits of politeness: therapeutic and courtroom discourse', *Multilingua*, 8: 101–129.

—— (2003) 'The new incivility: threat or promise?', in J. Aitchison and D. Lewis (eds) *New Media Language*. London: Routledge, pp. 36–44.

Larsen, E. (1980) *Wit as a Weapon: The Political Joke in History*. London: Muller.

Levinson, S. (1988) 'Putting linguistics on a proper footing: explorations in Goffman's concepts of participation', in P. Drew and A. Wootton (eds) *Erving Goffman: Exploring the Interaction Order*. Cambridge: Polity Press, pp. 161–227.

Littman, D. and Mey, J. (1991) 'The nature of irony: toward a computational model of irony', *Journal of Pragmatics*, 15(2): 131–151.

Louw, W. (1993) 'Irony in the text or insincerity in the writer? – the diagnostic potential of semantic prosodies', in M. Baker, G. Francis and E. Tognini-Bonelli (eds) *Text and Technology: In Honour of John Sinclair.* Amsterdam and Philadelphia: Benjamins, pp. 157–176.

Lyons, J. (1977) *Semantics.* Cambridge: Cambridge University Press.

McDonald, S. (1999) 'Exploring the process of inference generation in sarcasm: a review of normal and clinical studies', *Brain and Language,* 68: 486–506.

Mahood, M. (1979) *Shakespeare's Wordplay.* London: Methuen.

Martin, R. (1992) 'Irony and universe of belief', *Lingua,* 87(1–2): 77–90.

Merrison, A. (2002) Politeness in task-oriented dialogue. Online. Available: http://www.shu.ac.uk/wpw/politeness/merrison.htm

Miller, G. (1993) 'Images and models, similes and metaphors', in A. Ortony (ed.) *Metaphor and Thought.* Cambridge: Cambridge University Press, pp. 357–400.

Mindess, H. (1971) *Laughter and Liberation.* Los Angeles, CA: Nash.

Minsky, M. (1975) 'A framework for representing knowledge', in P.H. Winston (ed.) *The Psychology of Computer Vision.* New York: McGraw-Hill, pp. 211–277.

Morley, J. (2004) 'The sting in the tail: persuasion in English editorial discourse', in A. Partington, J. Morley and L. Haarman (eds) *Corpora and Discourse.* Bern: Peter Lang, pp. 239–255.

—— (2006) 'Lexical cohesion and rhetorical structure', *International Journal of Corpus Linguistics,* 11(3).

Nattinger, J. and DeCarrico, J. (1992) *Lexical Phrases and Language Teaching.* Oxford: Oxford University Press.

Norrick, N. (1993) *Conversational Joking: Humor in Everyday Talk.* Bloomington, IN: Indiana University Press.

—— (2003) 'Issues in conversational joking', *Journal of Pragmatics,* 35(9): 1333–1359.

O'Connell, D. and Kowal, S. (2004) 'Hillary Clinton's laughter in media interviews', *Pragmatics,* 14(4): 463–478.

Oller, J. and Streiff, V. (1975) 'Dictation: a test of grammar-based expectancies', *English Language Teaching Journal,* 30: 25–36.

Paolillo, J. (1998) 'Gary Larson's "Far Side": Nonsense! Nonsense!', *Humor: International Journal of Humor Research,* 11(3): 261–290.

Partington, A. (1998) *Patterns and Meanings.* Amsterdam and Philadelphia: Benjamins.

—— (2001) 'Corpus-based description in teaching and learning', in G. Aston (ed.) *Learning with Corpora.* Houston, TX: Athelstan, pp. 63–84.

—— (2003) *The Linguistics of Political Argument.* London: Routledge.

—— (2004) 'Utterly content in each other's company: semantic prosody and semantic preference', *International Journal of Corpus Linguistics,* 9(1): 131–156.

—— (2006) 'Metaphors, motifs and similes across discourse types: Corpus-Assisted Discourse Studies (CADS) at work', in A. Stefanowitsch and S. Th. Gries (eds) *Corpus-Based Approaches to Metaphor and Metonymy.* Berlin and New York: Mouton de Gruyter, pp. 267–304.

Partington, A., Morley, J. and Haarman, L. (eds) (2004) *Corpora and Discourse,* Bern: Peter Lang.

Pawley, A. and Syder, H. (1983) 'Two puzzles for linguistic theory: nativelike selection and nativelike fluency', in J. Richards and R. Schmidt (eds) *Language and Communication.* London: Longman, pp. 191–226.

Pilkington, J. (1992) '"Don't try to make out that I'm nice!": the different strategies women and men use when gossiping', *Wellington Working Papers in Linguistics,* 5: 37–60.

Pinker, S. (1997) *How the Mind Works*. Harmondsworth: Penguin.
Pomerantz, A. (1978) 'Compliment responses: notes on the co-operation of multiple constraints', in J. Schenkein (ed.) *Studies in the Organization of Conversation Interaction*. New York: Academic Press, pp. 79–112.
—— (1984) 'Agreeing and disagreeing with assessments: some features of preferred/dispreferred turn shapes', in J. Atkinson and J. Heritage (eds) *Structures of Social Action*. Cambridge: Cambridge University Press, pp. 57–101.
Provine, R. (2000) *Laughter: A Scientific Investigation*. New York: Viking.
Ragan, S. (1990) 'Verbal play and multiple goals in the gynaecological exam interaction', *Journal of Language and Social Psychology*, 9(1–2): 67–84.
Rapp, A. (1951) *The Origins of Wit and Humor*. New York: Dutton.
Raskin, V. (1985) *Semantic Mechanisms of Humor*. Dordrecht-Boston-Lancaster: D. Reidel.
Reah, D. (1998) *The Language of Newspapers* (Intertext series). London and New York: Routledge.
Redfern, W. (1984) *Puns*. Oxford: Blackwell.
Ritchie, G. (2004) *The Linguistic Analysis of Jokes*. London: Routledge.
Rowland, T. (1999a) 'The clinical interview: conduct and interpretation', in O. Zaslavsky (ed.) *Proceedings of the 23rd Conference of the International Group for the Psychology of Mathematics Education*, vol. 4. Haifa, Israel: Israel Institute of Technology, pp. 129–136.
—— (1999b) *The Pragmatics of Mathematics Education: Vagueness and Mathematical Discourse*. London: Falmer.
Ruch, W., Attardo, S. and Raskin, V. (1993) 'Towards an empirical verification of the General Theory of Verbal Humor', *Humor: International Journal of Humor Research*, 6(2): 123–136.
Rumelhart, D. (1976) 'Toward an interactive model of reading', in S. Dornic (ed.) *Attention and Performance 6*. New York: Academic Press, pp. 573–603.
Sacks, H., Schegloff, E. and Jefferson, G. (1978) 'A simplest systematics for the organization of turn taking for conversation', in J. Schenkein (ed.) *Studies in the Organization of Conversation Interaction*. New York: Academic Press, pp. 1–55.
Scannell, P. (1991) 'Introduction: the relevance of talk', in P. Scannell (ed.) *Broadcast Talk*. London: Sage, pp. 1–13.
Schaffer, R. (1982) Vocal clues for irony in English, unpublished PhD dissertation, Ohio State University.
Schama, S. (2000) *A History of Britain*, vol. 1 (Audiobook). London: BBC Books.
Schank, R. (1986) *Explanation Patterns: Understanding Mechanically and Creatively*. Hillsdale, NJ: Erlbaum.
—— (1991) *Tell Me a Story: A New Look at Real and Artificial Intelligence*. New York: Simon & Schuster.
Schank, R. and Abelson, R. (1977) *Scripts, Plans, Goals and Understanding*. Hillsdale, NJ: Erlbaum.
Schick Case, S. (1988) 'Cultural differences, not deficiencies: an analysis of managerial women's language', in S. Rose and L. Larwood (eds) *Women's Careers: Pathways and Pitfalls*. New York: Praeger, pp. 41–63.
Seto, K. (1998) 'On non-echoic irony', in R. Carston and S. Uchida (eds) *Relevance Theory: Applications and Implications*. Amsterdam and Philadelphia: Benjamins, pp. 240–255.
Sherzer, J. (1985) 'Puns and jokes', in T. van Dijk (ed.) *Handbook of Discourse Analysis, Discourse and Dialogue*, vol. 3. London: Academic Press, pp. 213–221.

Sinclair, J. (1982) 'Reflections on computer corpora in English language research', in S. Johannsson (ed.) *Computer Corpora in English Language Research*. Bergen: Norwegian Computing Centre for the Humanities, pp. 1–6.
—— (1987) 'Collocation: a progress report', in R. Steele and T. Threadgold (eds) *Language Topics: Essays in Honour of Michael Halliday*. Amsterdam and Philadelphia: Benjamins, pp. 319–331.
—— (1991) *Corpus, Concordance, Collocation*. Oxford: Oxford University Press.
—— (2004) *Trust the Text: Language, Corpus and Discourse*. London: Routledge.
Sperber, D. and Wilson, D. (1995) *Relevance*, 2nd edn. Oxford: Blackwell.
Stewart, S. (1995) Multiple functions of laughter in a Dominican Spanish conversation, paper presented at 'Language South of the Río Bravo Conference', Tulane University, January 1995. Online. Available: http://www.tulane.edu/~ling/LSoRB/Proc/Stewart.html (accessed 29 July 2004).
Stubbs, M. (1996) *Text and Corpus Analysis: Computer-assisted Studies of Language and Culture*. Oxford: Blackwell.
—— (2001) *Words and Phrases: Corpus Studies of Lexical Semantics*. Oxford: Blackwell.
Tannen, D. (1984) *Conversational Style: Analyzing Talk Among Friends*. Westport, CT: Ablex.
Tannen, D. and Wallatt, C. (1999) 'Interactive frames and knowledge schemas in interaction: examples from a medical examination/interview', in A. Jaworski and N. Coupland (eds) *The Discourse Reader*, pp. 346–366. London: Routledge. First published in *Social Psychology Quarterly* (1987) 50(2): 205–216.
Tholander, M. and Aronsson, K. (2002) 'Teasing as serious business: collaborative staging and response work', *Text*, 22(4): 559–595.
Thompson, G. (1996) *Introducing Functional Grammar*. London: Arnold.
Thompson, G. and Hunston, S. (2000) 'Evaluation: an introduction', in S. Hunston and G. Thompson (eds) *Evaluation in Text*. Oxford: Oxford University Press, pp. 1–27.
Toplak, M. and Katz, A. (2000) 'On the uses of sarcastic irony', *Journal of Pragmatics*, 32: 10, 1467–1488.
Ulmer, G. (1988) 'The puncept in grammatology', in J. Culler (ed.) *On Puns, The Foundation of Letters*. Oxford and New York: Blackwell, pp. 164–189.
Vuchinich, S. (1990) 'The sequential organization of closing in verbal family conflict', in A. Grimshaw (ed.) *Conflict Talk: Sociological Investigations of Arguments in Conversation*. Cambridge: Cambridge University Press, pp. 118–138.
Wells, J. (1982) *Accents of English*. Cambridge: Cambridge University Press.
Willis, P. (1981) *Learning to Labour: How Working Class Kids Get Working Class Jobs*. Farnborough: Saxon House.
Wilson, D. and Sperber, D. (1992) 'On verbal irony', *Lingua*, 87: 53–76.
Yarwood, D. (2004) *When Congress Makes a Joke: Congressional Humor Then and Now*. Lanham, MD: Rowman and Littlefield.
Zajdman, A. (1995) 'Humorous face-threatening acts: humor as strategy', *Journal of Pragmatics*, 23: 325–341.
Zgusta, L. (1967) 'Multi-word lexical units', *Word*, 23: 578–587.
Cambridge International Dictionary, 1st edn. (1995) Cambridge: Cambridge University Press.
Collins-Cobuild English Language Dictionary, 1st edn. (1987) London: Collins.
Oxford English Dictionary, CD-Rom version 3 (2002) Oxford: Oxford University Press.
Webster's Unabridged Encyclopedic Dictionary of English (1989) New York: Portland House.

Name index

Abelson, R. 29–42, 55, 242
Ahl, F. 112, 246
Allen, W. 2, 230, 246
Anderson, R. 38
Aronsson, K. 96, 145, 150, 152, 159, 162–166, 170, 175, 180, 228, 244
Attardo, S. 4, 13, 14, 22, 28–29, 42, 44, 47, 66, 74, 110, 113–115, 117–118, 124–126, 188, 210, 212–213, 218, 220–221, 231–232, 238

Bachorowski, J. 14
Baker, M. 52
Baldry, A. 15
Barbe, K. 190–191, 197, 203, 219, 228
Barlow, M. 53, 55
Bartlett, F. 27, 29
Bateson, G. 66, 68
Berger, A. 66
Best, A. 102
Biber, D. 74, 195, 245
Billig, M. 232
Bills, L. 88
Bolinger, D. 52, 123,
Boxer, D. 66, 94–95, 145, 147, 150, 173, 215
Brandreth, G. 127
Brown, G. 31, 34–35, 38, 59, 242
Brown, P. 18, 23, 62, 86, 88, 90–93, 96, 99, 103–109, 144–145, 173, 180, 205, 221, 226
Bryman, A. 4
Burgess, R. 4

Charniak, E. 31
Cherry, R. 86
Church, M. 183
Clark, T. 19
Clayman, S. 3, 19, 80–81, 102

Cockcroft, R. 81
Cockcroft, S. 81
Colston, H. 183
Conrad, S. 74, 195
Cook, G. 57, 66, 68–69, 112, 243
Cortés-Conde, F. 66, 94–95, 145, 147, 150, 173, 215
Crick, F. 55

DeCarrico, J. 55
Dews, S. 154, 183
DiMaio, S. 42, 44, 47, 126, 238
Drew, P. 22, 58, 144, 157, 160, 162–163, 167, 170, 228

Eder, D. 180

Fairclough, N. 133
Fanshel, D. 18
Fein, O. 188, 229
Ferguson, N. 241
Finegan E. 74, 195, 245
Foot, H. 16
Freud, S. 8, 40, 47, 49, 66, 116–117, 121–122, 138, 231, 238
Fry, W. 66, 68, 101

Galtung, J. 3
Gavioli, L. 92, 243
Gibbs, R. 183, 189, 210
Giora, R. 188, 206–207
Glenn, P. 16–18, 20, 92–94, 226, 229, 231–232
Goetz, E. 38
Goffman, E. 3, 18, 86, 90, 92, 101, 167, 197, 227, 245
Grainger, K. 66, 88, 92, 95, 145–147, 160, 180, 233
Greatbatch, D. 19, 102

Grice, H. 31, 33, 66–67, 138, 153, 188, 206, 220
Grotjahn, R. 242

Haarman, L. 4
Habermas, J. 59
Haiman, J. 212
Halliday, M. 59, 74, 187, 195
Hamamoto, H. 186–187, 210
Harris, S. 58, 59, 88
Hasan, R. 74
Hayworth, D. 233
Hempelmann, C. 42, 44, 47, 126, 238
Heritage, J. 2, 3, 58, 102
Hoey, M. 10, 53–54, 118, 119–120, 188
Holmes, J. 179
Holtgraves, T. 88
Hopper, R. 180
Huizinga, J. 65
Hunston, S. 46, 195–196, 218, 220
Hymes, D. 87

Jefferson, G. 15, 17, 23
Johansson, S. 74, 195, 245
Johnson-Laird, P. 38
Jorgensen, J. 154, 183, 216
Jucker, A. 102

Kaplan, J. 183
Kasper, G. 59
Katz, A. 154, 216
Kemmer, S. 53
Koestler, A. 23, 25–27, 33, 40–41, 43, 48, 110, 113, 132, 145, 225, 232, 234, 242, 244, 247
Kotthoff, H. 189, 203, 206–207, 220
Kowal, S. 20
Kreuz, R. 183

Labov, W. 18, 194
Ladefoged, P. 55
La Fave, L. 215
Lakoff, R. 59, 88
Larsen, E. 46
Leech, G. 74, 195, 245
Levinson, S. 3, 18, 23, 62, 86, 88, 90–93, 99, 103–109, 144–145, 167, 173, 180, 197, 205, 221, 226
Littman, D. 190, 219
Long, D. 183
Louw, W. 4, 223
Lyons, J. 43

McCarthy, M. 52
McDonald, S. 211, 222
Mahood, M. 110
Mannell, R. 215
Mansfield, G. 243
Martin, J. 195
Martin, R. 186–187, 199, 210, 222
Merrison, A. 62
Mey, J. 190, 219
Miller, G. 237
Mindess, H. 32
Minsky, M. 29, 66
Morley, J. 128, 195, 202, 217

Nattinger, J. 55
Norrick, N. 24, 66, 116–118, 132, 136, 138, 146, 183, 228

O'Brien, J. 183, 189, 210
O'Connell, D. 15, 20
Oller, J. 55
Owren, M. 14

Paolillo, J. 238
Partington, A. 3–6, 10, 20, 53, 88, 90, 99, 102–103, 106, 118, 127, 129, 140–141, 168, 227, 237, 245
Pawley, A. 53
Pilkington, J. 179
Pinker, S. 25–27, 40–41, 145
Pomerantz, A. 104, 181
Provine, R. 13, 16, 19, 82, 231, 233

Ragan, S. 66, 233
Rapp, A. 232
Raskin, V. 19, 27–29, 32–33, 39, 43–45, 47, 66–68, 114, 173, 225
Reah, D. 113
Redfern, W. 110–113, 115, 120, 124, 127, 237
Reppen, R. 74
Ritchie, G. 43–44, 48, 111, 114, 124, 126, 134, 225
Rowland, T. 88
Ruch, W. 44
Ruge, M. 3
Rumelhart, D. 31

Sacks, H. 17
Scannell, P. 76
Schaffer, R. 188
Schallert, D. 38
Schama, S. 240–241

Name index

Schank, R. 29–42, 55, 242
Schegloff, E. 17
Schick Case, S. 180
Schwartz, T. 188, 229
Seto, K. 12, 193, 209, 229
Sherzer, J. 17, 132
Sinclair, J. 6, 10, 50–53, 54–55, 121, 227
Smoski, M. 14
Sperber, D. 32, 118, 160, 183–188, 208, 210–211, 215–216, 219–221, 229
Stevens, K. 38
Stewart, S. 18
Streiff, V. 55
Stubbs, M. 4, 10
Syder, H. 53

Tannen, D. 17, 34, 66, 77
Tholander, M. 96, 145, 150, 152, 162–166, 170, 175, 180, 228, 244
Thompson, G. 59, 196, 220

Toplak, M. 154, 216
Trollip, S. 38

Ulmer, G. 112

Vuchinich, S. 171

Wallatt, C. 34, 66
Wells, J. 41, 122
Willis, P. 180
Wilson, D. 32, 118, 160, 183–188, 208, 210–211, 215–216, 219–221, 229
Winner, E. 154, 183

Yarwood, D. 19
Yule, G. 31, 34–35, 38, 59, 242

Zajdman, A. 94–95
Zgusta, L. 52

Subject index

absurd 42, 45, 48–49, 81, 174, 183
affect/affective face 18, 66, 88, 95, 97–98, 109, 145, 170, 181, 207, 222, 227, 235–236
affiliation 15, 18–20, 22, 80–81, 92–94, 97–99, 145, 150–151, 167–168, 170, 179, 181, 227, 229, 234, 244
aggression 16, 18, 21–22, 24, 65, 68, 85–87, 102–109, 132, 140, 145–146, 148, 150, 160–161, 164, 170–175, 179–181, 212–216, 231–236
alignment 18–20, 87, 143, 150–152, 167, 170, 181, 229, 244
ambiguity 19, 28, 33, 40, 48, 92, 94, 100, 112, 114, 118, 146, 164, 168, 204–205, 209, 242, 244
anecdotes 27, 66, 75, 111, 118, 228
Aristotle 2, 112, 232
audience laughter 13, 15, 19, 80–81, 92, 100, 106, 153, 167–169, 175, 181, 205
audience priming 116, 153, 168, 177

backtracking 28–29, 40, 48, 119–122, 230
bathos 26–27, 72, 74–75, 78–79, 100, 105, 116, 117, 126, 134–135, 157–158, 160–161, 169, 226, 230, 246–247
bisociation 23–27, 40–41, 48–49, 57, 65, 74, 81, 108–109, 113, 132, 157–158, 160, 162, 181, 190–191, 199, 202, 211, 218, 225–232, 235–236
blasphemy *see* religion
bona-fide communication 24, 66–68, 81, 100, 108, 149–150, 173, 238

children's jokes 41–42, 122, 127, 148–149, 221
clusters 10, 21
colligation 53–54, 120, 130

collocation 10–11, 53–54, 117–121, 124, 130–131, 149, 191, 213–214, 223
collocational principle *see* idiom principle
colourful language 62, 80–81, 136, 139, 166, 230
competence face 95, 97–98, 103, 109, 170–171, 206–207, 227, 235
complimenting 73, 87, 100, 103–105, 142, 166, 205, 245
concordance, concordancing 7–8, 10–13, 52, 65, 89, 147, 191, 193, 203, 216, 217, 243
Conversation Analysis 14, 15, 17, 195
Corpus-Assisted Discourse Studies (CADS) 3–6, 14, 229
cynical/cynicism 73, 81, 151–152, 160–161, 166, 194, 205, 207, 209, 213, 220, 228, 231

delexicalization 23, 118, 121–123, 138, 227
delivery 77, 82, 105, 109, 157, 163–164, 172, 173–176
dictionaries 20, 65, 89, 147, 212
disguise 88, 187
display 35, 68, 95, 100, 145, 149, 221

echo theory *see* irony
embarrassment 18, 21–22, 84, 85, 92, 93, 105, 108, 144, 147, 155, 156, 168, 171, 173, 175, 227, 233
evaluation 23, 44, 46–48, 60, 64, 73, 90, 100, 115 186–187, 194–212, 214, 218–224, 226, 228–231, 237, 241, 244
evolution 24, 69, 196, 231–233

Subject index

face, facework 18, 23–24, 49, 53, 59, 62, 82–109, 139, 142, 144–146, 149–175, 179–181, 189, 201, 204–207, 213–216, 221–222, 226–236, 243
fallibility *see* hitches and glitches; tease
fantasy 14, 41, 69–70, 72, 74, 79, 81, 94, 136, 156, 207, 226, 230, 236
fiction 36, 38–41, 68, 70, 186
footing(s) 3, 5, 245
frames 18, 65, 66, 79, 81, 102, 108, 149, 151, 153–154, 162–164, 167, 169, 171, 173, 181, 188–189, 207, 221–222, 226, 229–230

headlines 127–132
hitches and glitches 15, 83–86, 92–94, 97, 102, 108, 227, 234

idiom/idiom principle 50–56, 119, 124, 129–130, 227, 244
impropriety 17, 23, 44–49, 93, 97, 115, 127, 203, 218–219, 230, 234
incongruity 29, 43, 74, 157, 166, 190–191, 225–226, 231–232, 235
inferencing 37–41, 50–51, 55–56, 57, 96, 125–126, 181, 189, 199, 222, 225–226
in-group, out-group 11, 18, 68, 70, 82–105, 133, 170, 179, 209, 214–215, 220, 226–227, 231–232, 234, 243
in-joke 77, 99, 101, 106, 108, 152, 160, 175
in-script 70–72, 79, 96, 99, 101, 133, 152, 155–156, 169, 204, 215
institutional talk 2–3, 57–60, 88, 153, 227
insults 144, 150, 164, 173, 212, 215
intensification 13, 53, 120, 123–124, 193, 195, 201, 203, 210, 229
interactional *see* modes
interviews 3, 7, 18, 20, 34, 88, 95–96, 102–103, 105, 193, 201
intimacy 17, 82, 94–95, 100, 144–146, 163, 173, 181, 189
intonation 15, 74, 109, 149, 151, 157, 163, 174, 193, 205
irony 12–13, 24, 47, 49, 109, 112, 151–152, 155–156, 160–161, 166, 188–224, 228–229, 230, 240–241, 246; dramatic 186–187, 212, 246; echo theory 160, 183–187, 201, 210–211, 215–216, 218, 220–221, 229; explicit 190–195, 199–202, 212–213, 218, 228–229, 240–241;

implicit 199, 203–212, 218, 229; litotes – understatement 207–209, 218; one stage / two stages 188–189, 218, 222; paradoxical 198–199, 202; strong / weak 190–191, 197; verisimilar 187, 207–210, 219

Jewish jokes 47, 120, 231
jokes 1, 17, 19, 21, 25–49, 56, 66–67, 73, 82, 93, 96–98, 101, 110, 113, 117–122, 124–127, 132–133, 136, 139, 143–144, 147, 153, 158, 177, 179, 202–203, 213, 219, 225–226, 229–231, 234–236, 238; *see also* absurd; children's; in-jokes; Jewish; political; religion; scatology; sex; tricolon joke

lexical priming 53–54, 74, 114, 118–121, 123–124, 126, 130–131, 188, 223
lexicogrammar 50–56, 90, 121, 225
lexicography *see* dictionaries
lexicon – lexicology 50–56, 115, 118, 121, 126, 130–131, 223, 238
literature 1, 26, 39, 110, 127, 182, 183, 185, 217, 238, 247

memory 27, 29–30, 41, 50, 54–55
mental models 38–40, 51, 222, 225
metanalysis 111, 125–127, 142
metaphor 3, 5, 52, 68, 76, 80, 128, 131, 136, 139, 142, 188, 244
mimicry 68, 159–160, 166, 245
modes (transactional, interactional) 59–65, 76, 78, 81, 85, 100, 103, 105, 134, 136, 139, 155, 168, 215, 226, 229, 230
motivation 116–118, 128, 129–130, 132, 142–143

narratives 39–46, 49, 57, 69–75, 78–79, 81, 95, 97, 104, 115, 122, 126–127, 134–136, 152, 161–162, 172, 174, 187, 189–191, 194–195, 197, 199–203, 206–222, 225–226, 229–230, 235–236
nesting 54

open choice 50–56, 57, 119–120, 125, 226–227
opposition of scripts/narratives 28–29, 43–44, 46, 114
out-group *see* in-group

Subject index

parody 13, 64, 76–77, 79 134, 144, 208, 226, 247
performance 145, 172, 181, 216
personae 58, 70–71, 76, 79, 81, 94, 100, 109, 151, 165, 207, 209, 215, 226
phraseology/phraseological tendency 13, 53, 57, 74, 119, 124–125, 131, 226–227
play 18, 65–69, 71, 74–77, 79, 81, 94, 96–97, 101–102, 105, 108, 110, 146, 149–151, 153–154, 156, 158, 163–169, 171–174, 177, 207, 226, 230, 233, 243
po-face 15, 22, 162, 166–167
politeness 20, 23–24, 60, 85–109, 145–147, 153, 169, 189, 211, 219, 221, 226, 232–233, 235–236, 243
political jokes 46, 116, 124, 134–137, 142–143
preconstructed phrases 51–56, 119–124, 129–131, 135
priming *see* audience priming; lexical priming
puns 17, 23–24, 45, 110–143, 188, 227–228, 237–238, 242, 244, 246; *see also* word- and phraseplay

quality of humour 23, 35, 44, 113, 116–117, 132, 163, 227, 230–231, 236

reformulation 131, 134, 136, 140–141, 160, 167, 169, 214–216
register 6, 58, 74–80, 81, 101, 126, 154, 156, 158, 162, 166, 208, 226, 229–230, 233, 235, 243, 246–247
release theory *see* tension
relevance 32, 35, 188
relexicalization 23, 56, 119–126, 128, 130, 132, 135–138, 140–142, 174, 227–228, 242, 244
religion 26–27, 28, 40–41, 45, 75
Republican 6, 7, 11–12, 71, 73, 108, 150, 208
response to teasing *see* tease
reversal (of evaluation) 23, 44, 46–48, 73–74, 115, 191–192, 197, 201–212, 214, 218–224, 226, 229–231
rhetoric 1, 79, 81, 112–113, 141, 161–162, 171–172, 174, 179, 183, 193–195, 200–202, 205, 209, 211–212, 221, 226, 229
riddle 32, 112
rudeness 88, 144, 177

sarcasm 8, 12–13, 15, 24, 62, 66, 75, 78, 81, 94, 99, 101, 107–109, 112, 138, 143, 149, 151, 156, 166, 169, 171–172, 174–175, 179, 182–183, 189, 205–207, 209, 212–218, 220–222, 228–229, 236, 239, 246
scatology 45, 136
schema, schemata 23, 25, 27, 29, 31, 50, 53–56, 124–125, 130, 227
scripting 114, 118, 134–135
scripts, script theory 23, 26–46, 50–56, 57, 67, 72, 79, 96, 99, 101, 125, 133, 152, 155–156, 165, 169, 203–204, 211, 214, 225–226, 238, 242
self-deprecation 71, 79, 94–96, 98, 105, 108–109, 156, 166, 235
semantic preference 53–54, 118–119, 130
semantic prosody 90, 223–224
serendipity 12–13
sex 17, 40–41, 43–47, 69, 79–80, 147–148, 157, 231, 239
signalling 1, 18, 20, 66, 68, 93, 146, 163, 196, 227, 233–235
smile 14–16, 22, 92, 150, 157, 159, 173, 175, 181, 191, 213, 233
social control/correction 86, 144–146, 180–181, 232
stupidity 43, 46–49, 158, 190, 194, 200, 207, 211, 219, 235, 247
superiority 43, 49, 68, 98, 109, 152, 163, 174, 179, 230–232, 247

taboo 23, 45–46, 49, 105, 127
tease/teasing 11, 12, 13, 15, 18, 22, 14, 65, 66, 73, 81, 93–95, 97, 99–100, 127, 135, 142, 144–181, 191, 209, 210, 214–215, 228–230, 236, 244–246; cynicism tease 73, 160–162, 228; definitions 144–150; fallibility tease 155–159, 163, 172, 228; frustration tease 153–155, 181, 228; mimicry tease 159–160, 228; reactions to teasing 15, 162–170, 228
tension 49, 62, 100, 105, 108, 109, 151, 232–236
transactional *see* modes
transcription 2, 6, 14, 15, 66, 145
tricolon joke 42–43
troubles-talk 17–18, 22

unexpected 12, 25, 26–27, 34, 39, 41, 44, 45, 65, 67, 78, 83, 97, 114, 115, 122, 153–154, 160–161, 229, 230, 234, 236
upgrading 76, 78–80, 226, 230

verbal cascading 131–132
verbal duelling 113, 171–173, 228

word- and phraseplay 23–24, 49, 50, 54, 66, 110–143, 227–229, 244; argumentative/strategic wordplay 110, 136–138, 140–143; definitions 113–118; exact puns 113, 115–116, 127–129, 132, 237; linguistic mechanisms 118–127; motivation 116–117; non-exact (near) puns 114–116, 123, 127, 129–131, 132, 237; quality 113, 116–117, 132; reputation 110–113; syntagmatic puns 114, 134, 136, 142
WordSmith 8–10, 21, 66, 191, 242

Printed in Great Britain
by Amazon